The Post-Colonial Security Dilemma

The **ISEAS – Yusof Ishak Institute** (formerly Institute of Southeast Asian Studies) is an autonomous organization established in 1968. It is a regional centre dedicated to the study of socio-political, security, and economic trends and developments in Southeast Asia and its wider geostrategic and economic environment. The Institute's research programmes are grouped under Regional Economic Studies (RES), Regional Strategic and Political Studies (RSPS), and Regional Social and Cultural Studies (RSCS). The Institute is also home to the ASEAN Studies Centre (ASC), the Nalanda-Sriwijaya Centre (NSC), and the Singapore APEC Study Centre.

ISEAS Publishing, an established academic press, has issued more than 2,000 books and journals. It is the largest scholarly publisher of research about Southeast Asia from within the region. ISEAS Publishing works with many other academic and trade publishers and distributors to disseminate important research and analyses from and about Southeast Asia to the rest of the world.

The Post-Colonial Security Dilemma

Timor-Leste and the International Community

Rebecca Strating

YUSOF ISHAK INSTITUTE

First published in Singapore in 2019 by
ISEAS Publishing
30 Heng Mui Keng Terrace
Singapore 119614

E-mail: publish@iseas.edu.sg
Website: <http://bookshop.iseas.edu.sg>

All rights reserved. No part of this publication may be reproduced, stored in a retrieval system, or transmitted in any form or by any means, electronic, mechanical, photocopying, recording or otherwise, without the prior permission of the ISEAS – Yusof Ishak Institute.

© 2019 ISEAS – Yusof Ishak Institute, Singapore

The responsibility for facts and opinions in this publication rests exclusively with the author and her interpretations do not necessarily reflect the views or the policy of the publisher or its supporters.

ISEAS Library Cataloguing-in-Publication Data

Strating, Rebecca.
   The Post-Colonial Security Dilemma : Timor-Leste and the International Community.
   1. Timor-Leste—Foreign relations.
   2. National security—Timor-Leste.
   3. Self-determination, National—Timor-Leste.
   I. Title.
DS649.7 S89   2019

ISBN 978-981-4818-40-7 (soft cover)
ISBN 978-981-4818-41-4 (E-book PDF)

Typeset by International Typesetters Pte Ltd
Printed in Singapore by Markono Print Media Pte Ltd

CONTENTS

List of Tables   vii

Acknowledgements   viii

1. Introduction   1
2. The Struggle for Recognition: Territorialization, Self-determination and the Imagining of "East Timor"   35
3. The Politics of Recognition: East Timor and the International Community   59
4. Establishing Legitimacy: International State-building in East Timor   95
5. Timor-Leste's Aspirational Foreign Policy   123
6. Identity Hedging: Timor-Leste's Engagement with Intergovernmental Organizations   161
7. Timor-Leste's National Security Agenda   199
8. Securing Economic Sovereignty   235
9. International Reconciliation and Transitional Justice   272
10. Conclusion: Timor-Leste in the Changing Regional Order   303

Postscript 339

Bibliography 340

Index 387

About the Author 402

LIST OF TABLES

1.1	Key Foreign Policy Actors	16
3.1	Voting Record of Southeast Asian States in the UNGA on the Question of East Timor, 1975–82	71
3.2	Voting Records of the CPLP States in the UNGA on the Question of East Timor, 1975–82	75
4.1	List of International Missions in East Timor	99

ACKNOWLEDGEMENTS

There have been several names accorded to East Timor, including Portuguese Timor, Timor-Leste and Timor *Loro sa'e*. Upon achieving independence, the official title of the state became the Democratic Republic of Timor-Leste. The English term "East Timor" is used when discussing the pre-independence period, and "Timor-Leste" when describing the independent sovereign state.

Parts of the research in the book has been published earlier as journal articles. Chapter seven uses research from "East Timor's Emerging National Security Agenda: Establishing 'Real' Independence", *Asian Security* 9, no. 3 (2013): 185–210; chapter nine reproduces parts of "The Indonesia–Timor-Leste Commission of Truth and Friendship: Enhancing Bilateral Relations at the Expense of Justice", *Contemporary Southeast Asia* 36, no. 2 (2014): 232–61; and chapters two and three employ sections of "Contested Self-determination: East Timor and Indonesia's Battle over Borders, International Law and Ethnic Identity", *Journal of Pacific History* 49, no. 4 (2014): 469–94. I am grateful to the publishers for permission to reproduce sections of these articles in this book.

I am incredibly appreciative for the conversations I have shared with academics, politicians, international relations practitioners and others about Timor-Leste's foreign policy in Dili and beyond. I remain indebted to those who kindly read drafts and offered constructive criticism: Dr Jasmine Westendorf, Dr Beth Edmondson, Dr Benjamin Habib and Dr Kumuda Simpson. I am thankful for your wisdom, generosity and advice. A special thanks goes to Andrew Reynolds for providing excellent assistance in compiling data.

I am grateful to my tremendous colleagues and friends within the Department of Politics and Philosophy at La Trobe University for the ongoing support and useful and constructive discussions. In particular, I am thankful for the support of the Head of Department Associate Professor Gwenda Tavan. I am also grateful to the La Trobe School of Humanities and Social Sciences and College of Arts, Social Science and Commerce for providing funding for this research, La Trobe Asia and Professor Nick Bisley for the valuable advice and support, and to ISEAS Publishing for assistance over the course of completing the manuscript.

On a personal note, I would also like to acknowledge the ongoing support and good humour of my fabulous family and friends. In particular, this book would not have been written without the immeasurable generosity of my wonderful husband Lincoln: words fail to describe just how grateful I am every day for your encouragement, kindness and love.

1

Introduction

On 20 May 2002, the *República Democrática de Timor-Leste*/Democratic Republic of Timor-Leste became the first sovereign state established in the twenty-first century. International recognition of its sovereignty was confirmed when it became the 191st member of the United Nations (UN) in September 2002. This meant that a new, small, fragile state had entered the "international community".[1] For newly constituted states, such as Timor-Leste, sovereignty is the social status that provides political, economic and social freedom and confers upon them decision-making rights and capacities to pursue interests within the sphere of international relations.[2] New states become holders of governmental authority with a status equal to the great powers of international politics.[3] Timor-Leste's movement from occupied territory to sovereign state reflects a monumental shift in identity entailing new goals and interests, and necessitating new patterns of engagement with the international community.

The political history of the territory now known as "Timor-Leste" has been largely shaped by experiences with various forms of foreign intervention. For around 400 years, the eastern half of the island of Timor was subject to Portuguese colonialism. In 1960, Portuguese Timor was granted self-determination rights under international law as a non-self-governing territory. By 1975, a shift in policy allowed other Portuguese colonies to exercise self-determination, however, Portuguese Timor's decolonization process was halted when its neighbour, Indonesia, annexed its territory in 1975, leading to a twenty-four year struggle for independence. Indonesia's occupation delayed decolonization until 1999, when an internationally-sanctioned ballot resulted in Timor-Leste's separation.

Since 1999, Timor-Leste has been the subject of five UN peacebuilding missions and two international stabilization missions. While international state-building is not new, international recognition of Timor-Leste's sovereignty followed the most extensive period of state-building ever conducted by the UN. The most significant of these missions operated under the auspice of the United Nations Transitional Administration in East Timor (UNTAET). Present in Timor-Leste from 1999 until 2002, it was endowed with responsibility for the administration of the territory and possessed exclusive legislative and executive authority.[4] It was also mandated to provide immediate humanitarian and security assistance, build state institutions and public administration, restore the judicial system and promote "capacity-building" among local actors. The UNTAET's temporary role as *de facto* sovereign reflects a distinctive transition to independence. Not only was this mission unprecedented in its size, scope and mandate, it was also the high-water mark of UN state-building.[5] Following a political crisis in 2006, an International Stabilisation Force (ISF) and the United Nations Integration Mission in Timor-Leste (UNMIT) was introduced to establish internal security and order. From 2006 until 2012, Timor-Leste was again dependent upon a form of foreign intervention.

This book focuses on how Timor-Leste defines and pursues its national security interests, how leaders have positioned the Timorese state within the international community and their efforts to develop and guarantee autonomy. It argues that Timor-Leste's history of foreign intervention and dependence has shaped its approaches to the international community and identity-building as an international actor. This book analyses the historical evolution of Timor-Leste's international identity in the pre- and post-independence periods, and examines the ways the Democratic Republic of Timor-Leste (RDTL) has sought to advance its security interests in economic, geopolitical and diplomatic spheres. In so doing, it considers Timor-Leste's bilateral and multilateral engagements with other states, regional and intergovernmental organizations and key non-state actors and stakeholders.

This study contributes to the existing literature on the politics of Timor-Leste. Significant scholarly analysis has been devoted to the East Timorese independence movement,[6] the international state-building period,[7] the nature and success of various UN missions[8] and political and social development.[9] However, with a few key exceptions in the form of articles and book chapters, the international relations of independent Timor-Leste has been relatively neglected.[10] This book reflects the first comprehensive study of Timor-Leste's policies and discourses across a range of fields relevant to international relations, including foreign policy, security and defence, development and norms of international justice.

The primary aim of this study, however, is to contribute to the International Relations (IR) literature on foreign policy of small, new, weak states. Timor-Leste's development as a new state provides an opportunity to examine how a new state navigates international relations, engages with fellow states and tests international structures. While small states have achieved greater prestige and visibility than in any previous period, it remains the case that IR literature tends to be dominated by great, secondary or middle powers.

This book offers a contribution to the literature on the international preferences, behaviours and interactions of fragile, small and post-colonial states[11] by examining Timor-Leste as an actor within the international community. It draws upon two analytical frameworks for understanding Timor-Leste's search for security. The first relates to the types of security issues that poor, fragile and post-colonial states face, which are often quite different from those of established, developed states. In this study, the concept of state "security" encompasses externally focused military ("hard") security, internal security (social cohesion, political order and stability), non-traditional or asymmetric threats and economic viability. The second framework concerns the foreign policy of small states, including how they cope with vulnerability and the influences that shape their priorities, engagements and strategies in international relations. Timor-Leste's approach to the international community is syncretic insofar as it is influenced by realist and idealist traditions and tends to oscillate between perceptions of the international structural environment as cooperative and competitive. A degree of what Katzenstein and Sil describe as "analytical eclecticism" is hence necessary for understanding Timor-Leste's efforts to secure the state.[12] Such an approach can incorporate more of the complexity of real-world situations rather than employing one theory. As Wivel, Bailes and Archer point out in their comparative small state security, "the variations in historical, geopolitical and institutional contexts will affect the applicability of general theories to small state security across time and space".[13] The aim here is not to assume that "everything matters", but rather to uncover how different vectors impact on Timor-Leste's pursuit of security and independence and approaches to foreign policy.[14]

The analytical frameworks of weak state insecurity and small state foreign policy provide useful tools for understanding how Timor-Leste engages with the international community as it seeks to assert and defend its newfound political independence. As an international actor, Timor-Leste must operate within a system characterized by power dynamics that constrains its actions and decision-making. This study aims to understand how Timor-Leste exerts agency and makes foreign policy choices within this structural context, rather than focusing on overly determinist narratives of foreign domination and imposition.[15] In examining small, fragile states, this book considers the parameters of legitimate action for Timor-Leste, and its options for opening or closing the spaces for political manoeuvring in the pursuit of influence.[16] It also examines how Timor-Leste has sought to control its identity within the international community. These are important considerations for Timor-Leste because the relations and activities within the international community are integral for its political, economic and social development and the security of sovereignty and independence.

There have been a number of studies from a range of scholarly disciplines on national identity in Timor-Leste that have focused on multifaceted internal and external influences on national identity construction.[17] The distinction with this study is that it primarily focuses on Timor-Leste's international state-based identity construction using IR frameworks in order to examine its foreign policy interactions and orientations. Rather than examining only systemic factors in explaining "rational" activity (as a neo-realist might), this study views national interests as not objectively given but as influenced by various structural and unit level considerations, and subject to the identities of states.

Small states have agency in projecting desirable self-images to international publics. Identities are complex, multifaceted and historically contingent: it is through intersubjective interactions that states forge a sense of identity that is continually reconstructed. Interviews and informal discussions with politicians, ambassadors, bureaucrats, academics, journalists, NGO workers and others within and beyond Timor-Leste have helpfully contributed to the analysis of this book. However, this study focuses its attention primarily on foreign policy narratives, drawing upon English texts directed to the international community as the audience, including speeches, declaratory policy and government documents, as primary source data. These sources carry narratives that attempt to constitute the "self" as differentiated from others in the international community.[18] These stories about the "self" shape foreign policy action by making actions meaningful, framing the boundaries of what is possible and by legitimatizing or delegitimizing particular forms of behaviour. However, it is also important not to privilege narrative as "truth": for example, narratives and discourses can be used strategically by state actors through public diplomacy campaigns. Therefore, this study juxtaposes narratives against the actual actions and policies of the state, by using primary sources such as budgets, policy documents and voting records.

Timor-Leste's national identity and interests have been shaped by historical factors. In the context of past intervention and dependence, Timor-Leste's international relations have been increasingly determined by its leadership's pursuit of "real" independence' (i.e. "functional" or "actual" independence). Efforts to secure the Timorese state have been motivated by a desire to reduce its reliance upon others and to be "self-determining"; that is, to make decisions and govern free from foreign interference. This tension between Timor-Leste's desire for "real" political independence and the realities of dependence permeates all spheres of its international political, cultural and economic relations. As Rotberg points out, many of the world's newer nation-states "waver precariously between weakness and failure".[19] The dynamic between developing independence amid ongoing dependence that is often encountered by new, fragile states is used as a framework for examining Timor-Leste's search for security. Fragile states are those that struggle to meet the requirements of "Weberian statehood", typically defined by the exclusive control of a territorial jurisdiction through a legitimate monopoly on the use of force.[20] They are generally low income countries characterized by instability, weak institutions and low levels of political, social and economic development. Fragile states experience difficulties exerting effective governance or "empirical sovereignty", which refers to capacities of states to "be their own masters" and deliver "positive" political goods to citizens, including protecting people's safety, establishing rule of law, enabling access to basic social rights, such as health and education, and developing economic and physical infrastructure.[21] In the international realm, Timor-Leste self-identifies as a fragile, post-conflict state.[22] This book suggests that Timor-Leste experiences a "post-colonial security dilemma", which encapsulates the notion that internal insecurity — not external threats — poses the greatest challenge to Timor-Leste's capacities to exert genuine independence.

The Post-Colonial Security Dilemma

The realist IR tradition has often presented states as power-maximizers preoccupied with "national security", typically defined as the capacities of states to protect themselves from external threats presented by other states within an anarchical, self-help international political system. Within this anarchical structure — characterized by the absence of a higher authority — sovereign states are uncertain and fearful about the intentions of others, and work to expand their material power in order to alleviate their insecurity. These structural conditions of anarchy encourage "security dilemmas". As Herz describes it, the security dilemma arises when states strive to attain security from foreign attack and "are driven to acquire more and more power in order to escape the impact of the power of others".[23] One state's quest for security leads others to heighten their own security, producing a spiral effect which can ultimately result in conflict. Even though states can mitigate uncertainty through confidence-building, collective security arrangements, and knowledge sharing, the security dilemma remain quintessential to realist understandings of state security.[24]

Literature on weak or fragile states, however, has sought to problematize traditional understandings of the security dilemma in international relations. Scholars such as Buzan, Ayoob and Alagappa have argued that the security concerns of fragile states differ from those of great powers and developed states.[25] The concept of "functional" (i.e. actual or real) independence has concerned the capacities of states to maintain their sovereign status by protecting state boundaries and the societies they encompass. Realistically, most of the world's independent states cannot meet their security needs primarily through their own material capabilities.[26] Rather than small states being forced to meet security and functional requirements, their proliferation and survival suggest that traditional concerns around conquest and intervention are increasingly irrelevant.[27] Functional independence is not just about bolstering defence capacities to defend against foreign threat, it also requires establishing an orderly relationship between the state and society.[28] New post-colonial states are more likely to experience internal conflict and disorder than established industrialized states. Importantly, for fragile states, threats to security are more likely to emerge from *within* the state rather than from foreign sources.[29] The security dilemma for post-colonial states, according to Job, "arises in meeting internal rather than external threats".[30] In fragile states, security apparatuses compete for authority with substate actors, such as militia or rebel groups, and have little coercive power to control them. These internal security threats can be driven by a range of destabilizing domestic conditions, such as poverty, inequality, institutional weakness, regime instability, and identity conflicts.[31]

The security dilemma for fragile states is how they manage the internal and external threats to security. At its heart, the post-colonial security dilemma engages with fundamental political questions of how governments allocate scarce resources. Mainstream international relations suggests that weak, small states are more vulnerable in the international system, and therefore more conscious of external systemic constraints and the need to protect national security.[32] However, spending on traditional military resources to prevent and deter foreign attack can cause internal instability as it requires the diversion of funds away from other areas, such as health and education. Privileging defence spending when other states institutions are weak can also provide security institutions with disproportionate power, potentially destabilizing the balance of power between institutions and undermining rule of law. Essentially, the post-colonial security dilemma reflects the range of challenges facing new states, such as

Timor-Leste, as they try to secure the internal and external dimensions of state sovereignty.

The ways in which new states come into being affect their capacities to be functionally independent. Decolonization was a "revolution of sovereignty" that spread the modern state system across the globe.[33] Many post-colonial states that emerged after World War Two were established through law irrespective of whether empirical sovereignty could be established. Rapid decolonization changed the nature of sovereignty and membership of the international community, and consequently, various studies have sought to create typologies to explain the differences between states. While categories such as "modern" and "post-colonial" run the risk of reifying and homogenizing the identities of particular states, they are useful in highlighting the diversity in the nature and operation of state sovereignty and its different dimensions. Scholars such as Sorenson, Cooper and Clapham suggest that states can be divided into three highly generalized types: post-colonial (new, fragile states), modern (established, possessing internal and external sovereignty) and post-modern (member states of supranational institutions, in particular the European Union).[34] According to Krasner, there are also different types of sovereignty that states possess to differing degrees. International legal sovereignty is the recognition of sovereign statehood, Westphalian or Vattelian sovereignty is the rights to autonomy and non-intervention, and domestic (empirical) sovereignty is effective governance of society.[35] Jackson describes new post-colonial states as "quasi-states" that possess international legal (or "external") sovereignty but lack effective governance.[36] The struggle for fragile states has often been in realizing their autonomy, as recognition of external sovereignty did not, in many cases, translate into empirical sovereignty as new states struggled to establish and maintain internal order.[37]

The territorial arrangements of many small post-colonial states would have been unviable if it were not for the "normative benefits" of sovereign recognition and UN membership.[38] In the contemporary era, post-colonial states "are seldom recolonized, merged, or dissolved", partly because colonization has become illegitimate.[39] While there has been a tendency to view the capacity to defend territory and population from external threat as an essential component of sovereign statehood, the external sovereignty of post-colonial fragile states is generally protected through international regimes of recognition. Timor-Leste's statehood has been assured by an international constitution that privileges sovereignty and attendant norms of non-intervention as its foundational organizational principles. Nevertheless, survival, security and "real" independence remain the core drivers of Timor-Leste's international engagements. Ayoob suggests that elites in developing states are obsessed with security as a consequence of vulnerabilities that emerge from within and beyond the state.[40] State fragility has undermined the efforts of Timor-Leste to secure popular visions of sovereignty as "real" independence, signified by a lack of dependence upon others.

Traditional conceptions of territorial sovereignty has entailed a belief in the "impermeability" of fixed, "hard shell" boundaries which protected states from outside penetration and interference.[41] There have been various criticisms levelled at this "old-fashioned" concept of territorial sovereignty since the end of the Cold War.[42] Scholars have argued that sovereignty has become increasingly irrelevant due to transnational economic forces, interdependence and globalization;[43] supranational organizations, particularly the European Union, have de-territorialized political authority;[44] a range of non-traditional global issues and threats, such as climate change, transgress the "hard shell" of boundaries;[45] and, humanitarian intervention has limited the capacities of state governments to violate the basic rights of their population.[46] In the words of Chopra and Weiss, these arguments have suggested that sovereignty is not "sacrosanct"; that is, under certain conditions, the international community can legitimately override domestic jurisdictions.[47] Furthermore, scholarly debates have considered the extent to which sovereign states hold responsibilities to their own populations (and to citizens of other states) and whether rights to territorial sovereignty are contingent upon the protection of human rights.[48] These debates about sovereignty reflect various perspectives about the absoluteness of sovereignty, and the extent to which states (with diverse governing capabilities) can or should be considered independent entities.

This book engages with questions of how post-colonial states (re)produce sovereignty through foreign policy discourses, norms and behaviours. Independence movements, such as East Timor's, undermine the idea that sovereignty and territorial boundaries are irrelevant. For liberation movements, sovereignty remains the ultimate goal because it promises nations the ability to enact collective rights to self-determination. Since independence, Timor-Leste has pursued and promoted a form of territorial sovereignty. This book uses the term "absolute external sovereignty" to describe a notion of sovereignty as providing states with inviolable rights to political authority over a territorial jurisdiction. This conception of sovereignty draws heavily on norms of "non-interference", which bestows upon states the right to independently conduct domestic affairs free from foreign interference, criticism or even advice.[49] Ringmar argues that many post-colonial states are defenders of absolute "Westphalian" conceptions of sovereignty.[50] Burke, on the other hand, suggests that post-colonial states have not always defended an absolute state sovereignty concept.[51] He points to the contribution of new African and Asian nations in the development of the post-World War Two international human rights regime aimed at limiting the range of permissible governmental actions *vis-à-vis* their populations.[52] The vision of sovereignty presented by Timor-Leste's leaders is reminiscent of the central norms embedded in the Association of Southeast Asian Nations (ASEAN), an organization that has sought to protect principles of absolute sovereignty and non-interference. Timor-Leste's vision of absolute external sovereignty is shaped by its historical struggle for recognition and the means by which it became independent. For Timor-Leste, this aspiration is shaped by its history of external interventions from Portugal's colonialism and Indonesia's occupation through to the extensive UN missions.

In the twenty-first century, fragile states have been viewed as potential harbourers of terrorist networks, drug syndicates and people smuggling rings that threaten the security of established states.[53] This has rendered fragile states susceptible to intervention by powerful states defending their own national security interests. In Timor-Leste's case, internal conflict has precipitated prolonged peacebuilding efforts that have compromised its pursuit of independence and self-determination. The primary threat to "real" independence is state failure as internal insecurity has repeatedly given rise to foreign intervention in the guise of peace-building missions. As a post-conflict fragile state, the primary challenges to security and functional independence are largely internal. Yet, as this research demonstrates, Timor-Leste's governments have focused on traditional security concerns, such as building a military to deter foreign threat.

Small State Foreign Policy

As well as being a fragile state, Timor-Leste is also small, which is typically characterized by geography, population size and the degree of influence in international relations.[54] Within the UN Forum of Small States, population numbers vary from 10,000 to 10 million.[55] There are currently 107 member states of this informal grouping, meaning that the majority of the UN membership are classified as small states according to population. This problematizes the use of "smallness" as an analytical tool. With a population of approximately 1.25 million people, some studies would classify a population of Timor-Leste's size (e.g. less than 1.5 million) as a "micro-state".[56] However, this study positions Timor-Leste as small but not micro: in 2015, Timor-Leste possessed the 157th largest population of 217 states.[57] Although Timor-Leste shares some similar developmental concerns with its Pacific micro-state neighbours, it is considerably larger than Nauru (population of 10,000), Tuvalu (10,000) and Palau (21,000). In terms of territory size, Timor-Leste is 14,874 square kilometres, ranking 160th of 257 recorded territories.[58] Exacerbating Timor-Leste's small physical size is its geographical location between the much larger states of Australia and Indonesia.

Smallness can also reflect the perceived position of states within an international hierarchy of power. Small states lack coercive power and are more likely to be aid dependent. They cannot guarantee their own security by military means, they struggle to make an impact on the international system and generally pose little or no danger to neighbouring states.[59] Traditionally, power in international relations has been attributed to criteria such as size, military capabilities and gross domestic product (GDP).[60] It is not, however, the case that levels of influence accurately correspond with size. While sometimes small states are conflated with "weak" states in international relations,[61] this is conceptually confusing as weak states are also conflated with "fragile" states (wherein "weakness" relates largely to the internal face of sovereign statehood, not their power in international relations). The category of small states includes some of the world's most and least developed states, and wealth can provide small states with material capacities that are disproportionate to their size.[62] For Timor-Leste, its position in the international community needs to be understood through the combination of its physical smallness, its newness and relative weakness, both in terms of its external power *vis-à-vis* other states, and its internal capacities to govern effectively.

Foreign policy is comprised of those policies "oriented towards the external world" as state representatives seek to deal with other states and the broader international community.[63] Analysis tends to sit in two camps: systems versus domestic approaches. Systems approaches view foreign policy as disproportionately influenced by external factors, such as balance of power dynamics or international law.[64] In contrast, domestic approaches examine the roles of leaders, institutions and internal politics in shaping foreign policy. Small states do not necessarily act in similar ways because economic and human development, geopolitics, geography and resources, internal stability and state weakness, domestic politics and history and culture also shape the policies of small states. This research considers four key influences on Timor-Leste's foreign policy: structural (external) forces; domestic politics; multilateral organizations and the global "rules-based order"; and, culture and history. These influences shape Timor-Leste's national interests and strategies that leaders implement as they pursue their goals in international relations.

Systemic Factors

International relations has tended to favour powerful, geostrategically influential states because they have the greatest capacity to shape international systems. While constructivists have argued that the structural (environmental) factors that neo-realism focus on as explanatory factors are reified through the behaviours and interactions of states,[65] the extent to which small states may contribute to shaping these external factors — rather than having to cope with external contingencies — is an important consideration. Small states have typically had little capacity to shape their external structural environments. Historically, small states have been more likely than great powers to "die" given their structural "irrelevance".[66] This has created an impetus for small states to "struggle for existence".[67] Realism has suggested that weaker small states "must always be aware of the realities of power and entertain no naïve illustration about disregarding the distribution of power in international relations".[68] The focus on systemic features of the international community suggests that small states' vulnerability within the political environment forces an unambiguous preoccupation with survival.[69] Small size has been viewed as a "handicap to state action".[70] Waltz, for example, argues that small powers have fewer options and a smaller margin for error than great or middle powers.[71] Consequently, realists view small states as devoting significant foreign policy resources to guaranteeing survival.[72]

Smallness, weakness and newness create particular vulnerabilities that shape the actions and interactions of states such as Timor-Leste. In some cases, the best small states can do is to cope with immediate security concerns, leading to reactive approaches to foreign policy.[73] Under conditions of anarchy, it would make sense that small states should be even more invested in survival and self-help. However, as Sharman argues, international structures provide even the smallest states with "choices rather than imperatives".[74] Small states are actually able to "energetically wield many sovereign prerogatives" as international structures permit greater freedoms for small states than what conventional international relations assumes.[75] Yet, even though it is possibly the safest period for weak and small states in history as they enjoy legitimacy, sovereign recognition and relative safety from foreign aggression, in its international relations, Timor-Leste remains focused on guaranteeing its sovereign status.[76] Foreign policy making is shaped by threat perception and international outlook, and this is central to understanding the goals and behaviours of Timor-Leste.

One of the central concerns for small states is how to best ensure security within the international distribution of power and how they should engage with more powerful states. Should a small state like Timor-Leste seek a great power protector to underwrite its national security, or eschew formal alliances in order to defend its independence and autonomy? Neo-realist small state foreign policy analysis has tended to find, following Walt, that small states are more likely to reluctantly "bandwagon" with (i.e. form an alliance with) an aggressive great power than balance against it.[77] Sharman's research finds that small states delegate fewer prerogatives to alliances than some much larger states.[78] In contrast, Labs suggests that small states can also tend towards balancing behaviours.[79] How can the differences in these findings be explained from a structural viewpoint? For Mouritzen, what matters is how the external "constellation" of power dynamics and relations to strong powers in the "salient environment" affects the foreign policy of small states.[80] The immediate environment of a small state may constitute an adaptive acquiescent constellation (whereby small states accept certain rules and avoid agitating great powers), an alliance constellation (in which small states are closely tied to a great power and have limited freedom of activity) or a symmetrical constellation (in which small states have greater freedom as they play off competing great powers).[81] As these constellations create a logic of rational action, changes in external balance of power can have consequences for small state foreign policy. However, a purely structuralist account misses the ways in which the actions and behaviours of small states can contribute to constellations of power. How and why small states belong to one of these constellations may be determined by their own agency in developing relations with great powers.[82]

Timor-Leste's immediate security environment, as fleshed out in this book, is defined as Asia-Pacific, a theatre dominated by two great powers, the United States and China. Using Mouritzen's account, this environment could be considered a symmetrical constellation. However, there are other relatively powerful states that also shape Timor-Leste's immediate security environment: principally, its neighbours Indonesia and Australia, two states have significantly affected Timor-Leste's status in recent history. For the most part, Timor-Leste has avoided making bandwagoning or balancing decisions, and has resisted the idea of forming a formal alliance with its main benefactor, Australia (itself a formal ally of the United States). Instead, Timor-Leste has adopted a policy of "hedging" by diversifying its relationships and seeking to reduce dependence on any one state or bloc of states. Timor-Leste may not be able to avoid making a choice about great power relations in the future as the global balance of power distribution shifts. However, its foreign policy choices thus far have undermine conventional assumptions that small states "bandwagon" to guarantee security, and demonstrate the complexity of the emerging "multiplex" world order[83] and the interrelationships with and between middle and great powers that shape their salient security environment.

Domestic Politics

Mainstream international relations tends to assume that domestic politics and institutions play a smaller role in the foreign policy formation of small states than great powers. Handel, for example, argues that domestic determinants have less salience in small powers foreign policy making than systemic factors.[84] However, Leifer suggests that Southeast Asian states tend to use foreign policy to serve domestic political purposes and to maintain the dominant position of those who rule, which is "not unique in relation to the overall experience of Third World countries".[85] Research on other small Southeast Asian states has also argued that domestic politics, institutional frameworks and regime types play a role in influencing foreign policy choices, for example in how states perceive and balance against threats, or their preference-formation regarding multilateral engagements and diplomacy.[86] In Southeast Asia generally, there remains little known about actual processes of foreign policy formation due to the sheer nature of the subject.[87] However, the general trend is that decision-making authority is normally invested in a few individuals, and in some cases, only one person.[88] Similarly, in Timor-Leste, political decision-making is highly centralized. Like many post-colonial states, foreign policy in Timor-Leste has been generally dictated by influential political leaders. These leaders were diplomats or military leaders during the East Timorese resistance and independence movement, a legacy that has subsequently shaped Timor-Leste's interactions with the international community, the worldviews of foreign policymakers and the tensions that emerge between them.

Since independence, Timor-Leste's approach to the international community has been largely shaped by two leaders. The architect of its foreign policy approach in the early years of independence was Nobel Peace Prize winner Dr José Ramos-Horta, who became Timor-Leste's first foreign minister in 2002 as a member of the FRETILIN (Revolutionary Front of Independent East Timor) government. Ramos-Horta would ultimately become prime minister for a short time during the political crises in 2006, and was elected president from 2008–12. A skilled practitioner of international relations well-known for his advocacy of East Timor's independence on the global stage and at the UN, Ramos-Horta promoted an internationalist stance that was consistent with universal human rights, social democratic values and initiatives for promoting global peace. Following his loss in the 2012 presidential election to former army chief, Taur Matan Ruak, Ramos-Horta's influence declined within the decision-making apparatuses of the state. This has loosely corresponded with a movement against Ramos-Horta's internationalist worldview, towards the reassertion of Timorese culture in national political discourse.[89]

TABLE 1.1
Key Foreign Policy Actors

Timeframe	Government	Key Figures
2002–6	FRETILIN	President – Xanana Gusmão Prime Minister – Mari Alkatiri Minister for Foreign Affairs and Cooperation – José Ramos-Horta
2006–7	FRETILIN	President – Xanana Gusmão Prime Minister – José Ramos-Horta
2007–12	Alliance of the Parliamentary Majority (AMP)	President – José Ramos-Horta Prime Minister – Xanana Gusmão Minister for Foreign Affairs and Cooperation – Zacarias da Costa
2012–15	National Congress for Timorese Reconstruction (CNRT)	President – Taur Matan Ruak Prime Minister – Xanana Gusmão Minister for Foreign Affairs and Cooperation – José Luís Guterres
2015–17 (July)	National Unity Government	President – Taur Matan Ruak Prime Minister – Rui Maria de Araújo Minister for Planning and Strategic Investment – Xanana Gusmão Minister for Foreign Affairs and Cooperation – Hernâni Coelho
2017 (Dec)	FRETILIN	President – Fransisco 'Lu Olo' Guterres Prime Minister – Mari Alkatiri Minister for Foreign Affairs and Cooperation – Aurélio Guterres

The other key leader in Timor-Leste's international relations is Xanana Gusmão. Elected Timor-Leste's first president in 2002, Gusmão became prime minister, forming a coalition government headed by *Congresso Nacional de Reconstrução de Timor*/National Congress for Timor-Leste Reconstruction (CNRT) party in 2007, and the Alliance for Parliamentary Majority (AMP) in 2012. Gusmão retired from the prime ministership in early 2015, which led to the creation of a "unity government" that included members of the opposition FRETILIN party.

Most notably, FRETILIN's Dr Rui Maria de Araújo became the new prime minister. Gusmão, however, retained considerable political influence by virtue of his charismatic leadership that derives from his status as a national liberation hero. A more nationalist leader than Ramos-Horta, Gusmão has promoted Timorese national interests and has led criticisms of the West, international donors and the global economy. Gusmão, however, has demonstrated that he is more likely to pursue idealistic foreign policy strategies in the pursuit of domestic interests than the more pragmatic Ramos-Horta. The politics and personal interests of key leaders influence the foreign policy objectives and strategies of Timor-Leste.

At the time of writing (the end of 2017), the "unity government" had broken down following parliamentary elections in July. A parliamentary majority opposition led by Gusmão emerged, threatening the authority of the new FRETILIN-led minority government and blocking the passing of its national agenda through parliament.[90] This set the scene for new elections. This breakdown in consensus highlights the fluidity of the domestic political context, and although it is too soon to tell, may have internal security and foreign policy implications in the future.

Multilateralism and the Rules-Based Order

Sovereign states are expected to engage in an incredibly large and diverse range of political activities in the international realm. Small fragile states are viewed as constrained in their foreign policy options, having to rely upon soft measure strategies in the absence of hard, coercive power. One characteristic of small state foreign policy can include low participation in foreign affairs and prioritizing close relationships within their immediate region.[91] However, research has also demonstrated that small and underdeveloped states tend to exhibit a range of foreign policy behaviours when confronting their vulnerabilities within international relations. Even Waltz, somewhat contradictorily, suggests that small states face fewer constraints than more powerful actors because of a general lack of interest in their foreign policies.[92] Small states must use their limited foreign policy resources to promote survival and maximize their strategic options. As they lack opportunities to use coercive powers, they rely upon a range of relationships to advance their core interests, particularly if they choose not to rely upon an alliance with a great power. Timor-Leste has developed an ambitious foreign policy that incorporates a disproportionately large range of relations within various global, regional and cultural multilateral forums, including the UN. Rather than focusing on the immediate neighbourhood, Timor-Leste's international relations extends across multiple regions, including East and Southeast Asia, South Pacific, Europe and Africa. This expansive foreign policy reflects Timor-Leste's unique status as a Portuguese-language speaking, Catholic small island state geographically situated in Southeast Asia, and the support it received during the independence movement from former Portuguese colonies in Africa.

While traditional international relations theories tend to equate size with capabilities, it is not the case that small states are impotent victims of a hostile international political system.[93] While small states are often constrained in the ways that they can advance national security (for example, in building a military), in foreign policy small fragile states employ a range of disparate strategies to balance against threat.[94] Small weak states are driven to cooperate by engaging in multilateralism and promoting international law as they defend legal principles of sovereignty, recognition and non-intervention.[95] Furthermore, the assumption that survival is the *only* preoccupation of small states is undermined by the rich variety of actions and interactions they engage in. Some studies, for example, have highlighted the ways in which small states can be "norm entrepreneurs" by promoting particular worldviews across different policy areas.[96] Others have demonstrated how the international fora may be used to enhance status through diplomacy and international law.[97] Other interests are at stake than survival, including advancing economic interests and promoting values, ideologies or principles within the international community. Multilateral forums provide small states the space to advance their diverse interests.

The literature on small states suggests that because they are deprived of coercive options they are more likely to seek out multilateral organizations for security. As Bull argues, the multilateral system of rules, norms and laws provides order in the anarchical society.[98] The primary functions of this "global rules-based order" is to preserve sovereignty, protect weak states from the strong, and promote peace among them.[99] Small states receive protection from international laws, norms and principles, and are among the biggest promoters of rules-based multilateralism.[100] As many small states lack the resources to defend borders, they have an interest in ensuring peace and stability through support for a multilateral rules-based order and principles of collective security.[101] As a global multilateral system, the UN also preserves the foundational norms of sovereign equality through the "one nation, one vote" principle. Timor-Leste is a vocal supporter of international rule of law as it safeguards its sovereignty. For Timor-Leste, participation in the global normative order and liberal institutions is in its strategic interests as it relies upon the international community to guarantee recognition. However, Timorese leaders have also been critical of UN organizations and the international development sphere when it has suited their quest for autonomy and domestic political interests.

In some areas, Timor-Leste's governments have embraced "realist" notions of security as relying upon material defence capabilities as other states and actors in the international community pose potential threats. At the same time, Timor-Leste's leaders seek to develop a "legitimate" identity as a "successful" state that provides internal security and order, and respects the rights of its citizens, in order to protect the state from future foreign intervention. This requires complying with international law, gaining membership in international institutions, and cooperating with other states, international institutions and non-state actors. Timor-Leste's "activist" foreign policy strategies employ international discourses in areas such as human rights, democracy and sustainable development in order to validate the state, drawing upon public diplomacy skills that were developed by leaders through the independence movement. The need to be perceived as a legitimate actor within the international community has shaped both the construction of Timor-Leste's democratic political institutions, and its engagement with actors and structuring forces, such as international law.

History, Culture and Identity

Finally, Timor-Leste's foreign policy has been shaped by a distinctive mix of historical experiences: of being colonialized twice, pursuing political independence and experiencing delayed self-determination as a result of international state-building. This history has shaped

Timor-Leste's state-based identity, and impacted upon perceptions of security threats and national interests that underpin foreign policy decision-making. States tend to respond to geopolitical circumstances and threats in ways that reflect historical experiences, domestic political dynamics and relations with regional powers.[102] It is not just that Timor-Leste is juxtaposed between the larger Australia and Indonesia that creates a potential security threat; the perception of threat is also contingent upon the interventionist roles of these two states in Timor-Leste's past. The strategic culture of Timor-Leste has also been shaped by the key decision-makers that were former members of the independence and resistance movement who fought — with weapons and/or words — against Indonesian colonialism.

As a new state, Timor-Leste has strategically positioned itself within an international political order, a process which is partly shaped by identity concerns. Timor-Leste's state identity has been defined by insecurity as it has transformed from colony to a trustee state of the UN to an independent sovereign state. As Sahin has argued, an insecure state identity has contributed to shaping the foreign policy manoeuvres of Timor-Leste's leadership.[103] Timor-Leste's national identity has been subject to three dominant influences: Portuguese colonialism; the resistance movement against Indonesia; and, Catholicism. Timor-Leste's connections with Southeast Asian states to the west and the states of Melanesia to the east are, and continue to be, shaped by cultural and historical links as much as they are geopolitical realities. The ongoing prioritization of Portuguese-speaking countries also reflects these cultural and historical links.

However, identities in international relations are multifaceted; they are representations and beliefs about the state that are externally produced and distinct from (but overlap with) internal or "national" identities.[104] States are social beings that produce categories in order to explain the diversity among actors within the international community. For Timor-Leste, there are a number of identity signifiers that leaders draw upon to position the state within the international community: it is a fragile, "post-conflict" state that has pursued a "zero enemies" policy and projects its image as a "good international citizen". While leaders presented the state as being a social democracy that respects universal human rights for over a decade, this has now shifted to a Timorese-specific "consensus" democracy as Timor-Leste's leaders try to justify their unity government to the international community using democratic terms. Understanding the multifaceted nature of identity is important for considering the self-images that Timor-Leste seeks to promote within the international community.

Recently, scholars have been paying more attention to the importance that small states place on image and perception building.[105] Identities "are created through an interplay of... two alternative perspectives" held by the self and the other.[106] A theory of recognition acknowledges that states are not in full control of their identities as they are contingent upon recognition by peers (i.e. fellow states).[107] States engage in a process of identity-projection in order to have their self-images accepted by others, which reflects an ongoing "struggle for recognition" of status that does not end upon the attainment of sovereign status.[108] Yet, self-images may not be recognized by others, so states are increasingly invested in pursuing social power through image building as a form of "soft power".[109] They attempt to influence how other states view them within the international community by creating "narratives" that tell stories about who they are.[110] These narratives establish and reify social categories, identities and status.[111] Image projection strategies can support the security objectives of small states as they can help legitimize their identities and deter foreign interference.

This book uses the term "aspirational foreign policy" to describe the ways in which Timor-Leste's foreign policy is motivated by identity goals, and is characterized by aspirations to achieve social prestige. Timor-Leste's aspirational foreign policy involves the use of identity projection through the use of narratives. Timor-Leste's exceptionalism is revealed in the self-image it projects as a state-building "success" story as it has moved "from fragility to resilience".[112] Timor-Leste's aspirational foreign policy is partly related to material considerations as it seeks to transform Timor-Leste from a poor developing state to an upper middle income state by 2030.[113] Timor-Leste's aspirations, however, are not just about status and prestige as part of a "struggle for recognition"; it is also a strategy increasingly used by nationalist political leaders to defend the "self-determination" of the Timorese state. Importantly, leaders are not solely interested in avoiding intervention in order to defend the rights of the Timorese nation to make collective political decisions. Foreign policy is also motivated by "elites"[114] seeking to protect their own personal and political interests. This book examines these complex dynamics between the multiple internal and external factors that shape Timor-Leste's engagements with the international community.

Chapters Overview

The first section of this book discusses the establishment of the Democratic Republic of Timor-Leste as an independent sovereign state through the three waves of Portuguese, Indonesian and UN administration. It is impossible to understand Timor-Leste's foreign policy and engagements with the broader international community without first understanding the importance of the independence movement to the identity and interests of Timor-Leste. Its key interests are in fulfilling the dreams and aspirations of independence: securing the state against colonialism and intervention, ensuring "real" independence and guaranteeing self-determination. These aspirations reveal the key source of Timor-Leste's insecurity, which is the prospect of foreign intervention, whether it be by the UN, a multinational force or a hostile external actor.

Chapter two examines the ways in which Timor-Leste was cartographically "imagined" through processes of European colonialism, which territorially defined East Timor, and contributed to the establishment of international legal rights as a colonial entity, and, ultimately, a sense of national identity. Colonial borders constructed by the European states gave East Timor a status under international law as a colonial territory with attendant rights to self-determination. East Timor's independence movement used international law and norms to justify their claims to self-determination during the Indonesian occupation from 1975 until 1999. This highlights the importance of international laws and principles for establishing Timor-Leste's distinct identity and rights within the international community.

Chapter three examines the struggle for recognition during the years of Indonesia's occupation as East Timor's independence movement sought to persuade members of the international community to uphold principles of self-determination. This chapter examines the reactions and activities of international actors to the claims of the East Timorese independence movement for sovereign independence. It examines the contexts that shaped the independence movement (for instance, the Cold War), and analyses the activities of key states such as Portugal, Australia and Indonesia in relation to East Timor's aspirations for sovereignty. It also focuses on the international pressure that led to Indonesia's policy shift on the issue of East Timor's self-determination. It argues there were two key reasons for the recognition of East Timor's rights under international law: first, the independence movement linked its struggle with key human rights precepts embedded in international law; and second, Indonesia failed to persuade others in the international community that East Timor belonged to Indonesia. The history of this struggle has shaped independent Timor-Leste's engagements with the international community.

Chapter four examines the contribution of international state-building from 1999–2002 in developing Timor-Leste's state identity. Timor-Leste's attainment of sovereignty was permitted by the international community and supported through various state-building and peace-building activities.[115] New states are expected to conform to the pre-existing normative frameworks of the international community. Timor-Leste's political institutions were shaped by external actors, which has consequences — positive and negative — for the development of sovereign statehood. One of the challenges facing local and international state-builders was reconciling the tensions between Western, "Weberian" (centralized) state structures and local, customary forms of political authority and law. This international state-building period was crucial in establishing Timor-Leste as a liberal-democratic state, reflecting dominant international political ideologies. This period of intensive international intervention is important for explaining the subsequent desire for self-determination and "real" independence espoused by Timorese leaders.

The second part of this book examines Timor-Leste's international relations following its achievement of independence in 2002. Chapter five begins by examining the development of Timor-Leste's foreign policy. It examines key bilateral and multilateral engagements since independence. Broadly, the three key aims of Timor-Leste's foreign policy were initially to maintain friendships with Indonesia and Australia, pursue membership of international and regional organizations, particularly ASEAN, and establish relationships with a range of countries.[116] However, this chapter argues that Timor-Leste has increasingly pursued an expansive, "aspirational" foreign policy approach. In the international arena it has sought to project its preferred self-image as a successful liberal-democracy that respects multilateralism and international rule of law. A dominant foreign policy narrative of "fragile state exceptionalism" has emerged around the belief that Timor-Leste has overcome its history of conflict and colonialism to become a successful model state for other fragile and post-conflict societies.

Chapter six examines the types of international institutions Timor-Leste has sought to join, the types of interests that have been pursued in multilateral engagements and the nature of Timor-Leste's diplomatic priorities. It focuses particular attention on Timor-Leste's pursuit of ASEAN membership, an organization whose members also defend an absolutist conception of sovereignty. It also examines Timor-Leste's relations with the Community of Portuguese Speaking Countries (CPLP) and its Pacific Island neighbours, and its leadership role in the g7+ organization of fragile, post-conflict states. This chapter reveals the significance of common cultural, historical, developmental and regional connections underpinning Timor-Leste's efforts at international cooperation and participation in intergovernmental organizations.

In contrast, chapter seven looks at the ways leaders have presented an image of the international environment as insecure and competitive. It examines the types of external threats identified by leaders and the ways they have sought to protect the state against these threats. Since independence, Timor-Leste has sought to develop their defence capacities in line with conventional thinking about national security and "real" independence, even though internal security has been more problematic than external threats. The growth of a domestic military has influenced the foreign relations of Timor-Leste and has broader implications for understanding security and independence in post-colonial states. Timor-Leste's national security has been linked to a political history that includes collusion between Australia and Indonesia in denying the East Timorese nation its right to self-determination.

Upon independence, Timor-Leste became the poorest sovereign state in Southeast Asia. It has depended upon donations from a range of international aid donors, comprising state and non-state actors. Timor-Leste has relied upon international institutions such as the International Monetary Fund and the World Bank for the provision of essential services and resources. Chapter eight examines the ways that Timor-Leste has sought to articulate, protect and extend its economic sovereignty. This chapter focuses on Timor-Leste's ambitious pursuit of development advanced through a neoliberal agenda based on oil industrialization, free trade policies and direct foreign investment. Although it remains a low-income state, Timor-Leste is resource rich and resource dependent. Timor-Leste's short- to mid-term economic future depends upon gaining access to contested hydrocarbon reserves in the Timor Sea, in particular the Greater Sunrise gas field. Timor-Leste responded to this foreign policy challenge by engaging in an ambitious and risky "activist" strategy based on public diplomacy and use of international legal mechanisms. By the end of 2017 (at the time of writing), the development of Greater Sunrise remained under negotiation with Australia and commercial partners. A failure of diplomacy in this regard would likely re-invite intervention and aid dependence, perhaps within a decade. Even if development begins soon on Greater Sunrise, a failure to diversify the economy will have longer term consequences for development. This highlights the ways in which Timor-Leste's tactics may paradoxically undermine its capacities to guarantee independence.

Chapter nine examines Timor-Leste's relationship with international norms of justice. International justice is characterized by the global articulation of basic human rights and norms outlawing crimes against humanity. In the twenty-first century, an international obligation of states to pursue individuals who bear responsibility for gross violations of human rights has crystallized. Since the 1999 independence referendum, Timor-Leste has struggled to achieve substantive justice for the human rights violations committed during Indonesia's twenty-five-year *de facto* administration because many alleged perpetrators of rights violations have been shielded by Indonesia. Many civil society organizations have lobbied the international community to establish an independent international tribunal, but this has yet to occur. This chapter examines the 2008 Indonesia–Timor-Leste Commission of Truth and Friendship, which was the world's first bilateral Truth and Reconciliation Commission. Its formation provides insights into how Timor-Leste has sought to engage its closest neighbour and former colonial master and its pursuit of security through bilateral reconciliation. It also analyses the implementation of the Commission's recommendations by Indonesia and Timor-Leste, and concludes that the Commission was primarily a pragmatic political mechanism designed to support international priorities rather than principles of justice.

Finally, chapter ten examines future challenges for Timor-Leste in the Asian-Pacific region. It explains the strategic relationships successive governments have pursued in response to an uncertain regional balance of power in Asia. It argues that Timor-Leste has, and will likely continue to, engage in "strategic hedging" to cope with insecurities emerging from shifting structural power dynamics. The chapter finishes by considering what is likely to be a most significant factor contributing to Timor-Leste's insecurity: climate change. It examines Timor-Leste's contribution to global climate change cooperation, as well as key environmental challenges facing the state in the future. Timor-Leste's leaders have proven themselves to be skilled rhetoricians insofar as they adeptly use human rights and development vernaculars in their public diplomacy. Ultimately, however, the book demonstrates that undiversified economic policies, weak institutions and increasingly undemocratic governance combine to threaten the future viability of Timorese statehood. Timor-Leste's security and independence will not rely on growing its military capabilities or its aspirational foreign policy, it will depend upon sustainable social, economic and environmental policies that genuinely support the livelihoods of the citizens of Timor-Leste.

NOTES

1. The phrase "international community" is used to encapsulate a range of international actors, including states, intergovernmental and regional organizations.
2. David Strang, "Contested Sovereignty: The Social Construction of Colonial Imperialism", in *State Sovereignty as Social Construct*, edited by Thomas Biersteker and Cynthia Weber, p. 22 (Cambridge: Cambridge University Press, 1996).
3. Hans Agné, "The Politics of International Recognition: Symposium Introduction", *International Theory* 5, no. 1 (2013): 95.
4. United Nations Security Council (UNSC), "Resolution 1272", S/RES/1272, 25 October 1999.
5. See Joel Beauvais, "Benevolent Despotism: A Critique of UN State-building in East Timor", *New York University Journal of International Law and Politics* 33 (2001–2): 1101, 1104; Sue Downie, "UNTAET: State-building and Peace-Building", in *East Timor: Beyond Independence*, edited by Damien Kingsbury and Michael Leach, p. 29 (Clayton: Monash University Press, 2007); Aksuno Matsuno, "The UN Transitional Administration and Democracy Building in Timor-Leste", in *Democratic Governance in Timor-Leste: Reconciling the*

Local and the National, edited by David Mearns and Steven Farram, p. 53 (Darwin: Charles Darwin University Press, 2008); Ralph Wilde, "From Danzig to East Timor and Beyond: The Role of International Territorial Administration", *American Journal of International Law* 95, no. 3 (2001): 583; Toshi Nakamura, *Reflections on the State-Institution-Building Support in Timor-Leste: Capacity Development, Integrating Missions, and Financial Challenges*, p. 3 (United Nations Development Programme, Oslo Governance Centre, November 2004); Simon Chesterman, "East Timor in Transition: Self-determination, State-building and the United Nations", *International Peacekeeping* 9, no. 1 (Spring 2002): 45–49.

6. See Clinton Fernandes, *The Independence of East Timor: Multi-Dimensional Perspectives – Occupation, Resistance, and International Political Activism* (Brighton: Sussex Academic Press, 2011).

7. See Simon Chesterman, *You, the People: The United Nations, Transitional Administration, and State-Building* (Oxford: Oxford University Press, 2005); Dominik Zaum, *The Sovereign Paradox: The Norms and Politics of International State-building* (Oxford: Oxford University Press, 2007).

8. See Michael Butler, "Ten Years After: (Re) Assessing Neo-Trusteeship and UN State-building in Timor-Leste", *International Studies Perspectives* 13 (2012): 85–104; Aurel Croissant, "Perils and Promises of Democratization Through United Nations Transitional Authority: Lessons from Cambodia and East Timor", *Democratization* 15, no. 3 (2008): 649–48; Paulo Gorjão, "The Legacy and Lessons of the United Nations Transitional Administration in East Timor", *Contemporary Southeast Asia* 24, no. 2 (2002): 313–36; Jonathon Morrow and Rachel White, "The United Nations in Transitional East Timor: International Standards and the Reality of Governance", *Australian Year Book of International Law* 22, no. 1 (2002): 1–47.

9. See Ingram, Sue, Lia Kent and Andrew McWilliam, eds, *A New Era? Timor-Leste After the UN* (Canberra: Australian National University Press, 2015); Damien Kingsbury and Michael Leach, eds., *East Timor: Beyond Independence* (Clayton: Monash University Press, 2007); Michael Leach and Damien Kingsbury, eds., *The Politics of Timor-Leste: Democratic Consolidation After Intervention* (Ithaca: Cornell, 2014); David Mearns and Steven Farram, eds., *Democratic Governance in Timor-Leste: Reconciling the Local and the National* (Darwin: Charles Darwin University Press, 2008); Vandra Harris and Andrew Goldsmith, eds., *Security, Development and Nation-Building in Timor-Leste: A Cross-Sectoral Assessment* (Oxon: Routledge, 2011); Andrea Molnar, *Timor-Leste: Politics, History, and Culture* (London and New York: Routledge, 2010); Dennis Shoesmith, *The Crisis in Timor-Leste: Understanding the Past, Imagining the Future* (Darwin: Charles Darwin University Press, 2007).

10. Michael Leach and Sally Percival-Wood, "Timor-Leste: From INTERFET to ASEAN", in *The Australia–ASEAN Dialogue: Tracing 40 Years of Partnership*, edited by Baogang He and Sally Percival-Wood, pp. 67–85 (New York: Palgrave Macmillan, 2014); Nuno Canas Mendes, "Dilemas Indentitários e fatalidades geopoliticas: Timor-Leste entre o Sudeste Asiático e o Pacifico-Sul", in *Understanding Timor-Leste*, edited by Michael Leach, Nuno Canas Mendes, Antero B. da Silva, Alarico da Costa Ximenes and Bob Boughton, pp. 35–40 (Hawthorn: Swinburne Press, 2010); Selver Sahin, "Timor-Leste: A More Confident or Overconfident Foreign Policy Actor?" *Southeast Asian Affairs* (2012): 341–58; Selver Sahin, "Timor-Leste's Foreign Policy: Securing State Identity in the Post-Independent Period", *Journal of Current Southeast Asian Affairs* 33, no. 2 (2014): 3–25; Pedro Seabra, "The Need for a Reshaped Foreign Policy", in *The Politics of Timor-Leste: Democratic Consolidation After Intervention*, edited by Michael Leach and Damien Kingsbury, pp. 145–61 (Ithaca, NY: Cornell, 2014); Anthony Smith, "Constraints and Choices: East Timor as a Foreign Policy Actor", *New Zealand Journal of Asian Studies* 7, no. 1 (June 2005): 15–36; José Kei Lekke Sousa-Santos, "Acting West, Looking East: Timor-Leste's Growing Engagement with the Pacific Islands Region", in *Regionalism, Security and Cooperation in Oceania*, edited by Rouben Azizian and Carleton Cramer, pp. 110–12 (Honolulu: Asia-Pacific Centre for Security Studies, 2015); Ian Storey, *Southeast Asia and the Rise of China: The Search for Security*, chapter 14 (New York: Routledge, 2011); Rebecca Strating, "East Timor's Emerging National Security Agenda: Establishing 'Real' Independence", *Asian Security* 9, no. 3 (2013): 185–210; Rebecca Strating, "The Indonesia–Timor-Leste Commission of Truth and Friendship: Enhancing Bilateral Relations at the Expense of Justice", *Contemporary Southeast Asia* 36, no. 2 (2014): 232–61; Rebecca Strating, "Timor-Leste's Foreign Policy Approach to the Timor Sea Disputes", *Australian Journal of International Affairs* (2017); David Willis, "Timor-Leste's Complex Geopolitics: The Local, the Regional and the Global", in *Timor-Leste: The Local, the Regional and the Global*, edited by Sarah Smith, Nuno Canas Mendes, Antero B. da Silva, Alarico da Costa Ximenes, Clinton Fernandes and Michael Leach, pp. 237–43 (Melbourne: Swinburne University Press, 2016).
11. "Post-colonial" is a contested term in the literature, see Priya Chacko, *Indian Foreign Policy: The Politics of Post-Colonial Identity From 1947–2004*, p. 11 (Oxon: Routledge, 2012). Here I am using its conventional usage to refer to Timor-Leste as a state that had previously been subject to colonial administration.
12. Rudra Sil and Peter Katzenstein, "Analyical Eclectism in the Study of World Politics: Reconfiguring Problems and Mechanisms Across Research Traditions", *Perspectives on Politics* 8, no. 2 (2010): 412.

13. Anders Wivel, Alyson Bailes, and Clive Archer, "Setting the Scene: Small States and International Security", in *Small States and International Security: Europe and Beyond*, edited by Clive Archer, Alyson Bailes and Anders Wivel, p. 7 (Oxon: Routledge, 2014).
14. Ibid.
15. William Brown and Sophie Harman, "African Agency in International Politics", *African Agency in International Politics*, edited by William Brown and Sophie Harman, p. 2 (Oxon: Routledge, 2013).
16. Ibid.
17. See in particular Nuno Canas Mendes, "Multidimensional Identity Construction: Challenges for State-building in East Timor", in *East Timor: How to Build a New Nation in Southeast Asia in the 21st Century?*, edited by Christine Cabasset-Semedo and Frédéric Durand, pp. 19–30 (Thailand: Research Institute on Contemporary Southeast Asia, 2009); Nuno Canas Mendes, *Multidimensionalidade da Construção identitária de Timor-Leste* (Lisbon: ISCSP, 2005); Michael Leach, *Nation Building and National Identity in Timor-Leste* (Oxon: Routledge, 2017).
18. David Campbell, *Writing Security: United States Foreign Policy and the Politics of Identity* (Minnesota: University of Minnesota Press, 1998).
19. Robert Rotberg, "The Failure and Collapse of Nation-States: Breakdown, Prevention and Repair", in *When States Fail: Causes and Consequences*, edited by Robert Rotberg, p. 1 (New Jersey: Princeton University Press, 2004).
20. Max Weber, *From Max Weber: Essays in Sociology. Edited, with an Introduction by H.H. Gerth and C.W. Mills* (Oxon: Routledge, 1991).
21. Robert Jackson, *Quasi-States: Sovereignty, International Relations and the Third World*, pp. 5, 9 (Cambridge: Cambridge University Press, 1990). Rotberg, "The Failure and Collapse of Nation-States", pp. 1–4.
22. It is also classified in various rankings as fragile. For example, it ranked 35th of 178 states in *Foreign Policy*'s Fragile States Index in 2015. *Foreign Policy*, "Fragile States Index 2015", available at <http://foreignpolicy.com/fragile-states-index-2016-brexit-syria-refugee-europe-anti-migrant-boko-haram/> (accessed 20 February 2017).
23. John Herz, "Idealist Internationalism and the Security Dilemma", *World Politics* 2, no. 2 (1950): 157. See also Robert Jervis, "Cooperation under the Security Dilemma", *World Politics* 30, no. 2 (January 1978): 169–70.
24. Alan Collins, *The Security Dilemmas of Southeast Asia*, p. 2 (Hampshire: Palgrave Macmillan, 2000); Jervis, "Cooperation under the Security Dilemma", p. 172.
25. Barry Buzan, *People, States, and Fear: The National Security Problem in International Relations* (Chapel Hill: North Carolina, University of North Carolina Press, 1983); Muthiah Alagappa, "International Security in Southeast Asia: Growing Salience of Regional and Domestic Dynamics",

in *Security of Third World Countries*, edited by Jasjit Singh and Thomas Bernauer, pp. 109–49 (Aldershot: United Nations Institute for Disarmament Research, 1993); Mohammad Ayoob, *The Third World Security Predicament: State-Making, Regional Conflict, and the International System* (Boulder: Lynne Rienner, 1995).
26. Robert Keohane, "'Lilliputians' Dilemma: Small states in international politics", *International Organization* 23 (1969): 293.
27. Ibid., p. 560.
28. Buzan, *People, States, and Fear*, pp. 63–69.
29. Ayoob, *The Third World Security Predicament*, p. 7
30. Brian Job, "Introduction", in *The Insecurity Dilemma: National Security of Third World States*, edited by Brian Job, p. 12 (Boulder: Lynne Rienner Publishers, 1992).
31. Collins, *The Security Dilemmas of Southeast Asia*, p. 31.
32. See for example Miriam Fendius Elman, "The Foreign Policy of Small States: Challenging Neorealism in its Own Backyard", *British Journal of Political Science* 25, no. 2 (1995): 175–79.
33. Daniel Philpott, "Westphalia, Authority and International Society", *Political Studies* XLVII (1999): 577–78.
34. Christopher Clapham, "Degrees of Statehood", *Review of International Studies* 24 (1998): 143–57; Robert Cooper, *The Breaking of Nations: Order and Chaos in the Twenty-First Century* (London: Atlantic Monthly Press, 2003); Georg Sørenson, "An Analysis of Contemporary Statehood: Consequences for Conflict and Cooperation", *Review of International Studies* 23, (1997): 253–69.
35. Stephen Krasner, "Abiding Sovereignty", *International Political Science Review* 22, no. 3 (2001): 231.
36. Jackson, *Quasi-States*, pp. 5, 9.
37. Ibid., pp. 26–31. See also James Crawford, *The Creation of States in International Law*, 2nd ed. (Oxford: Clarendon Press, 2006); Jackson Robert and Carl Rosberg, "Why Africa's Weak States Persist: The Empirical and the Juridical in Statehood", *World Politics* 35, no. 1 (October 1982): 1–24.
38. Juan Federer, *The UN in East Timor: Building Timor-Leste, a Fragile State* (Darwin: Charles Darwin University Press, 2005).
39. Naeem Inayatullah, "Beyond the Sovereignty Dilemma: Quasi-States as Social Construct", in *State Sovereignty as Social Construct*, edited by Thomas Biersteker and Cynthia Weber, p. 60 (Cambridge: Cambridge University Press, 1996); Strang, "Contested Sovereignty", p. 25.
40. Ayoob, *The Third World Security Predicament*, p. 4.
41. John Herz, "Rise and Demise of the Territorial State", *World Politics* 9, no. 4 (1957): 473.
42. Simona Țuțuianu, *Towards Global Justice: Sovereignty in an Interdependent World*, p. 43 (The Hague: TMC Asser Press, 2013).

43. See, for example, Joséph Camilleri and Jim Falk, *The End of Sovereignty? The Politics of Shrinking and Fragmenting World* (Aldershot, UK: Edward Elgar, 2002); Kenici Ohmae, *The Borderless World: Power and Strategy in the Interlinked Economy* (New York: HarperCollins, 1994).
44. See, for example, Andrew Linklater, *The Transformation of Political Community* (Cambridge: Polity Press, 1998).
45. See, for example, Benjamin Habib, "Climate Change, Security and Regime Formation in East Asia", in *Non-Traditional Security in East Asia*, edited by Ramon Racheco Pardo and Jeffrey Reeves, pp. 49–72 (London: Imperial College Press, 2016).
46. See, for example, Jarat Chopra and Thomas Weiss, "Sovereignty is No Longer Sacrosanct: Codifying Humanitarian Intervention", *Ethics and International Affairs* 6, no. 1 (1992): 95–117.
47. Ibid.
48. Alex Bellamy, Paul Williams and Stuart Griffin, *Understanding Peacekeeping*, 2nd ed., p. 38 (Cambridge: Polity Press, 2010).
49. Amitav Acharya, *Constructing a Security Community in Southeast Asia: ASEAN and the Problem of Regional Order*, 3rd ed., p. 57 (London and New York: Routledge, 2014).
50. Erik Ringmar, "Introduction: The International Politics of Recognition", in *The International Politics of Recognition*, edited by Thomas Lindemann and Erik Ringmar, p. 7 (Boulder: Paradigm Publishers, 2014). For an explanation of Westphalian and Post-Westphalian approaches, see Bellamy, Williams and Griffin, *Understanding Peacekeeping*, pp. 36–39.
51. Roland Burke, *Decolonization and the Evolution of International Human Rights* (Philadelphia: University of Pennsylvania, 2010).
52. Ibid.
53. Stephen Krasner, "Sharing Sovereignty: New Institutions for Collapsed and Failing States", *International Security* 29, no. 2 (2004): 86; Rotberg, "The Failure and Collapse of Nation-States". See, for example, Liana Sun Wyler, *Weak and Failing States: Evolving Security Threats and U.S. Foreign Policy* (Congressional Research Service, 2008).
54. There is some contest in the literature regarding how to define a small state. Jeanne Hey, "Introducing Small State Foreign Policy", in *Small States in World Politics: Explaining Foreign Policy Behaviour*, edited by Jeanne Hey, p. 2 (Boulder: Lynne Rienner Publishers, 2003).
55. In contrast, the World Bank uses a threshold of 1.5 million people. See Andrea Ó Súilleabháin, *Small States at the United Nations: Diverse Perspectives, Shared Opportunities*, p. 3 (New York: International Peace Institute, May 2014).
56. For example, Ali Nasser Mohamed, *The Diplomacy of Micro-states*, Discussion Papers in Diplomacy, Netherlands Institute of International Relations, 2002, p. 1.

57. World Bank, "Population 2015", available at <http://databank.worldbank.org/data/download/POP.pdf> (accessed 30 January 2017).
58. Central Intelligence Agency, "The World Factbook Country Comparison: Area", available at <https://www.cia.gov/Library/publications/the-world-factbook/rankorder/2147rank.html> (accessed 30 January 2017).
59. Hey, "Introducing Small State Foreign Policy", p. 3.
60. Baldur Thorhallsson, "Small States in the UN Security Council: Means of Influence?", *The Hague Journal of Diplomacy* 7 (2012): 135.
61. See, for example, Elma, "The Foreign Policies of Small States", p. 172.
62. Ó Súilleabháin, *Small States at the United Nations*, p. 3; Thorhallsson, "Small States in the UN Security Council", p. 139.
63. Campbell, *Writing Security*, p. 44.
64. Hey, "Introducing Small State Foreign Policy", p. 8.
65. See, for example, Alexander Wendt, *Social Theory of International Politics* (Cambridge: Cambridge University Press, 1999).
66. Matthais Maass, "Small Enough to Fail: The Structural Irrelevance of the Small State as Cause of its Elimination and Proliferation since Westphalia", *Cambridge Review of International Affairs* (2017): 1.
67. Ibid.
68. Beth Edmondson and Stuart Levy, *International Relations: Nurturing Reality*, p. 16 (Frenchs Forest, NSW: Pearson, 2008).
69. Kenneth Waltz, *Theory of International Politics*, pp. 194–95 (Reading: Addison-Wesley, 1979).
70. Wivel, Bailes and Archer, "Setting the Scene", p. 3.
71. Ibid. For a thorough overview of neo-realism on small states, see Elman, "The Foreign Policies of Small States", pp. 175–79.
72. Hey, "Introducing Small State Foreign Policy", p. 5.
73. Zachary Abuza, "Laos: Maintaining Power in a Highly Charged Region", in *Small States in World Politics: Explaining Foreign Policy Behaviour*, edited by Jeanne Hey, p. 184 (Boulder: Lynne Rienner Publishers, 2003).
74. JC Sharman, "Sovereignty at the Extremes: Micro-States in World Politics", *Political Studies* 65, no. 3 (2016): 559.
75. Ibid.
76. Hey, "Introducing Small State Foreign Policy", p. 8.
77. Stephen Walt, *The Origins of Alliances*, pp. 21–31 (Ithaca: Cornell University Press, 1987).
78. Sharman, "Sovereignty at the Extremes", p. 561.
79. See Eric Labs, "Do Weak States Bandwagon?", *Security Studies* 1, no. 3 (1992): 383–416.
80. Hans Mouritzen, "Testing Weak-Power Theory: Three Nordic Reactions to the Soviet Coup", in *European Foreign Policy: The EC and Changing Perspectives*

in Europe, edited by Walter Carlsnaes and Steve Smith, p. 158 (London: Sage, 1994).
81. Hans Mouritzen, "Tension between the Strong and the Strategies of the Weak", *Journal of Peace Research* 28, no. 2 (1991): 219.
82. Christopher Browning, *Constructivism, Narrative and Foreign Policy Analysis: A Case Study of Finland*, p. 30 (Bern: Peter Lang, 2008).
83. Amitav Acharya, "After Liberal Hegemony: The Advent of a Multiplex World Order", *Ethics and International Affairs*, 8 September 2017, available at <https://www.ethicsandinternationalaffairs.org/2017/multiplex-world-order/> (accessed 5 January 2018).
84. Michael Handel, "Weak States in the International System", in *Small States in International Relations*, edited by Christine Ingebritsen, pp. 149–50 (Washington, University of Washington Press, 2006). See also ibid., p. 27.
85. Michael Leifer, "Southeast Asia", in *Foreign Policy Making in Developing States: A Comparative Approach*, edited by Christopher Clapham, pp. 17, 32 (New York: Praegar, 1977). See also Jurgen Haacke, "South-East Asia's International Relations and Security Perspectives", in *East and Southeast Asia: International Relations and Security Perspectives*, edited by Andrew T.H. Tan, p. 158 (Oxon: Routledge, 2013).
86. See, for example, Abuza, "Laos", pp. 176–80.
87. Leifer, "Southeast Asia", p. 35.
88. Ibid., p. 32.
89. Rui Graça Feijó, "Challenges to the Consolidation of Democracy", in *A New Era? Timor-Leste After the UN*, edited by Sue Ingram, Lia Kent and Andrew McWilliam, p. 61 (Canberra: ANU Press, 2015).
90. Rebecca Strating, "Timor-Leste in 2017: A State of Uncertainty", in *Southeast Asian Affairs 2018*, edited by Malcolm Cook and Daljit Singh (Singapore: Institute of Southeast Asian Studies: 2018).
91. Hey, "Introducing Small State Foreign Policy", p. 5.
92. Waltz, *Theory of International Politics*, pp. 72–73.
93. Handel, "Weak States in the International System".
94. Hey, "Introducing Small State Foreign Policy", p. 187.
95. Ibid., p. 8.
96. Christine Ingebritsen, "Norm Entrepreneurs: Scandinavia's Role in World Politics", *Cooperation and Conflict: Journal of the Nordic International Studies Association* 37, no. 1 (2002): 11–23.
97. Carsten-Andreas Schulz, "Accidental Activists: Latin American Status-Seeking at The Hague", *International Studies Quarterly* 61, no. 3 (2017): 612–22.
98. Hedley Bull, *The Anarchical Society: A Study of Order in World Politics* (London: Macmillan, 1977), p. 13.
99. Ibid., pp. 17–18.

100. Ó Súilleabháin, *Small States at the United Nations*, pp. 1, 5.
101. Ibid., p. 4.
102. See, for example, Jutta Weldes, Mark Laffey, Hugh Gusterson and Raymond Duvall, "Introduction: Constructing Insecurity", in *Cultures of Insecurity: States, Communities, and the Production of Danger*, edited by Jutta Weldes, Mark Laffey, Hugh Gusterson and Raymond Duvall, pp. 1–34 (Minnesota: University of Minnesota Press, 1999); Alexander Wendt, "Anarchy is What States Make of It: The Social Construction of Power Politics", *International Organization* 46, no. 2 (1992): 391–425. According to Katzenstein, "[t]he state is a social actor. It is embedded in social rules and conventions that constitute its identity and the reasons for the interests that motivate actors." See Peter Katzenstein, "Introduction: Alternative Perspectives on National Security", in *The Culture of National Security: Norms and Identity in World Politics* (New York: Columbia University Press, 1996), p. 23.
103. Sahin, "Timor-Leste's Foreign Policy", pp. 3–5.
104. Maxym Alexandrov, "The Concept of State Identity in International Relations: A Theoretical Analysis", *Journal of International Development and Cooperation* 10, no. 1 (2003): 40.
105. Thorhallsson, "Small States in the UN Security Council", p. 143.
106. Ringmar, "Introduction", p. 6.
107. Ibid., p. 11.
108. See, for example, Thomas Lindemann, *Causes of War: The Struggle for Recognition* (Colchester: ECPR Press, 2010).
109. Joseph S. Nye Jr., "Soft Power", *Foreign Policy* 80, Twentieth Anniversary (Autumn 1990): 167.
110. Jelena Subotić, "Narrative, Ontological Security, and Foreign Policy Change", *Foreign Policy Analysis* 12, no. 4 (2014): 612–13.
111. Ned Lebow, *Politics and Ethics of Identity: In Search of Ourselves*, p. 49 (New York: Cambridge University Press, 2012).
112. See chapter 5.
113. República Democrática de Timor-Leste (RDTL), *Strategic Development Plan*, p. 9 (Dili: Government of Timor-Leste, 2011).
114. There are some debates about whether the term "elite" is applicable to Timor-Leste, where there are a few economic elites, and the grouping is subject to high rates of turnover. See Julien Barbara, John Cox and Michael Leach, "Emerging Middle Classes in Timor-Leste and Melanesia: Implications for Development and Democracy", *In Brief* 57 (Canberra: Australian National University, 2014), p. 2. However, the term is used here to describe the small number of people in influential political leadership and economic positions in Timor-Leste. The term has value because a small core of people have disproportionate decision-making capacities and increased opportunities to obtain advantage from highly centralized authority structures.
115. Federer, *The UN in East Timor*, p. 4.
116. Storey, *Southeast Asia and the Rise of China*, p. 277.

2

The Struggle for Recognition: Territorialization, Self-determination and the Imagining of "East Timor"

The first section of this book examines the roles of states and the international community in establishing East Timor's sovereign identity. This chapter develops an understanding of how East Timor became "imagined" as a bounded political unit within the international community. The 1933 Montevideo Convention defined a state as an entity that possesses a permanent population, defined territory, government and capacity to enter into relations with other states.[1] "Territorialization" is the act of organizing territory, a process that is integral to the absolute external sovereignty concept. While it is contested in international relations, territorial sovereignty continues to provide the conceptual framework for demarcating those groups that possess rights to political authority in the international community from those that do not. The first stage of East Timor's statehood involved the creation of an internationally recognized territory through the partition of the island of Timor by regional European powers, Portugal and the Netherlands in the nineteenth century. East Timor's status as a bounded territory with a population was established externally; its identity was dependent upon the international community rather than developing through national consciousness shared by the people inhabiting the territory. The territorialization of East Timor is key to understanding how it achieved state sovereignty.

Timor-Leste is part of the *Lesser Sundas* (*Nusatenggara*) group of islands situated on the Eastern tip of the Indonesian archipelago.[2] Territorially, it shares the island of Timor with the Indonesian province of West Timor. East Timor's colonial history and borders are relevant to the international recognition of the right of self-determination. The border that splits "East" from "West" Timor is not an organic demarcation, but one driven by international forces, most notably the introduction of European colonialism[3] in the region in the seventeenth century. The East Timorese exclave Oecussi in the Indonesian province of West Timor, for example, reflects historical colonial settlement. This chapter examines the processes by which the territory of East Timor became "imagined" during the era of Portuguese colonialism. It does so by examining the border arrangements and international legal negotiations between the Portuguese and Dutch to divide the island of Timor into "East" and "West". The contemporary state and national identity of Timor-Leste owes its existence to European colonialism and international law.[4] Bounded territory provided the physical and social space for "imagining" the East Timorese political community.[5]

Internationally recognized borders were not created with reference to governance structures or identity groupings that existed on the island of Timor. International law as it developed over the twentieth century created normative instruments to decide which entities would hold sovereign political authority. Timor-Leste owes its sovereign status to the principles and practices of self-determination that developed during the post-World War Two period of mass global decolonization that saw the creation of sovereign states corresponding with boundaries established with imperial powers. These rights generally corresponded with colonial demarcation of territory. In other words, European colonialism was pivotal for deciding which "people" (i.e. the *self* in self-determination) were recognized as holding rights to self-determination under international law.

While East Timor held rights to self-determination, these legal entitlements were insufficient to guarantee international recognition of sovereignty. In 1974, a shift in policy by a new Portuguese government permitted most of its colonies to exercise self-determination. By 1975, East Timorese "elites" had begun the process of establishing political parties and self-government. In December 1975, East Timor was invaded by Indonesia, which occupied the territory until 1999. Throughout the occupation, East Timor's independence leaders used arguments based upon international law and norms to justify claims to political self-determination. In 1975 and 1976, representatives of East Timor's independence movement argued at the United Nations (UN) that Timor-Leste had legal rights to self-determination, and that consequently Indonesia's occupation was unlawful under international law. In response, Indonesia, through official state ministers and East Timorese representatives, argued that an act of self-determination had occurred. While East Timor had legal entitlements — and a defined territory and population — it was unable to give substance to these rights. East Timor's delayed independence was an anomaly in the post-World War Two decolonization period, where the primary definition of "peoples" in regard to self-determination was "that of non-European inhabitants of former colonies" (such as East Timor).[6] This "struggle for recognition" is important for understanding the genesis of Timor-Leste's state-based identity, as the historical and structural forces shaping its development have contemporary implications for foreign policy decision-making.

Territorialization and Statehood

This chapter, and the one that follows, consider the questions of how and why Timor-Leste became a member of the "sovereignty" club. This question primarily concerns the dilemmas of "sovereign recognition" — that is, why some political entities attain sovereign eligibility but others do not. The English School has argued that states form an "international society" in spite of the anarchical structure, which they shape and, in turn, are shaped by.[7] This international society is created through processes of mutual recognition: states are accorded political status as they recognize, and are recognized as, sovereign by other states. According to Philpott, an international society "constitution" could be said to exist in the mutually agreed upon norms that define the members of society, holders of political authority and their prerogatives.[8] However, these norms that legitimize some polities (but not others) are not always clear or coherent, and the "rules and practices" of sovereign recognition remain under-theorized in international relations.[9]

Debates in international relations and international law have concerned the criteria of statehood and whether these are fact-based/ empirical, or socially constructed. Declaratory recognition focuses on the material criteria of statehood and the recognition of empirical facts rather than identities.[10] The Montevideo Convention, for example, expresses a "declaratory" view of sovereign recognition in which attainment of sovereign status is recognized if a political entity demonstrates that it possesses the material features of statehood.[11] Recognition itself does not create the state: declaring a state sovereign is a mere formality.[12] Political independence is separate from recognition because it is a matter of "fact" rather than law: independence was a criterion of statehood and sovereignty was the legal incident.[13] Kelsen, for example, emphasizes "natural" statehood over juridical statehood as being integral to the creation of sovereign states.[14] By "natural" statehood, Kelsen means that entities were required to possess the material and civil features of sovereignty before becoming recognized.

International relations, on the other hand, has favoured a constitutive theory of recognition that perceives recognition as about socially constructed "facts" sustained and altered through interactions. Sovereignty is an identity status that is given meaning through social relations. According to Erman, "[a] political entity would not be *self*-determining without the inter-state dimension since such a 'self' is premised on others' recognition... There is an essential *relational* aspect of self-determination, without which statehood would not be a *status*."[15] While declaratory theories view statehood as a factual phenomenon, constitutive theories view it as "a normative phenomenon impregnated by practices of recognition".[16] Prior to World War Two, states were often recognized only when they had attained the pre-requisites of statehood. Since then, however, international legal recognition has been distinguished from "real" or "actual" independence, which refers to the minimal degree of real power necessary to qualify a state as functionally independent.[17] For new states, becoming a sovereign state is not contingent upon "real" or "actual" political independence, or the capacity to defend boundaries from foreign aggressors. New post-colonial states were created out of international law, which privileged the principle of national self-determination.[18] As Fabry notes, "the understanding of collective self-determination shifted from the actual establishment of independence by a self-identified political community to the entitlement of independence allotted by international society to particular categories of territorial entities in their existing borders".[19] This reflects a constitutive act of recognition, whereby international recognition was understood as the process through which states enter into being.[20]

At least some empirical features must be present in order for an entity to be recognized as a sovereign state.[21] Bartelson suggests that a "people" must display "some recognizably state-like qualities in order to be qualified as an object of possible recognition".[22] If some minimum requirements are not met then "the entity in question falls outside the epistemic range of possible objects of recognition".[23] Declaratory theory assumes that entities "fit" some objective criteria of statehood, yet, as Erman argues, the "basic 'fitting' features are themselves construed through relations, norms, and agreements established in international law".[24] The criteria of statehood are hence a mix of factual and social conditions that differ across unique recognition scenarios.

In the case of East Timor, the "facts" of statehood — territory, population, government — necessary for the attainment of sovereign status were not just *recognized* by international actors, but actively constructed through European colonialism and international law. According to Griffiths, territorial constitutions refer to "the normative, legal, and political factors that determine how state boundaries are produced", and how territory is delineated and constructed within the international system.[25] For East Timor, the territorial conditions necessary for statehood were externally constructed. There is a tendency to view recognition as the process by which a politically independent entity becomes formally recognized as sovereign, which then permits personhood under international law and engagement in diplomatic relations with other states. However, recognition is a culmination of multiple acts that occur across time and global political contexts. Recognition is historically and politically contingent: we need to understand how multiple "recognition" acts worked to construct the entity of "East" Timor. For East Timor, recognition acts included constructing a territorial identity, being accorded political rights to self-determination, exercising these rights (i.e. through a referendum), being formally recognized by other states and joining the UN (considered further in chapters three and four). According to Mendes' work on multidimensional identity construction, the gestation of a collectively imagined "East" Timor was the establishment of boundaries, which confirms the "existence of a political unit, defined by Portuguese colonialism not without tremendous effort to pacify all kingdoms in the Eastern part of the island".[26] The first step in understanding Timor-Leste's sovereignty, then, is to examine how the international community came to recognize two empirical features of statehood: territory and population.

Questions of self-determination require considering what constitutes the "self" that claims the rights to political independence.[27] As Krishna notes, "spacialization" has the effect of producing "self" and other/s. Political self-determination entails the right of a nation to put into place constitutional structures and decide matters concerning their own community. Territory matters insofar as the new constitution of international society that emerged during the decolonization period created new rules for state creation. Groups claiming self-determination must "have a territory to set the geographic boundaries... of its rule if it is to be self-governing".[28] Colonial borders were often arbitrarily drawn and did not necessarily reflect national or social groupings. Migdal, discussing decolonization generally, notes that "states could be carved out of anachronistic empires but somehow, once created, they did not disappear and their borders stayed intact".[29] Implicit in the national self-determination is a belief that nations or culture should form the basis of statehood; however, pre-existing juridical borders, drawn by colonial powers, were privileged ahead of national, ethnic or tribal affiliations. These boundaries were not "accidents of geography" or "divine cartography" but lands inhabited by colonial empire.[30] By cartographically defining "East" Timor, Portuguese colonialism contributed to a "mapped" imagining which ultimately underpinned its status under international law as a colony and provided the basis for its legal rights to self-determination.[31] This international political "imagining" of East Timor preceded the formation of a distinctive national identity.

Establishing Territory: Portuguese Colonialism (1701–1974)

Outlining the historical context can assist in developing a picture of how "East Timor" as a distinct territory and identity came into being, particularly given the ethnic and cultural diversity of the people co-existing on Timor Island. According to Forman, East Timor "manifests an ethnic heterogeneity which characterises the entire region from the Philippines to Australia and from the islands east of Papua New Guinea to the Malagasy Republic".[32] Successive migrations of people from Melanesia, continental Asia and islands to the West created an intricate convergence of cultures on Timor.[33] East Timor's linguistic diversity is partly due to its mountainous terrain, as diverse dialects emerged within geographically concentrated language groups. The original habitants of Timor were believed to have been the *Atoni* (or "*Vaiquenos*" in Portuguese) group who descended from Melanesia and inhabited the central highlands and the west of the island for centuries.[34] The *Atoni* spoke "*Vaiqueno*", while the Tetum-speaking *Belu* ethnic group were more recent arrivals, typically located on the southeast coast.[35] There are few links between Bahasa Indonesian and the languages of East Timor, and despite close geographical proximity to Indonesia, Indo-Javanese and Islamic culture were barely present on the island.[36]

The presence of geographically concentrated socio-political communities adds a layer of complexity in understanding East Timor's cultural composition. Ethno-linguistic diversity has been heightened by the differentiation of the East Timorese people "into atomistic political units comprising lineages and clans".[37] Affiliations were directed towards traditional and local authority structures as "the peoples of East Timor identified themselves as internally distinct".[38] Historically, East Timor was partitioned into forty-six *reinos/rais* (kingdoms), led by *liurais* (chiefs), a "tribal-traditional" organizational system that continues to determine the day-to-day life of many East Timorese.[39] Traube states the "people of East Timor took pride in their differences from one another, evoking language, myth, and customs as badges of their distinctive cultural identities".[40] While there were commonalities in the lifestyles and animist religion among the different groups, the clans had historically fought each other.[41] This traditional authority structure precluded unified opposition to Portuguese colonialism. Although there were intermittent challenges to the colonial administration from *Liurias*, these were driven predominantly by the decline in economic conditions and issues relating to the collection of taxation rather than objection to Portuguese colonial rule.[42]

Portuguese influence in the region began when they conquered Malacca in 1511, following which they made yearly visits to Timor for sandalwood.⁴³ The first recorded European settlers to the region were Portuguese Dominican Friars in 1566 who settled on the island of Solor, just north of Timor.⁴⁴ First settlement became populated with "Topasses" or "Black Portuguese", the offspring of Portuguese soldiers and sailors who married local women. The Topasses established themselves in what was then Lifau (now Oecussi), following a struggle with the Dutch over the sandalwood trade.⁴⁵ In 1701, the Portuguese claimed control over East Timor while the Dutch asserted control of Kupang in West Timor in 1653.⁴⁶ The power dynamics between the Portuguese and Dutch resulted in Portugal concentrating their attentions on the eastern side of the territory.⁴⁷

Negotiated borders between the Portuguese and the Dutch carved up the island of Timor and were crucial in developing two distinct political communities. During the eighteenth and nineteenth centuries, Timor was bifurcated into "Portuguese and Dutch spheres of influence" with several treaties during the nineteenth and twentieth centuries aiming to settle conflicts over borders with diplomatic agreements in 1851, 1859 and 1916.⁴⁸ These included the 1859 Colonial Boundary Treaty between the Netherlands and Portugal, which delimited the island but had left enclaves, including Portuguese Oecussi in West Timor and Maucatar in East Timor.⁴⁹ Further treaties followed in June 1893 (the Lisbon Convention) and 1904 in order to eradicate the existing enclaves but agreement was not reached on the status of Oecussi, as the population of Lifau, consisting largely of Topasses, elected to remain under Portuguese rule.⁵⁰ The "Sentenca Arbitral" concerning the boundaries between Dutch and Portuguese possessions was signed at The Hague on 3 April 1913 with both sides agreeing to submit the boundary dispute to international legal arbitration.⁵¹ On 25 June 1914, the Permanent Court of Arbitration resolved border disputes in favour of the Netherlands, and the final settlements in 1916 separated "Portuguese" (East) Timor from "West" Timor under international law.⁵²

Once political borders were settled by Portugal and the Netherlands, they developed a "solidity" which has determined contemporary understandings of "East" and "West" Timor.⁵³ There is debate among historians and anthropologists regarding the extent to which the partition corresponds with observable cultural distinctiveness between the two territories. Some argue that Portuguese and Dutch colonialism loosely matched existing social borders between the *Atoni* and *Belu* people. An eighteenth-century Portuguese source noted that the two main groups on Timor island "differed a great deal, making up as it were two provinces and two peoples".[54] Krieger suggests, "[t]his partition reflected the division of the island into two great kingdoms, both in turn divided into a number of principalities".[55] Durand also argues that the "two halves of Timor exhibit clear differences... which does not result from colonization alone".[56] He views the boundary demarcated in the eighteenth century as "in keeping with an old political and ethnolinguistic division".[57]

In contrast, Hägerdal contends that these were "artificial pseudo-ethnic divisions" promoted by the Portuguese.[58] The Portuguese transformed the provinces and "interpreted them according to the political landscape as they understood it. Some aspects of the division ran counter to indigenous Timorese perceptions."[59] The idea that there were two distinct "East" and "West" provinces is problematic, according to this view, because "[t]he purported ethnic demarcation... seems to be a Portuguese convention, influenced by the colonial networks of the European powers in this period".[60] Farram suggests that the geographical division is mostly arbitrary as the people who lived near the borders generally belonged to the "same ethnic groups" and there was "nothing inherently Dutch or Portuguese about the land, or the people, on either side of the border".[61] According to these perspectives, the partition was not a "natural" reflection of two distinctive societies, but a social construct driven by European imperialism.

Yet, whether or not the two sides of the island were or continue to be culturally distinct is largely irrelevant for the purposes of understanding how East and West Timor came to being. The partition of Timor was largely a consequence of "long-term military and diplomatic rivalry between the Dutch and the Portuguese".[62] The passing of time gave these colonial borders "respectability" regardless of how they were constructed.[63] As with many other post-colonial states, the colonial borders of East and West Timor that were "secured over the centuries by bullets and treaties" proved resilient because they reflected dominant international norms that developed in the second half of the twentieth century.[64] These boundaries preceded any sense of unified national consciousness between the inhabitants of "East Timor", reflecting the ways that European colonialism and international law contributed to the contemporary formation of Timor-Leste's state-based identity.

Self-determination under International Law

The principle of self-determination was integral to state-creation in the second half of the twentieth century as imperialism became illegitimated under international law. In 1960, the UN General Assembly's Declaration on the Granting of Independence to Colonial Countries and Peoples (Declaration on Decolonization) called for a "speedy and unconditional end" to colonialism.[65] The 1966 International Covenant of Economic, Social and Cultural Rights (ICESC) and the 1966 International Covenant of Political and Civil Rights (ICPRC) recognized self-determination as an "inalienable human right".[66] Both charters asserted that "all people have the right of self-determination", covering three distinct types of political rights: the right to freely determine political status; the right to freely pursue economic, social and cultural development; and the right to freely dispose of their natural wealth and resources.

Ideas of national self-determination support a vision of an international community comprising a plurality of free and equal nations as it enshrines the rights of individuals to live according to culturally-determined rules and norms.[67] Nations are perceived "ethical communities", with self-determination granting "peoples" the freedom to shape their political context and preserve culture, laws and customs.[68] For example, Philpott views self-determination as a legal arrangement that provides independence (or autonomy within a state) to groups and enables people's expressions of political will.[69] The principle of national self-determination is based upon a perceived right of a "people" to determine their own laws and customs according to their own cultural, political and social beliefs.[70] It entails the "collective right of a people to be itself" and freedom from foreign subjugation.

In affording a group of people the right to self-determination, the international community designated groups a particular identity through the allocation of collective rights based on their colonial history and the construction of recognized borders.[71] In many cases, colonial borders did not reflect traditional or tribal identities.[72] Often, state-creation also required the development of a collectively shared identity (a nation) that could bind diverse ethnic and religious groups within the artificial borders. Rules about political organizations and the legitimacy of internationally recognized boundaries instituted through colonialism forced entities seeking statehood to build nations within those constructed borders. The practices of nationalism took pre-existing administrative borders and constructed nations to fit within them. These boundaries created the space for the development of the independent entity identified as Portuguese Timor.

Indonesia achieved international recognition of sovereignty in 1948 through a combination of negotiated internal settlements and successful expulsion of the Dutch, and West Timor became a part of the new archipelagic state in 1949 as it was located within the colonial boundaries of Dutch rule.[73] East Timor was acknowledged under international law as "a non-self-governing territory" in the 1960 Declaration on Decolonization due to its status as a Portuguese colony.[74] This formal status bestowed upon non-self-governing territories, such as East Timor, the right to self-determination under international law.[75] It was assumed at the time that these territories would be at some stage given the option to decide their own political future: whether "they" would be politically independent or incorporated within another state. Insofar as the people of "East Timor" were accorded these rights, it was recognized they possessed a distinct identity by virtue of their unique experiences with European colonialism.

The emphasis on colonial boundaries in determining rights to independence favours some social groupings more than others. The formal finalization of colonial boundaries by the Portuguese and Dutch during the period of European colonialism was critical to developing two separate identities and determining the political future of East Timor.[76] The "mapped" imagining of East Timor facilitated the emergence of its international identity.[77] These international dimensions preceded the internal development of an East Timorese nation and were hence integral to East Timor's future achievement of sovereignty.

The Use and Abuse of the Self-Determination Principle

In 1962, the UN General Assembly Resolution 1807 reinforced the rights outlined in the Declaration of Decolonization by calling on Portugal to immediately recognize the right of the peoples of their territories under its administration, including East Timor, to self-determination and independence.[78] Portugal resisted attempts by members of the international community to give East Timor and its other colonies their right of self-determination, until 1974, when the Salazar-Caetano dictatorship was overthrown by the Portuguese Armed Movement (AMF) during the "Carnation Revolution".[79] The new Portuguese government quickly began the process of granting decolonization to all Portuguese provinces including East Timor.[80] This movement towards decolonization led to the creation of political parties in East Timor, including the pro-Portugal *União Democrática Timorense*/Timorese Democratic Union (UDT) and the pro-Independent *Associação Social Democratica Timorense*/Timorese Social Democratic Association (ASDT, later *Frente Revolucionária de Timor Leste Independente*/Revolutionary Front for an Independent East Timor or FRETILIN). This time also represented the beginnings of political consciousness among East Timor's small population of educated elites, many of whom would go on to become leaders of the resistance and independence movement and in independent Timor-Leste.

On 28 November 1975, following a brief civil war in East Timor (August–September), pro-independence political party FRETILIN unilaterally declared independence and established the Democratic Republic of Timor-Leste (RTDL). Three days before invading East Timor, the Indonesian government had declared a commitment to decolonization in Portuguese Timor and a respect for "the rights and responsibilities of the Portuguese government as the sole lawful authority in the territory".[81] Additionally, it noted a "moral obligation to protect the people in the territory of Portuguese Timor" to enable decolonization.[82] However, Indonesian troops were already occupying significant territory in East Timor and a full scale attack was imminent.[83] Internal tensions compelled a group of smaller East Timorese political parties, including the UDT, APODETI, KOTA and the *partido Trabalhista*, to refute FRETILIN's unilateral declaration of independence.[84] Indonesia's occupation on 7 December 1975 prevented East Timor from attaining collective self-determination rights in any meaningful sense.

Many reasons were offered by Indonesia for invading East Timor, which included (but were not limited to) East Timor's perceived communist aspirations; its size and geographic position; underdevelopment (as a result of Portugal's neglectful administration); FRETILIN's repeated border infractions; and potential security risks to Indonesia and the broader Southeast Asian region. Indonesia's annexation of East Timorese territory began in early December 1975 with an air and sea attack involving large numbers of troops.[85] On the first day of the invasion, atrocities were conducted by the Indonesian military, including summary executions and massacres of the civilian population.[86] FRETILIN's army, FALINTIL, had around 10,000 troops prepared to defend against the invasion using NATO-grade weapons left behind from the Portuguese occupation.[87] However, these proved inadequate for expelling the Indonesian military.

Immediately following its invasion of East Timorese territory on 7 December 1975, Indonesia used regional stability as a justification and painted FRETILIN "terror" as threatening Indonesian sovereignty.[88] Indonesia maintained it had not abandoned its "anti-colonial" credentials and repeatedly opposed Portuguese colonialism in East Timor. In a government statement released on 8 December 1975, Indonesia claimed that East Timorese independence had disturbed regional stability and declared support for Portuguese Timor decolonization "in a proper, orderly and peaceful manner".[89] Indonesia defended its invasion by arguing that it "in no way" reflected any "territorial ambition of the Republic of Indonesia".[90] On 10 December 1975, an Indonesian government statement blamed FRETILIN and Portugal for "prolonged chaos" and justified its actions in terms of national security: "the Fretilin has often violated Indonesian sovereignty, attacking and robbing Indonesians in Indonesian territory".[91] Four days later, another statement released by the Indonesian government reinforced the view that FRETILIN posed a security threat due to repeated violations of "the sovereignty of the Republic of Indonesia by attacks and raids which had cause loss of lives and property of the population".[92] These arguments reflected Indonesia's desire to justify its actions in East Timor.

Over the next few months, Indonesia attempted to establish East Timor's incorporation as an outcome of self-determination. On 17 December 1975, Indonesia released a declaration on the establishment of a provisional government in East Timor, procuring the signatures of the UDT, APODETI, KOTA and the *partido Trabhalhista*.[93] The provisional government, which was formed from rigged "elections" in which local rulers and people were rounded up by Indonesian officers, generally comprised of pro-Indonesia supporters.[94] On 3 May 1976, Jakarta reported that the East Timorese were "clamouring to join Indonesia".[95] Later in the same month, on 31 May, the provisional government formed a thirty-seven-member Popular

Representative Assembly to oversee a self-determination act "on behalf of the people of East Timor".[96] The assembly quickly and unanimously approved East Timor's integration into Indonesia. A distinctive political community formed as a result of Indonesian colonialism. During the occupation, an estimated 180,000 people in a population of 650,000 were killed in conflict or as a result of Indonesia's policy of starvation as this community resisted Indonesian rule and asserted collective rights of the nation to self-determination on the international stage.[97]

In 1975 and 1976, East Timorese supporters of Indonesia's annexation spoke at the UN in an attempt to justify Indonesia's actions. In July 1976, the East Timorese Provisional Government sent a cable to the Chairman of the UN Special Committee on Decolonization and the Special Envoy of the Secretary-General that the consultation "democratically expressed... [East Timor's] view on their future".[98] A member of the Provisional Government, Mario Carrascalão, invited "the United Nations Special Committee on Decolonisation, foreign embassies and journalists in Jakarta to come to Dili and see for themselves how determined we are to be reunited with our brothers", linking self-determination with the myth of shared kinship relations.[99] To other observers, the vote represented nothing more than a sham consultation. According to Australian consul James Dunn, the consultation was designed to present to the world a "façade of legitimacy to the seizure of the colony".[100] It was reminiscent of the 1969 "Act of Free Choice" in West Papua in which the Indonesian military handpicked and threatened 1,026 Papuan "representatives" who ultimately all voted in support of incorporation within Indonesia.

Indonesia's argument that East Timor had been accorded its rights to self-determination relied upon discrediting the pro-independence political party FRETILIN as a representative of the majority will in East Timor. At the UN, Indonesian representative Anwar Sani declared that FRETILIN "attempted to deny the proper exercise of the right to self-determination".[101] The "East Timor after Integration" booklet, produced by the Indonesian government, stated "the people of Indonesia could not stand idly by while a small minority in Timor, represented by FRETILIN, ruthlessly imposed its ideas by force of arms upon the majority of the Timorese".[102] A subsequent Indonesian government document reinforced the argument that the people of East Timor had democratically chosen to become a part of Indonesia. A number of Indonesian scholars, such as Sabana Kartasasmuta, reinforced this perception that the majority of East Timorese chose integration within Indonesia.[103] FRETILIN's declaration was described by Indonesia as "ignoring the opinion of the large majority of the people of East Timor who were represented by the other four parties".[104] Perhaps unsurprisingly, Indonesia failed to justify the large numbers of Indonesian troops in East Timor throughout its occupation. In fact, Indonesia denied altogether that armed forces had been deployed in East Timor for the purposes of territorial expansion.[105]

While Indonesia incorporated East Timor despite its history as a Portuguese colony, it simultaneously employed Dutch colonial borders to defend its sovereignty over contested territories, most notably West Papua. Indonesia denied any apparent contradiction between its annexation of East Timor and its opposition to anti-colonialism, arguing that they had no territorial claims and respected East Timor's right of self-determination.[106] The Portuguese were presented as the problem as the "real intention" of Portugal was to perpetuate colonialism in a new form.[107] In a state address delivered on 16 August 1976, President Suharto argued that:

> Time and time again we have stated that the East Timor problem is a question of self-determination. It is a problem of abolishing colonialism. The fate of the people of East Timor can only be decided by themselves and right there on the soil of East Timor.[108]

Thus, for Indonesia, the right of East Timorese to self-determination was never in contention; throughout the twenty-four years of occupation, they consistently held that the East Timorese had already participated in an act of self-determination, with the majority wanting to be a part of Indonesia.

Indonesia's occupation of East Timor remained problematic because an act of self-determination is required under international law to be democratic, arising from a "free and genuine expression of the will of the peoples concerned".[109] In 1996, an Indonesian government document declared that "the entire process was conducted in accordance with the traditional democratic principals [sic] of the East Timorese people, and in compliance with the relevant United Nations General Assembly resolutions".[110] For the self-determination ballot to be considered legitimate, a widespread perception that the results were representative of all adult East Timorese was required because international law perceives the right to self-determination as existing with the whole population and not a particular group.[111] The legitimacy of the annexation as an act of self-determination was consistently disputed by the East Timorese independence movement.

East Timor's international legal rights to self-determination rested upon its status as a non-self-governing territory. FRETILIN's representative at the UN, José Ramos-Horta, countered many of the arguments presented by Indonesia throughout East Timor's occupation. He argued that FRETILIN's independence declaration was supported by the majority of the population.[112] He discredited pro-Indonesian parties such as APODETI, claiming that they were "financed by Indonesia from the beginning of its existence... [and had] never enjoyed the sympathy of the people of East Timor".[113] In every year between 1975 and 1982, East Timor's right of self-determination was upheld by UN General Assembly resolutions.[114] These resolutions repeatedly called upon Indonesia to withdraw all forces from the territory and reaffirmed the inalienable right of the people of East Timor to self-determination and independence.

While the UN Security Council called upon all states to respect the inalienable rights of East Timor and the territorial integrity of Portugal, which remained recognized as the administering authority, this was not supported by actions that would persuade Indonesia to vacate East Timorese territory, such as sanctions or military intervention.[115] Marker suggests that the lack of support from neighbouring states made East Timor's independence movement unique.[116] Few states were prepared to recognize the legitimacy of the Democratic Republic of East Timor.[117] East Timor was thus unable to make its independence "real" because it lacked external support and was unable to expel Indonesian forces. Hence, both Indonesia and East Timor engaged in a campaign from 1975–99 to legitimize their respective claims to sovereignty over East Timorese territory in the eyes of the international community.

For decades East Timor's independence movement struggled to convert its legal rights to self-determination into sovereignty. Sovereign statehood is premised on "recognitive practices internal and external to the state that fulfil both declarative and constitutive functions".[118] The act of recognizing sovereignty is largely *political*, and there are myriad reasons why independence might be granted or denied.[119] While East Timor's legal status was similar to other Portuguese colonies, it could not persuade most states to recognize its sovereignty until the late 1990s. The next chapter examines the political factors that prevented East Timor from becoming independent and why they had limited support from the international community for over two decades.[120]

Conclusion

Portuguese colonialism was a key factor in forming East Timor's international identity. According to Timorese government spokesperson Agio Pereira, the Timorese "owe a debt" to the Portuguese settlers in East Timorese territory. Without this historical event, he argues that Timor-Leste would not have become an independent state: instead, it "would have surely become part of the Dutch East Indies, which later became the Republic of Indonesia".[121] It is a "paradox" that European colonialism "continues to shape the fate of nations": as a consequence of Portuguese intervention, Timor-Leste has "been able to carve out a unique identity and culture that in 2002 led to Timor-Leste being admitted as the 191st member state of the United Nations".[122] The international context was hence pivotal in "imagining" East Timor and ultimately led to the recognition of its sovereign status.

Legal self-determination rights are not based on ethnic identities but on territorial borders: the construction of recognized boundaries provides the jurisdiction for territorial sovereignty. Timor-Leste's rights bearing status was accorded under international law on the basis that it was recognized as a "non-self-governing territory", yet the fledgling nation's first attempts at becoming formally recognized as independent in 1974–75 were violently curtailed by Indonesia. Indonesia defended its occupation of East Timor by claiming that a legitimate act of self-determination had already taken place, and that the East Timorese had chosen to be incorporated by Indonesia. While self-determination did not automatically provide East Timor political independence, it did provide a solid legal basis for its sovereign claims. As any aspiring state would acknowledge, "declaring yourself a state and even functioning like a state does not make you a state unless the international community approves".[123] Powerful individual states can play important roles in deciding which entities will become recognized. The next chapter examines the actions and political interests of key states, such as Australia, the ASEAN states and the United States, in responses to the East Timorese independence movement. This history shapes Timor-

Leste's approaches to the international community, and is important for understanding narratives of absolute external sovereignty and the pursuit of "real" independence.

NOTES

1. Montevideo Convention on the Rights and Duties of States, 1933.
2. James Dunn, *Timor: A People Betrayed* (Milton, Queensland: The Jacaranda Press, 1983); pp. 1, 17; Jill Jolliffe, *East Timor: Nationalism and Colonialism* (St. Lucia, Qld: University of Queensland Press, 1978), pp. 12, 25, 27–28.
3. Some historical revisionist perspectives like to distance Portugal's pre-independence engagements with Timor-Leste from the concept of colonialism. Examples of this revisionism are detailed in later chapters. However, it is clear from an international relations perspective that Portugal's administration was an indirect form of colonialism. The territory was internationally referred to as "Portuguese Timor". Portugal was internationally acknowledged as the administrator of the territory until 1999 and was permitted to enter (or not enter, in the case of the Timor Sea) international treaties on behalf of the territory and people of East Timor.
4. Mendes, Nuno Canas "Multidimensional Identity Construction: Challenges for State-building in East Timor", in *East Timor: How to Build a New Nation in Southeast Asia in the 21st Century?*, edited by Christine Cabasset-Semedo and Frédéric Durand, p. 20 (Thailand: Research Institute on Contemporary Southeast Asia, 2009).
5. Robert Ewin, "Peoples and Political Obligation", *Macquarie Law Journal* 3 (2003): 21; Joe Painter, *Politics, Geography and 'Political Geography'* (London: Arnold, 1995), p. 53.
6. Hurst Hannum, *Autonomy, Sovereignty, and Self-Determination: The Accommodation of Conflicting Rights*, pp. 36–37 (Philadelphia: University of Philadelphia Press, 1990).
7. Barry Buzan, *From International to World Society? English School Theory and the Social Structure of Globalisation*, p. 8 (Cambridge: Cambridge University Press, 2004).
8. Daniel Philpott, "Westphalia, Authority and International Society", *Political Studies* XLVII (1999): 567.
9. Ryan Griffths, "Admission to the Sovereignty Club: The Past, Present and Future of the International Recognition Regime", *Territory, Politics, Governance* 5, no. 2 (2016): 3.
10. Eva Erman, "The Recognitive Practices of Declaring and Constituting Statehood", *International Theory* 5 (2013): 134.

11. See James Crawford, *The Creation of States in International Law*, 2nd ed., p. 436 (Oxford: Clarendon Press, 2006); Oyvind Österud, "The Narrow-Gate: Entry to the Club of Sovereign States", *Review of International Studies* 23 (1997): 175.
12. Richard Caplan, *Europe and the Recognition of New States in Yugoslavia*, p. 56 (Cambridge: Cambridge University Press, 2005); Hans Agné, "The Politics of International Recognition: Symposium Introduction", *International Theory* 5, no. 1 (2013): 97; Erman, "The Recognitive Practices of Declaring and Constituting Statehood", p. 132.
13. Juan Federer, *The UN in East Timor: Building Timor-Leste, a Fragile State*, p. 89 (Darwin: Charles Darwin University Press, 2005).
14. Cited in S.K. Verma, *An Introduction to Public International Law*, p. 96 (New Delhi: Prentice Hall of India, 2004).
15. Erman, "The Recognitive Practices of Declaring and Constituting Statehood", p. 145.
16. Ibid., pp. 134–35.
17. Robert Jackson and Carl Rosberg, "Why Africa's Weak States Persist: The Empirical and the Juridical in Statehood", *World Politics* 35, no. 1 (October 1982): 1–24.
18. Crawford, *The Creation of States in International Law*, p. 108. See Robert Jackson, "Quasi-States, Dual Regimes, and Neo-Classical Theory: International Jurisprudence and the Third World", *International Organization* 41, no. 4 (Autumn 1987): 541.
19. Mikulas Fabry, "Theorizing State Recognition", *International Theory* 5 (2013): 167.
20. Agne, "The Politics of International Recognition", p. 97.
21. Erman, "The Recognitive Practices of Declaring and Constituting Statehood", p. 144.
22. Jens Bartelson, "Three Concepts of Recognition", *International Theory* 5 (2013): 121.
23. Ibid., p. 121.
24. Ibid., p. 144.
25. Griffiths, "Admission to the Sovereignty Club", p. 3.
26. Mendes, "Multidimensional Identity Construction", p. 21.
27. Ewin, "Peoples and Political Obligation", p. 13; Hannum, *Autonomy, Sovereignty, and Self-Determination*, p. 30.
28. Ibid., p. 15.
29. Joel Migdal, "State Building and the Non-Nation-State", *Journal of International Affairs* 8, no. 1 (2004): 19.
30. Sankaran Krishna, *Postcolonial Insecurities: India, Sri Lanka and the Question of Nationhood*, p. 7 (Minneapolis and London: University of Minneapolis, 1999).

31. Benedict Anderson, "Imagining East Timor", *Arena* 4 (April–May 1993).
32. Dunn, *Timor*, p. 2.
33. Ibid., p. 2; Armando Marques Guedes, "Thinking East Timor, Indonesia and Southeast Asia", *Lusotopie* (2001): 315. Anthropological work on local communities in East Timor has been conducted by various scholars. See, for example, David Hicks, *Tetum Ghosts and Kin: Fertility and Gender in East Timor* (Long Grove, Illinois: Waveland Press, 2004); Brigette Clamagirand, "The Social Organization of the Ema of Timor", in *The Flow of Life: Essays on Eastern Indonesia*, edited by James J. Fox, pp. 134–51 (Cambridge, Mass: Harvard University Press, 1982); Andrew McWilliam and Elizabeth Traube, eds., *Land and Life in Timor-Leste: Ethnographic Essay* (Canberra: ANU Press, 2011); Elizabeth Traube, *Cosmology and Social Life: Ritual Exchange among the Mambai of East Timor* (Chicago: University of Chicago Press, 1986); H.G. Schulte Nordholt, *The Political System of the Atoni* (The Hague: Martinus Nijhoff, 1971).
34. Dunn, *Timor*, p. 4; Nordholt, *The Political System of the Atoni of Timor*.
35. Ibid., pp. 4, 17.
36. Ibid., p. 3.
37. Ramos-Horta in Extracts from the Debates of the UN Security Council Concerning UN Security Council Resolution 389 (1976). See Heike Krieger, *East Timor and the International Community: Basic Documents*, p. 96 (Cambridge: Cambridge University Press, 1997).
38. Damien Kingsbury, *East Timor: The Price of Liberty*, p. 32 (New York: Palgrave Macmillan, 2009).
39. Damien Grenfell, "Governance, Violence and Crises in Timor-Leste: Estadu Seidauk Mai", in *Democratic Governance in Timor-Leste: Reconciling the Local and the National*, edited by David Mearns and Stevens Farram, p. 88 (Darwin: Charles Darwin University Press, 2008).
40. Elizabeth Traube, "Mambai Perspectives on Colonialism and Decolonization", in *East Timor at the Crossroads: The Forging of a Nation*, edited by Peter Carey and G. Carter-Bentley, p. 44 (London: Cassell/Social Science Research Council, 1995).
41. Federer, *The UN in East Timor*, p. 211; Damien Kingsbury, *East Timor: The Price of Liberty*, p. 17 (New York: Palgrave Macmillan, 2009).
42. Dunn, *Timor*, p. 19; Geoffrey Gunn, *Timor Loro Sae: 500 Years*, p. 19 (Hong Kong: Livros do Oriente, 1999).
43. Helen Hill, *The Timor Story*, p. 1 (Melbourne: Timor Information Service, 1976).
44. Commission for Reception, Truth and Reconciliation (CAVR), *Chega! Final Report of the Commission for Reception, Truth and Reconciliation Timor-Leste*, chapters 3, 7 (Dili: CAVR, 2005); Jolliffe, *East Timor*, p. 23 and Hill, *The Timor Story*, p. 1.

45. Dunn, *Timor*, p. 18.
46. Krieger, *East Timor and the International Community*, p. xix.
47. CAVR, *Chega!*, chapter 3, 6; Kingsbury, *The Price of Liberty*, p. 32.
48. Colonial Boundary Treaty between the Netherlands and Portugal, signed at Lisbon, 20 April 1859. See Krieger, *East Timor and the International Community*, p. 1. See also Steven Farram, "The Two Timors: The Partitioning of Timor by the Portuguese and Dutch", *Studies in Languages and Culture of East Timor* 2 (1999): 52; Hans Hägerdal, "Servião and Belu: Colonial Conceptions and the Geographical Partition of Timor", *Studies on Asia* 3, no. 1 (Spring 2006): 63.
49. Permanent Court of Arbitration (PCA), "Arbitral Award Rendered in Execution of the Compromis Signed at The Hague, April 3, 1913, between the Netherlands and Portugal Concerning the Subject of the Boundary of a Part of their Possession in the Island of Timor", Paris, 25 June 1914.
50. Hill, *The Timor Story*, p. 2.
51. Dunn, *Timor*, p. 18.
52. PCA, "Arbitral Award Rendered in Execution of the Compromis Signed at The Hague, April 3, 1913".
53. Farram, "The Two Timors", p. 39.
54. Dunn, *Timor*, pp. 13–14.
55. Krieger, *East Timor and the International Community*, p. xix.
56. Frédéric Durand, *East Timor: A Country at the Crossroads of Asia and the Pacific, A Geo-Historical Atlas*, p. 48 (Chiang Mai: Silkworm Books and Bangkok: IRASEC, 2006).
57. Ibid., p. 48.
58. Hägerdal, "Servião and Belu", p. 49.
59. Ibid., p. 64.
60. Ibid., pp. 49–52.
61. Farram, "The Two Timors", p. 39.
62. Hägerdal, "Servião and Belu", p. 50.
63. Farram, "The Two Timors", p. 55.
64. Hägerdal, "Servião and Belu", p. 64.
65. United Nations General Assembly (UNGA), "Declaration on the Granting of Independence to Colonial Countries and Peoples", United Nations General Assembly Resolution 1514 (XV), 15th Session, 14 December 1960.
66. UNGA, "International Covenant on Civil and Political Rights", United Nations General Assembly Resolution 2200A (XXI), 16 December 1966; UNGA, "International Covenant on Economic, Social and Cultural Rights", United Nations General Assembly Resolution 2200A (XXI), 16 December 1966.
67. John Breuilly, *Nationalism and the State*, p. 4 (Manchester: Manchester University Press, 1982).

68. David Miller, *Citizenship and National Identity*, p. 27 (Malden, Massachusetts: Polity Press, 2000).
69. Daniel Philpott, "In Defense of Self-Determination", *Ethics* 105, no. 2 (January 1995): 353; Aleksandar Pavkovic and Peter Radan, *Creating New States: Theory and Practice of Secession*, pp. 200–1 (Hampshire: Ashgate, 2008).
70. Richard Falk, "The East Timor Ordeal: International Law and its Limits", in *Bitter Flowers, Sweet Flowers: East Timor, Indonesia and the World Community*, edited by Richard Tanter, Mark Selden and Stephen R. Shalom, p. 150 (Annandale, New South Wales: Pluto Press Australia, 2001).
71. Hannum, *Autonomy, Sovereignty and Self-Determination*, pp. 48, 49.
72. Thomas Franck and Paul Hoffman, "The Right of Self-Determination in Very Small Places", *New York University Journal of International Law and Politics* 8 (1975/76): 331, 334.
73. Krieger, *East Timor and the International Community*, p. xix.
74. UNGA, "Declaration on the Granting of Independence to Colonial Countries and Peoples".
75. Simon Chesterman, *You, the People: The United Nations, Transitional Administration, and State-Building*, pp. 42–43 (Oxford: Oxford University Press, 2005).
76. CAVR, *Chega!*, chapters 3, 8.
77. Anderson, "Imagining East Timor".
78. UNGA, *Territories under Portuguese Administration*, United Nations General Assembly Resolution 1807, 17th Session, 14 December 1962.
79. John Taylor, *East Timor: The Price of Freedom*, p. 25 (Annandale, New South Wales: Zed Books, 1999).
80. CAVR, *Chega!*, chapters 3, 14.
81. Republic of Indonesia, *Government Statements on the East Timor Question*, p. 5 (Jakarta: Department of Information, Republic of Indonesia: 1976).
82. Ibid., p. 8.
83. CAVR, *Chega!*, chapter 3, pp. 58–60.
84. Joint Proclamation by APODETI, UDT, KOTA and the Partido Trabilhista, Issued at Batugade, 30 November 1975. See Krieger, *East Timor and the International Community*, p. 40.
85. CAVR, *Chega!*, chapter 3, p. 60.
86. Ibid.
87. Ibid., chapter 3, p. 61. NATO stands for North Atlantic Treaty Organization.
88. Republic of Indonesia, *Government Statements on the East Timor Question*, p. 12.
89. Ibid., p. 9.
90. Ibid.
91. Ibid., pp. 15–16.
92. Ibid., p. 20.

93. Declaration on the Establishment of a Provisional Government of the Territory of East Timor, 17 December 1975. See Krieger, *East Timor and the International Community*, p. 44.
94. Dunn, *Timor*, p. 298.
95. Ibid., p. 301.
96. Declaration on the Establishment of a Provisional Government of the Territory of East Timor, 17 December 1975. See Krieger, *East Timor and the International Community*, p. 44.
97. Derek McDougall, "The Security-Development Nexus: Comparing External Interventions and Development Strategies in Timor-Leste and Solomon Islands", *Asian Security* 6, no. 2 (2012): 175.
98. Cable sent by the Provisional Government of East Timor to the Secretary-General of the United Nations, the Chairman of the Special Committee on Decolonization, and Mr Vittorio Winspeare Guicciardi, the Special Envoy of the Secretary-General, 1 June 1976. See Krieger, *East Timor and the International Community*, p. 44.
99. See Krieger, *East Timor and the International Community*, p. 45.
100. James Dunn, *The Timor Story*, p. 83 (Canberra: The Parliamentary Library Legislature Research Service, 1976).
101. Krieger, *East Timor and the International Community*, p. 63.
102. Republic of Indonesia, *East Timor After Integration*, p. 53 (Jakarta: Department of Information, 1983).
103. Sabana Kartasasmuta, *The Quest for a* Solution, p. 1 (Singapore, Crescent Design Associates, 1998).
104. Republic of Indonesia, *East Timor After Integration*, p. 49.
105. Republic of Indonesia, *Statement of the Government at the Republic of Indonesia on Portuguese Timor* (Indonesia: Departemen Luar Negeri, 10 December 1975).
106. Republic of Indonesia, *Government Statements on the East Timor Question*, pp. 23–25.
107. Suharto cited in Republic of Indonesia, *Facts about East Timor*, p. 9 (Jakarta: Dewan Peerwakilan Rakyat, 1989).
108. Ibid., p. 11.
109. Linton cited in CAVR, *Timor-Leste Self-Determination and the International Community: National Public Hearing 15–17 March 2004*, p. 11 (Dili: Commission of Reception, Truth and Reconciliation Production Team and Translation Unit, 2009).
110. Republic of Indonesia, *East Timor: Building for a Future: Issues and Perspectives*, pp. 1–2 (Jakarta: Department of Foreign Affairs, 1996).
111. Linton cited in CAVR, *Timor-Leste Self-Determination and the International Community*, p. 11.

112. United Nations Security Council (UNSC), "Debates Concerning UN Security Council Resolution 389 (1976)", Security Council Official Records, 31st year, 1909th meeting, 14 April 1976.
113. UNSC, *Debates Concerning UN Security Council Resolution 384 (1975)*, Security Council Official Records, 1864th meeting, 30th year, 15 December 1975.
114. See Krieger, *East Timor and the International Community*, pp. 53, 93.
115. Franck and Hoffman, "The Right of Self-Determination", p. 349.
116. CAVR, *Chega!*, chapter 7, pp. 1, 4, 80.
117. Jamsheed Marker, *East Timor: A Memoir of the Negotiations for Independence*, p. 8 (Jefferson: MacFarland, 2003).
118. Erman, "The Recognitive Practices of Declaring and Constituting Statehood", p. 131.
119. Christine Chwaszcza, "'Recognition': Some Analytical Remarks", *International Theory* 5 (2013): 163.
120. CAVR, *Chega!*, chapter 3, p. 61.
121. Agio Pereira, "2015 Timor-Leste Update: Keynote Speech by His Excellency Agio Pereira, Minister of State and of the Presidency of the Council of Ministers, Government of Timor-Leste", Australian National University, Canberra, 19 November 2015.
122. Ibid.
123. Griffiths, "Admission to the Sovereignty Club", p. 4.

3

The Politics of Recognition: East Timor and the International Community

Sovereignty is an identity status that is bestowed upon political entities by sovereign states. The last chapter examined East Timor's rights to self-determination under international law. Whether individual states decide to recognize these claims to political independence is often motivated by political factors rather than legal principles. This chapter examines the reactions of states and members of the broader international community to the sovereign claims of the East Timorese independence movement. It examines some of the key states that contributed to denying — and then ultimately permitting — Timorese sovereignty. These include Australia, the ASEAN states, the United States and China, as well as the less influential but culturally significant groupings of Portuguese-speaking countries and Pacific Island States. For decades, East Timor's right to self-determination was denied as powerful states interpreted its claims within the context of their own national interests. At a system-level, Cold War power dynamics contributed to how states assessed their own geostrategic interests *vis-à-vis* Indonesia and East Timor. While many states refused to provide Indonesia *de jure* recognition of sovereignty over East Timor — a notable exception was Australia — Indonesia possessed *de facto* recognition as it was, in all practical senses, the administering power in East Timor. While East Timor's claims were legitimated by the United Nations General Assembly (UNGA), it was not provided the material support from the international community to make those rights meaningful.

There were two key challenges for East Timor achieving political legitimacy. The first related to convincing the international community that self-determination was a human rights issue. This entailed two elements: the first was the use of international liberal discourses to persuade Western states that East Timor's independence would be necessary to protect people from human rights violations by Indonesia. The second element involved constructing a vision of the type of state that East Timor would become — namely, a liberal democratic state that would defend the social, economic and civic rights of citizens according to international law. These normative appeals to liberal rights were ultimately successful in eroding the collective *realpolitik* that had sustained Indonesia's rule. At a system-level, the end of the Cold War compelled an increase in international pressure against human rights abuses during the 1990s. Within this context, Indonesia's own democratization in 1998 replaced President Suharto's "New Order" regime with a new government initially headed by President B.J. Habibie, who would ultimately grant East Timor a vote for independence.[1] Indonesia was ultimately unable to persuade the international community that East Timor belonged in its republic, and this was a key reason why its incorporation policy failed.

The second challenge related to the development of distinctive East Timorese identity and history *vis-à-vis* Indonesia. Analysis of these identity debates provides insights into the relationships between social identity and political legitimacy, and the role of the international community in permitting rights to self-determination.[2] Actualizing East Timor's right to self-determination required the independence movement to present arguments that a separate nation existed that should be politically independent according to norms of national self-determination. Representatives from both East Timor and Indonesia set about projecting representations about East Timor's identity based upon different interpretations of cultural, historical and political affiliations.

East Timor and the International Community

East Timor's delayed independence was an anomaly in the post-World War Two order because boundaries generally provided colonies with admission to the sovereignty club.[3] Despite this, East Timor's legal arguments remained insufficient as individual states used *realpolitik* calculations to interpret their interests. Recognition is primarily an act of executive power by a central government of an individual state. Whether a government will be motivated to recognize sovereignty — or not — depends upon a plurality of "heterogenous facts" and discretionary legal, political, moral, economic and security considerations that can come into play within unique recognition scenarios.[4] States are often committed to advancing their national interests rather than promoting international principles and norms (which are often contradictory anyway).[5] For example, Taiwan has *de facto* authority but lacks external sovereignty as many states support the "One China Policy" wherein Taiwan is incorporated within China. Here, approaches to Taiwan's political status have been shaped by states' national interests and relationships with China. Similarly with East Timor, legal and moral considerations were outweighed by the political, economic and security concerns of influential states.

While states provided *de facto* recognition of Indonesia's rule, the United Nations (UN) never recognized Indonesian sovereignty over East Timor. As the last chapter pointed out, from 1975 until 1982, all eight UNGA Resolutions on the issue of East Timor's international status affirmed its legal right to self-determination.[6] This meant little in practice. International political factors for East Timor's delayed self-determination included the Cold War, the threat of communism and the prioritization of "friendly" relations with Indonesia by states such as the United States and Australia. Additionally, perceptions that East Timor was too underdeveloped and small to become a sovereign state hindered its claims.[7] These external factors enabled Indonesia to promote the idea that their occupation of East Timor was an irreversible *fait accompli*.[8] This section examines the responses of key states and blocs to East Timor's occupation and subsequent struggle for independence. It draws upon the Commission of Truth, Reception and Reconciliation (CAVR) Report *Chega!* to provide an official East Timorese account of the actions of these states apropos Timorese independence.

Australia

Since Indonesia's invasion in 1975, there has been considerable scholarship on Australia's roles, interests and responsibilities regarding East Timorese independence.[9] While Australian officials did not regard Australia as a party principle to the dispute, it held a strategic interest in preventing instability within the region.[10] Australia's policy positions on the question of East Timor's status had been formulated during the 1960s after the UN granted its status as a non-self-governing territory. Several characteristics would remain relatively constant across time and governments: concerns about the improbability of a viable state; the desire for Indonesian occupation; in principle support for self-determination; and, opposition to the use of military force. During 1974 and 1975, Australian Prime Minister Gough Whitlam actively supported East Timor's incorporation into Indonesia.[11] In September 1974, Whitlam told Indonesian President Suharto that he favoured integration in Indonesia as an acceptable arrangement.[12] Whitlam's perspective was underpinned by the paradoxical position that this integration should be the result of "the properly expressed wishes of the people of Portuguese Timor".[13] As *Chega!* states, "[i]ndependence was not an option".[14] Cotton suggests that Whitlam was driven by a principled opposition to colonialism.[15] In 1975, Whitlam publically declared his aversion to neo-colonialism, arguing that Australia has "no national obligation or interest in getting reinvolved in colonial or post-colonial affairs in Portuguese Timor at the very time when Papua New Guinea's imminent dependence is leading to the ending of our colonial role there".[16] However, there were other reasons offered: the potential risk it could pose to regional stability, whether it would become "the focus of attention" of China and the Soviet Union, scepticism about FRETILIN's politics, and the affect it would have on Australia's attempts to develop a new diplomacy towards ASEAN.[17] The government recognized that Australia could not act in isolation, and attempted to coordinate policy on regional issues with Southeast Asian states, most of whom did not support an independent East Timor.[18]

While expressing unwavering support for good relations with Indonesia and for an integrated East Timor, Whitlam remained concerned about East Timor's self-determination.[19] The Australian government and the Department of Foreign Affairs and Trade knew

Indonesia planned to incorporate East Timor, but the question was how it would be incorporated and whether Indonesia would use force.[20] While Indonesia preferred that Portuguese Timor join Indonesia voluntarily, the blueprint for incorporation outlined that the least preferable action — military invasion — would be taken if Indonesia's national security interests were threatened.[21] Although Whitlam disapproved of Indonesia's use of force to annex Timorese territory, Australia continued to maintain a policy of appeasing Indonesia. This was partly owing to Whitlam's reluctance to "exercise a quasi-colonial role", but also due to the influence of Australia's Ambassador to Jakarta, Richard Woolcott.[22] A cable from Woolcott said that Australia should accept occupation as a *fait accompli*, remove Australians from East Timor, disengage from the issue, minimize publicity and show "privately" its understanding to Indonesia.[23] Woolcott "unashamedly" argued that Australia would be better served by a Kissingerian realism rather than a principled "Wilsonian idealism", favouring relations with Indonesia ahead of principles of human rights and self-determination.[24] He was also concerned about how Australia could best gain access to Timor Sea oil resources.[25] In the government documents at the time, officials were repeatedly explicit about this being a choice between a "principled but ineffective posture" and pragmatic realism.[26] This tension was highlighted by the Australian government's weak reaction to the deaths of the "Balibo Five" — five Australian TV newsmen covering the Indonesian invasion of East Timor — in October 1975.[27] According to James Dunn, a former Australian consul to Portuguese Timor, the Australian government actively sought to minimize and discredit information on the Indonesian military operations so as to quell concerns within the Australian public.[28]

In 1975, Australia voted in favour of the UNGA resolution upholding East Timor's right to self-determination, then abstained for two years and voted against the resolutions from 1978 to 1982. The Australian government was advised by bureaucrats to remain as "uninvolved in the United Nations as compatible with domestic political factors and our international ties and responsibilities".[29] From 1974–99, Australia's policy was consistently shaped by *realpolitik* considerations driven by systemic forces that bound Australia's perceived security interests to Indonesia.[30] A stable Indonesia was, and remains, a first order concern in Australian foreign policy because of its need to defend the northern approaches "from which or through which any military attack on Australia would be launched".[31] While Australia may have claimed neutrality in the East Timor issue, Aubrey estimated that from 1972 to 1980 around AU$50.5 million in military aid was transferred from Australia to Indonesia in various forms, including aircraft, boats and training.[32] East Timorese self-determination could have provided the catalyst for "Balkinization" by inspiring other restive communities across the Indonesian archipelago to escalate their separatist demands, putting further pressure on the unity of the republic and presenting a regional security threat.

Australia's interests were also defined by security concerns understood through the prism of the Cold War. This partly pertained to Australia's prioritization of its security alliance with the United States, which also supported Indonesia's occupation. For example, Pentagon officials met with Australian Prime Minister Malcolm Fraser in August 1976 to warn him not to allow Australia's relations with Indonesia to deteriorate because U.S. security interests required Indonesian goodwill.[33] Not only did Indonesia pose direct and indirect threats to Australia, but an independent, fragile East Timor could potentially become a "Southeast Asian Cuba" and harbour hostile powers. These were not abstract concerns: during World War Two, Japanese occupation of the island of Timor constituted a threat to Australia given its close proximity to Australia's northern shores.[34]

Australia's national interest formation relating to the question of East Timor was also shaped by material and corporate considerations. Since the 1970s, successive Australian governments have sought to protect its interests in Timor Sea oil and gas deposits.[35] Oil companies such as BHP had lobbied Australia in support of Indonesia's invasion.[36] In 1978 Australia extended *de facto* recognition of Indonesian sovereignty of East Timor, which "slipped" into *de jure* recognition in 1979, as this allowed Australia to enter into oil negotiations with Indonesia.[37] Australia's *de jure* recognition was confirmed by the Labor Hawke Government in 1985. Through the 1980s until 1996, the Hawke/Keating government pursued Australia's strategic and economic interests in the Timor Sea and subordinated legal and moral concerns about East Timor's collective rights to self-determination.[38] According to *Chega!*, while Australia acknowledged East Timor's right to self-determination, Australia did not uphold it in practice.[39] *Chega!*

considered the *de jure* recognition in 1979 as having the "effect of consolidating and legitimising Indonesia's sovereignty" over East Timor.[40] Other Western states, such as Britain, Canada and New Zealand, were also accused of either being actively complicit in human rights violations in East Timor — pointing to Britain's supply of military arms to Indonesia — or indirectly complicit *via* their negligent diplomacy and passivity.[41] Like Australia, these particular states were also primarily concerned about their relations with the United States and Indonesia.

The United States

Like Australia, U.S. policy on East Timorese independence was initially formulated in the 1960s. In 1963, a U.S. Department of State policy document outlined that Portuguese Timor had "only one possible future", which was to be a part of Indonesia.[42] Nevertheless, the United States "would have to oppose" any effort by Indonesia to take the territory of Portuguese Timor by force.[43] U.S. interests on the question of East Timor's self-determination were largely driven by strategic concerns arising from the Cold War. After the 1965 coup against Indonesian President Sukarno, the United States sought closer economic and security ties with Indonesia as a strategically important non-communist ally in Asia. Indonesia had promoted the idea that Portuguese Timor would become a communist state, which played to U.S. concerns about the expansion of communism in Southeast Asia.[44] The geostrategic position of East Timor was also significant for the United States. North of the Timorese coastline is the Ombai-Wetar Strait, a trench deep enough to permit submerged nuclear submarines transiting between the West Pacific and Indian Oceans to avoid detection.[45] The strategic importance of the Ombai-Wetar Strait was also linked to impending Law of the Sea agreements.[46] Like Australia, the U.S. policy on Portuguese Timor was a consequence of realist calculations of national interest.

The United States preferred peaceful integration in accordance to principles of self-determination and expressed concerns about military actions. According to *Chega!*, the United States had known early in 1975 about Indonesia's incorporation plans and the likely use of force, and participated in joint military exercises in February of that year that were similar to the invasion of Dili in December.[47] Indonesian

President Suharto briefly discussed East Timor with U.S. President Gerald Ford during a visit to Washington in July 1975, assuring him that Indonesia would not use force.[48] On 6 December 1975, the day before Indonesian troops invaded East Timor, Ford and Secretary of State Henry Kissinger visited Suharto. The U.S. president was quoted as saying "we will understand and will not press you on the issue. We understand the problem and the intentions you have."[49] Kissinger was concerned about the negative image of the use of U.S.-made arms in the invasion but nonetheless emphasized that the plan should succeed "quickly".[50] It seemed neither state anticipated a long war — certainly not a twenty-four-year resistance campaign. The timing of the invasion was important for damage control: Kissinger told Suharto, "[i]f you have made plans, we will do our best to keep everyone quiet until the President returns home."[51] President Suharto effectively asked for, and received, U.S. approval for its military intervention.

The United States knew that its weapons were used during and after the invasion of Dili.[52] By 1975, it has been estimated that 90 per cent of Indonesian military equipment was manufactured in the United States.[53] In 1976, the United States doubled its military aid to Indonesia and continued to provide arms.[54] The Ford and Carter administrations actively supported Indonesia's military: while the Ford administration stopped arms supplies in line with congressional rulings in the six months after the invasion, military aid nearly doubled from US$83 million in 1975 to US$146 million in 1982, and the United States increased arms supplies after the invasion, including twelve F-12 fighter aircraft in 1986.[55] Successive U.S. governments deepened relations with Indonesia at the expense of East Timor's independence. Following a visit in 1993, for example, Washington's Ambassador to Indonesia informed the U.S. State Department that East Timor's "economic backwardness" was "remarkable" and that East Timor was "not ready, economically or politically, for independence".[56] This reflected the arguments also raised by Australia concerning the capacities of an independent East Timor to enact empirical sovereignty by effectively governing the territory and population.

In contrast to Australia, the United States did not need to provide *de jure* recognition for any treaty negotiations. Instead, it recognized Indonesia's *de facto* incorporation of East Timor in 1976.[57] The official policy formulated in 1975 was to maintain silence on Indonesia's actions.[58] It voted against every resolution in the UNGA except for its abstention in 1975, although it did vote in favour of United Nations Security Council (UNSC) Resolution 384 of 1975 which upheld East Timor's right to self-determination.[59] The United States also actively obstructed censure of Indonesia at the UN.[60] Like other Western countries, it was not until the late 1990s that the United States began to change its stance on Indonesia's occupation of East Timor.

ASEAN States

The Association of Southeast Asian Nations (ASEAN) was established in 1967 with the signing of the Bangkok Declaration by the five founding member states: Indonesia, Singapore, Malaysia, Philippines and Thailand. Brunei, Vietnam, Cambodia, Laos and Myanmar followed in the 1980s and 1990s. Geographically, Timor-Leste is considered part of Southeast Asia.[61] While East Timor does not "naturally" belong within Southeast Asia because regional identities are socially constructed, Guedes suggests that East Timor's cultural heterogeneity makes it both similar and different to other states in the Southeast Asian region.[62] East Timor's relations with the region prior to and after the invasion were largely determined by the preferences of ASEAN states to maintain positive engagements with Indonesia.

ASEAN's security in the 1970s concerned the regional political turbulence that stemmed from internal and external security challenges, including separatism and civil conflict, Western intervention in other Southeast Asian states such as Vietnam, and the ongoing efforts to secure and guarantee sovereignty. The foundational ASEAN states supported Indonesia's policy because they feared that an East Timorese state would attempt to establish a radical Marxist regime, which would potentially harbour communist enemies of Indonesia's New Order regime. The ASEAN states were concerned about an "Angolan type situation" (a major civil conflict) emerging in the Indonesian archipelago due to a "weak, potentially radical" independent East Timor.[63] Norms of "non-interference" as a constitutive component of sovereignty were also crucial to understanding ASEAN's justification for its support of Jakarta's decision to annex Timor-Leste.[64] Indonesia's invasion was seen as providing "stability" in a region experiencing communist insurgencies and conflict, and the principle of non-interference offered a "shield" for ASEAN states' consent.[65]

Of particular concern was maintaining peace between the ASEAN states, particularly in light of the *Konfrontasi* between Indonesia and newly independent Malaysia in the 1960s. As a consequence, the foundational ASEAN states supported East Timor's incorporation. While Thailand, Singapore and Philippine officials reportedly regarded the use of force as potentially embarrassing, their overriding concern was ensuring stable relations with Indonesia. The ambassadors of the four ASEAN states assured Australia that the use of force would not strain their relations with Indonesia, and that if such a circumstance were to arise, their governments would be "as helpful to Indonesia as they could be in the circumstances".[66]

Malaysia, in particular, consistently and staunchly defended Jakarta's invasion of Timor-Leste from the outset. It accepted military involvement if Indonesia considered it necessary, and it played a role in defending Indonesia at the UN.[67] Malaysia's diplomacy prior to the invasion of Dili emphasized that Portugal was "mainly to blame" for the conflict in the territory, and that an independent East Timor was "unviable".[68] In the UNSC debates regarding 1975 Resolution 384, Malaysia's representative held Portugal responsible for the situation in East Timor and supported Indonesia's capacity and willingness to provide the East Timorese with an act of self-determination.[69] This decision was motivated by Malaysia's interests in stifling liberation movements, incorporating Brunei within Malaysia, and avoiding conflict with Indonesia and fellow ASEAN states. Malaysian Prime Minister Abdul Razak Hussein expressed fears about a radical leftist regime emerging in East Timor and supported the invasion. He argued that if Timor became an independent communist state it would "endanger the security in the Southeast Asian region".[70] Malaysia became active in leading and organizing public support for Indonesia's occupation amongst ASEAN states and defending its legitimacy at the UN.[71]

Along with Thailand and the Philippines, Malaysia was one of ten states in the UNGA, besides Indonesia, that voted against the Algerian draft condemning the invasion in 1975. The Philippines also justified the invasion on the grounds that the "people of Portuguese Timor had invited Indonesia to help them".[72] The Philippines support for Indonesia was driven by its own self-interest, as it did not want to risk Indonesia's opposition to its suppression of Muslim dissidents in Mindanao and the Sulu archipelago.[73] During the UNSC debates on the

Timor question in 1976, ASEAN states were increasingly supportive of Indonesia's claims that a valid self-determination process had taken place.[74] In 1982, during the debates on what would be the last vote on the East Timor question in the UNGA, Malaysia argued that the question of East Timor "should never have been put on the agenda" and accused the UNGA Fourth Committee (Special Political and Decolonization Committee) of indulging in an "unnecessary" debate on an issue that, it contended, had been settled six years earlier.[75] Malaysia argued in 1993 that UN Human Rights Council resolutions on East Timor should be scrapped on grounds of non-interference, and Thailand attempted to postpone debates on the East Timor question in the UN.[76]

Of the original ASEAN states, Singapore was the least enthusiastic about Jakarta's annexation, at least initially. Singapore was concerned that Indonesia's invasion could create a dangerous precedent of "Timorization" that could threaten the integrity of other small states in the region.[77] However by the late 1970s, Singapore began voting against resolutions condemning Indonesia in the UNGA, which demonstrated Singapore's belief that the occupation was a *fait accompli*. In 1979, Singapore expressed its support of Indonesia's occupation in the Fourth Committee on economic grounds, arguing that significant improvements had been made in health, education and social amenities in East Timor.[78] Singapore was "satisfied" that the occupation had a "positive effect on the welfare of the population".[79] It also presented the view to the assembly that the Timorese support for the "new situation had been growing rapidly".[80] By 1982, Singapore was describing East Timor as an "integral part of Indonesia".[81]

The ASEAN states "actively provided both material and diplomatic support for Indonesia's annexation of East Timor".[82] Singapore, for example, helped spread anti-FRETILIN propaganda and prioritized the unity of ASEAN.[83] The ASEAN states also provided support to Indonesia in its attempts to suppress the activities of the independence movement within international civil society. Malaysian authorities arrested participants of an Asia-Pacific conference on East Timor in Malaysia on the grounds that they were "insensitive to Indonesia–Malaysia ties".[84] The Philippines was also hostile towards conferences organized by the East Timorese solidarity movement.[85] The decisions of ASEAN states were also determined by domestic political and business interests, and calculations of the national interest that placed positive relations with Indonesia ahead of concerns about East Timor's self-determination. Non-interference assisted ASEAN states to "localise and de-internationalize the issue", forming a barrier against the "new interventionism" that emerged in the 1990s.[86]

The association was founded upon a mutual desire of member states to avoid external intervention in the Southeast Asian region by the superpowers. Supporting "regional autonomy and collective self-reliance" would require minimizing both domestic and intra-regional conflict and the use of force.[87] The ASEAN emphasis on the rights of states to sovereignty, non-interference, territorial integrity and non-use of force emerged from the historical circumstances by which most ASEAN states become independent.[88] ASEAN was established during Indonesia's *Konfrontasi* against Malaysia, a rare example of use of force by a post-colonial Southeast Asian state against a neighbour.[89] Thus, Indonesia's annexation of East Timor through the use of force presented a particular problem for the ASEAN states. Given that the ASEAN Bangkok Declaration that formed the association affirms the rights of states to political independence and freedom from interference, it appears that the acceptance of Malaysia, Singapore, Thailand and the Philippines of Indonesia's annexation and the use of force run contrary to the founding norms of the association. Circumventing this inconsistency required supportive states to argue that a legitimate act of self-determination had taken place, even if it did not conform to the dominant mode of determining the will of the "people" in the international community. The apparent ambiguity of East Timor's political status that arose after the abandonment of the territory by Portuguese administrators was exploited by the ASEAN states as they supported Indonesia's occupation.

As Table 3.1 demonstrates, the voting records of those states that joined ASEAN after the final vote in the UNGA were mixed, and the only states that voted in favour of the resolutions condemning Indonesia were Laos and Vietnam. The approach of the other Southeast Asian states in privileging relations with Indonesia ahead of principles of anti-colonialism stood in direct contrast to many other Third World states that supported Timor-Leste's claims to self-determination. During the 1970s and 1980s, in the global political context of the Cold War, many developing states were part of the non-aligned movement (NAM) that avowedly supported principles of autonomy in

TABLE 3.1
Voting Record of Southeast Asian States in the UNGA on the Question of East Timor, 1975–82[1]

	1975	1976	1977	1978	1979	1980	1981	1982
Singapore	Abstain	Abstain	Against	Against	Against	Against	Against	Against
Malaysia	Against	Against	Against	Against	Against	Against	Against	Against
Thailand	Against	Against	Against	Against	Against	Against	Against	Against
Philippines	Against	Against	Against	Against	Against	Against	Against	Against
Cambodia*	Absent	For	Absent	Abstain	Absent	Against	Against	Against
Laos*	For	For	For	Abstain	For	For	Absent	For
Vietnam*			For	Absent	For	For	For	For
Myanmar*	Absent	Absent	Abstain	Abstain	Abstain	Abstain	Abstain	Abstain

* Not ASEAN members at the time
[1] Brunei was not independent until 1984. See Krieger, *East Timor and the International Community*, pp. 129–33.

international relations and self-determination for colonial and former colonial peoples. These principles were affirmed by the Bandung Conference of Asian-African states in 1955.[90] Evidently, the ASEAN states were driven by realist calculations in which national security interests superseded legal principles. For other developing states, however, maintaining good relations with Indonesia was less important than upholding the principle of self-determination as they had less to lose. This can be illustrated by contrasting ASEAN's voting record with that of the Portuguese-speaking grouping.

Portuguese-Speaking Countries

As East Timor's administrator, Portugal was at least partly responsible for East Timor's denied self-determination as it mismanaged the diplomacy before and after Indonesia's invasion. Portugal had not devised a clear plan for decolonization, it failed to allocate sufficient resources for managing negotiations and was focused on avoiding the internationalization of the issue. During the brief civil war between Timorese political parties in 1975, Portuguese administrators abandoned the territory, which opened up the space for Indonesia's invasion and contributed to East Timor's ambiguous political status. According to Ramos-Horta, in the mid-1970s Portuguese attitudes "ranged from condescending paternalism to outright disrespect for the rights of the people of East Timor to self-determination".[91] Portugal anticipated Indonesia's occupation and reduced its military presence just before the Indonesian intelligence-seeking mission *Operasi Komodo* began in December 1974.[92] By August 1975, Australian officials reported that the Portuguese had "decided to write off the Timor problem", predicting an early intervention.[93] For example, Portuguese and Indonesian officials met in Rome in November 1975 to discuss the question of Timor without involvement of either the UN or East Timorese.[94] At this meeting, the movement of Indonesian troops from West Timor to Portuguese Timor was not canvassed, even though Portugal had been presented with evidence that this was occurring.[95] Its own efforts to appease Indonesia backfired: for example, in statements released in late November, Portugal blamed FRETILIN for the situation without naming Indonesia.[96]

Only following Indonesia's annexation did Portugal defend East Timor's rights to self-determination and protest Indonesia's actions. Directly after the invasion, it cut diplomatic ties with Indonesia, appealed to the UNSC to obtain a cessation of Indonesia's military activities and defended its position as Portuguese Timor's "only legitimate authority".⁹⁷ During UNSC debates in 1975, Portugal did not recognize FRETILIN's unilateral declaration of independence and condemned Indonesia's "expansionist claims", use of force and violations of international law.⁹⁸ Despite these protests, *Chega!* argues that Portugal was largely ambivalent about East Timor, and had "generally failed to translate its principles into sustained practical support until late in the conflict".⁹⁹ Portugal's key objective during the 1970s and early 1980s was "to extricate itself from a situation it had helped to create, whilst at the same time arguing that it was ultimately neither responsible nor influential".¹⁰⁰ Portugal's officials defended its position, arguing that it had "encountered successive difficulties" which prevented self-determination.¹⁰¹ In contrast, the negligence permitted Indonesia's supporters to blame Portugal for the instability in the territory.

Chega! emphasized the failures of Portugal to "discharge its responsibilities" to the East Timorese people until later in the conflict.¹⁰² The turning point came in 1983 when General Ramalho Eanes was elected Portugal's president. He declared it was a common mission for all Portuguese-speaking nations to support East Timor, and packaged its self-determination as a foreign policy priority. While Foreign Minister Jaime Gama was "lukewarm" on the policy shift, new Prime Minister Mario Soares sided with Eanes, and declared Portugal's intention to help East Timor achieve its rights to self-determination.¹⁰³ An example of the renewed support for East Timorese resistance in the 1980s was the Portuguese withdrawal of its ambassador after the Australian Hawke government confirmed *de jure* recognition of Indonesia's sovereignty of East Timor in 1985. Portuguese representatives began making diplomatic representations on a range of international committees, and from 1983 were involved in official tripartite talks with Indonesia and the UN.¹⁰⁴ In the mid-1980s, Portuguese ascension to the European Economic Commission (EEC) and European Parliament created new opportunities for Portugal to gather support among European states.¹⁰⁵ In 1993, Portugal also succeeded in gaining a positive resolution of East Timor's self-determination in the UN Commission of Human Rights.¹⁰⁶

Perhaps Portugal's most significant action was in 1991 when it initiated proceedings against the Australian government in the International Court of Justice (ICJ) regarding its Timor Gap Treaty with Indonesia. In 1995, the court ruled that it could not deliver a verdict due to

Indonesia's non-involvement, but the judgement reaffirmed East Timor's self-determination rights under international law as both Australia and Portugal considered it a non-self-governing territory.[107] Ultimately, Portugal's diplomacy was instrumental to the success of the independence movement by keeping the issue on the international agenda, and in negotiating the terms of the referendum in the late 1990s.

The other Lusophone states were supportive of East Timor's self-determination from 1975. The *Comunidade dos Países de Língua Portuguesa*/ Community of Portuguese Language Countries (CPLP) — a grouping of states that share a common cultural background and language by virtue of their common experiences of Portuguese colonialism — were unanimously in favour of East Timor's self-determination, in contrast to the ASEAN states (see Table 3.2). Prior to Timor-Leste's independence, the CPLP comprised Brazil, Portugal, Angola, Mozambique, Cabo Verde (Cape Verde)/São Tomé e Príncipe (Sao Tome and Principe) and Guinéa-Bissau.[108]

During UN debates, the CPLP states condemned Indonesia's actions and supported East Timor's rights to a genuine act of self-determination. The condemnations of Indonesia employed fierce rhetoric: Mozambique described a "cruel genocide" and "brutal annexation", and criticized Indonesia's claims of a people's assembly as "farcical";[109] São-Tomé and Principe condemned Indonesia's "genocidal policy" and stood by the East Timorese in solidarity;[110] Cape Verde argued that Indonesia was guilty of "deliberate aggression and shameful integration" and "colonial expansionist policy", and compared it with Israel and South Africa;[111] and, Guinéa-Bissau also spoke of "genocide", saying that it was a "gross error" to claim that the East Timorese accepted Indonesia's presence.[112] These states consistently held that Indonesia violated principles of international law through the use of force and its obstruction of a legitimate act of self-determination. Angola and Mozambique raised East Timor in the Fourth Committee in 1993 as an unresolved issue and refused to consider the issue of East Timor's self-determination closed.

The CPLP states also provided material and diplomatic support to the East Timorese independence movement. In his memoir, José Ramos-Horta recounts the support of Portuguese-speaking states to the independence movement in his memoir.[113] He wrote that the five African Portuguese colonies had a "special understanding of the Timor problem" and their own victories "owed a lot to international

TABLE 3.2
Voting Records of the CPLP States in the UNGA on the Question of East Timor, 1975–82

	1975	1976	1977	1978	1979	1980	1981	1982
Portugal	For	For	For	For	For	For	For	For
Brazil	For	For		For	For	For	For	For
Angola			For	For	For	For	For	For
Mozambique	For	For	For	For	For	For	For	For
São Tomé and Príncipe	Absent	For	For	For	For	For	For	For
Guinéa Bissau	For	For	For	For	For	For	For	For
Cape Verde	Absent	For	For	For	For	For	For	For

solidarity".[114] FRETILIN had also developed links with Mozambican nationalist movement and political party FRELIMO (*Frente de Libertação de Moçambique*).[115] At a meeting in Praia in September 1982, Angola, Cape Verde, Guinéa-Bissau, Mozambique and São-Tomé and Principe condemned the genocide and occupation of East Timor, and reaffirmed solidarity in the struggle for independence.

The key factors explaining why the developing CPLP states had a different voting record is because they prioritized relations with Portugal, and — not being geographically or politically close to Indonesia — were prepared to deal with the potential bilateral damage. Importantly, the advocacy of African CPLP states reflected their own interest in maintaining the primacy of the self-determination principle as the normative foundation upholding their own sovereignty. The African CPLP states had recently emerged from Portuguese colonialism and shared with the East Timorese political elite the common historical background of liberation movements and the Portuguese language, which provided the basis of its solidarity. This shared heritage was also reflected in Brazil's contribution to UN debates in 1982: "Brazilians shared a common political past with the Maubere people of East Timor. Their country, along with five African nations with the same cultural background and speaking the same language, had become independent states and were now responsible members of the international community."[116] The voting patterns of the CPLP conform to the broader trends of developing countries voting in favour of liberation movements and self-determination principles that underpin the recognition of their own external sovereignty.

Ramos-Horta argued at the UN that 400 years of Portuguese colonialism had profoundly impacted upon the East Timorese identity, and this had accentuated the political barriers and cultural incongruence that separated the Indonesian and East Timorese people.[117] East Timor's *lingua franca*, Tetum, for example, was "strongly influenced" by the Portuguese language, and despite close geographical proximity, linguists generally agree there are few links between Bahasa Indonesian and the languages of East Timor.[118] Portugal also introduced Roman Catholicism to East Timor, although animism continued as the dominant spiritual and religious practice throughout the Portuguese administration. Portugal's assimilation policies also contributed to the large number of Portuguese Timorese in the territory.

Hull also suggests that the East Timorese did not have the same anti-colonial attitudes towards the Portuguese as the Indonesians held towards the Dutch due in part to Portugal's cultivation of a global "Lusophone family".[119]

However, East Timor's connection to this Lusophone family and Catholicism should not be overstated. During Portuguese colonialism, there were few changes to social life in East Timor which continued to be organized around animist religious traditions.[120] The reinvigoration of the Lusophone-Catholic cultural influence came from an unlikely source: Indonesia. Indonesian colonialism had the unintended effect of growing Catholicism across the territory: the Indonesian Pancasila ideology compelled subjects to choose an official religion, and the spread of Tetum developed though liturgy in church services during the resistance.[121] As later chapters demonstrate, this revivification of the Portuguese influences on national identity through the resistance movement would have consequences on how the future Timorese state would approach its international relations.

South Pacific Island States

While Timor-Leste is generally positioned geographically in Southeast Asia, anthropologically it is said to lie in a "transitional space" between maritime Southeast Asia and Oceania, comprised of three subcultural regions Melanesia, Polynesia and Micronesia.[122] This provides East Timor an identity connection to its South Pacific neighbours.[123] Some scholars, such as Robie, Gray and King, identified East Timor alongside other "Melanesian independence struggles" in the South Pacific, including in the Indonesian province of Irian Jaya (West Papua).[124] Alongside its long history of Portuguese contact, East Timor's Melanesian roots provided the basis of "othering" Indonesia in debates about the ethnographic boundaries between Southeast Asia and Melanesia.[125] This idea was sustained by the historical and anthropological literature that positions Melanesians as the original occupants of East Timor who were pushed inland by Indo-Malayan immigration. The geographic and cultural ambiguities of the "transition zone" were exploited by East Timor's independence leaders as it emphasized Melanesian influences in its society, associating East Timor with its "brother and sisters of the South Pacific Region" in addition to the Malay-Polynesian and Portuguese influences.[126] By 1976, Ramos-Horta was arguing that the

Timorese had "more ethnic and cultural affiliation not with Java to the west, but with Papua and New Guinea to the east".[127] The East Timorese independence movement looked to Pacific states for support, and participated in regional forums, such as the Vanuatu Conference for a Nuclear Free and Independent Pacific.[128] In so doing, they sought to separate East Timor's identity — its cultural composition and political history — from Indonesia.

While the East Timorese independence movement sought to link in with Melanesian states, key South Pacific states tended to support Indonesia by not voting in favour of resolutions. The Pacific voting record in the UNGA was much less consistent than the ASEAN states and the CPLP. Papua New Guinea voted against the resolutions from 1978–82. Fiji initially voted in favour, but, along with the Solomon Islands, voted against the resolution in the final 1982 vote after periods of either abstaining or being absent. The exception in South Pacific was Vanuatu, which did not have a vote until 1981. It voted in favour of the resolutions twice at a time when the "for" vote was declining in the UNGA and other South Pacific states had committed to an "against" vote. In 1982, Vanuatu's representative at the UNGA declared that it could not "ignore the dangerous precedent" of a bigger country using force against "a smaller and more vulnerable country".[129] Vanuatu "could not vote against the old colonialism and accept a new one", and was not convinced that an act of self-determination had occurred.[130] It actively refuted the suggestion that supporting the resolution would be contrary to national interests, instead choosing principles ahead of other concerns. Despite mainly comprising new post-colonial states, of the three main cultural and/or regional groupings Timor-Leste associates with — ASEAN, Portuguese-speaking countries and the Pacific — only the Lusophone world demonstrated consistent support for East Timor's rights to self-determination.

China and the Soviet Union

In defending its occupation of East Timor during the Cold War, Indonesia exaggerated the leftist tendencies in FRETILIN and positioned an independent East Timor as a risk of becoming communist. Given the concerns about FRETILIN's communist leanings, it might be assumed that the Communist powers of the time, the Soviet Union and China, supported a leftist liberation movement. Indeed,

FRETILIN's attempts to include China in its plans to secure international recognition of sovereignty compounded suspicions of "Maoist" influences in the organization.[131] Yet, Indonesia's assessment of the international dynamics prior to intervention concluded that the Soviet Union, like the United States, would provide no "significant reaction", and that any protest from China "would be routine and stereotyped" ("an obligatory reaction").[132] The Soviet Union — keen to avoid getting involved in the issue — merely declared that it would not support outside intervention and showed little interest in East Timor despite supporting other radical liberation movements and voting in favour of all eight resolutions.[133]

China initially provided support for East Timor's independence movement by denouncing Indonesia at the UN and describing its incorporation of East Timor as an act of expansionist, colonial aggression. China's representative expressed recognition of the Timorese state that FRETILIN had unilaterally declared sovereign by using the official name designated by FRETILIN — the Democratic Republic of East Timor — at the UN.[134] While China espouses ardent support the principle of sovereignty, it has a more ambiguous relationship with self-determination, particularly given its efforts to supress liberation movements in its own jurisdiction. China's initial support for East Timor was at least partly due to China's sour bilateral relations with Indonesia, which had been suspended following Suharto's 1965 coup and the subsequent purge of Communists in Indonesia. China consistently voted in favour of East Timor's independence from 1975–82.

The Success of the Independence Movement

As the previous discussion demonstrated, throughout the 1970s and 1980s, realist policies favouring the national interest shaped the perspectives of many states in relations to East Timor's status, even though the UN still considered East Timor as administered by Portugal. It seemed evident that the only way East Timor would attain political recognition of sovereignty would be to compel Indonesia to allow a self-determination ballot. By 1999, East Timor had secured this right to hold a legitimate, universally acknowledged act of self-determination. There are multiple, intersecting explanations for this policy shift by Indonesia. This section focuses on two key factors:

the changing normative environment of the international community after the Cold War, and the failures of Indonesia to persuade the international community that East Timor belonged within its republic. Throughout the 1980s, supporters of East Timor's independence struggled to maintain the issue on the international agenda as Indonesia sought to "normalize" the territory. During the 1990s, however, states, international organizations, such as the European Union and the United Nations, and civil society organizations played important roles in pressuring Indonesia to change its policies on East Timor.

There were several key events during this period that garnered significant international media attention for the East Timorese independence movement and contributed to arguments that this was a human rights issue. The demonstrations and international publicity that accompanied the visit of Pope John Paul II to Dili in 1989 contributed to the increased activities of Portugal and some of its European counterparts in the 1990s.[135] The Santa Cruz massacre in 1991, the arrest of Xanana Gusmão in 1992 and the awarding of the Nobel Peace Prize to Bishop Carlos Belo and Jose Ramos-Horta in 1996 shone a spotlight on the human rights situation in East Timor.[136] After Santa Cruz, for example, the UN National Human Rights Commission Special Rapporteur on Extrajudicial, Summary or Arbitrary Executions produced a report that condemned Indonesia's policy failures, compelling the UN into action on resolving the East Timor question and "internationalized" it.[137] The United States publically condemned the massacre, and Congress voted to withdraw funding for military training and cooperation.[138] A newly elected president, Bill Clinton, decided to ban the sale of small and light arms and other military equipment to Indonesia.[139]

The end of the Cold War had also blunted fears that East Timor would become a communist state. These events may not have substantially altered the interests of influential states, however, if they had not coincided with the rise of international liberal rights discourses. The era of "liberal triumphalism" that followed the end of the Cold War was characterized by enthusiasm for the project of democratization and human rights within the international community. This movement towards liberal rights encouraged states to move away from purely *realpolitik* assessments of their own national interest regarding the East Timor question.[140] The *Chega!* report argues that a significant factor of the resistance was its reconstruction as an "all-inclusive movement" committed to democracy and human rights.[141] The East Timorese independence movement sought to appeal to a minimum international "standard of civilization" that encompassed democracy and liberal ideals.[142] The manifestoes and peace plans of the independence movement after 1987 included commitments that an East Timorese state would be a liberal-social democracy and would guarantee civil, legal and socio-economic rights to its citizens.[143]

The use of liberal rights discourses appealed to the newly hegemonic ideologies shaping the laws, norms and practices of the international community. The independence movement used an activist "public diplomacy" campaign to win the "hearts and minds" of citizens within states in order to shape the interests of powerful Western states such as Australia and the United States: concerned citizens would apply grassroots pressure on their governments, who, in turn, would apply pressure on Indonesia. Organizations advocated within global civil society and the international diplomatic spheres contributed to this activist public diplomacy campaign, and assisted in reinforcing the illegitimacy of the Indonesian occupation. This style of activist public diplomacy has subsequently been replicated in some areas of foreign policy strategy by Timor-Leste (see chapter seven).

The changing international order also provided the context for Indonesia's democratization, which was instrumental in changing Indonesia's policy on East Timor's self-determination.[144] Indonesia's own pro-democracy movement (*Reformasi*) contributed to the fall of the Suharto regime in 1998, which opened up new opportunities for supporters of East Timorese independence to pressure Indonesian elites, including those activists operating within Indonesian civil society. In June 1998, amidst international and domestic pressure, new caretaker Indonesian President B.J. Habibie offered East Timor a "special status" within Indonesia, consisting of wide-ranging autonomy as an "end-solution to the question of East Timor".[145] This was widely rejected by the East Timorese.[146] In December 1998, Australian Prime Minister John Howard sent Habibie a letter encouraging him to enter into direct negotiations with the East Timorese and offered New Caledonia as a model of self-determination, insulting the Indonesians with its colonial connotations.

Indonesia experienced other forms of international pressure as its Western allies began to question East Timor's political status and human rights became "more prominent in Washington and Canberra's thinking".[147] On 27 January 1999, Habibie announced that he would allow a referendum in East Timor whereby rejection of the offered autonomy package would result in independence.[148] Habibie argued that if "the East Timorese still refused to accept integration [after twenty-five years], then norms of democracy and justice would suggest that they should peacefully exercise their right of self-determination".[149] While the purpose of the Howard letter was to confirm Australia's support of East Timor remaining part of Indonesia, it compelled an offended Habibie to offer a popular consultation providing the East Timorese a choice between independence or weak autonomy within the republic.[150]

There were several reasons why Habibie reversed Indonesia's stance on East Timor.[151] First, the new leader was under pressure from civil society to provide greater human rights and democracy, including to East Timor. Second, new political, social and economic forces were reordering Indonesia's priorities. Ali Alatas had famously described East Timor as a pebble in Indonesia's shoe: by 1997, the Asian Financial Crisis and the emergent processes of democratization meant that maintaining East Timorese territory was rendered less significant than the other pressures on the Republic. Third, Habibie had poor intelligence: it has been reported that Habibie thought that East Timor would choose autonomy. Finally, the pressure from international community meant that Indonesian leaders re-evaluated the costs of East Timor's incorporation. Habibie was also more open to concerns about Indonesia's international image than Suharto.

Ultimately, Indonesia failed to absorb East Timor within the Republic — its distinctiveness within and outside Indonesia, and the continuing repression of the East Timorese, enabled the independence movement to keep the issue on the international agenda long after Indonesia had taken control of the territory. As the previous chapter noted, in the international arena, Indonesia argued that East Timor had elected to become part of the Indonesian republic. Through various speeches and propaganda documents directed at international audiences, Indonesia developed an argument that its incorporation of East Timor reunited the Indonesian and East Timorese people who had been separated by centuries of European colonialism.[152] This rested upon ethnic-genealogical or "primordial" visions of nations as comprising people bound together through common descent and ancestry. Indonesia defended the importance of colonial borders as a way of maintaining sovereignty over provinces in which self-determination movements had flourished, including West Papua. However, by incorporating East Timor, Indonesia defied the borders created by the European imperialists to instead privilege a mythical historical order based on an alleged "brotherhood" and "kinship" shared between Indonesians and East Timorese.[153] As a former European colony determined to hold together its post-colonial archipelagic state, Indonesia was determined to distinguish between East Timor's annexation and European colonialism. Indonesia's narrative presented Indonesia as liberating East Timor from centuries of colonial rule.[154]

In the absence of meaningful support for legal self-determination rights, establishing the "nation" in the eyes of the international community became fundamental for the promotion of East Timor's sovereignty in the international community. This is reflected in Abel Guterres' statement that part of the independence struggle was to establish an East Timorese identity to the outside world.[155] FRETILIN's representative at the United Nations, José Ramos-Horta, hit back at Indonesia's essentialist arguments, countering that integration was against "the historical law of social dynamism"; while the Indonesian and East Timorese may have once shared a common cultural and ethnic identity, 400 years of colonialism had profoundly impacted upon the East Timorese identity.[156] East Timor was at a "different social, political and cultural stage as a result of a different and independent development".[157] Within East Timor, an "anti-colonial nationalism" emerged *vis-à-vis* Indonesia, which refers to a political movement seeking state power on the grounds of a common nationality characterized by a unique "cultural" identity.[158] As a political doctrine, it promulgates a belief that nations must be as politically independent as possible as "like should rule over like".[159] The struggle for recognition compelled an anti-colonial nationalist movement, and the concept of an East Timorese "nation" emerged as a focal point for the mobilization of national consciousness.[160]

Indonesia's failure to convince both domestic and international audiences that East Timor belonged within Indonesia was an important contributing factor to East Timor's ultimately winning the right to a valid exercise of self-determination. Philpott argues that the East Timorese national identity arose from a "unifying discourse of blood, soil and shared suffering".[161] In a 1992 article, Anderson suggested that "a profound sense of commonality" emerged among the East Timorese during Indonesian administration and this was compounded by the activities of the Indonesians.[162] The scale of violence employed by Indonesia hampered their aim of absorbing East Timor and Indonesian administrators in East Timor, "othered" the East Timorese by referring to them as "Tim Tim".[163] Given the lack of international support, the pursuit of East Timor's right to self-determination necessitated the construction of a unified, nationalized independence movement because part of self-determination's *raison d'être* is the preservation of a unique culture.[164] Proving East Timor's distinctiveness, that is, not being Indonesian, at once supported claims to self-determination and reinforced the establishment of an East Timorese nation. While political aspirations encouraged the development of national unity within East Timor, constructed images of a East Timorese nation were necessary in the international realm where the contest over self-determination played out. Ultimately, the battle over identity was a reflection of the importance of nation in this recognition scenario, even though East Timor's claims to political independence were based on its non-self-governing territory status justified by its colonial history.

Conclusion

The next chapter discusses East Timor's transition from Indonesian province to independent state that followed the referendum in 1999. For much of Indonesia's occupation of East Timor, the realist motivations of many states influenced their decision not to recognize East Timor's claims to self-determination. Later chapters in this book demonstrate how this history of seeking political recognition has contributed to Timor-Leste's relations with members of the international community. This struggle continues to be drawn upon in foreign policy discourse. As Agio Pereira stated in 2015, "[d]uring two and a half dark decades, as we fought for our independence, without external support — the world turned its back on us. Yet we fought on to ensure that the country that emerged from Portuguese-Timor did not fade away."[165] He continued: "Western powers including Australia, all assumed we would inevitably become part of Indonesia and rebuffed our efforts to become independent. They ignored 500 years of cultural heritage; and failed to allow the Timorese people the right to self-determination."[166] East Timor found most support from other postcolonial states, particularly Portuguese-speaking states. The representation of Portugal's colonization has been softened over time, such that it is now described as "cultural interaction" (see chapters five and six). This has overshadowed the long history of neglectful administration and initial complicity in Indonesia's occupation. Southeast Asian states generally supported fellow ASEAN member, Indonesia. This has not dissuaded Timor-Leste from seeking ASEAN membership following independence, choosing its Southeast Asia geographical connection ahead of the Melanesian cultural connection that was emphasized by the independence movement.

Under international law, East Timor's status as a non-self-governing territory should have ensured its rights to self-determination. Ultimately, the end of the Cold War was crucial to Timor-Leste's independence. The increased concern for democracy and human rights within the international community during the 1990s contributed to a shift in foreign policy direction of a number of states, including the United States, on the question of East Timor. The lack of international support necessitated the construction of a unified, nationalized independence movement.[167] Indonesia ultimately failed to convince the international community after twenty-four years that East Timor belonged within the Republic of Indonesia. East Timorese leaders such as José Ramos-Horta presented the case that East Timor held a separate cultural and national identity from Indonesia by virtue of its Portuguese colonial history and Melanesian roots. This was necessary for reinforcing East Timor's right to self-determination as a unique "nation" within the international community that possessed a particular cultural, historical and political heritage. This sense of distinctiveness has informed its international relations.

NOTES

1. Simon Chesterman, *You, the People: The United Nations, Transitional Administration, and State-Building*, p. 61 (Oxford: Oxford University Press, 2005); Simon Philpott, "East Timor's Double Life: Smells Like Westphalian Spirit", *Third World Quarterly* 27, no. 1 (2006): 142.

2. See Daniele Archibugi, "A Critical Analysis of the Self-Determination of Peoples: A Cosmopolitan Perspective", *Constellations* 10, no. 2 (2003): 488–505.
3. Hurst Hannum, *Autonomy, Sovereignty, and Self-Determination: The Accommodation of Conflicting Rights*, pp. 36–37 (Philadelphia: University of Philadelphia Press, 1990).
4. Christine Chwaszcza, "'Recognition': Some Analytical Remarks", *International Theory* 5 (2013): 163; Mikulas Fabry, "Theorizing State Recognition", *International Theory* 5 (2013): 166.
5. Stephen Krasner, "Recognition: Organised Hypocrisy Once Again", *International Theory* 5, no. 1 (2013): 171.
6. See Heike Krieger, *East Timor and the International Community: Basic Documents*, pp. 123–33 (Cambridge: Cambridge University Press, 1997).
7. Commission for Reception, Truth and Reconciliation (CAVR), *Chega! Final Report of the Commission for Reception, Truth and Reconciliation Timor-Leste*, chapter 7, pp. 1, 66 (Dili: CAVR, 2005).
8. Ibid., p. 67.
9. Cotton provides a thorough and insightful analysis of Australia's role. See James Cotton, *East Timor, Australia and Regional Order: Intervention and its Aftermath in Southeast Asia*, pp. 6–11 (London: RoutledgeCurzon, 2004). For a comprehensive record of Australian diplomacy from 1974–76, see Department of Foreign Affairs and Trade, *Australia and the Indonesian Incorporation of Portuguese Timor, 1974–1976*, edited by Wendy Way, Damien Browne and Vivianne Johnson (Carlton: Melbourne University Press, 2000).
10. Gough Whitlam, "The New Federalism: A Review of Labor's Programs and Policies", Speech by the Prime Minister, the Hon EG Whitlam QC PM, Opening Address to Conference of the Centre for Research on Federal Financial Relations, Australian National University, 27 August 1975.
11. Cablegram to Canberra, Jakarta, 3 September 1975. Department of Foreign Affairs and Trade, *Australia and the Indonesian Incorporation of Portuguese Timor, 1974–1976*, p. 376.
12. James Dunn, *Timor: A People Betrayed*, p. 143 (Milton, Queensland: The Jacaranda Press, 1983).
13. Record of Meeting between Whitlam and Soeharto, Yogyakarta, 6 September 1974. Department of Foreign Affairs and Trade, *Australia and the Indonesian Incorporation of Portuguese Timor, 1974–1976*, pp. 95–100; Cablegram to Canberra, Jakarta, 3 September 1975. Department of Foreign Affairs and Trade, *Australia and the Indonesian Incorporation of Portuguese Timor, 1974–1976*, p. 376.
14. CAVR, *Chega!*, p. 26.
15. Cotton, *East Timor, Australia and Regional Order*, pp. 8–9.
16. Whitlam, "The New Federalism".

17. See, for example, Record of Conversation between Whitlam and Soeharto, Townsville, 4 April 1975. Department of Foreign Affairs and Trade, *Australia and the Indonesian Incorporation of Portuguese Timor, 1974–1976*, pp. 95–97; José Ramos-Horta, *Funu: The Unfinished Saga of East Timor*, p. 82 (New Jersey: The Red Sea Press, Lawrenceville, 1987).
18. Cablegram to Canberra, Jakarta, 6 December 1975. Department of Foreign Affairs and Trade, *Australia and the Indonesian Incorporation of Portuguese Timor, 1974–1976*, pp. 601–3.
19. Record of Conversation between Whitlam and Soeharto, Townsville, 4 April 1975. Department of Foreign Affairs and Trade, *Australia and the Indonesian Incorporation of Portuguese Timor, 1974–1976*, pp. 95–100.
20. Cablegram to Canberra, Jakarta, 14 August 1975. Department of Foreign Affairs and Trade, *Australia and the Indonesian Incorporation of Portuguese Timor, 1974–1976*, p. 309.
21. Cablegram to Canberra, Jakarta, 10 July 1975. Department of Foreign Affairs and Trade, *Australia and the Indonesian Incorporation of Portuguese Timor, 1974–1976*, pp. 290–91.
22. Commonwealth of Australia House of Representatives, *Debates 76*, 26 August 1975, pp. 491–93.
23. Cablegram to Canberra, Jakarta, 17 August 1975. Department of Foreign Affairs and Trade, *Australia and the Indonesian Incorporation of Portuguese Timor, 1974–1976*, p. 314.
24. Cotton, *East Timor, Australia and Regional Order*, p. 9. See, for example, Department of Foreign Affairs and Trade, *Australia and the Indonesian Incorporation of Portuguese Timor, 1974–1976*, pp. 306–9, 313–14, 431–33.
25. Cablegram to Canberra, Jakarta, 17 August 1975. Department of Foreign Affairs and Trade, *Australia and the Indonesian Incorporation of Portuguese Timor, 1974–1976*, p. 314.
26. See, for example, Cablegram to Canberra, Jakarta, 6 December 1975. Department of Foreign Affairs and Trade, *Australia and the Indonesian Incorporation of Portuguese Timor, 1974–1976*, pp. 601–3.
27. CAVR, *Chega!*, p. 28.
28. Dunn, *Timor*, p. 250.
29. Submission to Willesee, Canberra, 21 August 1975. Department of Foreign Affairs and Trade, *Australia and the Indonesian Incorporation of Portuguese Timor, 1974–1976*, p. 324. See also Cablegram to Canberra, Jakarta, 29 August 1975. Department of Foreign Affairs and Trade, *Australia and the Indonesian Incorporation of Portuguese Timor, 1974–1976*, pp. 359–60.
30. For a detailed analysis of how Australia-Indonesian bilateral relations affected the East Timor issue, see Cotton, *East Timor, Australia and Regional Order*, pp. 22–48.

31. Cotton, *East Timor, Australia and Regional Order*, p. 22.
32. Jim Aubrey, "Viva Timor L'este: Beyond Silence Betrayal, Cowardice and Murder", *Arena* 40 (1999).
33. John Taylor, *East Timor: The Price of Freedom*, p. 74 (Annandale, New South Wales: Zed Books, 1999).
34. Cotton, *East Timor, Australia and Regional Order*, p. 4.
35. Ibid.
36. Taylor, *East Timor*, p. 75.
37. Department of Foreign Affairs and Trade, *Australia and the Indonesian Incorporation of Portuguese Timor, 1974–1976*, pp. xxviii, 839–40; Gareth Evans, "Indonesia and East Timor: Looking Back and Looking Forward", 27 September 1999, available at <http://www.gevans.org/speeches/speech442I&ET1999.html> (accessed 4 February 2017).
38. See Rebecca Strating, "Timor-Leste's Foreign Policy Approach to the Timor Sea Disputes", *Australian Journal of International Affairs* (2017).
39. CAVR, *Chega!*, chapter 7, pp. 1, 30.
40. Ibid.
41. See, for example, Sharon Scharfe, *Complicity: Human Rights and Canadian Foreign Policy* (Montreal, New York and London: Black Rose Books, 1996); Marie Leadbeater, *Negligent Neighbour: New Zealand's Complicity in the Invasion and Occupation of Timor-Leste* (Nelson: Craig Potton Publishing, 2006).
42. CAVR, *Chega!*, chapter 7, pp. 1, 52.
43. Ibid.
44. Ibid., p. 53.
45. Ian Storey, *Southeast Asia and the Rise of China: The Search for Security*, p. 282 (New York: Routledge, 2011).
46. Taylor, *East Timor*, p. 169.
47. CAVR, *Chega!*, chapter 7, pp. 1, 53.
48. Government of the United States, *Memorandum of Conversation: President Ford, President Suharto, Dr Henry A Kissinger, Lt General Brent Scowcroft and Mr Widodo*, 5 July 1975.
49. U.S. Department of State, "Telegram 1579 from the American Embassy in Jakarta", 6 December 1975.
50. Ibid.
51. Ibid.
52. U.S. National Security Council, "Indonesian Use of MAP Equipment in East Timor", Memorandum for Brent Scowcroft from Clinton E. Granger, 12 December 1975.
53. Taylor, *East Timor*, p. 169.
54. Jessica Howard, "Invoking State Responsibility for Aiding the Commission of International Crimes: Australia, the United States and the Question of East Timor", *Melbourne Journal of International Law* 2, no. 1 (2001).

55. Taylor, *East Timor*, p. 169.
56. U.S. Department of State, "East Timor and Human Rights in Indonesia: A Fresh Look", Telegram 02365 from U.S. Embassy Jakarta to State Department, 5 March 1993.
57. Testimony of Kenneth Quinn, Deputy Assistant Secretary of State. United States Senate, "Crisis in East Timor and U.S. Policy towards Indonesia", Hearing before the Committee on Foreign Relations, 102 Congress, 2nd session, 27 February and 6 March 1992.
58. See CAVR, *Chega!*, p. 55.
59. See Krieger, *East Timor and the International Community*, pp. 129–33.
60. Cotton, *East Timor, Australia and Regional Order*, p. 77.
61. Andrea Molnar, *Timor-Leste: Politics, History, and Culture*, p. 5 (London and New York: Routledge, 2010).
62. Armando Marques Guedes, "Thinking East Timor, Indonesia and Southeast Asia", *Lusotopie* (2001): 315, 317, 321. See also Nuno Canas Mendes, "Dilemas Indentitários e fatalidades geopoliticas: Timor-Leste entre o Sudeste Asiático e o Pacifico-Sul", *Understanding Timor-Leste*, edited by Michael Leach, Nuno Canas Mendes, Antero B. da Silva, Alarico da Costa Ximenes and Bob Boughton, pp. 35–40 (Hawthorn: Swinburne Press, 2010).
63. Cablegram to Canberra, Jakarta, 6 December 1975. Department of Foreign Affairs and Trade, *Australia and the Indonesian Incorporation of Portuguese Timor, 1974–1976*, pp. 601–3.
64. Cotton, *East Timor, Australia and Regional Order*, pp. 84–85; Lee Jones, *ASEAN, Sovereignty and Intervention in Southeast Asia* (Houndmills, UK: Palgrave Macmillan, 2012), pp. 59–61, 71–72.
65. Jones, *ASEAN, Sovereignty and Intervention in Southeast Asia*, pp. 60, 64–67.
66. Cablegram to Canberra, Jakarta, 27 March 1975. Department of Foreign Affairs and Trade, *Australia and the Indonesian Incorporation of Portuguese Timor, 1974–1976*, p. 231.
67. Cablegram to Canberra, Jakarta, 6 December 1975. Department of Foreign Affairs and Trade, *Australia and the Indonesian Incorporation of Portuguese Timor, 1974–1976*, pp. 601–3.
68. Record of Conversation between Whitlam and Tun Abdul Razak, Canberra, 15 October 1975. Department of Foreign Affairs and Trade, *Australia and the Indonesian Incorporation of Portuguese Timor, 1974–1976*, pp. 466–68.
69. Security Council Office Records, 30th year, 1864th meeting, 15 December 1975. See Krieger, *East Timor and the International Community*, pp. 67–68.
70. Jones, *ASEAN, Sovereignty and Intervention*, p. 68.
71. Ibid., p. 69.
72. Ibid., p. 69.
73. Department of Foreign Affairs and Trade, *Australia and the Indonesian Incorporation of Portuguese Timor, 1974–1976*, p. 225.

74. United Nations General Assembly (UNGA), *Fourth Committee*, 34th session, 16th meeting, 24 October 1979; Jones, *ASEAN, Sovereignty and Intervention*, p. 71.
75. UNGA, *Fourth Committee*, 37th session, 18th meeting, 10 November 1982.
76. Jones, *ASEAN, Sovereignty and Intervention*, p. 154.
77. Nicholas Tarling, *Regionalism in Southeast Asia: To Foster the Political Will*, p. 184 (Oxon: Routledge, 2006).
78. UNGA, *Fourth Committee*, 34th session, 15th meeting, 24 October 1979.
79. Ibid.
80. Ibid.
81. UNGA, *Fourth Committee*, 37th session, 13th meeting, 5 November 1982.
82. Jones, *ASEAN, Sovereignty and Intervention*, p. 72.
83. Ibid., p. 70.
84. Gecker cited in Alan Collins, *The Security Dilemmas of Southeast Asia*, p. 47 (Hampshire: Palgrave Macmillan, 2000).
85. Amitav Acharya, *Constructing a Security Community in Southeast Asia: ASEAN and the Problem of Regional Order*, 3rd ed., p. 58 (London and New York: Routledge, 2014); Collins, *The Security Dilemmas of Southeast Asia*, p. 47.
86. Jones, *ASEAN, Sovereignty and Intervention*, p. 157.
87. Acharya, *Constructing a Security Community in Southeast Asia*, p. 44; Collins, *The Security Dilemmas of Southeast Asia*, p. 30.
88. Association of Southeast Asian States (ASEAN), "Treaty of Amity and Cooperation in Southeast Asia", Denpasar, 1976. See Article 2: "In their relations with one another, the High Contracting Parties shall be guided by the following fundamental principles:
    a. Mutual respect for the independence, sovereignty, equality, territorial integrity and national identity of all nations;
    b. The right of every State to lead its national existence free from external interference, subversion or coercion;
    c. Non-interference in the internal affairs of one another;
    d. Settlement of differences or disputes by peaceful means;
    e. Renunciation of the threat or use of force;
    f. Effective cooperation among themselves."
89. Acharya, *Constructing a Security Community in Southeast Asia*, pp. 46–47.
90. Asian-African Conference of Bandung, "Final Communiqué of the Asian-African Conference of Bandung", Indonesia, 24 April 1955.
91. Ramos-Horta, *Funu*, p. 57.
92. Ibid., p. 48.
93. Cablegram to Canberra, Lisbon, 21 August 1975. Department of Foreign Affairs and Trade, *Australia and the Indonesian Incorporation of Portuguese Timor, 1974–1976*, p. 326.

94. Ramos-Horta, *Funu*, p. 60.
95. CAVR, *Chega!*, chapter 7, pp. 1, 13.
96. Ibid.
97. Ibid., p. 11; United Nations Security Council (UNSC), "Debates Concerning UN Security Council Resolution 384 (1975)", Security Council Official Records, 30th year, 1864th meeting, 15 December 1975.
98. UNSC, *Debates Concerning UN Security Council Resolution 384 (1975)*, Security Council Official Records, 30th year, 1864th meeting, 15 December 1975.
99. CAVR, *Chega!*, chapter 7, pp. 1, 12.
100. Taylor, *East Timor*, p. 172.
101. UNSC, "Debates Concerning UN Security Council Resolution 384 (1975)", Security Council Official Records, 30th year, 1864th meeting, 15 December 1975.
102. CAVR, *Chega!*, p. 15.
103. Taylor, *East Timor*, pp. 172–73.
104. Ibid., p. 173; Grayson Lloyd, "The Diplomacy on East Timor: Indonesia, the United Nations and the International Community", in *Out of the Ashes: Destruction and Reconstruction of East Timor*, edited by James J. Fox and Dionisio Babo-Soares, p. 79 (South Australia: Crawford House Publishing, 2000).
105. CAVR, *Chega!*, chapter 7, pp. 1, 14.
106. Ibid., p. 14.
107. International Court of Justice, "Case Concerning East Timor (Portugal v Australia): Judgement of 30 June 1995", 1995, available at <http://www.icj-cij.org/files/case-related/84/6951.pdf> (accessed 2 February 2017).
108. Equatorial Guinea joined in 2014.
109. UNGA, *Fourth Committee*, 34th session, 15th meeting, 24 October 1979; UNGA, *Fourth Committee*, 37th session, 20th meeting, 11 November 1982.
110. UNGA, *Fourth Committee*, 34th session, 16th meeting, 24 October 1979; UNGA, *Fourth Committee*, 37th session, 18th meeting, 10 November 1982.
111. UNGA, *Fourth Committee*, 37th session, 20th meeting, 11 November 1982.
112. UNGA, *Fourth Committee*, 34th session, 16th meeting, 24 October 1979; UNGA, *Fourth Committee*, 37th session, 18th meeting, 10 November 1982.
113. Ramos-Horta, *Funu*, pp. 102–3.
114. Ibid., pp. 103–4.
115. Record of Conversation between Whitlam and Tun Abdul Razak, Canberra, 15 October 1975. Department of Foreign Affairs and Trade, *Australia and the Indonesian Incorporation of Portuguese Timor, 1974–1976*, pp. 466–68.
116. UNGA, *Fourth Committee*, 37th session, 18th meeting, 10 November 1982.
117. Ibid.; UNSC, "Debates Concerning UN Security Council Resolution 384 (1975)", Security Council Official Records, 30th year, 1864th meeting,

15 December 1975. See Krieger, *East Timor and the International Community*, p. 66.
118. Geoffrey Hull, "East Timor and Indonesia: The Cultural Factors of Incompatibility", *Studies in Languages and Cultures of East Timor* 2 (1999): 59–61.
119. Ibid.
120. James Dunn, *Timor: A People Betrayed*, pp. 4–5 (Milton, Queensland: The Jacaranda Press, 1983).
121. Kerry Taylor-Leech, "Language and Identity in East Timor: The Discourses of Nation Building", *Language Problems and Language Planning* 32, no. 2, (2008): 158.
122. Frédéric Durand, *East Timor: A Country at the Crossroads of Asia and the Pacific, A Geo-Historical Atlas*, p. 30 (Chiang Mai: Silkworm Books and Bangkok: IRASEC, 2006).
123. Geoffrey Gunn, "The Five Hundred Year Timorese Funu", in *Bitter Flowers, Sweet Flowers: East Timor, Indonesia and the World Community*, edited by Richard Tanter, Mark Selden and Steven Shalom, p. 10 (Annandale: Pluto Press Australia, 2001); John Taylor, "Emergence of a Nationalist Movement", in *East Timor at the Crossroads: The Forging of a Nation*, edited by Peter Carey and G. Carter-Bentley, p. 22 (London: Cassell/Social Science Research Council, 1995).
124. David Robie, *Blood on their Banner: Nationalist Struggles in the South Pacific* (London: Zed Books, 1989), pp. 13, 273; Peter King, "Redefining South Pacific Security: Greening and Domestication", *The South Pacific: Problems, Issues and Prospects*, edited by Ramesh Thakur, pp. 45–64 (Hampshire and London: Palgrave Macmillan, 1991); Andrew Gray, "The People of East Timor and Their Struggle for Survival", in *East Timor: The Struggle Continues*, edited by Torben Retboll (Copenhagen: IWGIA International Work Group for Indigenous Affairs, 1984), p. 41.
125. See Rebecca Strating, "Contested Self-determination: East Timor and Indonesia's Battle over Borders, International Law and Ethnic Identity", *Journal of Pacific History* 49, no. 4 (2014): 469–94.
126. Ramos-Horta cited in Gunn, "The Five Hundred Year Timorese Funu", p. 5. See also Mendes, "Dilemas Identitários e fatalidades geopolíticas".
127. UNSC, "Debates Concerning UN Security Council Resolution 389 (1976)", Security Council Official Records, 31st year, 1909th Meeting, 14 April 1976.
128. Gray, "The People of East Timor and Their Struggle for Survival", p. 41.
129. UNGA, *Fourth Committee*, 37th session, 23rd meeting, 15 November 1982.
130. Ibid.
131. Rebecca Strating, *Social Democracy in East Timor*, chapter 1 (Oxon: Routledge, 2015).

132. Cablegram to Canberra, Jakarta, 10 July 1975. Department of Foreign Affairs and Trade, *Australia and the Indonesian Incorporation of Portuguese Timor, 1974–1976*, p. 291.
133. Ramos-Horta, *Funu*, p. 111.
134. UNSC, "Debates Concerning UN Security Council Resolution 384 (1975)", Security Council Official Records, 30th year, 1864th meeting, 15 December 1975.
135. CAVR, *Chega!*, chapter 7, pp. 1, 14.
136. Ibid.; for more on these events, see Strating, *Social Democracy in East Timor*, chapter 2.
137. Cotton, *East Timor, Australia and Regional Order*, pp. 53–54.
138. Clinton Fernandes, *The Independence of East Timor: Multi-Dimensional Perspectives – Occupation, Resistance, and International Political Activism*, pp. 92–93 (Brighton: Sussex Academic Press, 2011).
139. Ibid.; Brad Simpson, "Solidarity in the Age of Globalization: The Transnational Movement for East Timor and U.S. Foreign Policy", *Peace & Change* 29, nos. 3 & 4 (July 2004): 459.
140. Jones, *ASEAN, Sovereignty and Intervention in Southeast Asia*, pp. 151–52.
141. CAVR, *Chega!*, chapter 7, pp. 1, 94.
142. Strating, *Social Democracy in East Timor*.
143. Ibid.
144. Cotton, *East Timor, Australia and Regional Order*, p. 71.
145. Jamsheed Marker, *East Timor: A Memoir of the Negotiations for Independence*, p. 87 (Jefferson: MacFarland, 2003); John Ballard, *Triumph of Self-Determination: Operation Stabilise and United Nations Peacemaking in East Timor*, p. 26 (Connecticut: Praeger Security International, 2004).
146. Ibid.; CAVR, *Chega!*, chapter 3, p. 126; Lloyd, "The Diplomacy on East Timor", p. 85.
147. Thomas Ambrosio, "East Timor Independence: The Changing Nature of International Independence", in *Transforming East Asian Domestic and International Politics: The Impact of Economy and Globalization*, edited by R. Compton, p. 115 (Aldershot: Burlington, 2002).
148. CAVR, *Chega!*, chapter 3, p. 130.
149. Habibie cited in Marker, *East Timor*, p. 128.
150. Iain Henry, "Unintended Consequences: An Examination of Australia's 'Historic Policy Shift' on East Timor", *Australian Journal of International Affairs* 68, no. 1 (2014): 52, 53.
151. For a fuller account of the reasons why Indonesia shifted policy, see Strating, *Social Democracy in East Timor*, chapter 2.
152. See Strating, "Contested Self-determination".
153. Ibid.

154. Goto Ken'ichi, "Multilayered Postcolonial Historical Space: Indonesia, the Netherlands, Japan and East Timor", Creation of a New Contemporary Asian Studies Working Paper 2, p. 1 (Tokyo: Waseda University, 2004).
155. Guterres cited in CAVR, *Timor-Leste Self-Determination and the International Community: National Public Hearing 15–17 March 2004*, p. 21 (Dili: Commission of Reception, Truth and Reconciliation Production Team and Translation Unit, 2009).
156. Ramos-Horta cited in Krieger, *East Timor and the International Community*, p. 66.
157. UNSC, "Debates Concerning UN Security Council Resolution 384 (1975)", Security Council Official Records, 30th year, 1864th meeting, 15 December 1975. See ibid., p. 66.
158. John Breuilly, *Nationalism and the State*, p. 3 (Manchester: Manchester University Press, 1982).
159. Andreas Wimmer, "Who Owns the State? Understanding Ethnic Conflict in Post-Colonial Societies", *Nations and Nationalism* 3, no. 4 (1997): 635; Breuilly, *Nationalism and the State*, p. 3.
160. Breuilly, *Nationalism and the State*, p. 3.
161. Simon Philpott, "Post-Colonial Troubles: The Politics of Transitional Justice", in *Timor-Leste: Challenges for Justice and Human Rights in the Shadow of the Past*, edited by William Binchy, p. 136 (Dublin: Clarus Press, 2009).
162. Benedict Anderson, "Imagining East Timor", *Arena* 4 (April–May 1993): 17.
163. David Wurfel, "Democracy, Nationalism and Ethnic Identity", in *Democratization and Identity: Regime and Ethnicity in East and Southeast Asia*, edited by Susan Henders, p. 202 (Plymouth: Rowman and Littlefield Publishers, 2004); Krieger, *East Timor and the International Community*, p. 178.
164. Robert Ewin, "Peoples and Political Obligation", *Macquarie Law Journal* 3 (2003): 17.
165. Agio Pereira, "2015 Timor-Leste Update: Keynote Speech by His Excellency Agio Pereira, Minister of State and of the Presidency of the Council of Ministers, Government of Timor-Leste", Australian National University, Canberra, 19 November 2015.
166. Ibid.
167. Ewin, "Peoples and Political Obligation", p. 17.

4

Establishing Legitimacy: International State-building in East Timor

This chapter examines the period of international state-building that Timor-Leste underwent prior to achieving political independence. While Indonesia had provided some education, schools and roads over the twenty-four years of occupation — which it sought to contrast with the neglectful Portuguese administration — the ability of East Timor to function as an autonomous state after the popular consultation was severely limited. Political, economic and social realities would render it impossible for Timor-Leste to establish governance structures and rule of law across the territory without extensive international assistance. While East Timor was not necessarily a "blank slate", it faced significant challenges: the legal system had to be rebuilt virtually from scratch, there was an absence of administrative experience as the public service had consisted of mainly Indonesian personnel who fled after the 1999 ballot and the formal economy was underdeveloped.

While previous chapters discussed international processes of recognition, this chapter examines the ways in which East Timor's sovereignty became contingent upon developing a functional liberal-democratic state. It examines the role of international state-building in East Timor from 1999–2002, focusing on the International Force for East Timor (INTERFET) and the United Nations Administration in East Timor (UNTAET).[1] East Timor's experiences with international state-building reflected a desire on behalf of key members in the international community to shape the identity of the new state and develop effective governance structures and capacities. There were several state-building goals in East Timor. The first was to establish "empirical sovereignty", which, as mentioned in the introduction, entails the capacities of states to establish political order and security within a territorial jurisdiction and provide their population "civil and socio-economic goods".[2] The second was to transform East Timor into a liberal-democratic state. These two goals are not necessarily compatible as liberal peace-building interventions have often struggled to build the conditions for democracy to take hold in societies unused to democratic rule. Nevertheless, the international state-building demonstrates that political recognition of East Timor's state sovereignty was conditional on the establishment of liberal-democratic institutions.

New states enter an international community with pre-existing normative frameworks with which they are expected to conform. The preferences of industrially-dominant developed states shape the norms that structure behaviours within the international community and influence the expectations of new states regarding the nature of legitimate statehood.[3] Establishing a liberal-democratic state highlights the demands of establishing a particular kind of state-based identity that is linked with domestic governance. East Timor's state-building period demonstrates the ways in which new states in the international community are increasingly pressured to conform to liberal and democratic ideals. That East Timor's political institutions were shaped by external actors has consequences — positive and negative — for the development of sovereign statehood. The size and scope of the United Nations (UN) mission in East Timor provided a unique model for international state-building in the twenty-first century, one that has not since been repeated. This chapter examines East Timor's relations with the international community during the intervention.

Establishing Legitimacy: International State-building in East Timor

While processes of international state-building have been detailed extensively in the literature, understanding these dynamics are important for the arguments presented in later chapters regarding the effects of international intervention on Timor-Leste's international relations. This chapter highlights the demands of self-determination that are characterized by the engagements of East Timorese leaders with international state-builders. Self-determination continues to be a central concern for Timor-Leste's international relations as it has sought to reduce its dependence upon international donors. In examining the narratives about state-building experiences, it appears that they have consolidated a view that dependence compromises the authority and the autonomy of the state.

The International Community Intervenes

As the previous chapter detailed, East Timor's independence movement was ultimately successful in being granted the right to hold a legitimate, internationally sanctioned ballot to collectively decide political status. In August 1998, conferences between Indonesia, Portugal and the UN began discussing models of self-determination, without East Timorese representation.[4] It was decided that East Timor would not automatically attain sovereign status after the popular consultation. Rather, the 5 May agreements assigned the UN the task of temporarily administering East Timor if the population rejected Indonesia's autonomy proposal.[5] In August 1999, a popular consultation was held under the auspices of the United Nations Mission in East Timor (UNAMET) in which 78.5 per cent of voters elected for East Timor to become independent from Indonesia.[6] UNAMET relied upon the contributions of a number of states, including Australia, the United States and a few ASEAN states. Following the popular consultation, the first priority was ensuring security in East Timor. The 5 May agreements had placed the Indonesian military (TNI) in charge of security, however prior to the consultation, supporters of autonomy had attacked civilians, burned homes and buildings and intimidated people in an effort to manipulate the outcome.[7] After the ballot, the violence rapidly escalated.

It became evident that the TNI was not only unwilling to avert the impending humanitarian crisis, but actively implemented a "scorched earth campaign" known as "Operation Clean Sweep" with the assistance of the pro-Indonesia East Timorese militia.[8] During the three weeks following the vote, it was estimated that 70 per cent of the physical infrastructure was deliberately burned or rendered uninhabitable across East Timor, and street-by-street burnings destroyed 95 per cent of some areas.[9] An estimated two thousand East Timorese were killed during Operation Clean Sweep, and around 400,000 people (approximately half the population) were forced to flee their homes.[10] An estimated 230,000–250,000 people were forced across the border into West Timor, with those who remained taking refuge in the mountains of East Timor.[11] The actions of the Indonesian military and pro-Indonesia militia severely compounded the pre-existing challenges that would face the new state. They also precipitated demands for the international community to intervene in the humanitarian crisis as Indonesia failed to fulfil its security responsibilities under the May 5 agreements.

The post-ballot violence led to an international outcry and calls for a multinational peacekeeping force in East Timor. International pressure further increased when the UN sent a mission to East Timor and Jakarta on 6 September 1999.[12] Indonesia initially rejected calls for a multinational force, arguing it could handle the security situation.[13] In the days following the referendum, Australian diplomats worked in international forums such as the UN to secure support for intervention from other states, including New Zealand, the United Kingdom and Canada.[14] Various world leaders sought to pressure Indonesia, including U.S. President, Bill Clinton, who exerted economic pressure through sanctions and issued warnings to Indonesia to stop the violence, and the International Monetary Fund, who threatened to withdraw much needed loans.[15] A United Nations Security Council (UNSC) delegation also worked to persuade Indonesia to accept a peacekeeping force.[16] There were debates within the Australian public about whether or not the Australian government should have foreseen the events of September 1999 and pushed for an earlier intervention, but no state would commit to sending forces into East Timor without Indonesia's consent.[17] On 7 September, Martial Law was instituted in East Timor, and five days later, international pressure forced Indonesian President B.J. Habibie to request a multinational peacekeeping team in East Timor.[18] This included statements on 9 and 10 September from U.S. President Bill Clinton condemning the violence and emphasizing the need for an international security force.[19]

Establishing Legitimacy: International State-building in East Timor 99

TABLE 4.1
List of International Missions in East Timor

Name	Date	Type of Mission	Mandate	Role/s
UNAMET	June–October 1999	Political	UN Security Resolution 1246	Oversee the popular consultation and transition period following the popular consultation.
International Force for East Timor (INTERFET)	September 1999–February 2000	Multinational Peacekeeping Force	UN Security Council Resolution 1264	Restore peace and security in East Timor; protect and support UNAMET in carrying out its tasks; facilitate humanitarian assistance operations.
United Nations Transitional Administration in East Timor (UNTAET)	October 1999–May 2002	Peacekeeping	UN Security Council Resolution 1272	Provide security and maintain law and order throughout the territory of East Timor; establish an effective administration; assist in the development of civil and social services; ensure the coordination and delivery of humanitarian assistance, rehabilitation of humanitarian assistance, rehabilitation and development assistance; support capacity-building for self-government; assist in the establishment of conditions for sustainable development.
United Nations Mission of Support in East Timor (UNMISET)	May 2002–May 2005	Peacekeeping	UN Security Council Resolution 1410	Provide assistance to core administrative structures critical to the viability and political stability of East Timor; provide interim law enforcement and public security; assist in developing the East Timor Police Service (ETPS); contribute to the maintenance of the new country's external and internal security.

TABLE 4.1 (continued)

Name	Date	Type of Mission	Mandate	Role/s
United Nations Office in East Timor (UNOTIL)	May 2005–August 2006	Political	UN Security Resolution 1599	Support the development of critical state institutions; support further development of the police force; bolster the development of the Border Patrol Unit (BPU); provide training in observance of democratic governance and human rights; review progress on those fronts.
United Nations Integrated Mission in East Timor (UNMIT)	August 2006–December 2012	Peacekeeping	UN Security Resolution 1704	Support the government in consolidating stability; enhancing a culture of democratic governance; facilitating political dialogue among Timorese stakeholders; fostering social cohesion.
International Stabilisation Force (ISF)	May 2006–April 2013	Multinational Peacekeeping Force	Requested by Timor-Leste's government; UN Security Resolution 1704	Fully cooperate with and provide assistance to UNMIT for the implementation of its mandate (see above).

On 15 September, the UN authorized the establishment of INTERFET, which arrived in East Timor on 20 September 1999.[20] The UNSC Resolution 1264 made INTERFET temporarily responsible for restoring peace and security. This reflects the domestic security dilemma facing East Timor. International Relations has tended to characterize the domestic jurisdictions of states as orderly, while the outside case as anarchical due to the absence of a higher authority. The conditions of uncertainty that arise from anarchy and encourage a traditional security dilemma can also be present *within* states. As Zaum argued, "[d]omestically, security dilemmas are at the heart of weak institutions in the aftermath of conflict: histories of conflict and low levels of trust and interaction between different groups make the interpretation of their motives more difficult, fuel uncertainty about their motives, and limit their ability to cooperation".[21] INTERFET would need to establish credible security guarantees to resolve the conflict arising from the internal conditions of "anarchy".

Of INTERFET's 12,600 troops, nearly half (5,521) were Australian.[22] The reversal of Australia's position on East Timor was staggering. As the previous chapter argued, Australia was reluctant to support an independent East Timor until just before the ballot. Compelled by domestic pressure and a looming refugee crisis, Foreign Minister Alexander Downer sent a letter to the UN Secretary-General on 14 September stating Australia's willingness to accept a leadership role.[23] Leach and Percival-Wood put the cost of Australian Defence Force involvement in the peacekeeping mission at A$2.9 billion from 1999–2002, funded by a special levy on high income earners.[24] Australia's leadership was also a result of its purported "deputy sheriff" role to the United States in the region. Both the United States and Britain had encouraged Australia to take a greater role in the region since World War Two. U.S. President Bill Clinton noted that the U.S. alliance with Australia was a key factor in his decision to exert pressure on Indonesia. The United States provided logistics, equipment and intelligence to support Australia. Even so, Australia's "logistic systems were fully stretched" and would have run into "severe difficulties" if Indonesia's forces were more confrontational.[25] The United States refusal to put boots on the ground in East Timor highlighted the problems of Australia's over-reliance on the U.S. alliance in the security domain.

Some positioned INTERFET as a product of Australian neo-colonialism, and it was criticized for arrogance, insensitivity to local needs and placing Australia's national interests first.[26] Indonesia was not pleased with Australia's involvement in INTERFET: on 16 September 1999, Indonesia protested by withdrawing from the 1995 Australia–Indonesia Security Arrangement. The criticism of INTERFET as purely a product of Australian neo-colonialism, however, neglects the contributions of other states to the peacekeeping effort, especially those from Southeast Asia. Twenty-two states contributed to the mission, and around 2,500 troops were from ASEAN states.[27] The second-largest contributor was Thailand, which deployed 1,580 personnel. Constrained by constitutional limitations, Japan contributed funding of around US$100 million, and Japanese forces would ultimately serve with the UN peacekeeping forces.[28] Cotton also points to South Korea's decision to contribute as "a major step forward" in assembling INTERFET.[29]

Asian participation was crucial for off-setting the arguments that INTERFET was a "Western" intervention. Another mistaken perception was that ASEAN states were "paralysed" because of the norms of non-interference, and that they had "hesitated" in adopting a leadership role.[30] However, ASEAN states contributed more to the peacekeeping forces than what is commonly acknowledged, and the founding members in particular became more supportive of peacekeeping forces as the humanitarian situation deteriorated after the ballot. Dupont, for example, wrote in 2000 that ASEAN states were wary of alienating Indonesia, but had nonetheless played "a significant political and military role" in conflict resolution.[31] As the previous chapter noted, ASEAN states were supportive of Indonesian sovereignty of East Timor, yet the violence in East Timor created concerns about Western intervention in the region.[32] Southeast Asian states have generally resisted the doctrine of humanitarian intervention, which are designed to protect citizens against severe human rights violations.[33] While Narine suggests that ASEAN states were unable to act due to non-interference principle, it is the case that founding ASEAN states did contribute to peacekeeping in East Timor.[34]

Like other states, the participation of individual ASEAN states in INTERFET was contingent upon a UN mandate.[35] The fortuitously-timed APEC leaders' summit in Auckland on 11–12 September 1999 contributed intense pressure on Indonesia to request international assistance.[36] Cotton argues that APEC provided the means for persuading regional states, such as the Philippines and Thailand, to support an intervention in East Timor.[37] The founding ASEAN states had made personnel contributions to UNAMET, and the chief political officer was Singaporean.[38] While newer ASEAN states, such as Vietnam and Myanmar, refused to contribute to the intervention, Singapore, Malaysia, Thailand and the Philippines offered to provide troops, which Indonesia initially rejected.[39] ASEAN states also demanded that the result of the ballot be respected. Thailand's Foreign Minister Surin Pitsuwan gathered support for ASEAN peacekeeping.[40] ASEAN assistance demonstrated support for Jakarta insofar as it attempted to minimize control of Australia in the peacekeeping mission.[41]

The response of ASEAN to the crisis in East Timor in 1999, which Indonesia held responsibility for, was a test for its conflict avoidance role in the region.[42] ASEAN states were concerned that INTERFET could "set a precedent for Western interference in the internal affairs of other member states using the norm of humanitarian intervention as justification", particularly as other member states shared similar concerns regarding separatism and civil conflict.[43] Indonesian President Habibie asked ASEAN states to be involved in INTERFET.[44] Thailand, the Philippines, Malaysia and Singapore participated, with the financial assistance of Australia and Japan, and around a quarter of the force were from ASEAN states.[45] While participation of individual states was mixed, critically, involvement in the crisis in East Timor was necessary for ASEAN's central goal of avoiding other states intervening in the region.[46] Far from avoiding a leadership role, Malaysia pressed to be appointed the commander of the UNTAET force that would replace INTERFET, but the East Timorese strongly opposed it on the grounds that Malaysia was too sympathetic to Indonesia.[47] Thai Major General Songkitti Jaggabatara became the deputy commander of INTERFET.[48] UNTAET military and civilian police included personnel from ASEAN states such as Malaysia, Singapore and Thailand.[49] ASEAN personnel comprised around one-fifth of the UNTAET peacekeeping force, which was initially commanded by a Philippine, Lieutenant General Jaime de los Santos, with an Australian, Michael Smith, as deputy.[50]

One interpretation of ASEAN's role is that intervention did not constitute a shift in the regional normative order because East Timor's status was politically ambiguous.[51] Jones suggests that the founding ASEAN states in particular were primarily concerned with limiting the unrest in Indonesian territories. Ultimately, the norm of non-interference was subordinate to national interests for those states who were concerned that the unrest could spread to their territories. That commitment to non-interference is not necessarily "iron-clad" if the security interests of ASEAN states are contravened.[52] By the time international intervention appeared inevitable, Indonesian Defence Minister Wiranto said that Indonesia wished to see "overwhelming ASEAN forces, coming to help restore the deteriorating situation'".[53] Indonesia's President Habibie requested that ASEAN take commandership of the peacekeeping force, suggesting that Indonesia understood the inevitability of an international intervention. This request, however, came after the foundational ASEAN states had already began organizing their peacekeeping contributions.[54] While Haacke argues that ASEAN would not have sent forces if not for Indonesia's consent, this was no different to the Western states, such as Australia and the United States, whom also waited for Habibie's consent prior to taking action.[55]

By the time INTERFET arrived, "Operation Clean Sweep" had created a humanitarian crisis that presented significant obstacles for re-establishing law and order. In addition to the dire humanitarian situation, the physical destruction also presented issues for the establishment of political institutions necessary for statehood.[56] As Beauvais suggests, "all semblance of government and financial institutions essentially had ceased to exist".[57] Members of the Indonesian administration in East Timor fled, creating a "governance vacuum" that threatened to exacerbate the humanitarian crisis.[58] International assistance was required to protect human security in East Timor and to create the social and political conditions necessary for establishing functional independence. The international political community therefore played a greater role than simply permitting and supporting the sovereignty of the new post-colonial state: it actively participated in establishing the necessary conditions for empirical sovereignty.

Empirical Sovereignty and International Legitimacy

As previous chapters discussed, post-World War Two decolonization often resulted in the establishment of fragile states defined by the recognition of their sovereign status rather than their capacity to meet the "objective" criteria of statehood.⁵⁹ In the early 1990s, Jackson argued that decolonization had produced "quasi-sovereign" states: those entities that possessed international legal recognition of sovereignty (*de jure* sovereignty) — which encompassed attendant rights to non-intervention — but lacked the abilities to effectively rule their population (*de facto* sovereignty) and "act as responsible members of the international community".⁶⁰ In the twenty-first century, the concern with this "gap" has been encapsulated by the extensive literature by scholars classifying states as "failed", "failing", "fragile", "weak" and so forth. Helman and Ratner were the first to use the term "failed state" in 1993 to describe those states that are "utterly incapable of sustaining... [themselves as members] of the international community".⁶¹ Some scholars suggest the "Weberian" state has become the ideal form by which post-colonial states are evaluated — and often found wanting.⁶² Critics of the term "failing state" suggest that it reflects "a schoolmarm's scorecard according to linear index defined by a univocal Weberian endstate".⁶³ While this is a reasonable point, acknowledging the "gaps" in authorities and institutions reflects the modern realities of many states. While a multitude of different terms have flourished to capture the gaps between internal and external sovereignty, these states have in common the inability or unwillingness to meet sovereign responsibilities "generally understood as delivering 'core functions to the majority of its people'".⁶⁴ It is Western states that have typically had the power to decide the international standards of domestic political organizations.⁶⁵

Typically, legitimate statehood has been expressed in Weberian terms as those communities which (successfully) claim the "monopoly of the legitimate use of physical force within a given territory".⁶⁶ For Weber, states' control of violence within their territory is essential for establishing political order and rule of law.⁶⁷ Wesley and Ottaway argue that international state-builders have perceived their mission as implementing "Weberian" structures within new states irrespective of existing local political structures.⁶⁸ New states are supposed to model themselves upon old, established states. However, as Ghani and Lockhart point out, the problem of establishing legitimate statehood extends well beyond controlling the use of force. Political order relies upon possessing political authority, meaning the "rightfulness to rule", and is largely derived from citizens' belief in the moral legitimacy of key state institutions and leaders.⁶⁹ States must also perform specific functions in social, political and economic spheres to be considered "legitimate". The international community has developed norms to prevent states using coercive force alone to establish security, and so new states have undergone state-building to "close the gap" between *de jure* recognition and *de facto* capabilities.⁷⁰

In the post-World War Two period of decolonization, self-determination rather than functioning independence was privileged. As Helman and Ratner argued, the idea that "states could fail — that they could be simply unable to function as independent entities — was anathema to the *raison d'être* of decolonization and offensive to the notion of self-determination. New states might be poor, it was thought, but they would hold their own by virtue of being independent."⁷¹ While sufficient internal capacity was traditionally a feature of state-creation, it became far less significant for recognition of states during the decolonization period of the second half of the twentieth century. For many post-colonial states, the accordance of statehood was not contingent upon internal capabilities to govern autonomously and independently.

In contemporary international societies, some entities are "regarded as legitimate candidates for self-determination" while others remained "outside the scope of both legal and moral recognition by virtue of being seen as too weak, rogue or undemocratic".⁷² However, many states remain weak, rogue and undemocratic: Krasner points out that "understanding the actual practice of recognition is a puzzle because many of the political entities in the international environment, recognized, unrecognized, and partially recognized do not conform with the ideal-typical conception of sovereign statehood".⁷³ As the previous chapter argued, many states did not recognize East Timor's rights to political independence partly because they were concerned about the "viability" of an East Timorese state. This stands in contrast with states that decolonized regardless of internal capacities to govern. The 1960 Declaration of Decolonization explicitly states that "[i]nadequacy of political, economic, social or educational preparedness should never serve as a pretext for delaying independence".⁷⁴ Yet, it had been decided in the talks between Portugal, the UN and Indonesia that if the result of the popular consultation in August 1999 was East Timorese independence, the international community would play a role in preparing the new state for sovereignty. This signified a shift in the ways that new states would be "midwifed" into existence, with recognition contingent upon a period of institution building.⁷⁵

International state-builders in East Timor were required to construct political institutions and create the conditions necessary for democratization. The agreement between the UN, Portugal and Indonesia in the case of independence was to follow UNAMET with a successor mission, UNAMET II, a larger UN presence. In 2000, the UN would create a transitional authority (UNAMET III) to oversee the "gradual" withdrawal of Indonesia in the territory.[76] The humanitarian crisis following the popular consultation rendered this plan irrelevant, as Indonesian personnel fled the territory creating a political vacuum in East Timor. The state-building phase began in earnest in 2000 with the introduction of the UNTAET (see Table 4.1). Officially a peacekeeping mission, it had an extensive state-building mandate to construct political institutions including elections and the electoral system, the judiciary, military and police.[77] The mandate of the UNTAET also included: providing security and maintaining law and order throughout the territory of East Timor; establishing an effective administration; assisting in the development of civil and social services; ensuring the coordination and delivery of humanitarian assistance, rehabilitation and development assistance; supporting capacity building for self-government; and assisting in the establishment of conditions for sustainable development.[78] This was an exercise in creating a modern state virtually from the ground up. State-building in East Timor reflected a concern that East Timor would function effectively once its sovereignty was internationally recognized.

Timor-Leste's external sovereignty was linked to its capacities to enact particular responsibilities *vis-à-vis* its population: creating political order, providing public goods and ensuring democratic governance and human rights. The post-colonial security dilemma is partly characterized by the problems facing fragile states in establishing functional sovereignty and managing security threats that emerge from within state borders rather than beyond them. In International Relations scholarship, though, "functional independence" has traditionally concerned the capacities of states to maintain their sovereign status by preserving "national security". Achieving this requires bolstering capacities to defend citizens from foreign threats and creating an orderly relationship between the state and the society it encompasses.[79] While the international community seeks specific kinds of "rational-legal" authority that emerge from practices of democratic governance, traditional authority rests upon "an established belief in the sanctity of immemorial traditions and the legitimacy of the status of those exercising authority under them".[80] In terms of identity formation, one of the challenges faced was reconciling the tensions between Western, "Weberian" (centralized) state structures and local, customary forms of political authority and law.[81]

The capacity of state institutions to exert control over violence remains a key test of state legitimacy as it is generally recognized as necessary for the exercise of empirical sovereignty. Thus, state-building in Timor-Leste was an exercise in creating the institutions of a modern state, consisting of legally constituted institutions capable of creating order. Federer notes that Timor-Leste had their sovereignty "bestowed upon them and legally protected by the international community", which contrasts with how old, established states acquired sovereign status.[82] Timor-Leste's development of sovereignty — both in terms of their practical ability to possess "supreme" authority over population and territory and their recognized international legal identity — relied on the assistance of the international community. State-building in Timor-Leste demonstrated new roles for the international community in assisting self-determination and providing independence, despite the twenty-five-year period of delayed independence that preceded it. Contemporary post-colonial states are offered institutional protection to ensure the sanctity of recognition, even if norms of non-intervention are at times broken. In other words, sovereign identity generally remains secure for post-colonial states although many lack the capacities to defend themselves from external threats or to ensure internal order.

Building a Liberal-Democracy: The Challenges of Participation and Self-determination

Extensive literature has been devoted to the problems of the international community engaging in democracy building and "liberal peace-building" as a way of developing empirical sovereignty in fragile states.[83] There are two dominant paradigms for understanding how authority is exercised and how power and decision-making capabilities are distributed during state-building missions. The "authoritarian" vision of state-building asserts the necessity of the nation rescinding self-determination for a period of time.[84] Dominant criticisms of liberal peace-building have targeted "neo-trusteeship" as a form of "post-modern imperialism" as multinational coalitions "take over" the governance of post-conflict states for an indefinite amount of time.[85] Critics argue that neo-trusteeship establishes "self-perpetuating dependency relationships" in which the affected population is left unable to meet the challenges of administering their post-conflict societies. The second model of "participatory intervention" demonstrates a concern for inculcating "local ownership" through the full and active participation of local actors in decision-making for the durability of newly built institutions.[86] A UN review of peacebuilding architecture in 2010, for example, emphasized more local participation, civil society participation and field knowledge in future peacebuilding.[87] Much of the focus of state-building in East Timor would concern the best ways to balance these two models to ensure the state would survive after independence and fulfil its obligations as a member of the international community.

A realist explanation of neo-trusteeship presents it as a method of mitigating potential security risks to world major powers that arise from state fragility as conflicts spill over borders, and transboundary crime networks and terrorist organizations flourish in the absence of monopolized violence and rule of law.[88] Normative theorists, on the other hand, have sought to move beyond paradigms of self-interested utility maximization. These scholars have sought to examine the roles of norms in justifying interventions, understanding peacebuilding as a corollary of the post-Cold War normative shift that elevated democracy and human rights issues and challenged "traditional conceptions of sovereignty and non-intervention".[89] While UNTAET did not involve a violation of sovereignty, this observation does point to the paradox of state-building missions that aim to establish the exercise of internal self-determination while simultaneously denying it.[90]

Under UNSC Resolution 1272, the state-builders were mandated to establish liberal-democratic institutions in East Timor.[91] As Franck argues, the global "democratic entitlement" entails a belief that meaningful political representation and participation is necessary for the realization of self-determination. Notions of democratic legitimacy connect collective self-determination rights with individual rights to political participation.[92] In Franck's view, governments were increasingly aware that their legitimacy depended upon meeting normative expectations of the international community *vis-à-vis* democratic governance and basic human rights.[93] According to Bartleson, the notion that entities must be democratic in order to be recognized performs a "discriminatory function" in international politics.[94] The concept of "sovereignty as responsibility" reflected the dominance of liberal-democracy within the international community.[95] States were increasingly viewed as responsible for enabling "positive sovereignty" by guaranteeing basic human rights, developing democratic institutions and a functioning public service, and adhering to international law and norms.[96]

While sovereign legitimacy has become increasingly contingent upon the democratic credentials of new states, there is a question about the extent to which this demand curtails states' rights to non-interference and self-determination.[97] Theoretically, international state-building should respect self-determination principles by allowing the people to choose the particular form of government they wish to implement. A key criticism was that international state-builders in East Timor regarded the territory as a "blank slate" and ignored pre-existing socio-political structures.[98] Advocates of "participatory intervention" recommended a longer-term period of transition based on extensive citizenry participation, providing "time for an indigenous paradigm to coexist with, or to gradually transform during the creation of, modern institutions".[99] The UNTAET's requirement to build a democracy in East Timor raised the potential problem of these new, rational-legal "modern" institutions clashing with "traditional" forms of socio-political organization.[100] A mismatch between the expectations of the international community and those of domestic society is potentially problematic. As Migdal notes, "strong societies" can provide challenges to the capacities of states to exert effective governance.[101] If new institutions have to compete with existing non-democratic institutions or are not accepted as legitimate then this can undermine the capacities of states to exert control within their territorial jurisdictions. This points to the tensions that can arise between domestic and international conceptions of legitimacy as the "right to rule", as well as to the problems that arise when new political institutions are seen by people as "foreign" or "imposed".

Another key criticism of the UNTAET was the apparent lack of participation, although this tended to relate to two different types of participation: those of independence leaders who wished to have a greater authoritative role, and those of "civil society" who wanted more opportunities for ordinary East Timorese to contribute to decision-making. The state-building period provided for "shared sovereignty" between the UNTAET and the East Timorese, however, the power balance was considerably weighted in favour of the UNTAET. Its transitional administrator, Sergio Vieira de Mello, was given *de facto* sovereign power, leading Beauvais to describe the temporary regime as "benevolent despotism".[102] A key complaint of East Timorese leaders and commentators was that authority was not adequately "shared".[103] Even Vieira de Mello conceded that the UNTAET was unable to involve the East Timorese to the extent that they were entitled.[104] Initially, the UNTAET viewed itself as exercising authority on behalf of the East Timorese, with local actors expected to provide consultation and advice without having any actual decision-making capabilities.[105] Even though the UN mandated that the East Timorese in decision-making were to be major stakeholders in transition, initially the Timorese were disempowered, which reinforced the ongoing denial of self-determination.[106] These criticisms asserted that the UNTAET failed to engage effectively with the National Congress for Timorese Reconstruction (CNRT) and FRETILIN due to its desire to follow principles of political impartiality.[107]

East Timorese resistance leaders wanted full and active participation in shaping the institutions of the new state, however these expectations were unfulfilled at the beginning.[108] As it progressed, the UNTAET was compelled to "Timorize" transitional processes as the state-building model was increasingly criticized for being authoritarian rather than participatory. The first stage was the establishment of the fifteen-member National Consultative Council (NCC) in December 1999.[109] Liberation leader Xanana Gusmão described it as "tokenistic" because it only held an advocacy role, as decision-making authority continued to remain invested in the Transitional Administrator.[110] Civil society organizations also argued that the NCC "not only deprived Timorese people of the chance to practice decision-making during the transition, but created an atmosphere of mistrust and disempowerment".[111] In July 2000, the UNTAET responded to these complaints by creating a thirty-three (later thirty-six) member National Council designed to give greater political authority to East Timorese leaders and enhance political participation.[112] However, this did little to alleviate perceptions that decision-making remained invested in international actors. Gusmão again accused the UNTAET of failing to share power in practice and four members of the newly established "cabinet", the East Timor Transitional Administration, threatened to resign.[113] In March 2001, the National Democratic Institute reported that many East Timorese thought that the UNTAET's attempts at community consultation were inadequate and the National Council was not representative.[114]

The final stage of the "Timorization" process was the election of an eighty-eight-member Constituent Assembly on 30 August 2001 that would draft East Timor's constitution and provided the Democratic Republic of Timor-Leste — formally recognized in May 2002 as a sovereign state — with its first government. These elections reflected a shift away from the UNTAET's previously centralized, imperious approach to state-building towards a more participatory model. The National Constitution, drafted by the Constituent Assembly, established the framework for a liberal, social-democratic state with little intervention from international state-builders. While this conformed to the expectations of the international community, it is not accurate to say that UNTAET imposed democracy and human rights on the East Timorese. In fact, various manifestoes and peace plans promised to institute a liberal, social democratic form of government.[115] As the previous chapter argued, these commitments were reflective of the ways that the independence movement used an activist public diplomacy campaign to present a future state as one that would respect dominant liberal norms.

The UNTAET highlighted the inherent contradiction of state-building missions that defer and undermine self-government in the bid to support it. The problem of fragile states has sought some scholars to reassess principles of sovereignty, including re-thinking trusteeship or international tutelage models as ways of overcoming the challenges that arise from state weakness. Krasner, for example, has argued that a shared sovereignty arrangement — which violates Westphalian/Vattelian principles of sovereignty — might work to support collapsed or weak states.[116] The haste with which UNTAET left East Timor demonstrates that a long-term neo-trusteeship model was undesirable to both state-builders and Timorese elites. According to Federer, it was ideals of absolute external sovereignty that "drove the UN to engage only in a speedy transitional administration, aimed at finding a local power elite to take over the responsibilities of conventional sovereignty".[117] The lack of time and resources was a key challenge in the international state-building effort in East Timor.[118]

The system of absolute external sovereignty that has given rise to *quasi-states* has favoured political elites, particularly in resource rich states with weak institutions and poor records of corruption. Timorese political leaders were unsatisfied with sharing power with the UN during the state-building period. Xanana Gusmão, for example, was critical of the international actors in the territory, arguing that the East Timorese were:

> not interested in a legacy of cars and laws, nor are we interested in a legacy of development plans for the future designed by [people] other than East Timorese. We are not interested in inheriting an economic rationale which leaves out the social and political complexity of East Timorese reality. Nor do we wish to inherit the heavy decision-making and project implementation mechanisms in which the role of the East Timorese is to give their consent as observers, rather than the active players we should start to be.[119]

In December 2000, Gusmão outlined his preferred political transition calendar: a constitution would be debated, drafted and adopted within ninety days, and the UN withdrawn by the end of 2001.[120] Civil society organizations were concerned that a lack of time would hinder opportunities for citizenry participation. In his 2001 New Year's speech, Gusmão demanded Timorese self-government and a hasty end to UNTAET.[121] Notably, he also appeared to question the project of democracy-building, and the link between democracy and sovereign recognition when he said: "[w]hat seems to be absurd is that we absorb standards just to pretend we look like a democratic society and please our masters of independence".[122] By 2001 a number of political elites were keen for self-government, and for UNTAET to leave East Timor as soon as possible to fulfil the promises of political independence.

The system of sovereign states privileges external sovereignty as the predominant expression of self-determination. The transition to the United Nations Mission of Support in East Timor (UNMISET) and then United Nations Office in East Timor (UNOTIL) after the recognition of Timor-Leste's sovereignty in 2002 clearly demonstrated the UN efforts to move away from the neo-trusteeship that characterised the

UNTAET period while continuing to support Timor-Leste's empirical statehood (see Table 4.1). The UNMISET reflected a significant reduction in personnel and presence in East Timor. Timorese leaders continued to resist UN overtures and increasingly asserted independence from UNMISET.[123] While UNTAET was initially described as a model of state-building, as chapter six discusses further, a crisis in 2006 necessitated the introduction of another peacekeeping mission — United Nations Integrated Mission in East Timor (UNMIT)[124] — and the International Stabilisation Force (ISF). This crisis revealed the challenges facing the UNTAET in establishing empirical sovereignty in East Timor, as the security crisis that emerged in part due to weak institutions rendered Timor-Leste again vulnerable to foreign intervention.[125]

Presidential elections in May 2002 saw independence leader Xanana Gusmão become East Timor's first president. East Timor's first National Parliament, dominated by political party FRETILIN, was promulgated on 20 May 2002 after two and half years of international administration. According to Gusmão, on this day Timor-Leste *"regained* our sovereignty, which meant that we had the power to decide the future of the people and of the country" [my emphasis].[126] Despite fair criticism of "hubristic" state-building, however, there seems to be little doubt that the challenges facing Timor-Leste after the 1999 referendum necessitated extensive international assistance. The UNTAET provided an example of what Krasner describes as "autonomy compromised by recognition": in order for Timor-Leste to secure sovereign recognition it was compelled to again delay the exercise of its rights to collective self-determination by submitting to another — albeit of a different nature — form of foreign intervention.[127] Recognition of East Timor's sovereignty by members of the international community was hence conditional on the acceptance and development of institutions of government that conform to contemporary international standards of effective and democratic statehood. Nevertheless, there were significant tensions that arose between the need to establish a functioning democratic state and the demands of East Timorese leaders and civil society for greater autonomy and decision-making capacities. It is posited in later chapters that this contributed to the ways that leaders have guarded political independence and non-intervention principles in international relations, as foreign policy decisions and discourses reflect the efforts of leaders to reduce dependence on international donors.

Conclusion

These last three chapters have sought to place Timor-Leste's pursuit of sovereign recognition in historical context because its experiences with colonialism, denial of independence and international intervention have shaped its engagements with the international community following independence. Timor-Leste's desire for "real" independence — the lack of dependence on other actors and the absence of foreign intervention — has permeated all spheres of its international political, cultural and economic relations and foreign policy discourse. On the subject of the role of the international community in assisting Timorese statehood, Timorese leaders tend to deliver mixed messages. In a speech delivered in Malaysia, Xanana Gusmão argued that:

> Timor-Leste received the care and the solidarity of the international community. From September 1999 to the Restoration of Independence we had a strong military and political presence by the international community, including our brothers and sisters from Malaysia. This presence enabled the transitional administration of the territory, under the banner of the UN.[128]

However, to domestic audiences, Timorese politicians have increasingly taken to populist criticism of UN international assistance.[129] In a 2011 article in *Tempo Semanal*, for example, Timor-Leste's Defence Minister Julio Tomas Pinto described a later UN mission as "dumb":

> The people together with Timor-Leste's leadership know what Timor-Leste needs to do, and it's not what other people want to have done in this beloved country. That is why we need to hold firm to the principle *"to do what we (Timor Leste) need to do, rather than what others want"*, so as to prevent the manipulative doctrine, which others have brought and tried to force Timor-Leste to implement.[130]

The following chapters demonstrate how this history of international intervention has shaped Timor-Leste's international relations since its achievement of independence in 2002.

The next chapter demonstrates how Timor-Leste seeks to demonstrate its liberal-democratic credentials in order to establish its legitimacy within the international community. According to Gusmão, "our people proved to the world to be worthy of the respect that we all owe and know. It is the respect that we, one of the world's smallest states, is starting to garner for our solid work to consolidate peace and to take our place as an open democracy in the international community".[131]

This can be understood as one strategy to avoid future international intervention. Timor-Leste's leaders justify their actions by using discourses of liberal-democracy and international rule of law. This is symbolic of the leadership's aspiration to maintain their liberal-democratic image within the international community.

NOTES

1. For deeper explanation about the role and mandate of UNTAET, see Norrie McQueen, "United Nations Transitional Administration in East Timor (UNTAET)", in *The Oxford Handbook of UN Peacekeeping Operations*, edited by Joachim Koops, Noorie McQueen, Thierry Tardy and Paul Williams, pp. 642–55 (Oxford: Oxford University Press, 2015).
2. Robert Jackson, *Quasi-States: Sovereignty, International Relations and the Third World*, pp. 5, 9 (Cambridge: Cambridge University Press, 1990).
3. Rebecca Strating and Beth Edmondson, "Beyond Democratic Tolerance: Witch Killings in Timor-Leste", *Journal of Current Southeast Asian Affairs* 34, no. 3 (2015): 45; Dominik Zaum, *The Sovereign Paradox: The Norms and Politics of International State-building* (Oxford: Oxford University Press, 2007).
4. James Cotton, *East Timor, Australia and Regional Order: Intervention and its Aftermath in Southeast Asia*, p. 90 (London: RoutledgeCurzon, 2004).
5. Markus Benzing, "Midwifing a New State: The United Nations in East Timor", *Max Planck Yearbook of United Nations Law* 9 (2005): 310–11.
6. UNAMET was established on 11 June 1999 by the UN Security Council Resolution 1246.
7. Damien Kingsbury, "The TNI and the Militias", in *Guns and Ballot Boxes: East Timor's Vote for Independence*, edited by Damien Kingsbury, p. 69 (Clayton, Victoria: Monash Asia Institute, 2000).
8. Jarat Chopra, "The UN's Kingdom of East Timor", *Survival* 42, no. 3 (Autumn 2000): 27.
9. Commission for Reception, Truth and Reconciliation (CAVR), *Chega! Final Report of the Commission for Reception, Truth and Reconciliation Timor-Leste*, chapter 3, p. 145 (Dili: CAVR, 2005); Chopra, "The UN's Kingdom of East Timor", p. 27; Geoffrey Robinson, *East Timor 1999 Crimes against Humanity*, p. 44 (United Nations Office sof the High Commissioner for Human Rights, July 2003); United Nations Office of the Commissioner of Human Rights, "Report of the Commission for Inquiry on East Timor to Secretary-General" United Nations General Assembly, A/54/726, S/2000/59, January 2000.
10. Robinson, *East Timor 1999*, p. 1; Joel Beauvais, "Benevolent Despotism: A Critique of UN State-building in East Timor", *New York University Journal*

of International Law and Politics 33 (2001–2): 1103; CAVR, *Chega!*, chapter 3, p. 145.
11. Robinson, *East Timor 1999*, p. 42.
12. CAVR, *Chega!*, chapter 3, p. 150.
13. Grayson Lloyd, "The Diplomacy on East Timor: Indonesia, the United Nations and the International Community", in *Out of the Ashes: Destruction and Reconstruction of East Timor*, edited by James J. Fox and Dionisio Babo-Soares, p. 100 (South Australia: Crawford House Publishing, 2000); Dionisio Babo-Soares, "Political Developments Leading to the Referendum", in *Out of the Ashes: Deconstruction and Reconstruction of East Timor*, edited by James Fox and Dionisio Babo-Soares, p. 72 (Hindmarsh, South Australia: Crawford House Publishing, November 2003).
14. Cotton, *East Timor, Australia and Regional Order*, pp. 95–96.
15. Lloyd, "The Diplomacy on East Timor", p. 101.
16. Cotton, *East Timor, Australia and Regional Order*, p. 96.
17. CAVR, *Chega!*, chapter 3, p. 149.
18. Lloyd, "The Diplomacy on East Timor", p. 101.
19. CAVR, *Chega!*, chapter 7, pp. 1, 61.
20. United Nations Security Council (UNSC), "Resolution 1264", S/RES/1264, 15 September 1999. See also Ian Martin, *Self-Determination in East Timor: The United Nations, the Ballot, and International Intervention* (Boulder, Colorado: Lynne Rienner Publishers, 2001).
21. Dominik Zaum, "International Relations Theory and Peacebuilding", in *Routledge Handbook in Peacebuilding*, edited by Roger Mac Ginty, p. 112 (Oxon: Routledge, 2013).
22. Felicity Rogers, "The International Force in East Timor: Legal Aspects of Maritime Operations", *University of New South Wales Journal of International Law* 37 (2005); Michael Leach and Sally Percival-Wood, "Timor-Leste: From INTERFET to ASEAN", in *The Australia–ASEAN Dialogue: Tracing 40 years of Partnership*, edited by Baogang He and Sally Percival-Wood, p. 73 (New York: Palgrave Macmillan, 2014).
23. Benzing, "Midwifing a New State", p. 308.
24. Leach and Percival Wood, "Timor-Leste", p. 74.
25. Cotton, *East Timor, Australia and Regional Order*, p. 87.
26. Chris Bickerton, "State-Building: Exporting State Failure", *Arena Journal* 32 (2009): 112; Sam Pietsch, "Australian Imperialism and East Timor", *Marxist Interventions* 2 (2010): 7–38.
27. Rogers, "The International Force in East Timor"; Shaun Narine, *Explaining ASEAN: Regionalism in Southeast Asia*, p. 173 (Boulder: Lynne Rienner, 2002).
28. Leach and Percival Wood, "Timor-Leste", pp. 73–74; Cotton, *East Timor, Australia and Regional Order*, pp. 73–74.

29. Cotton, *East Timor, Australia and Regional Order*, p. 73.
30. See Narine, *Explaining ASEAN*; Benzing, "Midwifing a New State", p. 310.
31. Alan Dupont, "ASEAN's Response to the East Timor Crisis", *Australian Journal of International Affairs* 45, no. 2 (2000): 163.
32. Narine, *Explaining ASEAN*, p. 172.
33. Cotton, *East Timor, Australia and Regional Order*, p. 163; Lee Jones, *ASEAN, Sovereignty and Intervention in Southeast Asia* (Houndmills, UK: Palgrave Macmillan, 2012), p. 163.
34. Narine, *Explaining ASEAN*, p. 173.
35. Jurgen Haacke, "South-East Asia's International Relations and Security Perspectives", in *East and Southeast Asia: International Relations and Security Perspectives*, edited by Andrew T.H. Tan, p. 160 (Oxon: Routledge, 2013).
36. Benzing, "Midwifing a New State", pp. 307–8.
37. Cotton, *East Timor, Australia and Regional Order*, p. 95.
38. Jones, *ASEAN, Sovereignty and Intervention in Southeast Asia*, p. 158.
39. Ibid., pp. 159–60; Narine, *Explaining ASEAN*, pp. 173–74.
40. Leach and Percival Wood, "Timor-Leste", p. 73.
41. Jones, *ASEAN, Sovereignty and Intervention in Southeast Asia*, pp. 151, 162; Narine, *Explaining ASEAN*, p. 173; Nicholas Tarling, *Regionalism in Southeast Asia: To Foster the Political Will*, p. 211 (Oxon: Routledge, 2006).
42. Dupont, "ASEAN's Response to the East Timor Crisis", p. 163.
43. Ibid., pp. 164–65.
44. Alan Collins, *The Security Dilemmas of Southeast Asia*, p. 38 (Hampshire: Palgrave Macmillan, 2000).
45. Dupont, "ASEAN's Response to the East Timor Crisis", p. 165.
46. Ibid., p. 168.
47. Narine, *Explaining ASEAN*, p. 173; Leach and Percival Wood, "Timor-Leste", p. 73.
48. Cotton, *East Timor, Australia and Regional Order*, pp. 79–80
49. Ibid., pp. 72, 74.
50. Dupont, "ASEAN's Response to the East Timor Crisis", p. 168.
51. Cotton, *East Timor, Australia and Regional Order*, p. 88.
52. Jones, *ASEAN, Sovereignty and Intervention in Southeast Asia*, pp. 163, 169.
53. Ibid., p. 150.
54. Ibid., p. 162.
55. Ibid., p. 160.
56. Robinson, *East Timor 1999*, p. 44.
57. Beauvais, "Benevolent Despotism", p. 1104.
58. Ibid., p. 1109.
59. Max Weber, *From Max Weber: Essays in Sociology. Edited, with an Introduction by H.H. Gerth and C.W. Mills*, p. 328 (Oxon: Routledge, 1991).

60. Jackson, *Quasi-States*, chapter 1; Ashraf Ghani and Clare Lockhart, *Fixing Failed States: A Framework for Rebuilding a Fractured World*, pp. 3–4 (Oxford: Oxford University Press, 2009).
61. Gerald Helman and Steven Ratner, "Saving Failed States", *Foreign Affairs* 89 (Winter 1992–93): 33.
62. Sankaran Krishna, *Postcolonial Insecurities: India, Sri Lanka and the Question of Nationhood*, p. 5 (Minneapolis and London: University of Minneapolis, 1999).
63. Those who criticize "failed state discourses" often do so on the basis that it cannot encapsulate the diversity of the states it seeks to describe. See Charles T. Call, "The Fallacy of the 'Failed State'", *Third World Quarterly* 29, no. 8 (2008): 1491–507.
64. Jackson, *Quasi-States*, p. 199.
65. Jens Bartelson, "Three Concepts of Recognition", *International Theory* 5 (2013): 107–29.
66. Weber, *From Max Weber*, p. 78.
67. Ibid.
68. Michael Wesley, "The State of the Art on the Art of State Building", *Global Governance* 14 (2008): 374; Marina Ottaway, "Rebuilding State Institutions in Collapsed States", *Development and Change* 33, no. 5 (2002): 1002.
69. Muthiah Alagappa, "Introduction", in *Political Legitimacy in Southeast Asia: The Quest for Moral Authority*, edited by Muthiah Alagappa, pp. 2–3 (Stanford: Stanford University Press, 1995).
70. Ghani and Lockhart, *Fixing Failing States*, p. 7.
71. Helman and Ratner, "Saving Failed States".
72. Bartelson, "Three Concepts of Recognition", p. 124.
73. Stephen Krasner, "Recognition: Organised Hypocrisy Once Again", *International Theory* 5, no. 1 (2013): 171.
74. United Nations General Assembly (UNGA), "Declaration on the Granting of Independence to Colonial Countries and Peoples", United Nations General Assembly Resolution 1514 (XV), 15th Session, 14 December 1960.
75. Benzing, "Midwifing a New State".
76. Ibid., p. 306.
77. Simon Chesterman, *You, the People: The United Nations, Transitional Administration, and State-Building*, p. 5 (Oxford: Oxford University Press, 2005).
78. UNSC, "Resolution 1272", S/RES/1272, 25 October 1999.
79. Barry Buzan, *People, States, and Fear: The National Security Problem in International Relations*, pp. 63–69 (Chapel Hill: North Carolina, University of North Carolina Press, 1983).
80. Weber, *From Max Weber*, p. 328.
81. See Strating and Edmondson, "Beyond Democratic Tolerance".
82. Juan Federer, *The UN in East Timor: Building Timor-Leste, a Fragile State*, p. 4 (Darwin: Charles Darwin University Press, 2005).

83. There is an extensive literature on liberal state-building. See, for example, Simon Chesterman, Michael Ignatieff, and Ramesh Thakur, eds., *Making States Work: State Failure and the Crisis of Governance* (Tokyo and New York: United Nations University, 2005); Patrick Sutter, "State-Building or the Dilemma of Intervention: An Introduction", in *Facets and Practices of Statebuilding*, edited by Julia Raue and Patrick Sutter, p. 5 (Leiden: Martinus Nijhoff Publishers, 2009); Roland Paris, "Saving Liberal Peacebuilding", *Review of International Studies* 36, (2010): 339; Francis Fukuyama, *State-Building: Governance and World Order in the Twenty-First Century* (Ithaca: Cornell University Press, 2004); Roland Paris and Timothy Sisk, eds., *The Dilemmas of Statebuilding: Confronting the Contradictions of Postwar Peace Operations* (New York: Routledge, 2009); Roland Rotberg, ed., *When States Fail: Causes and Consequences* (Princeton, New Jersey: Princeton University Press, 2003).
84. Bickerton, "State-building", p. 105.
85. James Fearon and David Laitin, "Neo-Trusteeship and the Problem of Weak States", *International Security* 28, no. 4 (2004): 12.
86. Stephen Ryan, "The Evolution of Peacebuilding", in *Routledge Handbook in Peacebuilding*, edited by Roger Mac Ginty, p. 27 (Oxon: Routledge, 2013).
87. United Nations Peacebuilding Commission, "Review of the United Nations Peacebuilding Architecture", A/64/868, 2010.
88 See, for example, Stephen Krasner, "Sharing Sovereignty: New Institutions for Collapsed and Failing States", *International Security* 29, no. 2 (2004): 84–85.
89. Zaum, "International Relations Theory and Peacebuilding", p. 108.
90. Dominik Zaum, "The Authority of International Administrations in International Society", *Review of International Studies* 32 (2006): 456. See David Chandler, *Empire in Denial: The Politics of Statebuilding*, p. 41 (London: Pluto Press, 2006).
91. UNSC, "Resolution 1272".
92. Rebecca Strating, *Social Democracy in East Timor* (Oxon: Routledge, 2015).
93. Thomas M. Franck, "The Emerging Right of Democratic Governance", *The American Journal of International Law* 86, no. 1 (January 1992): 46.
94. Bartelson, "Three Concepts of Recognition", p. 123.
95. Alex Bellamy, "Kosovo and the Advent of Sovereignty as Responsibility", in *Kosovo, Intervention and Statebuilding: The International Community and the Transition to Independence*, edited by Aidan Hehir, p. 40 (Oxon: Routledge, 2010); Zaum, *The Sovereign Paradox*, p. 234; Chandler, *Empire in Denial*, pp. 36–40.
96. Zaum, *The Sovereign Paradox*, pp. 38, 226.
97. Michael Reisman, "Sovereignty and Human Rights in Contemporary International Law", *American Journal of International Law* 84, no. 4 (1990): 866–76.

98. Chesterman, *You, the People*, pp. 136.
99. Jarat Chopra and Tanja Hohe, "Participatory Intervention", *Global Governance* 10 (2004): 289.
100. See Tanja Hohe, "The Clash of Paradigms: International Administration and Local Political Legitimacy in East Timor", *Contemporary Southeast Asia* 24, no. 3 (December 2002): 569–89.
101. Joel Migdal, *Weak Societies and Strong States* (Princeton: Princeton University Press, 1988).
102. Beauvais, "Benevolent Despotism".
103. Ibid and Chopra, "The UN's Kingdom of East Timor".
104. de Mello cited in Chesterman, *You, the People*, p. 138.
105. UNSC, "Report of the Secretary-General on the Situation in East Timor", RES/1999/1024, 4 October 1999, pp. 7–8.
106. UNSC, "Report of the Secretary-General on the United Nations Transitional Administration in East Timor", S/2000/53, 26 January 2000, p. 10.
107. Randall Garrison, *The Role of Constitution-Building Processes in Democratization Case Study: East Timor*, p. 9 (Stockholm: International Institute for Democracy and Electoral Assistance, 2005); Chesterman, *You, the People*, p. 135; Paulo Gorjão, "The Legacy and Lessons of the United Nations Transitional Administration in East Timor", *Contemporary Southeast Asia* 24, no. 2 (2002): 316; Rui Graça Feijó, *Dynamics of Democracy in Timor-Leste, 1999–2012*, chapter 2 (Amsterdam: Amsterdam University Press, 2016).
108. Butler, "Ten Years After", p. 92.
109. United Nations Transitional Administration in East Timor, "On the Establishment of a National Consultative Council", UNTAET/REG/1999/2, 2 December 1999.
110. Mark Dodd, "Gusmão Gives UN Team a Serve: 'We Don't Want a Legacy of Cars'", *Sydney Morning Herald* (10 October 2000).
111. La'o Hamutuk, *The La'o Hamutuk Bulletin* 6, no. 13 (August 2005).
112. United Nations Transitional Administration in East Timor, *On the Establishment of a National Council*, UNTAET/REG/2000/24, 14 July 2000.
113. Anthony Smith, "East Timor: Elections in the World's Newest Nation", *Journal of Democracy* 15, no. 4 (April 2004): 149.
114. Jim Della-Giacoma, *Timor Loro Sa'e is Our Nation: A Report on Focus Group Discussions in East Timor*, p. iv (Dili: National Democratic Institute for International Affairs and East Timor NGO Forum's Working Group on Electoral Education, March 2001).
115. Strating, *Social Democracy in East Timor*.
116. Krasner, "Sharing Sovereignty", p. 119.
117. Federer, *The UN in East Timor*, p. 18.
118. Chesterman, *You, the People*.

119. Dodd, "Gusmão Gives UN Team a Serve", cited in Chesterman, *You, the People*, p. 183.
120. Joanne Wallis, *Constitution Making During State Building*, p. 80 (New York: Cambridge University Press, 2014).
121. David Edelstein, "Foreign Ministries, Sustainable Institutions", in *The Dilemmas of Statebuilding: Confronting the Contradictions of Postwar Peace Operations*, edited by Roland Paris and Timothy D. Sisk, p. 86 (Oxon: Routledge, 2009).
122. Xanana Gusmão, "New Year's Message", Dili, 31 December 2000.
123. Butler, "Ten Years After", pp. 85–86.
124. For more on UNMIT, see McQueen, "United Nations Integrated Mission in Timor-Leste (UNTAET)".
125. For a deeper discussion on political institutions and democratization, and in particular the role of semi-presidentialism, see Lydia Beuman, *Political Institutions in Timor-Leste: Semi-Presidentialism and Democratization* (London: Routledge, 2015).
126. Xanana Gusmão, "Timor-Leste and ASEAN Perspectives and Challenges", Address by His Excellency the Prime Minister and Minister of Defence and Security, Kay Rala Xanana Gusmão, Sabah, Malaysia, 2 April 2014.
127. Krasner, "Recognition", p. 174.
128. Gusmão, "Timor-Leste and ASEAN Perspectives and Challenges".
129. See Simon Roughneen, "Aid and Independence", *The Diplomat*, 29 September 2011.
130. Julio Tomas Pinto, "UNMIT Mission: Development or Destruction", *Tempo Semanal*, 7 June 2011.
131. Cited in Agio Pereira, "The Challenges of Nation-State Building", in *A New Era? Timor-Leste After the UN*, edited by Sue Ingram, Lia Kent and Andrew McWilliam, p. 19 (Canberra: ANU Press, 2015).

5

Timor-Leste's Aspirational Foreign Policy

Since becoming a new state in 2002, Timor-Leste's foreign policy approach has been driven by the twin demands of guaranteeing survival and asserting political independence. Particular insecurities and constraints arise from being a small power. The "post-colonial security dilemma" reflects the need for small, new, weak states to diminish their reliance upon other states by pursuing a concept of absolute external state sovereignty as "real" independence. The tensions between dependence and independence are reflected in Timor-Leste's efforts to secure state sovereignty through its international relations, national defence policy and development strategy. This book argues that the historical experiences of the denial of self-determination and international state-building outlined in the previous chapters helped shape Timor-Leste's foreign policy approach, threat perceptions and subsequent engagements with the international community. Perhaps the greatest limitation is its inability to independently guarantee its own security. Small states are limited by what they can achieve in their international relations and have few opportunities to shape the international structures they inhabit.[1] Like most small, new states,

Timor-Leste's core national interest is survival, and it must use foreign policy as a way of negotiating its vulnerabilities and insecurities.[2] Yet, even the smallest and weakest states have options in pursuing core national interests. The question is how small states can maximize their capacity for strategic manoeuvring and decrease reliance on relationships that give rise to imperatives rather than choices.

This chapter examines the formation of Timor-Leste's foreign policy. The initial challenges were determining its place in the world and defining its strategic national interests. Three key objectives have driven Timor-Leste's international relations:

1. Develop good relations with states in the region, particularly Australia and Indonesia;
2. Pursue membership of regional and international organizations;
3. Establish relationships with those beyond the immediate neighbourhood.

Timor-Leste's foreign policy objectives emphasize a collaborative and cooperative approach to international relations in support of the key interest of survival. Initially, Timor-Leste's foreign policy was designed to support nation-building goals. Xanana Gusmão, for example, argued that "Timor-Leste is not only a small country; we are also the youngest nation in the Asia Pacific. Precisely because we are small, and because we are young, it is important that we work together with our neighbours to improve the lives of our people and the human development of our region."[3] Over time, however, Timor-Leste has increasingly pursued an expansive foreign policy approach as it has applied for membership in a number of regional and international institutions and established diplomatic missions in every inhabited continent across the globe. The diversified approach seeks to avoid dependence on any one state or bloc of states by eschewing formal alliances.

Securing the state entails projecting a legitimate identity in the international community to protect and guarantee political recognition of sovereign status, an imperative that gives rise to Timor-Leste's "aspirational foreign policy". While smallness and newness are factors in Timor-Leste's international relations, this chapter also focuses on material considerations that offer aspirational drivers of foreign policy. Timor-Leste's approach is partly driven by its ambitions of transforming from a "lower-middle income country" (as classified by the World Bank in 2015) to an upper-middle income state by 2030.[4] However, it is also driven by ideational ambitions that are motivated by identity goals of achieving social prestige. For Timor-Leste, aspirational foreign policy is revealed in the ways leaders seek recognition of its preferred self-image as a development success story through a narrative of "foreign policy exceptionalism". This chapter also examines Timor-Leste's approach to international norms and global issues, particularly through its activities as one of the newest members of the United Nations (UN). In this forum, Timor-Leste can project its desired identity to the broader international community. This section examines Timor-Leste's voting record at the UN and its stance on key global issues of human rights, disarmament and self-determination, and discusses its attempts to shift from aid recipient to donor through policies of humanitarianism.

Negotiating Vulnerability: Security and Sovereignty

Like many post-colonial states, Timor-Leste's lack of economic or military might renders it a fragile state. There are twin dimensions to this: in external relations, the term "weak state" encapsulates the vulnerabilities of states with limited capacity to exert power in the international system. The term also describes states that are internally "weak" insofar as they do not meet traditional standards of statehood. As the introduction noted, since the 1990s, there has been considerable attention devoted to the question of how weak states "survive" in the anarchical international political system. One answer to this question, as examined in early chapters, is the ways in which the international normative order of twentieth-century decolonization has permitted the external sovereignty of new post-colonial states. This provided opportunities for nations that would not have been able to independently guarantee their own independence to become members of the international community. The weaker the state — in terms of size and capacities to effectively govern — the more likely it will rely upon external recognition and assistance.[5] The post-colonial security predicament arises from a lack of "stateness", as this renders weak states vulnerable to external coercion and intervention from more powerful states.[6] Ayoob argues that the primary concern of developing states in their international relations is reducing their vulnerabilities.[7] Elites in developing post-colonial states "see Westphalian values in their pristine form [i.e. absolute external sovereignty] as the greatest normative and ideological bulwark against both domestic and foreign threats to states and regimes".[8] Hence, the foreign policies of weak states are often driven by a desire to guarantee their sovereign identity.

As a small island state in Southeast Asia, Singapore's foreign policy approach provides a useful comparison for Timor-Leste. In terms of both population and territory size, as well as geographical location, Singapore employs a small state foreign policy. While Singapore's population is now 5.5 million, it was 1.8 million in 1965 when it became independent, and it is less than half the territorial size of Timor-Leste. Similar to Timor-Leste, Singapore's initial foreign policy was driven by a concern about its much larger neighbours. Both Timor-Leste and Singapore experienced severe "vulnerabilities" following independence. Prior to independence, Singaporean statehood was also widely considered non-viable, for reasons owing to a lack of natural resources.[9] However, Singapore now wields disproportionate power to its small size in its international relations. Consequently, Timor-Leste's Ministry of Foreign Affairs and Cooperation identified Singapore as a model for Timor-Leste's foreign policy.

Singapore's concern with territorial sovereignty was partly derived from the manner by which it became independent. Like Timor-Leste, its history of colonialism has shaped its perceptions of external threats. The only other example of successful separatism in Southeast Asia besides Timor-Leste, Singapore's independence was unique as it was the incorporating state — Malaysia — that enforced independence upon Singapore.[10] Singapore faced the political reconciliation between Indonesia and Malaysia, which, according to Leifer, became a major factor in Singapore's outlook:

> The transformation, virtually overnight, from being a constituent unit of Malaysia — then confronted by Indonesia — to becoming a small, vulnerable and conspicuously Chinese island state, and then of suffering the rapprochement of its more powerful Malay neighbours was politically traumatic.[11]

Foreign policy formation in Singapore was shaped by the insecurities that arose from its state formation and the Southeast Asian power politics of the time. Similarly, the regional dynamics that prevented Timor-Leste's self-determination, and the mechanisms by which Timor-

Leste became independent through an invasive international state-building period has similarly coloured Timor-Leste's insecurities.

Singapore's foreign policy was dominated by concerns about survival as a consequence of its small state vulnerability, and Singapore has not taken its sovereignty for granted.[12] According to Singaporean leader Lee Hsien Loong, the price of the survival of small states is "eternal vigilance".[13] Some scholars view Singapore's approach to foreign policy as very much in keeping with the realist tradition.[14] Ganesan, for example, views Singapore's foreign policymakers as prioritizing self-help through national development and balancing of major powers in the region as core elements of its survival strategy.[15] Its realist behaviour is a consequence of the vulnerabilities arising from its small physical and population size "wedged" between two larger states, similar to Timor-Leste.[16] Yet, in contrast to Singapore, Timor-Leste's survival [i.e. its status as a sovereign state] has been underwritten by the international community since 1999. Its perceived security challenge pertains largely to its capacities to fulfil the ideals of absolute external sovereignty by securing the state against foreign intervention.

This focus on absolute external sovereignty is not unique among post-colonial states. According to Leifer, Singapore's foreign policy practice is "compatible with a strong commitment to the cardinal rule of international society: namely the sanctity of national sovereignty no matter how small and insignificant the state".[17] Indeed, other Southeast Asian states also define security in terms of their own survival.[18] The sovereignty principles of territorial integrity, non-intervention and equality provided guarantees for former colonial territories that they could maintain their independence despite their inability to defend themselves from military attack or meet substantive criteria of empirical statehood.[19] Stronger states have less need for the "equal sovereign" principle than new states. Sovereignty provides a mechanism through which weak states protect themselves from the strong.[20] As the following analysis highlights, the desire for political independence is a key driver of Timor-Leste's interactions with the broader international community. It seeks to consolidate a consistent "sense of self" by securing state sovereignty as the constitutive basis of its legitimate "state personhood".[21] For both Singapore and Timor-Leste, the experiences of becoming independent have shaped the culture and rhetoric of their foreign policy.[22]

During Timor-Leste's state-building period, a national constitution was developed by a democratically elected Constituent Assembly that provides the framework for Timor-Leste's relations with other states, and articulates its core national interests in relation to sovereignty. Article 8 of Timor-Leste's National Constitution presents a particular vision of sovereignty in the context of its international relations:

> On matters of international relations, the Democratic Republic of East Timor shall govern itself by the principles of national independence, the right of the Peoples to self-determination and independence, the permanent sovereignty of the peoples over their wealth and natural resources, the protection of human rights, the mutual respect for sovereignty, territorial integrity and equality among States and the non-interference in domestic affairs of other States.[23]

The protection of state sovereignty remains Timor-Leste's core national interest. Timor-Leste's 2011 Strategic Development Plan (SDP) argued that the central objective of foreign policy is "to protect and promote, at an international level, the fundamental interests of the people of Timor-Leste and to safeguard and consolidate the independence of our nation".[24] The sixth government stated in its 2012–17 blueprint, "[o]ur foreign policy seeks to protect and to promote the vital interests of the Timorese people, thereby safeguarding the independence, sovereignty and territorial integrity of our Nation".[25] These declaratory policy documents tie Timor-Leste's sovereignty with its capacities to exert political independence.

While the language of sovereignty is similar to that used around sovereignty in international law and organizations, the emphasis on "non-interference in domestic affairs" is notable. After twenty-four years of struggle for independence, drafters were understandably concerned with preserving Timor-Leste's hard-fought rights to collective self- determination. Typically, sovereignty is said to confer rights to "non-intervention". This reflects a belief that military intervention or direct involvement in the territorial jurisdictions of states is a violation of sovereignty.[26] The "non-interference" discourse, in contrast, is preferred by ASEAN states. Non-interference ostensibly provides states the rights not to be publically judged or criticized for domestic policies, for instance in the case of human rights violations or democracy, although this principle has been weakened.[27] It is not necessarily the case that post-colonial states share an absolutist concept of state sovereignty: the African Union, for example, articulates a right to intervention in the Constitutive Act of the Union.[28] In Timor-Leste's case, constitutional drafters favoured the concept of "non-interference" that is similar to that employed by ASEAN (see chapter six). Rhetoric, history and national mythologies constitute the political imagining of sovereignty as an absolute, inviolable and sacrosanct enabler of self-determination.

Fragile State Exceptionalism

For Timor-Leste, discourses of struggle and resistance provide continuity from the past to the present, and Timor-Leste's history of colonialism shapes state-based identity, interests and interactions. While International Relations tends to assume that once independence is gained, states become less concerned with recognition, states' desire for status recognition and respect can be important for understanding their motives and behaviours of states. States attempt to project a desired image that may or may not be recognized by others, and can even "appear to act against their material interests in pursuit of some particular identity-based goal".[29] This suggests that through international actions, narratives and rhetoric, the representatives of states deliberately project an image that they wish to be recognized by the international community. Narratives of identity matter because Timor-Leste has limited foreign policy options to pursue its goals. One of its core foreign policy strategies is "public diplomacy", which encompasses dynamics of image-making in international relations and reflects the role of public relations in international relations as a form of soft power.[30] Narratives are representative tools that assist states in projecting self-images to the international community. A "legitimate" identity can help protect the sovereignty and non-interference rights of small, weak states.

According to Clunan, the aspirations of political elites can "play a central role in shaping which historical legacies are incorporated into national identities and national interests".[31] She argues that historical memory plays a role in shaping these aspirations, which in turn contribute to the social construction of national identities and interests.[32] Among powerful states, for example, aspirations are reflected in the U.S. belief in its "exceptionalism", Russian attempts to regain international great power status, or China's efforts to absolve the state of its historical humiliations. For Timor-Leste, its national self-image is shaped by beliefs about its international status as a successful example of state-building. Consequently, a central foreign policy narrative is that of "fragile state exceptionalism", which inculcates the idea that Timor-Leste has overcome its history of colonial oppression to emerge as a model state for other post-conflict societies.

Timor-Leste's dominant foreign policy narratives relate to the means by which it became independent, and employ discourses of "heroism", "struggle" and "resistance" to project Timor-Leste's state-based identity. Within Timor-Leste, the independence struggle continues to be integral to Timorese nationalism, particularly through the spread of Catholicism and the lingua franca, Tetum (see chapter six).[33] Resistance discourses and images feature heavily in Timor-Leste's museums, monuments and in the National Constitution. Monuments around Timor-Leste's capital of Dili tend to evoke particularly masculine displays of heroism and courage during the resistance struggle. The National Museum in Dili is singularly devoted to detailing the resistance movement; written on its entrance walls is the famous independence motto "To Resist is to Win!" Similarly, within the international realm Timorese representatives draw extensively on historical experiences of occupation and resistance. As one example, Gusmão, told an audience in fellow new state South Sudan:

> [d]espite the cost, we held on to our dream of freedom. Our motto was "To Resist is to Win" and our occupiers were to learn that, despite terrible suffering, our spirit and our solidarity could not be broken. We were inspired by campaigns against colonial rule in Africa which showed us the way. And so, we fought a guerrilla war in the mountains and valleys of Timor.[34]

Common themes in international speeches also include "courage", "resilience" and "solidarity". For example, Gusmão argued that the struggle for self-determination has left the pages of Timor-Leste's history "marked with bloodshed; but they are also coloured by heroic deeds and humbling acts of sacrifice, and the final chapter tells of success as we achieved our dream of independence".[35] It is evident within foreign policy discourse that the resistance provides the basis for (re)constructing Timor-Leste's external national identity and aspirational foreign policy.

The struggle for recognition of Timor-Leste's state-based identity is also reflected in the ways it seeks to present the state as a development success story. On the one hand, Gusmão recognized the fragility of the Timorese state:

> Our people sacrificed so much for the cause of independence and self-determination. They have suffered unspeakable acts of violence and hardship. And while we prevailed against all odds, and with little international support, too many still suffer every day from extreme poverty and miserable living conditions. They deserve more. When we became an independent nation we started with nothing. We had no money, no experience of nation building and we lacked the core infrastructure necessary to support a modern and productive economy.[36]

More recently, however, foreign policy speeches have been coloured by a narrative of exceptionalism regarding its state-building project. Former Prime Minister Rui Maria de Araújo presents Timor-Leste's national identity as distinctive within the international community:

> it is this identity of ours, this common sense of values, feelings and solidarity that makes us stand out in the international community and that gave us the courage and the resilience to fight for the right to self-rule. It was this unique culture and this unique identity that made Timor-Leste fight to regain its independence for twenty-four years, after it was taken away from us in 1975.[37]

Timor-Leste's leaders commonly refer to the journey from colonial occupation to statehood as a movement *from fragility to resilience*.[38] After independence, Timor-Leste's central concern has been its transformation from a fragile state to a "successful" state: a stable, prosperous nation that could resist interference in domestic affairs from external actors.

This narrative presents Timor-Leste's progress as "remarkable", and its transition from "conflict to development" "difficult but successful".[39] Timor-Leste is described by key leaders as "a development success story".[40] According to the narrative, owing to the determination of Timorese people and the support of its "international friends… Timor-Leste has established a vibrant and free democracy, a tolerant and peaceful society and the foundations for sustained economic growth and development progress."[41] This narrative presents Timor-Leste as exceptional within the context of other new fragile states. This exceptionalism is also prominent in the ways Timor-Leste has increasingly sought to carve out a leadership role for itself among the fragile state cohort (see chapter six). The narrative presents Timorese self-determination as the principle reason for its success. For example, Gusmão argued that Timor-Leste's transition from *fragility to resilience* was possible because the Timorese "took control and ownership of our future. We know that we still face many challenges and that the process of State building is ongoing. But we have a plan and we have the same commitment to developing our nation as we did to freeing it."[42] According to this story, crises in Timor-Leste were largely the result of the interference of foreign donors and the stifling of self-determination, but success in overcoming crises was due to the Timorese people. The continuation of Timor-Leste's success story relies upon maintaining its independence.[43] The narrative of fragile state exceptionalism that underpins foreign policy discourse is hence linked to the desire of Timor-Leste to avoid foreign intervention, and its promotion of self-determination. These themes are picked up in later chapters.

The Evolution of Timor-Leste's Foreign Policy Approach

As mentioned above, the key national interest defining Timor-Leste's foreign policy was guaranteeing recognition of state sovereignty and was initially oriented towards urgent nation-building imperatives.[44] This included using international relations to establish itself as a successful liberal-democratic state under rule of law.[45] During the first FRETILIN government, Timorese politician and academic Dionisio Babo-Soares recommended that Timor-Leste "intensify both multilateral and bilateral relations with all countries, with particular emphasis on those with the ability and interest to provide assistance in the development of its human capital, security and economy".[46] After all, good relations with other states was necessary because Timor-Leste "cannot survive on its own".[47] The Constitution mandates that Timor-Leste's relations with other states be principally based on "friendship and cooperation". These objectives remain central.[48]

In the first years of statehood, Timor-Leste's foreign policy approach was mobilized around supporting the internal institutional- and nation-building project to guarantee recognition of its state-based legitimacy in the eyes of the international community. Insecurity arose from Timor-Leste's transition from a dependent colony, to the subject of a unique form of international neo-trusteeship and finally, to a new state searching for its position in the international political order. Hence, for the first years of independence, foreign policy was largely directed towards internal goals of political development and establishing its international identity through dialogue and collaboration. To this end, a key priority was strategic positioning: that is, how to position Timor-Leste in relation to its neighbours, in the region and globally. This included dealing with key identity questions: how Timor-Leste views its own identity, how it views its neighbours, the region and the international community, how Timor-Leste perceives international laws and norms, and developing principles for relations with others. Timor-Leste's foreign policy was driven by a need to establish itself as a "credible actor in the regional setting", but also in maintaining relationships with major international donors that would continue to support Timor-Leste's state- and nation-building processes.[49]

As an early example of declaratory policy, the key foreign policy objectives outlined in the 2002 National Development Plan (NDP) included "strengthening regional and international political, economic, cultural and scientific cooperation and relations".[50] Araújo described Timor-Leste as "a friend of everyone".[51] This approach is reminiscent of the guiding doctrine of its much larger neighbour, Indonesia, under Susilo Bambang Yudhoyono of "A Million Friends and Zero Enemies". The development plan reflected Timor-Leste's desire to be a cooperative, responsible and collaborative international actor, fleshing out the main objective outlined in the Constitution, namely to maintain friendship and cooperation with neighbouring countries, and with the rest of the world; maintain "special" links with the Community of Portuguese Speaking Nations (CPLP); establish diplomatic relations; and, maximize support for the social and economic development of Timor-Leste. The last objective highlights the importance of using foreign affairs to consolidate Timorese state and nation in the initial years of independence. The objectives would be achieved by systematically expanding diplomatic representation, pursuing south-south and regional cooperation, and fostering relations with Portuguese-speaking states.

Timor-Leste's foreign policy follows that path of other small states in seeking "comprehensive and collective engagement" through "peaceful dialogue and collective action".[52] According to Gusmão, "[d]ialogue, the asset of diplomacy, is the only weapon that can deal with the problems of our time. As such, sharing security challenges in our region will contribute to improve strategic trust between countries in the region."[53] In another speech he argued that states need to focus on maintaining respectful and positive relationships: "We need to see international leaders moving beyond words of good faith to taking constructive actions — and participating in real dialogue and active engagement — in the best interests of our common security."[54] Timor-Leste's leaders and declaratory policy emphasized the importance of dialogue and diplomacy, and cooperation and collaboration in international affairs.

The focus on "friendship and cooperation" in Timor-Leste's foreign policy approach is due in part to the complex geopolitics of Timor-Leste's position in the world. To understand foreign policy behaviour, it is important to consider the influence of the unique geographic features of each state and their physical location. Great and middle power states in the Asia-Pacific region, including the United States, China, Australia and Indonesia have long held geostrategic interests in the eastern half of Timor island.[55] In 2015, Timor-Leste's then-Minister for Defence Cirilo José Cristovão stated that small countries are "more often than not neglected or obliterated from the bigger picture when discussing the contemporary geo-strategic theatre".[56] Geopolitically, Timor-Leste's security interests are shaped by its location in the Asia-Pacific. The complex geopolitics of small states such as Timor-Leste and Singapore — their relative size and proximity to larger and potentially antagonistic states — has contributed to an emphasis on vulnerabilities in foreign policy formation. This region has become increasingly defined by the emergent great power competition between the United States and China. The great power rivalry has strategic consequences for Timor-Leste's international relations. As chapter three pointed out, the Ombai-Wetar Strait to the north of Timor-Leste is used by U.S. submarines, a scenario that would not be lost on China.[57] Indeed, China has sought to develop its relations with Timor-Leste through the provision of aid grants and military support as part of its efforts to balance U.S. influence in Southeast Asia (see chapter ten).[58]

The first crucial objective for Timor-Leste is managing its relations with Indonesia and Australia, as these states occupy an important place in Timor-Leste's foreign policy.[59] Having good bilateral relations with its powerful neighbours has been presented as "an imperative, rather than a choice".[60] Indonesia and Australia continue to be sources of insecurity and dependence. In the past, both states have demonstrated a willingness to intervene in the territory to support their own national interests, a history which shapes the perception of security threats. Timor-Leste's leaders in foreign policy have long recognized that its independence would rely upon Indonesia and Australia. Smith suggests that Timorese foreign policy was firmly focused on both Australia and Indonesia in order to "protect itself".[61] In any case, a key interest for Timor-Leste was to avoid becoming party to any geopolitical disputes between its two neighbours, which do not always share common interests or strategic goals.[62]

Indonesia continues to have significant geopolitical relevance to Timor-Leste. The republic dominates Timor-Leste's geography insofar as it surrounds its "western, northern and eastern flanks, and shares its only land border, totally encapsulating the enclave of Oecussi and the majority of its maritime border".[63] Timor-Leste is dependent on Indonesia for imports, particularly food, support for ASEAN membership and other diplomatic objectives, border security and guaranteeing territorial integrity.[64] Indonesia's close proximity to Timor-Leste means it has strategic interests in ensuring security and development in order to mitigate the potential for border disputes, terrorism or refugees. Both Gusmão and Foreign Minister José Ramos-Horta adopted a conciliatory stance towards Indonesia from the beginning.[65] As a consequence of this reliance, Timor-Leste has adopted a pragmatic realist approach to its relations with Indonesia (see chapter nine).

Timor-Leste's relations with Australia are also defined by geopolitical proximity and ongoing dependence, as Australia is Timor-Leste's significantly larger southern neighbour and its main aid provider. Timor-Leste's fragility and dependence was best exemplified by its request for Australia to provide security during the 2006 political crisis (see chapter seven). Australia's interests in Timor-Leste are security related: it is concerned about the security implications of weak states in the neighbourhood. Timor-Leste's weak statehood raises traditional security fears for Australia including the potential of a hostile power getting a foothold in the territory and setting up military bases, as well as transnational crime and security threats, including terrorism, money laundering and refugees. In the 2016 Australian Defence White Paper, one of the three equally-weighted strategic defence interests was in a "secure nearer region", including

Timor-Leste as a main security partner.[66] Australia's main interest is ensuring that a foreign military power seeking influence in smaller, weaker states in the region could not do so "in ways that could challenge the security of our maritime approaches or transnational crime targeting Australian interests".[67] Australia's interventions in Timor-Leste have been largely driven by its own security interests.[68] Australia also has economic objectives as it seeks to guarantee its claim to the Timor Sea oil and gas reserves. A group of security studies experts predicted in 2002 that Timor-Leste would develop friendlier relations with Australia than Indonesia.[69] This did not materialize. Over time, Timor-Leste's bilateral relations with Australia actually deteriorated largely due to its dispute over the resources in the Timor Sea over which both states claim an interest. As chapter eight demonstrates, while good relations with Australia seems like an imperative, since 2010, Timor-Leste has employed a range of strategic choices in the search of a better deal on Timor Sea boundaries and hydrocarbon resources which have both belied its material vulnerabilities and challenged relations with Australia.

Nevertheless, in the first few years of independent statehood, foreign policy was based on a double-barrelled neighbourhood policy of "comprehensive and collective engagement" that appeases Indonesia while shoring up support from Australia and other Western states.[70] Timor-Leste was predicted to produce a "benign" foreign policy as a small state that "does not represent a threat or source of concern to no one".[71] This lack of influence and attention can actually provide greater room for small states to manoeuvre in foreign policy than larger and/or more geopolitically significant states, including middle powers such as Australia and Indonesia. Given Timor-Leste's fragility, the priority would be in establishing the best possible relationships with other state actors. According to Babo-Soares, "[a]s a fledgling and poor country, Timor-Leste developed a 'modest' but 'progressive' approach to foreign policy, defined by an active diplomacy and international cooperation to 'safe-guard the interests of Timor-Leste'".[72] What has resulted, however, could perhaps be more accurately described as an "aspirational foreign policy", as Timor-Leste has increasingly developed an expansive approach that does not necessarily correspond with its limited resources.

The 2011 SDP articulated a more "outward looking"[73] vision of foreign policy than the 2002 NDP, which was much more inwardly focused on how foreign policy could support state-building. The SDP focuses more specifically on positioning Timor-Leste on international relations issues such as conflict, collective security and the global economy. The plan stated:

> As a small nation in a highly strategic geographic location, Timor-Leste's security will depend upon forging strong relationships with our neighbours and friends, making a positive contribution to a stable and peaceful region, and participating in global peacekeeping missions and cooperative international forums and initiatives. Having an outward looking, collaborative approach to foreign policy will encourage our people to take pride in the development of Timor-Leste, attract international investors and generate greater opportunities for economic advancement.[74]

This expansive foreign policy is articulated by Araújo: "In addition to the relationships of diplomacy and friendship that we have been establishing with virtually every country in the world, we are increasingly taking part in international forums, so as to share our challenges and accomplishments."[75] Timor-Leste's aspirational foreign policy has shifted away from inward-looking state- and nation-building purposes to growing its foreign policy reach and consolidating its enhanced presence on the global stage. This highlights the increasing confidence among Timor-Leste's foreign policymakers.[76]

While Timor-Leste recognized the importance of relations with Australia and Indonesia, it has also pursued relations in a number of other spheres in order to hedge against its reliance on its powerful neighbours. Timor-Leste's second objective was pursuing membership of international and regional organizations, particularly the Association of Southeast Asian Nations (ASEAN) and the Community of Portuguese-Language Speaking Countries (CPLP). Timor-Leste has prioritized membership of ASEAN because of its geographical location: the territory was part of ASEAN when East Timor was occupied by Indonesia. From a realist perspective, the particular emphasis on the CPLP is surprising given that it is a language and cultural association with little strategic or economic power. Yet, it reflects the multifaceted influences on Timor-Leste's state-based identity, particularly Portugal and CPLP's support during the resistance, the choice of Portuguese as the official language and the significance of Catholicism within Timorese society.[77] In fact, article 8 (3) of the Constitution demands that Timor-Leste prioritize relations on the basis of the Portuguese language. Importantly, as a document that reflects values and identity, the Constitution's specific mention of Portuguese-speaking nations explicates a cultural bond as a result of the support offered to the East Timorese independence movement (see chapters three and six). Timor-Leste has developed special ties with both its former colonizers, Portugal and Indonesia. In some way this is not unusual: other post-colonial states have also been supported by former occupiers.[78] Even though these relationships were born from power imbalance, and tended to reinforce patterns of dependence, they remained central to the foreign policies of many colonial states. Clapham suggests that with many post-colonial African states, relationships with the former colonizer could be "difficult" and resentful as they carried "a constant reminder of the colonial past, and could never be entirely divorced from a sense of subordination".[79] What is striking is Timor-Leste's eagerness to pursue friendly relationships with its former colonizers for pragmatic and cultural reasons.

The third objective was to establish relationships with a range of countries beyond its immediate neighbours, including in the Pacific, Americas, Northeast Asia and Africa. Timor-Leste's foreign policy emphasizes the importance of bilateralism and it has established diplomatic relations with more than 100 states.[80] The sixth government reaffirmed the "constitutional principle of having friendly relations with all countries in the world, regardless of their size, location or ideology".[81] A security report written in 2002 anticipated that there would be three key building blocks in terms of Timor-Leste's bilateral and multilateral relationships: Australia and Indonesia, ASEAN states and Portuguese-speaking states.[82] As it has developed, however, Timor-Leste's foreign policy operates primarily in six key relational circles:

1. Indonesia and Australia;
2. ASEAN states;
3. Portuguese-speaking states;
4. Pacific Island states
5. China and the United States
6. The global south (i.e. g7+ countries).

Timor-Leste's interactions within these circles reflect its efforts to diversify allegiances and partnerships for the purposes of avoiding dependence on any one state or group.[83] Alongside those listed above,

Timor-Leste emphasizes cooperation with the United States, China, Japan, South Korea, the European Union (EU), and friends in Africa.[84] In 2002, Ramos-Horta stated that China was the new state's "closest possible ally", offering the history of China's recognition of the republic created in 1975 as a reason for this closeness (see chapter ten).[85] The SDP also identified three "special relationships" with New Zealand, Cuba and Ireland.[86] Cuba, in particular, has shown Timor-Leste "great solidarity", and been a significant donor of medical aid through the delivery of doctors and scholarships, as well as contributing to eradicating illiteracy.[87] A special mention was also made of Timor-Leste's relationship with the Vatican, reflecting Timor-Leste's close cultural association with the Roman Catholic Church.[88]

In terms of bilateral relationships, the SDP highlighted Timor-Leste's aspirational foreign policy as it promised at least thirty international embassies, primarily in Asia-Pacific and "proportional representation" in America, Africa and Europe by 2030. According to Timor-Leste's 2016 state budget papers, over US$7 million was allocated to maintaining foreign embassies, consulates and permanent missions, plus over US$13 million in salaries in the Ministry of Foreign Affairs and Cooperation.[89] In 2016, US$6 million was also allocated to purchasing a building for its embassy in Singapore.[90] Timor-Leste has embassies in all ASEAN states and three other major Asian states: Japan, South Korea and China. It also has embassies in four CPLP states: Portugal, Brazil, Angola and Mozambique. Also included are the Vatican, Australia, New Zealand, South Africa, the EU, the United States and the United Kingdom. Additionally, Timor-Leste funds consulates in Denpasar, Kupang, Sydney, Darwin and Atambua, and permanent missions in New York, Geneva and CPLP/UNESCO. Overall, the 2016 state budget allocated US$26,375,000 to the Ministry of Foreign Affairs and Cooperation, more than the Ministry of Agriculture, even though the majority of Timorese citizens rely upon subsistence farming.[91] This again demonstrates the ways in which Timor-Leste has become more ambitious and its vision of international affairs has looked beyond its immediate neighbourhood and the CPLP states.[92] Importantly, Timor-Leste has also increasingly sought leadership roles in the international community, including becoming a founding member of the g7+ grouping of fragile and conflict-affected countries (see chapter seven).

International Citizenship: Timor-Leste at the United Nations

"International citizenship" refers to the nature of states as members of an international community.[93] The concept seeks to understand how states act as citizens with rights and responsibilities, and how they behave in reference to the overarching norms and values espoused by the international community. The architect of "good international citizenship", Gareth Evans, described it as "the area of foreign policy in which community values most influence the pursuit of national interests".[94] States' interests in international citizenship are distinct from traditional concepts of national interest and reflect "purposes beyond" the nation.[95] The values of the international community generally concern a belief in multilateralism and collective security, support for human rights, democracy and poverty alleviation, and defending the so-called "global rules-based order".[96] As part of its international citizenship, Timor-Leste has promised to: establish relations of friendship and cooperation; settle conflicts peacefully; pursue disarmament; support collective security; and create "a new international economic order" to ensure global peace and justice.[97]

Prior to Timor-Leste's independence, the person who would go on to be the principal architect of Timor-Leste's foreign policy approach, José Ramos-Horta, articulated a foreign policy vision for Timor-Leste that emphasized key principles of international citizenship.[98] According to Babo Soares, having Ramos-Horta as a leading thinker "generated a high profile" for Timor-Leste in diplomatic circles. In advocating for Timorese independence, Ramos-Horta espoused an agenda of peace, promising that an East Timorese state would follow a Costa Rican model of eschewing a standing army. It would work towards the "total demilitarisation of the entire East Asia and Pacific regions", establish a "Zone of Peace" around East Timor, and would submit to all international human rights treaties for ratification. These pre-independence declarations indicate the use of international discourses of peace and human rights to support Timor-Leste's statehood claims, essentially committing the future state to good international citizenship and demonstrating deference to the legal order that had provided Timor-Leste's rights to self-determination.

Timor-Leste's history at the UN and other international fora during the independence movement informed its approach to multilateralism and good international citizenship. Timor-Leste's international diplomacy preceded its achievement of independence as diplomacy and international solidarity were important tools of the resistance.[99] The SDP, for example, presents the independence movement as the basis for Timor-Leste's international diplomacy:

> Since the beginning of our struggle for independence, Timor-Leste has had a significant impact well above our size in the international arena through the efforts of a handful of extraordinarily gifted statesmen and women. These courageous individuals were engaged in the international arena pursuing the goal of a free and independent State of Timor-Leste. The embryonic diplomatic service we established in 2001 drew upon the experience of these people... it was through the United Nations that we were able to resolve our struggle for independence.[100]

Former President Taur Matan Ruak highlighted that the newly-established Timor-Leste capitalized on "resistance diplomacy", which had affirmed Timor-Leste's identity on the global stage.[101] Politician Agio Pereira also suggested that Timor-Leste's leaders have "a unique and keen understanding of the UN and the international community... Timor-Leste takes seriously its role as an international citizen and strives to be a good one, given our singular experience."[102] These statements signal both the importance of the solidarity movement in informing Timor-Leste's approach to foreign policy as an independent state, and the optimistic sense that its influence is disproportionate to its small size.

Timor-Leste's Constitution forms the basis for Timor-Leste's engagements with the global normative order, including the UN, international law and regimes. The context of international state-building was important for ensuring that the Constitution would commit Timor-Leste to guaranteeing human rights and abiding by international law, consequently contributing to the document that guides Timor-Leste's foreign policy.[103] Ramos-Horta asserts that the "very liberal and humanist Constitution" is one of the most progressive in the world.[104] Pereira also proudly presents the Constitution as

> one of the finest examples of liberal constitutions in the world. It is a constitution that the people take pride in. The respect for law and human decency is enshrined in the constitution and the objectives of the state are in accord with the most valued principles of the UN.[105]

Ideas that human rights norms are "imposed" upon developing states tend to neglect the agency of representatives within those states, and the ways in which developing states use human rights discourses in order to establish regime legitimacy in international relations. In Timor-Leste's case, the independence movement linked its resistance struggle to human rights, a process that has been important in forming Timor-Leste's state-based identity as a liberal-democratic state that conforms to international rule of law (see chapter four).

Timor-Leste promotes the rules-based architecture because it supports sovereignty.[106] As a small state, Timor-Leste relies upon the principles of multilateralism and collective security to defend national interests against potential aggressors. Collective security refers to the principle that a violation of the sovereignty of one state is a violation for all states. Both the SDP and the programme of the sixth government emphasized multilateralism and the rules-based order for Timor-Leste's foreign policy. They emphasized the UN General Assembly and other relevant intergovernmental organizations that seek to protect "universal principles in terms of peoples and states living together, such as human rights and democracy, environment, the fight against international terrorism, other transnational crimes and crimes against humanity".[107] As Thorhallsson argues, "[s]mall states, like other states, aspire to, and achieve UN membership in order to receive official approval and international recognition of their independence and sovereignty, particularly in instances of decolonization".[108] The UN as a guarantor of sovereignty through collective security is thus perceived to be crucial to the interests of small, weak and new states.

Small state UN diplomacy faces challenges such as limited resources, difficulties accessing and negotiating vast amounts of information and smaller delegation sizes. Timor-Leste, for example, had just three diplomats in its UN mission in 2014. The United States, in contrast, had over 150 officials.[109] This presents challenges for small states in terms of being across the extensive set of issues that the UN must negotiate. Nevertheless, multilateral forums can provide small states an opportunity to play an international role that is disproportionate to size.[110] This can be enhanced by the formation of blocs and alliances that defend and promote shared interests. The opportunities to build allegiances, lobby particular interests and cooperate on issues in the UN make it attractive to small states.[111] Timor-Leste, for example, is a member of the Alliance of Small Island

States (AOSIS), which strives to advance the special interests of vulnerable small island states on issues such as climate change.[112] The AOSIS has been cited as effective negotiators on climate change issues, and has influenced the formation of the global development agenda, including policies such as the Sustainable Development Goals (SDG).[113] Timor-Leste is also a member of the Small Island Developing States (SIDS), a special unit within the UN Secretariat Division for Sustainable Development, and the G77, among a range of other informal coalitions that seek to promote common interests.

Like other small states, Timor-Leste is committed to preservation and promotion of world peace and the prevention of the use of force in conflict resolution, fundamental principles reflected in the Non-Aligned Movement (NAM).[114] Timor-Leste became a member of NAM in February 2003.[115] This Cold War relic promotes independent foreign policies for states not aligned with any major bloc or military alliance, and seeks to enhance international security by advocating for more inclusive and democratic systems of collective decision-making.[116] This grouping of 120 developing states coalesces around principles of national independence, anti-imperialism, defence of self-determination, disarmament and a restructuring of the economic order. At the 17th Non-Aligned Summit, Timorese Foreign Minister Hernâni Coelho emphasized the importance of maintaining political independence. He was reported as saying:

> [m]any of the new NAM members are free and independent countries which were former colonies of Western powers. However, our work is not finished. We are still facing the challenges of our founders and we must keep alive the spirit of the movement and improve solidarity between each other.[117]

The interesting point here is that independence has not automatically freed Timor-Leste from the bonds of colonialism. These non-alignment narratives can be viewed as a form of "soft idealism" as they reveal the normative elements of Timor-Leste's foreign policy discourse.

While identity projection through discourses reflects particular norms and values, it is important to question whether foreign policy behaviours conform to the rhetoric of state leaders. This next section analyses Timor-Leste's voting record at the United Nations General Assembly (UNGA) based on a data set compiled that included every successful resolution that required a vote from the 64th session (2009) to the 70th session (2015).[118] This timeframe was selected because during the 54th to 64th sessions, Timor-Leste did not cast a vote for around one-third of the time, reflecting the challenges that small states face in developing national positions on the range of UNGA resolutions and being available to vote on all resolutions.[119] Only a small number of resolutions are voted upon each year. These "roll-call" votes pertain to controversial, highly politicized issues. The data set recorded the votes of the following states and regional blocs: Timor-Leste, Australia, the United States, all ASEAN states, all CPLP states, New Zealand, Canada and key EU states. The aim is to consider how Timor-Leste votes in relation to other voting blocs, and how this might contribute to identity formation in the global normative order. Importantly, these "blocs" are often not unified. While some small states are beholden to others in UN voting (i.e. the Marshall Islands, Palau and Micronesia are committed to consulting the United States on foreign affairs), the analysis suggests that Timor-Leste has pursued an independent policy on voting in the UN.[120] Timor-Leste has been "sensitive" to its neighbour's views, making "every effort to harmonise our foreign and security policies with those of our ASEAN neighbours" and not deviating from the ASEAN view when there is a consensus.[121] However, Timor-Leste has also been responsive to some of the human rights issues favoured by Western states.

A number of patterns are clear in the voting record data. First, Timor-Leste is inclined to vote in favour of resolutions. In 2015, for example, of the 74 resolutions that passed Timor-Leste voted in favour of 68. Of the remaining resolutions, Timor-Leste recorded five non-votes, and one abstention. In over 400 resolutions over the time period, Timor-Leste recorded only two dissenting votes, both on "combating defamation of religion".[122] In this, Timor-Leste voted against ASEAN and China, and with Western states, including Portugal, Australia, the United States, New Zealand and Canada. Critics of this resolution, including human rights groups, argue that it is essentially an "international blasphemy law".[123] This resolution reveals splits between the Western bloc and some developing and Islamic states. The overarching pattern is that Timor-Leste is more likely to vote yes (when it votes). Philippines, Indonesia, Singapore and CPLP states (except Portugal) also had either no or very few (under 15) dissenting votes. In contrast, China had 25 dissenting votes, Portugal 81, Australia 142 and the United States over 200, demonstrating that Timor-Leste — like many post-colonial developing states that comprise the UNGA — are more amenable to passing resolutions than more powerful and/or developed states. The correspondence between Timor-Leste and other states depends on the issue; for example, Timor-Leste often votes against Western states on resolutions relating to "the right to development", "promotion of a democratic and equitable international order" and "towards a New International Economic Order". The analysis below provides a brief overview of voting patterns relating to three global issues that emerge in UNGA voting: the death penalty, nuclear proliferation and self-determination.

On the first issue, Timor-Leste's Constitution prohibits the death penalty, which stands in contrast with some ASEAN states that employ the death penalty and support its use in the international arena. On the three resolutions concerning a moratorium on the death penalty, Timor-Leste voted yes alongside Australia, New Zealand, Canada, CPLP and Western European states. This was a point of contrast between Timor-Leste and ASEAN states, which split across yes, no and abstain, and China shifted between no and abstain. This fits with the profile of Southeast Asian states regarding their use of the death penalty. Cambodia, Timor-Leste, and the Philippines are fully abolitionist in law and practice; Brunei, Laos, Myanmar do not employ the death penalty in practice; and Thailand has an unofficial moratorium in place. Singapore, Malaysia, Vietnam and Indonesia continue to employ the death penalty, albeit with various levels of enthusiasm.[124] On this issue, Timor-Leste voted in alignment with the Western bloc (excluding the United States) and CPLP. The death penalty highlights the diversity of opinion among ASEAN states, therefore the extent to which Timor-Leste could align its vote with ASEAN (as a cohesive bloc) on this issue is irrelevant.

On the issue of nuclear disarmament, Timor-Leste generally votes in favour. From 2010 to 2015, of the 105 relevant resolutions passed, Timor-Leste voted in favour of 99 (Timor-Leste recorded a non-vote for all related resolutions in 2009). The voting records of most other states was much more mixed: Portugal, China, Europe and Australia generally voted against, or abstained, in a number of relevant resolutions each year. Timor-Leste had the highest degree of correspondence in voting patterns among the CPLP states (with the exception of Portugal) and most of the ASEAN states, particularly the

Philippines, Singapore and Malaysia. In 2015, for example, Timor-Leste voted in favour of all 27 resolutions promoting disarmament and weapons restrictions. It differed only once from Indonesia, Laos, Cambodia and Brazil. This is in contrast with Portugal, which voted no or abstained for more than half the number of votes. The voting record demonstrates a general tendency to side against weapons proliferation. This is in line with foreign policy declarations, but also reflects Timor-Leste's status as a small state which like to be concerned about the capacities of larger, wealthier states to develop weapons for security reasons. It is thus little surprise that it is the CPLP states, mostly small post-colonial developing states, that align most closely with Timor-Leste's vote.

Timor-Leste's actions at the UN have broadly supported principles of self-determination. Timor-Leste formally recognized Kosovo as an independent state in 2012, and voted in favour of Kosovo's independence at the 63rd session of the UNGA. It has voted yes to all but one of the 37 roll-call votes concerning non-self-governing territories, decolonization and independence from 2009 to 2015. Timor-Leste's voting practices here largely corresponded with ASEAN and CPLP states, as well as China and Australia. On these issues European states, Portugal, the United Kingdom and the United States are split. However, Timor-Leste's voting practices on resolutions concerning Palestine have been mixed. Resolutions are generally bundled into two groups: at the beginning of each session there are roughly six resolutions pertaining to Palestine's self-determination rights. Later, there is another bloc of around nine resolutions that pass on refugees, human rights and settlements. In the first round from 2009 to 2015, Timor-Leste has tended to vote in favour of resolutions supporting Palestine. Across 44 resolutions, Timor-Leste voted 25 times in favour (2009 was an anomaly; there were 6 absent votes). Since 2011, Timor-Leste's voting record became more consistent: it tended to abstain in the two resolutions supporting the inalienable rights of Palestine (except in 2016), but vote in favour of the less contentious resolutions. The data demonstrates that Timor-Leste was more willing to favour resolutions than European states including Portugal. In contrast, the United States and Canada consistently dissented, and Australia is generally split between no and abstaining, which reflects close ties to Israel. Timor-Leste was less inclined to favour stronger resolutions against Israel than other post-colonial states: for example, CPLP states mostly voted yes, and China and ASEAN voted yes to all but one. Overall, Timor-Leste tended to vote with China and the developing CPLP and ASEAN states.

In the second bundle of Palestine votes from 2009–15, Timor-Leste almost consistently supported the resolutions, along with ASEAN, China and CPLP countries. Australia tended to be divided across voting yes, no or abstaining, and Canada and the United States, along with Israel, were the most reluctant to approve the resolutions. Across 65 resolutions in seven years, Timor-Leste voted in favour of all but seven. Each year Timor-Leste abstained from resolutions that establish the UN special committee to investigate Israeli practices affecting Palestinian human rights. Most members of the NAM tend to vote in favour of the special committee, whereas Timor-Leste's voting record replicates the European states. As for Timor-Leste's commitment to liberation movements, the UN voting record on Palestine suggests that Timor-Leste's support is not unequivocal, however has been mostly in favour of resolutions supporting self-determination and human rights.

The National Constitution reflects the history of the independence movement as it commits the state to "extending solidarity" to peoples struggling for self-determination, and providing political asylum to persecuted members of liberation movements.[125] In practice, this support for self-determination has manifested in different ways according to the context as pragmatic realist interests rub against normative principles. Timor-Leste supports the Saharawi Republic in Western Sahara and has shown its recognition of independence by engaging with the interim government.[126] At the UN Timor-Leste's representatives have advocated on behalf of the Western Saharan struggle for self-determination, drawing parallels with Timor-Leste's own resistance movement.[127]

This support sits in contrast with West Papua. According to leaders, Western Sahara is similar to East Timor's situation prior to independence whereas West Papua is different. Ramos-Horta, for instance, insists that "[s]olutions for the betterment of the people of West Papua, ending any human rights abuses, economic, social exclusion of West Papuans have to be realised in the context of Indonesian sovereignty".[128] This argument relies upon defence of colonial boundaries: whereas West Papua was a part of the Dutch sphere of influence, Timor-Leste was administered by Portugal, which gave it particular rights to self-determination under international law as a non-self-governing territory (see chapter two). This view privileges international legal principles of self-determination but brushes aside human rights abuses in the territory. As chapter three argued, human rights violations alongside principles of self-determination provided an important defence of East Timor's rights to independence. Timor-Leste's view is that Indonesia should find a peaceful solution on West Papua. This is a similar stance to the one taken by Australia to West Papua, and to East Timor when it was occupied by Indonesia.

In an act of "Melanesian solidarity", seven small Pacific Island states spoke out for West Papua in UNGA debates in 2016, and the Pacific Island Coalition on West Papua was formed to support its independence. Timor-Leste's refusal to support West Papua is a point of contrast from its Pacific Island neighbours, and reflects its pragmatic realist prioritization of its relationship with Indonesia, a foreign policy orientation that contributed to the denial of East Timor's independence for over two decades (see chapters three and nine). This is not the only example of where realist calculations have overridden support for the principle of self-determination. On the subject of Taiwanese independence, for example, Timor-Leste "firmly" adheres to a One China policy in order to appease the more powerful China (see chapter ten).[129]

In summary, Timor-Leste's engagement with particular global issues at the UN and more broadly conform to a diversified foreign policy approach as Timor-Leste does not consistently align with either Western or ASEAN states. The tendency to vote in favour of most resolutions is also suggestive of a lack of clear policy discernment that may reflect limited human resource capabilities. Unlike some other small Pacific states that are allied to the United States, such as Micronesia and Palau, Timor-Leste has not compromised its vote in the UN in order to appease a more powerful alliance partner or secure aid. However, the issue of self-determination also demonstrates that Timor-Leste is not always principled, but that certain imperatives — such as friendly relations with Indonesia — may provoke a more "realist", interest-led approach, even when the Constitution obliges Timor-Leste to stand in solidarity with independence movements.

Timor-Leste's Humanitarianism and Democracy Promotion

The final section of this chapter examines Timor-Leste's activities in providing humanitarian assistance and contributing peacekeepers to humanitarian missions in other regions. The SDP envisages that by 2020 "Timor-Leste will be recognised as a model and reference on regional conflict resolution and peace building" and by 2030 "Timor-Leste will have assumed a position of global peacemaker and mediator" with security apparatuses capable of being "fully utilised" by the UN.[130] This ambition is also integrated within the national defence force agenda (see chapter seven). In 2011, Ramos-Horta asserted that "Timor-Leste police officers have served and are serving with the United Nations in the Balkans and Africa."[131] He also stated that Timor-Leste army engineers were also scheduled for deployment in a peacebuilding mission in Lebanon.[132]

Timor-Leste also contributes foreign aid to states, many of whom are far wealthier than Timor-Leste. In 2011, Ramos-Horta stated that: "[a]s poor as we are, we have nevertheless provided humanitarian assistance to countries, rich and poor, afflicted by natural calamities. We have provided in cash support to victims of natural disasters in Indonesia, Myanmar, China, Madeira Islands (Portugal), Haiti, Brazil and Australia, totalling close to US$5 million in the last three years."[133] In 2004, Timor-Leste provided humanitarian assistance to communities in Indonesia affected by the Boxing Day Tsunami and this was viewed as an important step in reconciliation between the two states.[134] The 2016 state budget allocated US$1.5 million to support elections in São Tomé and Príncipe.[135] In August 2016, Timor-Leste's government donated 1.25 million euros to support Portugal to assist in fighting bush fires and 750 thousand euros for humanitarian relief.[136] This is a considerable amount of money, considering the entire 2016 state budget was less than US$2 billion, and over two thirds of the population live on less than US$2 a day.[137] This was also not the first time Timor-Leste had provided aid to its much wealthier former colonizer: in 2013, 740,000 euros was donated to help Portugal repair fire damage.[138] This was reported in the Portuguese press as reflecting Timor-Leste's affection for Portugal.[139]

Peacekeeping contributions reflect an aspirational foreign policy as they assist in developing Timor-Leste's image as a "successful" liberal-democratic state. Timor-Leste has been active in the international democracy-building. According to Araújo, it provided "decisive support to the elections and the restoration of constitutional order in Guinea-Bissau".[140] At the 2013 Bali Democracy Forum, Gusmão announced that he and Mari Alkatiri visited Guinea-Bissau with the intention of determining if there was anything they could do to assist putting it back on the path to democracy. According to Gusmão, Timor-Leste "wanted to show" how it has "overcome a bitter history of animosity to work together for the good of our people in the context of a robust democracy".[141] Part of securing the state is establishing a legitimate state identity to assist in avoiding foreign intervention. An interesting element of Timor-Leste's national strategic study — *Force 2020* — is the importance of "nation-branding strategies". It argues that "Timor-Leste must create, and continue to develop, new elements of national identity that project its image to the world", one of which is to "contribute, by means of the participation of the Armed Forces, in peacekeeping missions of the UN and other international bodies".[142] Timor-Leste's efforts at democracy promotion can be interpreted as a strategy of identity projection directed to the international community.

One interpretation for this generosity again links back to a sense of international responsibilities and citizenship. Its own independence, after all, was in part due to the support of small, weak states in the UN and international civil society. Hence, Timor-Leste's leaders reflect upon the "generosity of the many nations around the world" that supported the development of its statehood.[143] However, it is also possible to interpret these actions as part of Timor-Leste's aspirational foreign policy. These gestures fit with Timor-Leste's narratives relating to its move from fragility to resilience, such that Timor-Leste can be viewed as an aid donor rather than recipient. Part of this aspirational foreign policy also demonstrates an interest in becoming a leader among developing states. In 2013, Gusmão argued: "We celebrated the 11-year anniversary of the Restoration of our Independence and our nation is now moving towards greater international engagement, as we look beyond our shores to how we can contribute to the global community."[144] Its leadership of the g7+ group of eighteen fragile and conflict affected nations, according to Gusmão, reflects Timor-Leste's "responsibility to support other fragile nations of the world".[145] This theme is picked up in the next chapter.

While Timor-Leste's leaders seek to defend its democratic credibility abroad, questions emerged about Timor-Leste's democratic credentials in the domestic sphere. This includes criticisms of the sacking of Portuguese judges in 2014, attempts to restrict media and journalistic freedoms by using punitive defamation laws, and the emergence of a National Unity government in 2015, formed under the doctrine of "Consensus Democracy", which discouraged opposition in favour of "stability".[146] Former President Taur Matan Ruak argued that Timor-Leste's highly centralized system had created an autocratic government under the guise of "national unity" that privileges and consolidates the power of wealthy elites. He argued that the "family and friends of brother Xanana and brother Mari have benefited both from state contracts".[147]

Importantly, the emphasis that was placed on "national values" in the Consensus Democracy narrative can be interpreted as a critique of state-building and "imposed" institutions, and reflects a determination of elites to reassert Timorese sovereignty and minimize the interference of the international community.[148] This was not necessarily new. According to Feijó, Ramos-Horta's defeat in the first round of the 2012 presidential elections "has been read as a signal of the Timorese fatigue with an internationally driven agenda, and the two candidates that made it to the final round converged in praising the Timorese own values and the need to bring them to a more prominent place in the political arena".[149] This highlights the particular significance of Ramos-Horta in initially shaping Timor-Leste's foreign engagements, particularly its internationalist approach to global issues such as human rights, collective security and self-determination. After 2015, Timorese leaders defended its National Unity regime as a legitimate, albeit culturally specific form of Timorese-style democracy.[150] This reflects the importance of identity-building and image projection as a way of bolstering support for statehood within the international community. By the end of 2017, this unity among key elites had broken down, revealing the fragility of Timor-Leste's domestic political order.

Conclusion

Since 2002, Timor-Leste has become an increasingly confident and vocal foreign policy actor.[151] Critics have pointed out that the government's "grand schemes" do not account for Timor-Leste's size or development status, and there has not been "a clear and precise framework through which Timorese foreign policy could be easily categorized or evaluated".[152] While arguably, a range of factors and political dynamics contribute to the short-, mid- and long-term goals and activities of all foreign policy actors, Timor-Leste's approach and orientation lacks consistency. This book attempts to make sense of this inchoate approach by using the post-colonial security dilemma lens. That Timor-Leste seeks an "independent" foreign policy and to portray itself with greater foreign policy maturity and international leadership is part of the aspirational state-based identity. Relations reflect both the pragmatic realities of international donorship and geostrategic positioning (i.e. good relations with Indonesia and Australia) as well as the cultural and historical influences that established Timor-Leste's "unique" identity. The sixth government was aware of the problem of limited personnel, and made plans to scale back Timor-Leste's diplomatic presence.[153] It remains to be seen what the future governments will prioritize in foreign policy.

Future chapters highlight how identity and history have shaped Timor-Leste's foreign policy objectives which rely on realist and idealist approaches depending on specific issues and the actors involved. For example, chapters seven and nine highlight the "realist" underpinnings of Timor-Leste's military build-up and pragmatic friendship with its neighbour Indonesia. In contrast, chapter six examines the cooperative and interdependent nature of Timor-Leste's foreign policy through its intergovernmental engagements. Indeed, one of the emerging features of Timor-Leste as an international actor is the adoption, at times, of an "activist foreign policy" approach. Chapter eight indicates that Timor-Leste's approach on the Timor Sea issue has been driven by an optimistic approach to Australia that contrasts its pragmatic realist approach to Indonesia. The next chapter examines how Timor-Leste has sought to hedge against its dependence on its larger neighbours by prioritizing regional associations.

NOTES

1. David Willis, "Timor-Leste's Complex Geopolitics: The Local, the Regional and the Global", in *Timor-Leste: The Local, the Regional and the Global*, edited by Sarah Smith, Nuno Canas Mendes, Antero B. da Silva, Alarico da Costa

Ximenes, Clinton Fernandes and Michael Leach, p. 238 (Melbourne: Swinburne University Press, 2016).
2. Christopher Clapham, *Africa and the International System: The Politics of State Survival* (Cambridge: Cambridge University Press, October 2009), p. 6.
3. Xanana Gusmão, "Timor-Leste's Role and Future in a Rising Asia Pacific", Singapore, 4 June 2013.
4. República Democrática de Timor-Leste (RDTL), *Strategic Development Plan* (Dili: Government of Timor-Leste, 2011).
5. Clapham, *Africa and the International System*, 11.
6. Mohammad Ayoob, *The Third World Security Predicament: State-Making, Regional Conflict, and the International System*, p. 4 (Boulder: Lynne Rienner, 1995).
7. Ibid., p. 3.
8. Ibid., pp. 3-4.
9. Michael Leifer, *Singapore's Foreign Policy: Coping with Vulnerability*, p. 4 (London: Routledge, 2000).
10. Ibid., p. 27.
11. Ibid., p. 23.
12. Ganesan, "Singapore: Realist cum Trading State", in *Asian Security Practice: Material and Ideational Influences*, edited by Muthiah Alagappa, p. 579 (California: Stanford University Press, 1998).
13. Cited in ibid., p. 579.
14. See Leifer, *Singapore's Foreign Policy*, p. 5.
15. Ganesan, "Singapore: Realist cum Trading State", p. 579.
16. Leifer, *Singapore's Foreign Policy*, p. 1.
17. Ibid., p. 6.
18. Amitav Acharya, "Regionalism and Regime Security in the Third World: Comparing the Origins of the ASEAN and the GCC". In *The Insecurity Dilemma: National Security of Third World States*, p. 144 (Boulder: Lynne Rienner, 1992).
19. Clapham, *Africa and the International System*, p. 17.
20. Ibid., p. 17.
21. Jennifer Mitzen, "Ontological Security in World Politics: State Identity and the Security Dilemma", *European Journal of International Relations* 12, no. 3 (2006): 342.
22. Leifer, *Singapore's Foreign Policy*, p. 15.
23. Constituent Assembly, *Constitution of the Democratic Republic of Timor-Leste*, article 8 (Dili: Democratic Republic of Timor-Leste, 2002).
24. RTDL, *Strategic Development Plan*, p. 171.
25. RDTL, "Program of the Sixth Constitutional Government 2015–2017" (Dili: Government of the Democratic Republic of Timor-Leste, 6 March 2015).
26. See Robin Ramcharan, "ASEAN and Non-Interference: A Principle Maintained", *Contemporary Southeast Asia* 22, no. 1 (2000): 60.

27. Ibid.
28. Organisation of African Unity, "Constitutive Act of the African Union", Lome, Togo, 11 July 2000; Roland Burke, *Decolonization and the Evolution of International Human Rights* (Philadelphia: University of Pennsylvania, 2010).
29. Erik Ringmar, "Introduction: The International Politics of Recognition", in *The International Politics of Recognition*, edited by Thomas Lindemann and Erik Ringmar, p. 11 (Boulder: Paradigm Publishers, 2014); Brian Greenhill, "Recognition and Collective Identity Formation in International Relations", *European Journal of International Relations* 14, no. 2 (2008): 344.
30. Evan Potter, "Canada and the New Diplomacy", *International Journal* 58, no. 1 (2002/3): 44.
31. Anne Clunan, *The Social Construction of Russia's Resurgence*, pp. 3–4 (Baltimore: The Johns Hopkins University Press, 2009).
32. Ibid., pp. 8–9.
33. Michael Leach, "The Politics of History in Timor-Leste", in *A New Era? Timor-Leste After the UN*, edited by Sue Ingram, Lia Kent and Andrew McWilliam, p. 41 (Canberra: Australian National University Press, 2015). For more on the internal dynamics of nation-building, see Michael Leach, *Nation Building and National Identity in Timor-Leste* (Oxon: Routledge, 2017).
34. Xanana Gusmão, "Sharing Experiences", Lecture by His Excellency the Prime Minister of the Democratic Republic of Timor-Leste Kay Rala Xanana Gusmão, Juba, South Sudan, 2 December 2013.
35. Xanana Gusmão, "Peace Building and State Building: From Fragility to Resilience", Lecture by His Excellency the Prime Minister of the Democratic Republic of Timor-Leste Kay Rala Xanana Gusmão at the Lee Kuan Yew School of Public Policy at the National University of Singapore, Dili, 18 September 2013.
36. Xanana Gusmão, "Harnessing National Resource Wealth for Inclusive Growth and Economic Development", Keynote Address by His Excellency the Prime Minister Kay Rala Xanana Gusmão, Dili, 4 June 2013.
37. Rui Araújo, "Speech by His Excellency the Prime Minister of the Democratic Republic of Timor-Leste at the Dinner Celebrating the 40th Anniversary of the Proclamation of Independence and the 500 Years of the Interaction between Two Civilisations: Timor-Leste and Portugal and the Affirmation of the Timorese Identity", Oecusse, Timor-Leste, 27 November 2015.
38. Gusmão, "Peace Building and State Building: From Fragility to Resilience".
39. Rui Araújo, "Keynote Speech by His Excellency the Prime Minister Dr Rui Maria de Araújo at the Inaugural Meeting of the Pacific Island Regional Initiative of the Alliance for Financial Inclusion", Dili, 7 May 2015; Xanana Gusmão, "Peace and Capable Institutions as Stand-alone Goals in the

post-2015 Development Agenda", Keynote Address by His Excellency the Prime Minister Kay Rala Xanana Gusmão at the High-Level Ministerial Lunch Meeting, New York, 22 September 2014.
40. Xanana Gusmão, Address by His Excellency the Prime Minister Kay Rala Xanana Gusmão to the 2014 Timor-Leste Development Partners' Meeting, Dili, 25 July 2014; Gusmão, "Peace Building and State Building: From Fragility to Resilience".
41. Xanana Gusmão, "Peace, Security and Human Development", Address by His Excellency the Prime Minister Kay Rala Xanana Gusmão on the Occasion of the World Summit 2014, Seoul, 10 August 2014.
42. Gusmão, "Peace Building and State Building: From Fragility to Resilience".
43. See Xanana Gusmão, "State Building: The Timor-Leste Experience in a Southeast Asian Context", Address by His Excellency the Prime Minister Kay Rala Xanana Gusmão at the Vietnam University, Hanoi, Vietnam, 3 September 2013.
44. Pedro Seabra, "The Need for a Reshaped Foreign Policy", in *The Politics of Timor-Leste: Democratic Consolidation After Intervention*, edited by Michael Leach and Damien Kingsbury, p. 145 (Ithaca, NY: Cornell, 2014). See the East Timor Planning Commission, *National Development Plan* (Dili: Planning Commission, May 2002).
45. Dionisio Babo-Soares, "The Future of Timor-Leste's Foreign Policy", in *A Reliable Partner: Strengthening Australia-Timor-Leste Relations*, ASPI Special Report 39, p. 21 (Canberra: Australian Strategic Policy Institute, April 2011).
46. Ibid., p. 23.
47. Ibid., p. 22.
48. See Asian Dvelopment Bank (ADB), "Regional Cooperation and Integration Assessment", *Timor-Leste: Country Partnership Strategy (2016–2020)*, available at <https://www.adb.org/documents/timor-leste-country-partnership-strategy-2016-2020> (accessed 14 February 2017).
49. Seabra, "The Need for a Reshaped Foreign Policy", p. 146
50. East Timor Planning Commission, *National Development Plan*, p. 107.
51. Channel NewsAsia, "EXCLUSIVE: 'We are Friends with Everyone', says Timor Leste's New Prime Minister", 21 March 2015.
52. José Kei Lekke Sousa-Santos, "Acting West, Looking East: Timor-Leste's Growing Engagement with the Pacific Islands Region", in *Regionalism, Security and Cooperation in Oceania*, edited by Rouben Azizian and Carleton Cramer, p. 111 (Honolulu: Asia-Pacific Centre for Security Studies, 2015).
53. Xanana Gusmão, "Timor-Leste and ASEAN: Perspectives and Challenges", Address by His Excellency the Prime Minister and Minister of Defence and Security, Kay Rala Xanana Gusmão, Sabah, Malaysia, 2 April 2014.
54. Gusmão, "Timor-Leste's Role and Future in a Rising Asia Pacific".
55. Willis, "Timor-Leste's Complex Geopolitics", p. 238.

56. Cirilo José Cristóvão, "Emerging Challenges to Small State Security in the Asia-Pacific", 14th Asia Security Summit, The IISS Shangri-La Dialogue, Singapore, 30 May 2015; Willis, "Timor-Leste's Complex Geopolitics", p. 38.
57. Ian Storey, *Southeast Asia and the Rise of China: The Search for Security*, p. 282 (New York: Routledge, 2011).
58. Loro Horta, "Timor-Leste: The Dragon's Newest Friend", *Irasec Discussion Papers* no. 4 (May 2009).
59. Agio Pereira, "The Challenges of Nation-State Building", in *A New Era? Timor-Leste After the UN*, edited by Sue Ingram, Lia Kent and Andrew McWilliam, p. 27 (Canberra: ANU Press, 2015); Storey, *Southeast Asia and the Rise of China*, p. 277.
60. RDTL, "Program of the Sixth Constitutional Government 2015–2017".
61. Anthony Smith, "Constraints and Choices: East Timor as a Foreign Policy Actor", *New Zealand Journal of Asian Studies* 7, no. 1 (June 2005): 17.
62. Miguel Santos Neves, Kusnanto Anggoro, José Amorim Dias, Alan Dupont, Francios Godement, Dato Hassan, Carolina Hernandez, Tim Huxley, Riefqi Muna, Roque Rodrigues, Leonard Sebastian and Kusuma Sntiwongse, *The Security of East Timor in the Regional Context Report*, p. 8 (Lisbon: Institute of Strategic and International Studies, 2002); Sousa-Santos, "Acting West, Looking East", p. 110.
63. Willis, "Timor-Leste's Complex Geopolitics", p. 238.
64. Rebecca Strating, "The Indonesia-Timor-Leste Commission of Truth and Friendship: Enhancing Bilateral Relations at the Expense of Justice", *Contemporary Southeast Asia* 36, no. 2 (2014): 242.
65. Neves et al., *The Security of East Timor in the Regional Context Report*, p. 23.
66. Commonwealth of Australia, *2016 Defence White Paper*, p. 17 (Canberra: Department of Defence, 2016).
67. Ibid., p. 69.
68. Willis, "Timor-Leste's Complex Geopolitics", p. 239.
69. Neves et al., *The Security of East Timor in the Regional Context Report*, p. 8.
70. Smith, "Constraints and Choices", p. 15.
71. Neves et al., *The Security of East Timor in the Regional Context Report*, p. 9.
72. Babo-Soares, "The Future of Timor-Leste's Foreign Policy", pp. 22, 25.
73. RDTL, *Strategic Development Plan*, p. 171.
74. Ibid.
75. Rui Araújo, "Speech by His Excellency the Prime Minister on the Occasion of the Swearing-In of the Sixth Constitutional Government", Lahane Palace, Dili, 6 February 2015.
76. Selver Sahin, "Timor-Leste: A More Confident or Overconfident Foreign Policy Actor?" in *Southeast Asian Affairs 2012*, edited by Daljit Singh and Pushpa Thambipillai, pp. 341–58 (Singapore: Institute of Southeast Asian Studies, 2012).

77. See Nuno Canas Mendes, *Multidimensionalidade da Construção identitária de Timor-Leste* (Lisbon: ISCSP, 2005).
78. Clapham, *Africa and the International System*, p. 17.
79. Ibid., pp. 77, 80.
80. ADB, "Regional Cooperation and Integration Assessment".
81. RDTL, "Program of the Sixth Constitutional Government 2015–2017".
82. Neves et al., *The Security of East Timor in the Regional Context Report*, p. 32.
83. RDTL, *Strategic Concept for Defence and National Security* (Dili: Ministry of Defence, 2016).
84. Araújo, *Swearing-In of the Sixth Constitutional Government*.
85. Jill Jolliffe, "East Timor says China is its Closest Ally", *The Sydney Morning Herald*, 11 July 2002.
86. RDTL, *Strategic Development Plan*, p. 174.
87. Ibid., p. 174.
88. RDTL, "Program of the Sixth Constitutional Government 2015–2017".
89. RDTL Ministry of Finance, *State Budget 2016: Book One* (Dili: Democratic Republic of Timor-Leste, 2016).
90. Ibid., p. 49.
91. Ibid.
92. Sahin, "Timor-Leste"; Seabra, "The Need for a Re-shaped Foreign Policy", p. 145.
93. To be distinguished from a global citizen, which refers to an individual who identifies as part of a global rather than national community.
94. Gareth Evans, "Foreign Policy and Good International Citizenship", 6 March 1990, available at <http://www.gevans.org/speeches/old/1990/060390_fm_fpandgoodinternationalcitizen.pdf> (accessed 26 March 2017).
95. Ibid.
96. RDTL, *Strategic Concept for Defence and National Security*.
97. RDTL, *Strategic Development Plan*, p. 170.
98. Awarded 1996 with Carlos Belo. See Babo-Soares, "The Future of Timor-Leste's Foreign Policy", p. 22.
99. East Timor Planning Commission, *National Development Plan*, pp. 115, 118.
100. RDTL, *Strategic Development Plan*, pp. 170–171
101. Taur Matan Ruak, "State of the Nation", Speech by His Excellency Taur Matan Ruak to the National Parliament, Dili, 20 September 2016.
102. Pereira, "The Challenges of Nation-State-Building", p. 28.
103. United Nations Security Council (UNSC), "Resolution 1272", S/RES/1272, 25 October 1999; José Ramos-Horta, "Why Timor-Leste Should Join ASEAN Now", *East Asia Forum*, 16 May 2011.
104. Ramos-Horta, "Why Timor-Leste Should Join ASEAN Now".

105. Pereira, "The Challenges of Nation-State-Building", pp. 19–20.
106. Rui Araújo, *Remarks by His Excellency the Prime Minister of the Democratic Republic of Timor-Leste Dr Rui de Araújo at the Atlantic Council*, Washington D.C., 21 June 2016.
107. RDTL, "Program of the Sixth Constitutional Government 2015–2017"; RDTL, *Strategic Development Plan*, p. 171.
108. Baldur Thorhallsson, "Small States in the UN Security Council: Means of Influence?" *The Hague Journal of Diplomacy* 7 (2012): 142.
109. Andrea Ó Súilleabháin, *Small States at the United Nations: Diverse Perspectives, Shared Opportunities*, p. 11 (New York: International Peace Institute, May 2014).
110. Ibid., p. 1.
111. Thorhallsson, "Small States in the UN Security Council", p. 159.
112. Alliance of Small Island States (AOSIS), *25 Years of Leadership at the United Nations*, 2015, available at <http://aosis.org/wp-content/uploads/2015/12/AOSIS-BOOKLET-FINAL-11-19-151.pdf> (accessed 14 February 2017).
113. Ó Súilleabháin, *Small States at the United Nations*, p. 9.
114. RDTL, "Program of the Sixth Constitutional Government 2015–2017".
115. Babo-Soares, "The Future of Timor-Leste's Foreign Policy", p. 26.
116. Non-Aligned Movement, "Members of the Non-Aligned Movement", available at <http://www.nam.gov.za/media/040802b.htm> (accessed 14 February 2017).
117. *Xinhua*, "Spotlight: Non-Aligned Movement Takes Stance on UN Reform, Terrorism, Multilateralism", 19 September 2016.
118. All of the data compiled for this data set is available from the United Nations, "General Assembly Resolutions", available at <http://www.un.org/en/sections/documents/general-assembly-resolutions/index.html> (accessed 14 February 2017) and UNGA, "Voting Records", available at <http://www.un.org/en/ga/documents/voting.asp> (accessed 14 February 2017).
119. Diana Panke, *Unequal Actors in Equalising Institutions: Negotiations in the United Nations General Assembly*, p. 77 (London: Palgrave Macmillan, 2013).
120. Ó Súilleabháin, *Small States at the United Nations*, pp. 3–4; Thorhallsson, "Small States in the United Nations Security Council", p. 145.
121. Ramos-Horta, "Why Timor-Leste Should Join ASEAN Now".
122. United Nations General Assembly (UNGA), *Combating Defamation of Religions*, A/RES/64/156, 8 March 2010 and UNGA, *Combating Defamation of Religions*, A/RES/65/224, 11 April 2011.
123. L. Bennett Graham, "No to an International Blasphemy Law", *The Guardian*, 26 March 2010.
124. United Nations Office of the High Commissioner for Human Rights, *Moving Away from the Death Penalty: Lessons in Southeast Asia* (Bangkok: United Nations, 2013).

125. Constituent Assembly, *Constitution of the Democratic Republic of Timor-Leste*; Hilary Charlesworth, "The Constitution of East Timor", *International Journal of Constitutional Law* 1, no. 2 (2003): 330. See also RDTL, *Strategic Concept for Defence and National Security*.
126. Babo-Soares, "The Future of Timor-Leste's Foreign Policy", p. 27.
127. UNGA, "Fourth Committee Approves Five Consensus Texts Reaffirming Inalienable Right to Self-determination and Independence", GA/SPD/482, 10 October 2011; UNGA, "Fourth Committee Approves 20 Texts for General Assembly Action, Passing 4 by Recorded Vote, 16 by Consensus", GA/SPD/612, 10 October 2016.
128. Australian Broadcasting Corporation (ABC), "East Timor's Former President José Ramos Horta says West Papua 'part of Indonesia'", *ABC News*, 23 July 2015; Jolliffe, "East Timor says China is its Closest Ally".
129. José Ramos-Horta, "Address by the Hon. José Ramos Horta to The Lowy Institute for International Policy", Sydney, 29 November 2004; RDTL, "Joint Statement between the People's Republic of China and the Democratic Republic of Timor-Leste on Establishing Comprehensive Partnership of Good-Neighbourly Friendship, Mutual Trust and Mutual Benefit", Minister of State and of the Presidency of the Council of Ministers and Official Spokesperson for the Government of Timor-Leste Press Release, Dili, 14 April 2014.
130. RDTL, *Strategic Development Plan*, p. 175.
131. Ramos-Horta, "Why Timor-Leste Should Join ASEAN Now".
132. Ibid.
133. Ibid.
134. Seabra, "The Need for a Reshaped Foreign Policy", p. 146.
135. RDTL Ministry of Finance, *State Budget 2016: Book One*, p. 49.
136. Jornal de Notícias, "Timor-Leste aprova doação a Portugal de dois milhões de euros para ajuda aos fogos", *Jornal de Notícias*, 10 August 2016.
137. World Bank, "Poverty Headcount Ratio at National Poverty Lines: Timor Leste", available at <http://data.worldbank.org/indicator/SI.POV.NAHC?locations=TL> (accessed 14 February 2017).
138. Bruno Simões, "Timor doa dois milhões de euros a Portugal para ajudar a combater incêndios", *Negocios*, 10 August 2016.
139. Ibid.
140. Araújo, *Swearing-In of the Sixth Constitutional Government*. See also RDTL, *Strategic Concept for Defence and National Security*.
141. Xanana Gusmão, "Consolidating Democracy in a Pluralist Society", Address by His Excellency the Prime Minister Kay Rala Xanana Gusmão on the Occasion of the Bali Democracy Forum, Bali, 7 November 2013.
142. RDTL, *Force 2020*, 2007, p. 14, available at <https://www.locjkt.or.id/Timor_E/pdf/Forca202007.pdf> (accessed 11 February 2017). This includes

projecting national identity in sports, music, arts, industrial brands and the Nobel Peace Prize internationally. In one interesting example, the Timorese football team was banned from the Asian Cup by the Asian Football Confederation for falsifying documents of Brazilian players. See Asian Football Confederation, "Federacao Futebol Timor-Leste Expelled From AFC Asian Cup 2023", available at <http://www.the-afc.com/media/federacao-futebol-timor-leste-expelled-from-afc-asian-cup-2023-34508> (accessed 22 March 2017).
143. Gusmão, "Consolidating Democracy in a Pluralist Society".
144. Gusmão, "Timor-Leste's Role and Future in a Rising Asia Pacific".
145. Gusmão, "Consolidating Democracy in a Pluralist Society".
146. Rui Graça Feijó, "Challenges to the Consolidation of Democracy", in *A New Era? Timor-Leste After the UN*, edited by Sue Ingram, Lia Kent and Andrew McWilliam, p. 62 (Canberra: ANU Press, 2015); United Nations Office of the Commissioner of Human Rights, "UN Human Rights Expert Urges Timor-Leste to Reconsider Dismissal of International Judges and Prosecutors", 25 November 2014; Paul Cleary, "E Timor Civil Society on Skid Row: President", *The Australian*, 12 March 2016; Jose Belo, "East Timor Elites Try to Muzzle Media", *Crikey*, 23 June 2014.
147. Cleary, "E Timor Civil Society on Skid Row".
148. Feijó, "Challenges to the Consolidation of Democracy", p. 62.
149. Ibid., p. 61.
150. Agio Pereira, "2015 Timor-Leste Update: Keynote Speech by His Excellency Agio Pereira, Minister of State and of the Presidency of the Council of Ministers, Government of Timor-Leste", Australian National University, Canberra, 19 November 2015.
151. Sahin, "Timor-Leste", p. 341.
152. Seabra, "The Need for a Reshaped Foreign Policy", pp. 155, 160.
153. RDTL, "Program of the Sixth Constitutional Government 2015–2017".

6

Identity Hedging: Timor-Leste's Engagement with Intergovernmental Organizations

As a small new state, one of Timor-Leste's initial foreign policy priorities was to strategically position itself within the international community. The term "hedging" typically refers to ways small and medium states employ policies of balancing and engagement in their relations with powerful states. Hedging acts as an "insurance policy" as states "cultivate a middle position that forestalls or avoids having to choose one side… at the obvious expense of another".[1] In its engagements with multilateral regional and cultural associations, Timor-Leste has employed a form of "identity hedging" as it has diversified its relationships and sought to avoid dependence on any one state or bloc. Small states, such as Timor-Leste, use multilateral engagements as a way of maximizing their strategic options in international relations. According to declaratory policy, Timor-Leste considers its geographical position as "highly strategic" and views the protection of its natural resource wealth and security as dependent upon "maintaining good relationships with our neighbours and friends".[2] This chapter focuses on Timor-Leste's engagements with intergovernmental regional and cultural associations. Upon independence, Timor-Leste aspired to join as many multilateral organizations as possible.[3]

As highlighted in chapter two, Timor-Leste's leaders have emphasized its cultural distinctiveness arising from centuries of migration and occupation, and its geographical location in the "transition zone" between Southeast Asia to the west and Oceania to the east. During his Nobel Peace Prize acceptance speech, José Ramos-Horta argued that, "East Timor is at the crossroads of three major cultures: Melanesian, which binds us to our brothers and sisters of the South Pacific Region; Malay-Polynesian binding us to Southeast Asia; and the Latin Catholic influence, a legacy of almost 500 years of Portuguese colonisation."[4] He argued that Timor-Leste would retain close ties with Portugal and seek membership in the Association of Southeast Asian Nations (ASEAN) and South Pacific Forum "within days" of independence because Timorese leaders were conscious of the need to "co-exist" with its eastern and western neighbours.[5] In a 2014 speech, Xanana Gusmão also emphasized the importance of Timor-Leste's geopolitical positioning in "creating bridges with Europe, Africa and Latin America".[6] This cultural distinctiveness is viewed by leaders as providing Timor-Leste opportunities to facilitate unique relationships between and across different states and regional associations. It also reflects the ways in which collective identity formation is not "organic" but a consequence of choices made by leaders as they interpret the best interests of the state.

This chapter focuses on Timor-Leste's application to become a member of ASEAN, a regional grouping comprising diverse, mostly post-colonial states that has embedded defensive concepts of sovereignty, territorial integrity and rights to non-interference as key constitutive norms. While concepts of absolute external sovereignty are defended by many post-colonial states, these are given particular prominence within ASEAN as its *raison d'être* and the central principle guiding behaviours and processes.[7] One of the core interests is to build regionalism based on common interests of confirming and preserving the principle of sovereignty and non-interference. Multilateral forums and international law can provide "one of the best guarantees of survival for small states in the post-World War II period".[8] For a small state, such as Timor-Leste, ASEAN offers a "largely non-coercive neighbourhood" for pursuing development and security interests.[9]

This chapter also examines Timor-Leste's role in the Community of Portuguese Speaking Countries (CPLP), and highlights the ways in which common cultural and language ties established through colonialism have facilitated international cooperation. This chapter reveals the significance of common cultural, historical and regional connections underpinning international cooperation and participation in institutions, which is central to constructivist approaches to international relations. However, it also reflects the ways that new states seek membership in institutions in order to promote their strategic interests. Timor-Leste's engagement with forums of the Pacific Island states, including the Pacific Island Forum (PIF), as well as the g7+, also reveal the importance of shared interests and common vulnerabilities in collective identity formation.

"Identity hedging" supports Timor-Leste's aims to develop an independent foreign policy, enhance capacities to shape international affairs as a small state, and expand opportunities for influence and leadership as a component of the "fragile state exceptionalism" narrative outlined in the previous chapter. Engagement in intergovernmental organizations is attractive for small new states as they can inculcate a sense of solidarity and collectivism, and provide spaces for smaller states to exert diplomatic and soft power influence and to form blocs in relation to international issues. As Acharya notes, the usefulness of regionalism lies "in its potential to enhance the bargaining power of small and weak states in their dealings with the Great Powers".[10] Importantly, these regional and cultural associations allow Timor-Leste to buffer against the influence of its more powerful neighbours, Indonesia and Australia, emphasizing again that Timor-Leste has choices as well as imperatives.

Pursuing ASEAN Membership

ASEAN membership is described as the "cornerstone" of Timor-Leste's foreign policy. While resistance leaders preferred membership in both ASEAN and PIF, exclusionary rules restricted against "double membership".[11] Forced to choose, Timor-Leste's leaders decided to pursue membership in the more influential ASEAN, and leaders have often publically praised the association as "an international success story" for its role in "establishing a region of peace, cooperation and development".[12] In 2002, Timor-Leste successfully applied for ASEAN observer status. The first foreign policy target in the 2011 Strategic Development Plan (SDP) was for Timor-Leste to possess full membership of ASEAN, starting with establishing embassies in all ASEAN countries by 2015.[13] It envisaged that by 2020, Timor-Leste would be a key member of ASEAN, outlining an aspiration to be recognized as experts in "economic development, small-nation management, good governance and aid effectiveness and delivery".[14] In March 2011, Timor-Leste's Foreign Minister, Zacarias Albano da Costa, strategically but unsuccessfully applied for formal membership to ASEAN when Indonesia was chair.[15]

By the end of 2017, Timor-Leste has still yet to achieve ASEAN membership.[16] Minister for Foreign Affairs and Cooperation, Hernâni Coelho, reaffirmed Timor-Leste's commitment, pointing to its "intensive preparations to boost its institutional capacity and human capital to participate in ASEAN activities".[17] ASEAN membership presents onerous requirements for small states. In 2015, Timor-Leste only had six embassies in Southeast Asia. In 2016, it established four more in order to fulfill the membership requirement of having an embassy in all ASEAN states. Timor-Leste also created a dedicated government portfolio to ASEAN membership (the Secretary of State to ASEAN), and established an ASEAN secretariat in Dili. As part of Timor-Leste's charm offensive, Xanana Gusmão visited each of the ASEAN countries from 2013, using public speaking opportunities to praise ASEAN's role in regional and global affairs.

While full membership has eluded it, Timor-Leste has been involved in ASEAN-based organizations. In 2005, it became a member of the ASEAN Regional Forum (ARF) which comprises sixteen other members besides Timor-Leste and the ten ASEAN states: its ten dialogue partners (Australia, Canada, China, the European Union, India, Japan, New Zealand, South Korea, Russia and the United States), one ASEAN observer (Papua New Guinea), plus North Korea, Mongolia, Pakistan, Bangladesh and Sri Lanka.[18] The ARF diffuses ASEAN norms and principles about collective security and conflict avoidance beyond the ASEAN states.[19] Timor-Leste also participates in other components of Asia's regional governance architecture, including in the Bali Democracy Forum, the Shangri-La Dialogue (an international forum for regional and security defence issues and cooperation) and the Jakarta International Defence Dialogue.[20] However, other ASEAN-affiliated dialogue forums, including the East Asia Summit (EAS), do not include Timor-Leste.[21] In 2007, Timor-Leste signed the Treaty on Amity and Co-operation (TAC) established by ASEAN.

One of the defining features of ASEAN's composition is the diversity of its member states in terms of culture and ethnicity, language, political systems, size, development and history. According to the Bangkok Declaration of 1967, ASEAN membership is available to all states in the Southeast Asian region.[22] Admission requires consensus by the ASEAN summit on the recommendation of the Coordinating Council.[23] As a regional organization, ASEAN is a boundary setting organization, but there is a tension between "spatial" and "political" Southeast Asia. "ASEAN" has become increasingly synonymous with "Southeast Asia".[24] Ortuoste argues that East Timor was excluded from ASEAN during Indonesia's occupation.[25] Perhaps politically this is true, however it is not the case spatially: East Timor was included geographically as a province of Indonesia. As such, Timor-Leste has a strong claim to belonging to Southeast Asia. Yet it acceded to the TAC as a state outside of Southeast Asia.[26] As Emmerson notes, the creation of Timor-Leste created a problem for the relationship between "spatial" and "political" Southeast Asia; unless the Southeast Asian region had shrunk, ASEAN could "no longer claim to represent all of Southeast Asia".[27] Given the conceptual conflation of ASEAN and Southeast Asia, as long as Timor-Leste does not belong to ASEAN, its sense of regional identity and belonging remains ambiguous.

The prospect of Timor-Leste's entry into ASEAN was met with a mixed response by member states as they held "technical" and "non-technical" concerns about its membership.[28] The ASEAN Charter stipulates that membership is conditional on four factors: geographical location, recognition by other states, agreement to be bound by the ASEAN Charter, and ability and willingness to carry out obligations of membership.[29] While the first three membership conditions have been met, the fourth condition has proved challenging. Technical concerns relate to the resources, funds and personnel that Timor-Leste requires to fulfil membership obligations. Along with opening foreign missions in all ten member states, having officials in ASEAN Secretariat, and establishing a Permanent Secretary of State for ASEAN, Timor-Leste acceded to over sixty legal agreements and make the necessary domestic adjustments to ensure compliance and coordination across the whole of government.[30] In relation to human resource capabilities, Timor-Leste was required to demonstrate that it had sufficient English-speaking diplomatic staff as representatives for the one thousand annual meetings which ASEAN states are expected to attend.[31] Other ASEAN states have been assisting Timor-Leste to build up English skills as few Timorese diplomats read and write in English.[32]

Singapore proposed a thorough review of Timor-Leste's membership application, and feasibility studies examined the implications of Timor-Leste's accession to the ASEAN Political Security Community (APSC), the ASEAN Economic Community (AEC) and the ASEAN Socio-Cultural Community (ASCC). The 2016 Joint Communique of the 49th ASEAN Foreign Ministers' Meeting in Vientiane noted that all three feasibility studies on accession have been completed.[33] The first two studies showed that Timor-Leste's human resources needed "capacity-building" to "boost economic growth and skills".[34] At the end of 2017, the application remained with the ASEAN Coordinating Council Working Group (ACCWG), the final stage before official membership processes begin.[35]

Emmerson suggests that ASEAN's reluctance to allow Timor-Leste membership was actually due to "non-technical" concerns pertaining to its security, economic development, and, importantly, whether its foreign policy agenda might be "too heavily influenced by outsiders, notably Australia and Portugal".[36] Similarly, Dupont suggests that Timor-Leste's earlier prevarication on whether to join PIF, as well as its prioritization of relations with Portugal sent a message to the Southeast Asian states that Timor-Leste was only "lukewarm" about joining ASEAN.[37] It appears that Timor-Leste's expansive, aspirational foreign policy approach is one factor in its delayed entry into ASEAN.

Singapore is the most vocal opponent of Timor-Leste's membership. It is concerned that Timor-Leste would burden ASEAN with requests for financial support and hinder the progress of ASEAN economic community building. According to Gusmão:

> We are aware of our limitations and of the challenges imposed on us to become an asset to ASEAN. However, being the youngest and poorest country in the region, Timor-Leste sees membership in ASEAN as a way to multiply opportunities for its own development. Ultimately, this will benefit both the member countries and the Community as a whole.[38]

Laos also expressed concerns about Timor-Leste's capacities to fulfil membership obligations, despite Timor-Leste's greater gross domestic product (GDP) per capita than Laos, and its higher Human

Development Index ranking than Laos, Cambodia and Myanmar.[39] Leaders have sought to reassure ASEAN states that Timor-Leste would "not beg for economic or financial support".[40] They have also argued that Timor-Leste's entry will provide benefits to the regional community.

At the beginning of 2017, the signs regarding Timor-Leste's accession into ASEAN appeared positive as the organization signalled its willingness to increase Timor-Leste's involvement in related activities. In 2016, Timor-Leste held the ASEAN People's Forum (APF) for Southeast Asia civil society organizations because Laos was reluctant to do so. In 2017, the Philippines held the ASEAN Chair and was reportedly "very keen to bring the region's young democracy into its embrace".[41] Like the 2016 Joint Communique, the 2017 Joint Communique of the 50th ASEAN Foreign Ministers' Meeting in Manila again announced that Timor-Leste would participate in more ASEAN meetings for capacity building.[42] While this sounded optimistic, the similar wording in the communiques suggested that Timor-Leste's progression had stalled. The ASEAN requirement for consensus means that all states will need to agree with Timor-Leste's accession. In 2018, the chair is Singapore, the state least supportive of Timor-Leste's entry. This is likely to slow down the momentum for Timor-Leste's ASEAN membership.

It is important to consider that it has only been six years since Timor-Leste first formally applied for membership. It took twenty years of regular engagement with Cambodia before it was admitted.[43] ASEAN states are also more cautious now given the dilemmas presented by Myanmar's membership and the demands for an ASEAN response to human rights abuses by the military regime. Timor-Leste's entry into ASEAN would constitute its fourth enlargement. The controversial entry of Cambodia, Vietnam, Laos and Myanmar in the 1990s raised serious concerns that the gaps between economic and diplomatic capacity would adversely impact upon regional integration and community-building processes.[44] These structural inequalities in economic diplomatic capabilities "will not be helped by adding an eleventh member".[45] While Indonesia initially had concerns about Timor-Leste's membership due to instability, weak economic development and human resource capacity, Timor-Leste's membership bid has relied upon its friendly relationship with Indonesia, who, as ASEAN largest state, is considered a regional leader. Jakarta has publically endorsed Timor-Leste's ASEAN ambitions. Joining ASEAN was part of Timor-Leste's efforts to assure Indonesia that it would not become a "Trojan horse" for another powerful state, a prospect that Indonesia has long viewed as inimical to its own national security interests.[46] In the contemporary global order, Timor-Leste's neighbours are concerned about the capacities of China to establish a foothold in Timor-Leste. Former ASEAN Secretary-General Rodolfo Severino reported Ramos-Horta — frustrated with the slow processes of ASEAN accession — "darkly" saying in 2004 that Timor-Leste's relations might make ASEAN "nervous", then referring to its relations with China in the energy sector.[47]

Less critical analysis has been paid to the reasons why Timor-Leste — as a small weak state — might seek ASEAN membership, particularly in relation to the project of image-making in international relations and the desire to secure its state identity. The historical relationship between ASEAN states and the Timorese independence movement does not immediately suggest that ASEAN is a natural fit for Timor-Leste. As chapter three noted, the ASEAN states played an active role in supporting Indonesia's annexation of Timor-Leste. Foundational states consistently privileged good relations with Indonesia over East Timor's collective rights to self-determination.[48]

In public declarations, Timor-Leste's leaders highlight a number of different motivations for pursuing ASEAN membership. The primary reason relates to the perceived benefits of belonging to a "security regime". Neves et al. suggested in 2002 that Timor-Leste would be prone to external intervention the longer it remained excluded as it constituted "a weak link for ASEAN".[49] It was therefore considered in Timor-Leste's best interest to choose ASEAN as a more productive and influential security forum than the PIF. Since its establishment, scholars and analysts have disagreed about the role of ASEAN in providing regional security and economic prosperity. ASEAN's critics have long accused ASEAN of being a "talk shop" incapable of resolving conflicts. Realists consider regional security to be dependent upon relations with the great powers and broader balance of power and alliance dynamics. ASEAN sceptics point to the role of the U.S. military presence in the Asia-Pacific as underwriting regional order. Constructivists, however, see ASEAN as a "security community" that establishes Southeast Asia's collective norms and identity through processes of socialization and a culture of "dialoguing".[50] These norms shape ways of thinking and acting, and contribute to the establishment of order through patterned and predictable diplomatic engagements in the Southeast Asian region.[51]

According to Secretary of State for ASEAN, Roberto Soares, Timor-Leste's decision to join was predicated on strategic geopolitical interests.[52] The value of ASEAN for the small state lies in the ways that it can ameliorate regional security risks through collective security arrangements. Crucially, membership in ASEAN could provide Timor-Leste with a forum to promote its interests in regional security discussions. A comparison can be drawn with Singapore's foreign policy, which has devoted "considerable diplomatic resources and energy" to agenda-setting in multilateral contexts in order to mitigate geopolitical vulnerabilities.[53] According to Acharya, realists underestimate the role of ASEAN in promoting Singapore's interests and foreign policy.[54] He argues that Singapore's reliance on ASEAN for ensuring its sovereignty, through the principle of non-intervention and non-use-of-force, is consistent with neoliberal institutionalism rather than realism.[55] Similarly, Timor-Leste's pursuit of ASEAN membership reflects a belief that multilateralism can support its foreign policy goals of survival, independence and non-interference.

Timor-Leste's representatives present ASEAN as a useful pathway for advancing its economic development plans. ASEAN membership would mean joining the newly established AEC, the manifestation of ASEAN's goal of creating an integrated single market. The hope is that ASEAN would allow Timor-Leste to extend regional links beyond Indonesia and establish commercial relationships with strong economies. For example, Gusmão has argued:

> [a]t a time of global economic weakness, the Asian region continues to make incredible progress. It is home to emerging economies that are driving world growth, lifting millions from poverty and shifting international economic and strategic weight to our region. And Southeast Asia is a central part of this remarkable Asian transformation. The ASEAN group of nations together have a larger economy than India, Singapore has consolidated its place as a global financial centre and Indonesia is one of the great emerging economies of the world.[56]

Some commentators have questioned the economic benefits of ASEAN, suggesting that Timor-Leste would be better off pursuing bilateral relations with "more powerful friends like China, New Zealand and Australia" than joining an "increasingly irrelevant and ineffective" group (see chapter eight).[57]

Timor-Leste's pursuit of ASEAN membership reflects its desired position in international relations. Timor-Leste's future is tied up with ASEAN as it views itself as part of Southeast Asia. According to Gusmão, "[w]e feel like an integral part of our neighbourhood and have a strong sense of regionalism and solidarity with our Southeast Asian Nations".[58] Even though ASEAN is most clearly defined by its diversity, Timor-Leste does share some similarities with ASEAN states, including a post-colonial background (with the exception of Thailand). The foreign policies of Southeast Asian states have in common a concern for territorial unification and political centralization.[59] These states have generally placed great emphasis on sustaining colonial territories although support for East Timor's incorporation within Indonesia was a key exception. As Leifer notes, this policy was driven in part by concerns that East Timorese independence would encourage separatist tendencies in the outer regions of Indonesia.[60]

This shared background assists in explaining the normative reasons why ASEAN membership is attractive to Timor-Leste. Constitutive norms are the stable and routinized patterns of thinking and behaving that are replicated in ASEAN's extensive sets of declarations and social rituals that guide the practice of member states.[61] ASEAN's constitutive norms are inextricably linked to its formation, as founding states were principally engaged in "developmental nationalism" and pre-occupied with internal nation- and state-formation processes, including establishing a unifying national identity and political ideology, consolidating domestic security and regime legitimacy and, crucially, lessening dependence upon other states or international institutions.[62] Like most others in ASEAN, the legitimacy of Timor-Leste as a new political construct is based on "colonial inheritances".[63] In this context, development nationalism was preoccupied with anti-colonialism, self-determination and national consolidation.[64] Foundational members were also concerned about external intervention from superpowers.[65]

Key norms are embedded in the 1967 Bangkok Declaration, 1976 TAC and Declaration of ASEAN Concord.[66] These documents reinforce the sovereign rights of member states to political independence, territorial integrity and self-determination, attendant rights to non-interference in internal affairs and non-use of force. As Beeson argues, the commitment to non-interference in domestic affairs needs to be understood in the context of the "troubled intra-regional context from which ASEAN emerged and the very real concerns about domestic stability that confronted ASEAN's elites during their formative years".[67] The principle of non-interference took on a "special importance" for post-colonial ASEAN states due to their struggles to become recognized as politically independent.[68] Indeed, it is possible to trace similarities between the post-colonial Southeast Asian states of the 1960s and Timor-Leste following its separation from Indonesia. Timor-Leste's leaders have emphasized the common experiences of European colonialism and the difficult political transitions to independence experienced by most Southeast Asian states.[69]

There are also geostrategic vulnerabilities shared by Timor-Leste and small states, such as Singapore and Brunei, who, like Timor-Leste, have much larger archipelagic neighbours (Malaysia). Principles of non-interference and non-use of force help alleviate the acute sense of vulnerability experienced by small states in the region and provide them with a forum within which they could seek to influence "like-minded countries on issues of mutual interest".[70] Norms can and do evolve over time, and there have been a number of examples where ASEAN states have contravened or promoted policies that could have potentially weakened the non-interference principle (for example, Indonesia's suggestion in 2003 of establishing an ASEAN peacekeeping force).[71] While the application of sovereignty principles may at times be selective, they remain important in explaining ASEAN regionalism and its attractiveness to Timor-Leste.[72]

Like Timor-Leste, ASEAN states tend to be protective of the absolute external sovereignty concept as opposed to more limited conceptions of sovereign entitlements. Externally generated norms such as sovereignty are mediated within local contexts in a process of "constitutive localization"; that is, adapting international norms to suit the Southeast Asian context.[73] The post-colonial sensitivities of Southeast Asian states around sovereignty, intervention and security reflect the historical context of ASEAN's formation. ASEAN was borne from a desire to constrain the "belligerence" of Indonesia as a consequence of *Konfrontasi*,[74] which remains an important security interest of Timor-Leste. According to Bellamy and Beeson, "[w]hat we now think of as Southeast Asia has been exposed to historical forces over which the region has generally had little control. As a consequence, the states of the region have been preoccupied with shoring up sovereignty and consolidating domestic security."[75] The equating of non-interference with non-criticism was driven by the concern of founding ASEAN states that public criticism of Jakarta could enhance the likelihood of confrontation. They also feared the disintegration of the Indonesian archipelago, which would weaken security and economic prospects in the region.[76] The turbulent history of colonialism and conflict in the region explains the salience of non-interference and non-use of force principles that Timor-Leste upholds.[77]

The parameters for what constitutes "interference" — and by extension, violations of sovereignty — are broad. According to Acharya, there are four components to non-interference: (1) not criticizing the actions of states towards their people; (2) criticizing states that do breach non-interference; (3) not recognizing or supporting rebel or separatist groups threatening to overthrow existing governments; and (4) providing support to governments seeking to quell subversive elements.[78] From 1975–99, Timor-Leste was one such "subversive element". These non-interference principles render political independence and autonomy sacrosanct, and as such, ASEAN's regionalism enhances rather than limits sovereignty. Indeed, Xanana Gusmão views ASEAN as:

> a dynamic and united community, with leaders that safeguard the collective interests of the nations, guided by ethical considerations and valorising assistance rather than dependence between States. As a result of its experience and its relationship with the International Community, *particularly as a recipient of aid, Timor-Leste views ASEAN as a model of integration that preserves the emancipation of its countries and the dignities of their peoples*. Lastly, and because I believe that ASEAN's great success is based on mutual respect, without pretentions of dominance or condescendence [my emphasis].[79]

This passage reflects the ways in which the ASEAN community presents an empowering vision of sovereign independence for Timor-Leste's leaders. It again raises a key theme of Timor-Leste's foreign policy discourse: the rejection of dependence and dominance. ASEAN is juxtaposed against the broader "international community" (i.e. Western-dominated organizations and donor states); it is viewed as preserving the "dignities" of peoples, in contrast to the international actors that engage in condescending aid delivery and state-building in fragile countries.

ASEAN is a prolific, dialogue-focused regional organization, but one within which a small state such as Timor-Leste might be able to exert political influence. ASEAN embeds bilateralism at the heart of its multilateralism. The "ASEAN way" is a contested term that seeks to encapsulate regionally-based standards of informality, consensus decision-making and consultation built upon the constitutive norms of absolute external sovereignty. Some view ASEAN decision-making processes as socio-cultural norms unique to Southeast Asia, although Acharya notes that the ASEAN way more likely resulted from "incremental socialization".[80] While it differentiates itself from the "sabre-rattling, gunboat diplomacy" of the West, critics view the demands of consensus as obstructing ASEAN's capacity to resolve disputes or make decisions, as the organization cannot adequately confront difference of opinion.[81] However, the high importance placed on "dialogue" and "collaboration" conforms to the foreign policy preferences of Timor-Leste mentioned in the previous chapter, wherein knowledge sharing can assist in alleviating security dilemmas. The informality of the ASEAN way reflects the unwillingness of states to cede authority to the organization. The ASEAN Secretariat, for instance, is deliberately less powerful than the national ASEAN secretariats located within the foreign ministries of member states.[82] Importantly, the socio-cultural foundations of ASEAN — both in terms of its guiding norms and processes of decision-making — constitute a "soft-institutionalism" in which ASEAN is a weak organization that is subordinate to the self-interest of "strong" member states. As Narine notes, sovereignty norms actually mitigate against the establishment of a strong regional identity in Southeast Asia.[83] While some form of "imagined community" might be said to exist, this is relatively weak as its inability to respond effectively to events demonstrates a lack of strategic alignment across some issues.

In terms of norms, the non-interference principle corresponds more closely to the aims of the Timorese state, and leaders have shown a pragmatic willingness to sideline human rights activism as it seeks ASEAN membership. It is true that the promotion of human rights and democracy in international public discourses has, in the past, clashed with the ASEAN way. Tarling, for example, suggests that the human rights activism of independence leaders such as Ramos-Horta "was something of an obstacle" in its pursuit of ASEAN membership.[84] Criticism of Myanmar's military junta by East Timorese leaders for human rights violations and support for Burmese pro-democracy advocate Aung San Suu Kyi was viewed as contravening the cardinal rule of non-intervention.[85] However, ASEAN states have also grappled with how to respond to Myanmar, including Singapore, which also criticized reports of violence against protestors.[86] Timor-Leste's representatives have noticeably softened criticism of Myanmar's military regime for fear that it would jeopardize its membership prospects.[87] Ramos-Horta, for instance, welcomed Myanmar's foreign minister to Dili in 2010, professing the need to deepen relations with Myanmar.[88] This willingness to subordinate principles in the pursuit of its strategic interests reflects Ramos-Horta's pragmatic approach to foreign policy.

The SDP argues Timor-Leste's ASEAN membership aspirations reflect the wishes of its leaders and people.[89] However, Timor-Leste's pursuit of ASEAN membership has not been without controversy. There are reasonable questions to be asked about whether ASEAN membership is the best use of Timor-Leste's limited diplomatic capacities. It is also dubious whether Timor-Leste would benefit substantially from economic relationships and free trade agreements (see chapter eight). More broadly, the weaknesses of ASEAN in decision-making and capacity for action is likely to be exacerbated by global shifts of power that directly affect the allegiances supporting the liberal "rules-based order" that regional peace and stability is predicated upon. To this end, Timor-Leste's diversified foreign policy avoids reliance on ASEAN membership as a guarantor of security. While ASEAN has been considered by some as a nascent security community, one must also consider how "peace" in Southeast Asia and the broader Asia-Pacific neighbourhood has also been underwritten by post-World War Two alliance networks. The inherent weaknesses of the ASEAN way indicates that it will struggle to develop unified responses to a rising China if the United States substantially pivots away from the Asia-Pacific. Chapter ten considers Timor-Leste in the context of changing regional dynamics in the twenty-first century in further detail.

The Pacific Island Region

There has been some debate about whether Timor-Leste should abandon ASEAN membership and instead build on the common connections and interests shared with Pacific Island states pertaining to their level of development and socio-cultural composition.[90] In reality, Timor-Leste's relationships with Pacific Island states are already significant, and through the use of public narratives, representatives continue to culturally link Timor-Leste with the Pacific Islands. As chapter three examined, the East Timorese independence movement sought to distance Timor-Leste's "national identity" from Indonesia by emphasizing Melanesian roots. The South Pacific Forum (now PIF), however, lacked the power, security influence and wealth of the ARF and ASEAN.[91] Nevertheless, Timorese leaders have emphasized Timor-Leste's "solidarity" with the Pacific Islands. This solidarity is further confirmed by shared experiences of state-building, aid delivery and intervention: for instance, the Solomon Islands was also subject to Australian intervention in the security sector.[92]

Timor-Leste holds special observer status in the South Pacific's primary multilateral organization, the PIF,[93] but reportedly made a formal application for membership in 2014 following a change of rules on non-regional membership.[94] While PIF membership might not be assured, Timor-Leste is a co-founding member and donor partner of the Pacific Islands Development Forum (PIDF). This organization was established in 2013 as a way for Fiji to engage Pacific leaders after it had been suspended from the PIF. Timor-Leste joined the PIDF in July 2016, but claims co-founding member status.[95] The PIDF conceptualizes three pillars of sustainable development as economic growth, social development and environmental sustainability.[96] The basis of PIDF was establishing new modes of regionalism, partnerships and approaches to development, and focusing on "green growth in blue economies", sustainable development concerns and "special cultural bonds" and "regional kinships".[97] It puts the environmental imperatives to address climate change at the core of the agenda and the aims of establishing green economies reflect the mutual environmental vulnerabilities of the small island states owing to climate change.

This version of regionalism emphasizes the Pacific Islands Developing States (PSIDS) as core membership, including Timor-Leste, as it purports to represent Pacific Islander people, values and identity and rejects "top down bureaucracy".[98] Timor-Leste's leaders take its membership of PIDF seriously, committing $250,000 to PIDF activities in 2014.[99] At the inaugural summit, Prime Minister Xanana Gusmão, gave the keynote address, and urged other state leaders to take greater ownership of development and be agents of change.[100] The emphasis here is on the capacities of states to be politically independent and self-determining, and the PIDF places specific emphasis on "empowering the People of the Pacific".[101] Engagement with multilateral forums of the Pacific Islands allows Timor-Leste another space for critiquing the development assistance it has received from the international community.

By centring on PSIDS, the PIDF included Timor-Leste in its definition of "Pacific countries" but excluded developed, Western PIF members Australia and New Zealand. China has been growing its influence through foreign assistance, presenting a challenge to Australia's leadership role in the region. While perhaps not overtly challenging the PIF, the PIDF operates in a different sphere of influence as Russia and China are strong backers of the PIDF. O'Keefe highlights key trends influencing the strategic setting that has given rise to this "new Pacific Diplomacy", including the rising power of China, Russia's renewed interest in the Pacific, challenges to traditional models of regionalism and the emergence of Fiji as an increasingly confident foreign policy actor.[102] A diverse collection of states, such as Indonesia, India, Israel, the United Arab Emirates and Turkey, are also vying for increased influence in the Pacific.[103] The PIDF provides Timor-Leste with another strategy for diversifying its relations, mitigating its dependence upon Australia and expanding opportunities to "bridge" across regions. However, as Asia-Pacific emerges as another battleground in the contest between security and economic orders, these shifting balance of power dynamics are likely to have destabilizing effects on the region, presenting problems for Timor-Leste's security environment (see chapter ten).

Timor-Leste has also sought greater influence and engagement with other groupings in the regional architecture such as the Melanesian Spearhead Group (MSG), the Southwest Pacific Dialogue and the Secretariat of the Pacific Community (SPC).[104] Timor-Leste is an observer of the MSG, a forum of four Pacific states that receives substantial funding from China. According to the SDP, the aim of Timor-Leste's foreign policy is to be more "active in these regional organisations to ensure our national interests are appropriately represented".[105] As Timor-Leste shares similar political, cultural and developmental circumstances with Pacific Island states, there is plenty of "scope for mutually beneficial knowledge sharing on issues such as governance, capacity development, economic policy, and natural resource management".[106] Indeed, Timor-Leste is increasingly looking towards the East in its international engagements. This can be interpreted as a form of identity hedging, as Timor-Leste seeks to expand its influence within the Pacific region and engage with great powers as an "insurance policy" against dependence on Australia. Importantly, the PIDF is seen as an organization that rejects "neo-colonialism", which corresponds to Timor-Leste's foreign policy narratives regarding political independence and self-determination.

The Lusophone Connection

While Timor-Leste's geography places it at the crossroads between Southeast Asia and the Pacific, 400 years of Portuguese colonialism has shaped Timor-Leste's approach to international relations. In the national constitution and declaratory policy, the Timorese state prioritizes the maintenance of "privileged relations" and "special ties" with Portuguese-language speaking countries.[107] This dedication to the Lusophone connection with Portugal and its former colonial outposts in Africa and Latin America is given prominent expression in Timor-Leste's enthusiastic participation in the intergovernmental cultural organization, the CPLP.[108] Timor-Leste's particular emphasis on relations with Portugal replicates the "special relationship" between Portugal and its former African colonies, the continuation of which is a central function of the CPLP.[109]

The CPLP is a grouping of states that share a common cultural background and language by virtue of their common experiences of Portuguese colonialism and "Lusitanization"; that is, the spread of Portuguese colonial ideology.[110] The principle concern of the CPLP is maintaining and consolidating unity among Lusophone countries. One of its key instruments is the International Institute of Portuguese Language, which is a transnational language institution that began in 1989.[111] The CPLP itself was formed in 1996, and Timor-Leste joined in 2002. While Timor-Leste places a great deal of significance on the CPLP, it is very small compared with other multilateral organizations with a small staff and "meagre" budget (EUR 1.2 million in 2008).[112] This reflects the fact that the majority of member states are impoverished (in spite of the wealth of natural resources in some states), and that the largest state, Brazil, does not prioritize the forum.

According to the *Declaração Constitutiva da Comunidade dos Países de Língua Portuguesa* (the "Statutes"), the CPLP reflects the "special relationship" between member states based primarily on a common language. Any state can be a CPLP member as long as it has Portuguese as an official language. According to Sousa and Pinto, there are a number of components to the "Lusophony" that underpins the CPLP. They are:

1. a geo-linguistic space comprising states that have Portuguese as an official language;
2. "a sentiment, a memory of a common past, a partition of common culture and history"; and,
3. a set of institutions that work to advance Portuguese language and culture.[113]

Portuguese-speaking states are remarkably diverse in size, political regime type, ethnic and religious diversity and economic development, and are also subject to different modes of Portuguese colonialism. According to Makoni and Severo, the heterogeneity of CPLP member states precludes them from forming a "community", even though this is suggested by the English translation of its name.[114] Even the concept of a "Portuguese language" is complicated by hybridization, as well as the reality that Portuguese is spoken within CPLP societies to very different degrees. Thus, while CPLP is a multilateral organization, it is not a regional grouping like ASEAN or PIF. The CPLP member states are geographically dispersed across four continents. Half of the CPLP are members of other language and cultural-based associations such as the Commonwealth and the *Organisation Internationale de la Francophonie* (OIF). CPLP has largely focused on cultural association as the basis of relations, and the shaping of linguistic and cultural policies of member states. According to the "Statutes", the purpose of the CPLP is deepening friendship, diplomatic coordination and cooperation.[115] The objectives are to encourage political and diplomatic consultation and cooperation in all policy fields,[116] and to promote and diffuse the Portuguese language, specifically through the International Institute of Portuguese Language.[117]

Timor-Leste emphasizes this weak cultural association because it can enable the exertion of leadership and soft power diplomacy. One of the core interests is pursuing influence in the international sphere through the diffusion and affirmation of Portuguese language, and through cultural activities and exchanges.[118] These activities enable the exercise of soft power, which rests upon the "attractiveness" of culture, political values and foreign policies of states to others.[119] Language is associated with national culture and identity as well as collective identity formation, and the image that states wish to project to the broader international community. Timor-Leste's choice of Portuguese as an official language has consequences for image-making and branding as it identifies Timor-Leste as a Lusophone state, a unique status in Southeast Asia. Like most other CPLP states, the Timorese state is plurilingual: its official languages are Portuguese and Tetum, with business languages of English and Bahasa Indonesian. While most people in Timor-Leste speak Tetum — which is in the process of becoming standardized — it is specific to Timor-Leste and so provides little assistance in relating with the wider world through international trade and diplomacy, which is critical for the capacity of the small state to survive.

The relationship between the Portuguese-speaking elites was consolidated through the independence movement as the CPLP states supported East Timor's resistance (see chapter three). Timorese Minister Agio Pereira argues that CPLP support was "one of the most important factors in our victory in the struggle against the illegal occupation of East Timor by Indonesia, which occurred with the full connivance of successive Australian governments".[120] Portuguese was the language of the international independent movement as it "facilitated the critical fraternal relationship with the independence movements of Portugal's African colonies".[121] However, Portuguese-influenced Tetum increasingly became a *lingua franca* within East Timor as it spread through Catholic liturgy during the resistance against Indonesia, and the younger generation of resistance fighters were taught Bahasa Indonesian. Even before Indonesia's invasion, very few East Timorese spoke Portuguese as schooling was limited to the privileged class.[122] The adoption of Portuguese as the official language was controversial because the number of Portuguese speakers in 2000 was estimated somewhere between 5 and 20 per cent.[123] In 2004, Portuguese literacy ranked well behind Indonesian and Tetum in all districts, with less than 20 per cent of the population able to speak, read or write in Portuguese.[124] Commentary in the Australian and Indonesian press argued against the adoption of Portuguese while advocating for English and/or Bahasa Indonesian as dominant languages in the media.[125] The decision of the National Congress for Timorese Reconstruction (CNRT) to make Portuguese the official language served the political and symbolic purpose of distinguishing the new state from Indonesia and Australia.[126]

Portuguese remains a "foreign language" to the majority of East Timorese and a language of the privileged elite.[127] The choice of language enabled older resistance fighters to maintain power at the expense of the younger, Indonesia-educated generation. Portugal and Portuguese citizens were significant contributors to the CNRT, with the government providing 240 million of the CNRT's 300 million Euro income in the 2000 financial year. Following Gusmão's announcement that Portuguese would become the official language in February 2000, in July Gusmão declared to a delegation of representatives from CPLP states in Maputo, Mozambique, that East Timor would join the CPLP upon independence.[128] The Portuguese government invested heavily in the revival of the Portuguese language in Timor-Leste, including establishing a cooperation programme that allocated 46 million Euros to fund the education sector.[129] Timor-Leste's choice of Portuguese and its pursuit of CPLP membership is demonstrative of the power of the elite in external identity construction, as well as the effective diplomacy and soft power influence of Portugal before and during the international state-building period.

Constructivism examines the ways shared identity and culture informs relationships between states and the formation of collective identities in international relations, which is relevant for understanding Timor-Leste's focus on CPLP relations.[130] As chapter three identified, the narratives adopted by leaders of the East Timorese independence movement positioned Portuguese colonialism as a boundary marker distinguishing East Timor culturally, ethnically and historically from Indonesia. Gusmão, for instance, points to the importance of Portugal for providing Timor-Leste its national identity and its political independence in explaining the CNRT's choice of Portuguese as the official language in 2000: "if the Portuguese [had] left many years ago... the Dutch would have taken this area and we would have become Indonesia. We have them to thank for our own national identity."[131] Following independence, Portuguese language and historical connection remained influential within domestic and international realms of Timor-Leste's nation-state identity formation, and distinguishing Timor-Leste culturally from its larger neighbours.

The efforts of the successive Portuguese governments in supporting Timor-Leste's independence and state-building efforts have resulted in Timorese leaders increasingly recasting historical relations with Portugal as cultural "ties", "interactions" and "meetings" rather than as primarily an act of European colonialism entailing political domination and economic exploitation. For example, in his swearing-in speech in 2015, current Prime Minister Rui Maria de Araújo outlined a foreign policy vision for Timor-Leste to continue to promote "our historical *ties of friendship* with Portugal [my emphasis]".[132] Gusmão defined the Portuguese landing in Oecusse in 1515 as a *"meeting of civilization and cultures* that shaped the destiny of a People, a Country and a Nation [my emphasis]".[133] Celebrations were held from 1 October to 27 November 2015 for the "500 Years of the *Interaction* of Two Civilisations: Timor-Leste and Portugal and Affirmation of the Timorese Identity [my emphasis]".[134] This "affirmation" began when Portuguese missionaries first met with the people and leaders of Oecusse. At the unveiling of a monument in Oecusse on 30 November 2015, President Taur Matan Ruak designated Oecusse as the birthplace of Timorese identity, arguing that "[it] was here that our relationship with the Portuguese people began and where it blossomed, thus shaping our identity — an identity built on two important pillars: the Portuguese language and Catholicism."[135] These discourses obfuscate the colonial role of the Portuguese in Timorese history.

Not all Timorese considered the 500th anniversary of Portuguese colonialism worth celebrating. In response to criticisms, Pereira argued that what is often overlooked is the rare sense of "common identity and solidarity" that emerged "despite many negative aspects of colonialism and imperialism", and that Timor-Leste extends solidarity because it acknowledges "that the Portuguese people were also oppressed by the Portuguese empire".[136] This suggests that Timor-Leste's relationship with Portuguese-speaking countries is based on a common culture and religion, and shared historical experiences of Portuguese colonialism. Certainly, the emphasis on the Lusophone world recognizes the relationships that were established during the independence movement, but tends to revise history to the advantage of Portuguese foreign policy, which Taylor describes as offering "too little, too late".[137]

Neoliberal understandings of Timor-Leste's emphasis on the CPLP focuses on the ways in which the CPLP brings Timor-Leste closer to regional powers. For example, Seabra suggests that Timor-Leste's entry into CPLP provided the new state with "another way of gaining international recognition" as it "implied" that Timor-Leste had alliances with the regional powers of Brazil and Angola, as well as the European Union through Portugal.[138] Sahin also emphasized that

CPLP membership "provided the Timorese government with access to European funds for national development through Portugal".[139] CPLP hence provides a small state such as Timor-Leste with another forum to engage with economic global powers such as the European Union and China. Leach suggests that Timor-Leste's motives for choosing the Portuguese language are partly economic, as China has increased its influence among African CPLP states through energy diplomacy and economic and trade cooperation, encouraging Portuguese-language schools in Macau.[140] Yet, if it were purely economic motives that decided language policy, English would have been the natural choice; not only is it the global business language, it is also the language of ASEAN, which is central to Timor-Leste's trade and foreign policy. This suggests cultural rather than economic motives are more compelling in explaining the Lusophone connection, as well as the strategic interest in maintaining its unique identity *vis-à-vis* Australia and Indonesia.

Timor-Leste's CPLP emphasis can also be interpreted as part of its strategic positioning and identity-hedging, entailing pragmatic realist calculations regarding its small state foreign policy. The CPLP allows Timor-Leste to consolidate international recognition of its sovereign identity while using international forums to defend or advance its national interests. The CPLP provides an alternative space from ASEAN for Timor-Leste to exert diplomatic influence, and provides Timor-Leste a way of establishing a useful bridge across different language and cultural blocs. CPLP membership is hence presented by Timorese leaders as an asset rather than a liability in Timor-Leste's pursuit of ASEAN membership. Additionally, CPLP membership may provide Timor-Leste with greater autonomy and flexibility in foreign policy.

Constructivism also emphasizes the role of norms in identity construction in international relations. Like Timor-Leste, the CPLP uses activist discourses to explain its role in reinforcing the social bonds of "solidarity and fraternity" among member states.[141] The CPLP also conceives of itself as playing a role in the dissemination of, and socialization of member states to, normative principles around democracy, peace, rule of law, governance, respect for human rights and social justice. Like ASEAN, member states' commitment and adherence to these principles is uneven; the organization's newest member, Equatorial Guinea, is home to one of the world's most enduring dictatorships.[142] Nevertheless, CPLP has increasingly added democracy- and peace-building to its agenda, including conducting election observation missions in member states such as Guinea Bissau, São Tomé and Principe.[143]

Portuguese-speaking Ministers of Defence have adopted protocols for coordinating defence activities, including joint military exercises, training forces, defence knowledge sharing and strengthening the internal military capabilities of member states.[144] The defence agenda of the CPLP is largely driven by the agenda of Portugal's government, and there were accusations that Portugal exhibited "neo-colonial behaviour" in African peace processes.[145] This should be an area of concern for Timor-Leste as it reflects the ways that the CPLP is a vehicle for Portuguese interests, as it attempts to "frame its post-colonial relationships" in a European way.[146] Over recent years, the CPLP has increased its interest in security and politics in addition to language and culture, and these sorts of missions appear to be a priority of the CPLP in the future.[147] This provides Timor-Leste with opportunities to develop defence cooperation, share its knowledge and experiences in state-building and export its narrative of fragile state exceptionalism.

The CPLP has provided Timor-Leste opportunities for international leadership, a key aspect of its aspirational foreign policy. Timor-Leste's leaders are committed to "ongoing participation in the intercontinental programs and activities of the CPLP".[148] The SDP envisaged that by 2015, Timor-Leste would be playing "a leading role in the CPLP".[149] Indeed, in 2014, Timor-Leste began its two-year presidency of the CPLP. During this time, leaders attempted to extend the economic component of the organization, including possibilities for joint exploration and production of oil and gas.[150] During Timor-Leste's tenure as chair, the CPLP drafted over twenty resolutions and initiated activities revolving largely around human rights, democracy and the sustainable development goals. Gusmão argued that "Timor-Leste had the political conditions to promote a serious and honest discussion that leads to a sustainable economic development plan for its member States."[151] This suggests that Timor-Leste aspires for the organization to have a greater role in international relations, expanding the areas of concern from largely cultural matters to include economic concerns and energy cooperation as Timor-Leste's leaders try to leverage their competitive advantage in oil and gas. It also sought to align Timor-Leste's interests with those of other states in order to advance common goals and a shared vision. The aim is to capitalize on the CPLP, even aligning positions in UN voting, particularly on issues such as agriculture and fisheries. Most importantly, the CPLP has played an important function in the establishment and consolidation of Timor-Leste's unique identity within the international community.

g7+: Activist Foreign Policy and "International Solidarity"

One initial strategy Timor-Leste employed in its international affairs was to leverage the international sympathy that developed throughout the independence campaign to assist the new state consolidate its statehood.[152] Now, Timor-Leste's foreign policy appears focused on establishing its decision-making agency in the development domain and adopting a leadership role among other "fragile states".[153] The clearest example of this is in Timor-Leste's engagement in the g7+, a voluntary organization of nineteen self-identified "fragile" states co-founded by Timor-Leste.[154] The concept of solidarity continues to be used in the declaratory policy as a way of explaining Timor-Leste's networks, associations and relations, committing Timorese governments to support and consolidate the g7+ grouping to support weaker states by knowledge-sharing in international development dialogues.[155]

The g7+ was established as a response to "inadequate and inappropriate international approaches to the poorest countries".[156] It emerged as a response to the Organisation of Economic Cooperation and Development's (OECD) efforts to increase dialogue on aid effectiveness in fragile states, including the 2005 Paris Declaration on Aid Effectiveness, the 2007 Principles for Good International Engagement in Fragile States and Situations and the 2009 Monitoring of the Principles for Good International Engagement in Fragile States.[157] The "New Deal for Engagement in Fragile States" was a joint initiative of the g7+ states that emerged from the International Dialogue on Peacebuilding and Statebuilding held in Dili in April 2010 and presented at the Fourth High Level Forum on Aid Effectiveness in Busan in November 2011.[158] The main goal was "developing a country-led and country-owned new paradigm for aid intervention, adapting the way in which this aid would be 'managed, designed and delivered' in 'fragile states'".[159] The New Deal emphasized the importance of development solutions based on national ownership and inclusivity. Timor-Leste self-nominated to pilot the "New Deal".

The New Deal emphasized the need for new "development architecture" tailored to fragile contexts, including the importance of empowering women, youth and marginalized groups, encouraging "inclusive and participatory political dialogue" and building "constructive state-society" relations.[160] This rejects a "one size fits all", top-down approach to development, instead favouring "inclusive country-led and country-owned transitions out of fragility based on a country-led fragility assessment developed by the g7+ with the support of international partners, a country-led one vision and one plan, a country compact to implement the plan".[161] Implicit is a criticism of international aid delivery and intervention. The emphasis on country-led and owned development plans within fragile contexts symbolizes a rejection of imposed development plans that render developing states dependent upon international donors. The principal policy concern was to ensure that the needs of fragile and conflict affected states were reflected in the development agenda, and to enable a forum for developing states to cooperate and collaborate on their engagements with donor partners and hold the global development agenda to account.[162] While this forum reflects a mutual interest in critiquing orthodox global development models, and presents an alternative vision, the policy prescriptions of g7+ are still largely driven by economic liberal ideology.[163]

Although a contested term in Timor-Leste, its engagement in these developing institutions has identified the state as "fragile" and "post-conflict".[164] Disgraced former Finance Minister Emilia Pires was the chair of g7+[165] and following its inception, Helder Da Costa became the director of the g7+ Secretariat based in Dili.[166] This makes the g7+ an interesting case study in how states such as Timor-Leste have "internalised and reinterpreted the 'fragile state' classification, and how they have exploited the concept for their own strategic purposes".[167] As Siqueira argues, state fragility discourses "have power in themselves, as they are reproduced and applied in ways not originally envisaged, with consequences that are often different or more powerful than anticipated".[168] Timor-Leste's representatives are keen to share their knowledge about the "do's and don'ts" of state-building and post-conflict development.[169] As Gusmão states, it was during Timor-Leste's state-building processes that leaders "noticed that the international agencies of support and the United Nations pursued the wrong approaches to development in fragile and post-conflict countries".[170] The adoption of a fragile state identity permits Timor-Leste to take up a leadership and knowledge sharing role through the g7+, which broadly corresponds to its aspirational development policies.

Another key aspect is the role of the g7+ in providing fragile post-conflict states with a "voice" to shape the post-2015 development agenda. In its leadership role, Timor-Leste aims to shape collective responses to international development. The g7+ slogan "Goodbye Conflict, Welcome Development", for example, is a motto in Timorese political discourse.[171] Timorese Prime Minister Xanana Gusmão has also been a global spokesperson for the g7+. To the United Nations Security Council, Gusmão declared:

> The general goal of the 'g7+' is to awaken leaders and peoples so that they may reacquire ownership of their processes, viewed within a long term perspective without losing sight of the characteristics of each country and their priorities, and without forgetting to focus also on the need for a better control and adjustment over outside help, requiring greater transparency by donors and beneficiaries.[172]

In this statement, it is clear that issues of "ownership" of development processes are at the heart of the g7+ criticism of existing engagements with the international aid community.

In 2013, Timor-Leste chaired a Dili International Conference themed "Development for All: Stop Conflict, Build States and Eradicate Poverty" on the post-2015 development agenda in February 2013.[173] The conference was attended by government and civil society representatives from forty-seven states, including the g7+, Pacific Island states and Portuguese-speaking African countries.[174] Nearly fifty states backed the deal, including eighteen in the g7+.[175] The aim was to shape the global development goals that would follow the Millennium Development Goals (MDGs).[176] Gusmão emphasized the importance of the g7+ in allowing developing states' agency and active participation in global development dialogue, which he argued has been controlled by established states.[177]

This conference produced the "Dili Consensus", which argued that "business as usual is not an option". The Dili Consensus appeared to reject neoliberal models promoted by the Washington Consensus as well as the MDGs. It sought to establish the priorities of member states for the post-MDG development agenda, and advocated a "new" development deal based on inclusive "country-led consultative processes", sustained political leadership and commitment to good governance.[178] The emphasis on self-determination was reflected in the belief that "national ownership of the development agenda is imperative" for sustainable and enduring progress.[179] The Dili Consensus rejected aid conditionalities, instead arguing that development partnerships be based on "mutual trust" and "inclusive" economic growth, and that they recognize the importance of climate change (see chapter ten).[180] The Dili Consensus underscored the importance of "participatory national consultations and self-assessments as the basis for defining our national development priorities, and acknowledge the critical role of political leadership and sustained political commitment in realising our goals".[181] These development narratives can be contrasted with Timor-Leste's key economic policies outlined in chapter eight.

The Dili Consensus employed the discourses of "inclusive" economic growth, achieved through "pro jobs and pro poor" policies that put in place social protection policies and programmes that identify and support those suffering the greatest hardships, including the elderly and people with disabilities.[182] Timor-Leste's Prime Minister Xanana Gusmão closed the conference with a speech asking for "development by all, for all".[183] In the words of Gusmão, Timor-Leste associates its identity with other post-colonial fragile states: "We now walk together. We have shared our stories and histories, from across Asia, Africa and the Pacific. And while each nation is unique, we are bound by similar challenges, and a shared desire to contribute to the discussions on the global development agenda."[184] According to the g7+, "we are not trying to change it [the fragile state label], but to redefine it and use our definition by assessing ourselves". As Rocha De Siqueira notes, this reflects the ways in which the g7+ reappropriated the "fragile state" label.[185] For Timor-Leste, this has provided an opportunity to promote its fragile state exceptionalism that underpins its aspirational foreign policy.

Conclusion

Timor-Leste's engagement with intergovernmental organizations reflects the aspirational and expansive foreign policy detailed in the last chapter. The SDP articulated the goal for Timor-Leste to become a member of ASEAN with "recognized expertise in economic development, small-nation management, good governance and aid effectiveness".[186] According to Roberto Soares, ASEAN membership would "further safeguard Timor Leste's own independence and sovereignty, and of course, peace and stability in our region".[187] ASEAN is also viewed as important for regional political stability and preserving non-intervention sovereignty norms, reflecting Timor-Leste's own definition of sovereignty entitlements. Through the history of ASEAN it is possible to perceive similar threat perceptions held by small post-colonial states relating to foreign intervention. In Timor-Leste's case, those fears relate to its two powerful neighbours. Timor-Leste's ASEAN membership is a strategic move linked to Timor-Leste's "search for an identity" *vis-à-vis* Indonesia and Australia.[188]

This chapter has demonstrated how Timor-Leste has engaged in a form of "identity hedging" through its engagements with multilateral organizations. Its socio-cultural, linguistic and historical ties to Lusophone countries means the CPLP is afforded great weight in Timor-Leste's foreign policy agenda despite the constrained scope of its activities in security or economic spheres. Identity hedging is a risky strategy because it can make Timor-Leste's commitment to Southeast Asia region look weak, yet, according to Xanana Gusmão, Timor-Leste's "special historical and ongoing ties and relationships across the globe", including the CPLP, will benefit the ASEAN community.[189] Here, Timor-Leste's foreign policy seeks to leverage its unique relationships and geopolitical position to best advantage, as identity hedging may enable Timor-Leste to strategically bridge across different groupings. Timor-Leste's diversified intergovernmental engagements risks spreading diplomatic resources too thinly, a situation that will be intensified in the future given the human resource capabilities and training required for participation in ASEAN. Its activities as chair of the CPLP, and its leadership and knowledge-sharing within the g7+, demonstrate the ways in which Timor-Leste projects its self-image as a successful developing state that has moved "from fragility to resilience", and is now capable of leadership in the development sphere. However, Timor-Leste's ongoing economic and political vulnerabilities could potentially have significant consequences for the capacities of governments to maintain internal security and development goals. This is discussed further in the next chapters.

NOTES

1. Evelyn Goh, "Understanding 'Hedging' in Asia-Pacific Security", *Pacnet* 43, p. 1 (Honolulu: Pacific Forum CSIS, 2006).
2. República Democrática de Timor-Leste (RDTL), "Program of the Sixth Constitutional Government 2015–2017" (Dili: Government of the Democratic Republic of Timor-Leste, 6 March 2015).
3. Pedro Seabra, "The Need for a Reshaped Foreign Policy", in *The Politics of Timor-Leste: Democratic Consolidation After Intervention*, edited by Michael Leach and Damien Kingsbury, p. 146 (Ithaca, NY: Cornell, 2014).
4. José Ramos-Horta, "Ramos-Horta – Nobel Lecture", 10 December 1996, available at <https://www.nobelprize.org/nobel_prizes/peace/laureates/1996/ramos-horta-lecture.html> (accessed 21 July 2014).
5. José Ramos-Horta, *Towards a Peaceful Solution in East Timor*, 2nd ed., p. 21 (Sydney: ETRA, 1997).
6. Xanana Gusmão, "Timor-Leste and ASEAN: Perspectives and Challenges", Address by His Excellency the Prime Minister and Minister of Defence and Security, Kay Rala Xanana Gusmão, Sabah, Malaysia, 2 April 2014.
7. Erik Ringmar, "Introduction: The International Politics of Recognition", in *The International Politics of Recognition*, edited by Thomas Lindemann and Erik Ringmar, p. 7 (Boulder: Paradigm Publishers, 2014).
8. Amitav Acharya, *Singapore's Foreign Policy: The Search for Regional Order*, p. 7 (Singapore: World Scientific Publishing/Institute of Policy Studies, 2008).
9. Ibid., p. 8.
10. Amitav Acharya, *Constructing a Security Community in Southeast Asia: ASEAN and the Problem of Regional Order*, 3rd ed., p. 51 (London and New York: Routledge, 2014).
11. Ramos-Horta cited in Selver Sahin, "Timor-Leste's Foreign Policy: Securing State Identity in the Post-Independent Period", *Journal of Current Southeast Asian Affairs* 33, no. 2 (2014): 10. See also Nuno Canas Mendes, "Dilemas Indentitários e fatalidades geopoliticas: Timor-Leste entre o Sudeste Asiático e o Pacifico-Sul", in *Understanding Timor-Leste*, edited by Michael Leach, Nuno Canas Mendes, Antero B. da Silva, Alarico da Costa Ximenes and Bob Boughton, pp. 35–40 (Hawthorn: Swinburne Press, 2010).
12. Gusmão, "Timor-Leste and ASEAN: Perspectives and Challenges".
13. RDTL, *Strategic Development Plan*, p. 175 (Dili: Government of Timor-Leste, 2011).
14. Ibid.
15. Seabra, "The Need for a Reshaped Foreign Policy", pp. 157–58.
16. Kavi Chongkittavorn, "Will Timor-Leste Finally Join ASEAN in 2017?", *Reporting ASEAN*, available at <http://www.aseannews.net/will-timor-leste-finally-join-asean-2017a/> (accessed 12 February 2017).

17. Sally Percival-Wood, "Timor-Leste's ASEAN Aspirations Can Benefit From Pragmatic Indecision", *Australian Outlook*, 29 May 2015.
18. Department of Foreign Affairs of Trade, Australian Government, "ASEAN Regional Forum (ARF)", available at <http://dfat.gov.au/international-relations/regional-architecture/Pages/asean-regional-forum-arf.aspx> (accessed 12 February 2017).
19. On the ARF see Rodolfo Severino, *The ASEAN Regional Forum* (Singapore: Institute of Southeast Asian Studies, 2009); Ralf Emmers, "The Influence of the Balance of Power Factor within the ASEAN Regional Forum", *Contemporary Southeast Asia* 23, no. 2 (2000): 275–91.
20. RDTL, *National Strategic Concept of Security and Defence* (Dili: Ministry of Defence, 2016).
21. Department of Foreign Affairs of Trade, Australian Government, "East Asia Summit", available at <http://dfat.gov.au/international-relations/regional-architecture/eas/pages/east-asia-summit-eas.aspx> (accessed 12 February 2017).
22. Association of Southeast Asian Nations (ASEAN), "The ASEAN Declaration (Bangkok Declaration)", Bangkok, 8 August 1967.
23. ASEAN, *ASEAN Charter*, p. 9 (Jakarta: ASEAN Secretariat, 2015).
24. Donald E. Weatherbee, *International Relations in Southeast Asia: The Struggle for Autonomy*, 2nd ed. (Lanham, Maryland: Rowman & Littlefield Publishers Inc., 2010), p. 18.
25. Maria Ortuoste, "Timor-Leste and ASEAN: Shaping Region and State in Southeast Asia", *Asian Journal of Political Science* 19, no. 1 (2011): 10.
26. Ibid.
27. Donald Emmerson, "Challenging ASEAN: A Topological View", *Contemporary Southeast Asia* 29, no. 3 (2007): 427.
28. See Rodolfo Severino, *Southeast Asia in Search of an ASEAN Community*, pp. 76–78, 81–82 (Singapore: Institute of Southeast Asian Studies, 2006).
29. ASEAN, *ASEAN Charter*, p. 9.
30. Asian Development Bank (ADB), "Regional Cooperation and Integration Assessment", *Timor-Leste: Country Partnership Strategy (2016–2020)*, available at <https://www.adb.org/documents/timor-leste-country-partnership-strategy-2016-2020> (accessed 14 February 2017).
31. Selver Sahin, "Timor-Leste: A More Confident or Overconfident Foreign Policy Actor?", in *Southeast Asian Affairs 2012*, edited by Daljit Singh and Pushpa Thambipillai, p. 350 (Singapore: Institute of Southeast Asian Studies, 2012).
32. Chongkittavorn, "Will Timor-Leste Finally Join ASEAN in 2017?".
33. ASEAN, "Turning Vision into Reality for a Dynamic ASEAN Community", Joint Communiqué of the 49th ASEAN Foreign Ministers' Meeting, Vientiane, 24 July 2016.

34. Chongkittavorn, "Will Timor-Leste Finally Join ASEAN in 2017?".
35. Edmund Sim, "Wrap-up of the 2016 ASEAN Summit(s)", *ASEAN Economic Community Blog*, 7 September 2015, available at <http://aseanec.blogspot.com.au/2016/09/wrap-up-of-2016-asean-summits.html> (accessed 12 February 2017).
36. Emmerson, "Challenging ASEAN", p. 427.
37. Alan Dupont, "ASEAN's Response to the East Timor Crisis", *Australian Journal of International Affairs* 45, no. 2 (2000): 169.
38. Gusmão, "Timor-Leste and ASEAN: Perspectives and Challenges".
39. United Nations Development Programme (UNDP), *Human Development Report 2015*, p. 49 (New York: UNDP, 2015).
40. José Ramos-Horta, "Why Timor-Leste Should Join ASEAN Now", *East Asia Forum*, 16 May 2011.
41. Chongkittavorn, "Will Timor-Leste Finally Join ASEAN in 2017?".
42. ASEAN, "Turning Vision into Reality for a Dynamic ASEAN Community"; ASEAN, "Partnering for Change, Engaging the World", Joint Communiqué of the 50th ASEAN Foreign Ministers' Meeting, Manila, Philippines, 5 August 2017.
43. Din Merican, "Cambodia's Engagement with ASEAN: Lessons for Timor-Leste", *CICP Working Paper* 14, p. 7 (Cambodia: Cambodian Institute for Cooperation and Peace, 2007).
44. Prashanth Parameswaran, "When Will Timor-Leste Join ASEAN?", *The Diplomat*, 6 October 2016.
45. Percival-Wood, "Timor-Leste's ASEAN Aspirations Can Benefit From Pragmatic Indecision".
46. Sahin, "Timor-Leste's Foreign Policy", p. 12.
47. Severino, *Southeast Asia in Search of an ASEAN Community*, p. 79.
48. Dupont, "ASEAN's Response to the East Timor Crisis", p. 164.
49. Miguel Santos Neves, Kusnanto Anggoro, José Amorim Dias, Alan Dupont, Francios Godement, Dato Hassan, Carolina Hernandez, Tim Huxley, Riefqi Muna, Roque Rodrigues, Leonard Sebastian and Kusuma Sntiwongse, *The Security of East Timor in the Regional Context Report*, p. 38 (Lisbon: Institute of Strategic and International Studies, 2002).
50. See Alice Ba, *(Re)Negotiating East and Southeast Asia: Region, Regionalism and the Association of Southeast Asian Nations*, p. 5 (California: Stanford University Press, 2009).
51. Acharya, *Constructing a Security Community in Southeast Asia*, pp. 5–8.
52. Sasha Passi, "New Kid on the Bloc?" *ASEAN Focus*, 5 December 2013, available at <http://focus-asean.com/east-timor-focus-asean/> (accessed 18 June 2014).
53. Leifer, *Singapore's Foreign Policy*, p. 8; Acharya, *Singapore's Foreign Policy*, p. 8.
54. Acharya, *Singapore's Foreign Policy*, p. 5.

55. Ibid., pp. 5–6.
56. Xanana Gusmão, "Timor-Leste's Role and Future in a Rising Asia Pacific", Singapore, 4 June 2013. See also Agio Pereira, "The Challenges of Nation-State Building", in *A New Era? Timor-Leste After the UN*, edited by Sue Ingram, Lia Kent and Andrew McWilliam, p. 24 (Canberra: ANU Press, 2015).
57. Mong Palatino, "ASEAN Needs Timor-Leste", *The Diplomat*, 6 June 2011.
58. Gusmão, "Timor-Leste's Role and Future in a Rising Asia Pacific".
59. Michael Leifer, "Southeast Asia", in *Foreign Policy Making in Developing States: A Comparative Approach*, edited by Christopher Clapham, p. 21 (New York: Praegar, 1977).
60. Ibid., p. 26.
61. Ba, *(Re)Negotiating East and Southeast Asia*, p. 39.
62. Alan Collins, *The Security Dilemmas of Southeast Asia*, p. 30 (Hampshire: Palgrave Macmillan, 2000); Acharya, *Constructing a Security Community in Southeast Asia*, p. 57.
63. Muthiah Alagappa, "International Security in Southeast Asia: Growing Salience of Regional and Domestic Dynamics", in *Security of Third World Countries*, edited by Jasjit Singh and Thomas Bernauer, pp. 109–10 (Aldershot: United Nations Institute for Disarmament Research, 1993).
64. Ba, *(Re)Negotiating East and Southeast Asia*, p. 65.
65. Collins, *The Security Dilemmas in Southeast Asia*, p. 30; Acharya, *Constructing a Security Community in Southeast Asia*, p. 44.
66. ASEAN, "Treaty of Amity and Cooperation in Southeast Asia", article 2, Denpasar, 1976.
67. Mark Beeson, "ASEAN's Ways: Still Fit for Purpose?", *Cambridge Review of International Affairs* 22, no. 3 (2009): 336.
68. Acharya, *Constructing a Security Community in Southeast Asia*, p. 43.
69. Gusmão, "Timor-Leste's Role and Future in a Rising Asia Pacific".
70. Acharya, *Constructing a Security Community in Southeast Asia*, p. 47.
71. Lee Jones, *ASEAN, Sovereignty and Intervention* (Houndmills, UK: Palgrave Macmillan, 2012), p. 178; Mely Cabellero-Anthony, *Regional Security in Southeast Asia: Beyond the ASEAN Way* (Singapore: Institute of Southeast Asian Studies, 2005).
72. Collins, *The Security Dilemmas in Southeast Asia*, p. 36.
73. See Amitav Acharya, *Whose Ideas Matter? Agency and Power in Asian Regionalism* (Ithaca and London: Cornell University Press, 2009).
74. Acharya, *Constructing a Security Community in Southeast Asia*, p. 47.
75. Alex Bellamy and Mark Beeson, "The Responsibility to Protect in Southeast Asia: Can ASEAN Reconcile Humanitarianism and Sovereignty?" *Asian Security* 6, no. 3 (2010): 265.

76. Dupont, "ASEAN's Response to the East Timor Crisis", p. 164.
77. Acharya, *Constructing a Security Community in Southeast Asia*, pp. 56–57.
78. Ibid.
79. Gusmão, "Timor-Leste and ASEAN: Perspectives and Challenges".
80. Acharya, *Constructing a Security Community in Southeast Asia*, pp. 44, 69.
81. Collins, *The Security Dilemmas in Southeast Asia*, pp. 32, 35; Acharya, *Constructing a Security Community in Southeast Asia*, p. 66.
82. Collins, *The Security Dilemmas in Southeast Asia*, p. 33; Acharya, *Constructing a Security Community in Southeast Asia*, p. 63.
83. Shaun Narine, *Explaining ASEAN: Regionalism in Southeast Asia*, pp. 1–3 (Boulder: Lynne Rienner, 2002).
84. Nicholas Tarling, *Regionalism in Southeast Asia: To Foster the Political Will*, p. 211 (Oxon: Routledge, 2006).
85. See Ramos-Horta, *Towards a Peaceful Solution*, p. 24.
86. Emmerson, "Challenging ASEAN", pp. 427, 441.
87. Ortuoste "Timor-Leste and ASEAN", p. 16.
88. Seabra, "The Need for a Reshaped Foreign Policy", p. 157
89. RDTL, *Strategic Development Plan*, p. 172.
90. Leonard Sebastian C., "Timor-Leste's Road to ASEAN Membership", *In Asia* (San Francisco: The Asia Foundation, 9 March 2011); José Kei Lekke Sousa-Santos, "Acting West, Looking East: Timor-Leste's Growing Engagement with the Pacific Islands Region", in *Regionalism, Security and Cooperation in Oceania*, edited by Rouben Azizian and Carleton Cramer, p. 117 (Honolulu: Asia-Pacific Centre for Security Studies, 2015).
91. Neves et al., *The Security of East Timor in the Regional Context Report*, p. 35.
92. Gusmão, "Timor-Leste's Role and Future in a Rising Asia Pacific".
93. Pacific Islands Forum Secretariat, "The Pacific Islands Forum", available at <http://www.forumsec.org/pages.cfm/about-us/> (accessed 14 February 2017). Established in 1971, its membership comprises Australia, Cook Islands, Federated States of Micronesia, Fiji, Kiribati, Nauru, New Zealand, Niue, Palau, Papua New Guinea, Republic of Marshall Islands, Samoa, Solomon Islands, Tonga, Tuvalu, Vanuatu, and, since September 2016, French Polynesia and New Caledonia.
94. ADB, "Regional Cooperation and Integration Assessment", p. 2.
95. Ruby Taylor, "Timor-Leste is PIDF Newest Member", *The Fiji Times Online*, 19 July 2016.
96. Pacific Island Development Forum, "Pacific Island Development Overview", available at <http://pacificidf.org/overview/> (accessed 12 December 2016).
97. Sandra Tarte, "A New Pacific Regional Voice? The Pacific Islands Development Forum", in *The New Pacific Diplomacy*, edited by Greg Fry and Sandra Tarte, p. 80 (Canberra: ANU Press, 2015).

98. Ibid., pp. 81, 85.
99. RDTL, "Timor-Leste Participates in the Second Summit of the Pacific Islands Development Forum (PIDF) in Fiji", Press Release, 23 June 2014.
100. Tarte, "A New Pacific Regional Voice?", p. 84.
101. Pacific Island Development Forum, "Pacific Island Development Overview".
102. Michael O'Keefe, "The Strategic Context of the New Public Diplomacy", in *The New Pacific Diplomacy*, edited by Greg Fry and Sandra Tarte, p. 125 (Canberra: ANU Press, 2015); Roman Madaus, "The Bear Returns to the South Pacific: Russia Sends Arms to Fiji", *The Diplomat*, 9 April 2016.
103. O'Keefe, "The Strategic Context of the New Public Diplomacy", p. 126.
104. Sousa-Santos, "Acting West, Looking East", p. 111.
105. RDTL, *Strategic Development Plan*, p. 172.
106. ADB, "Regional Cooperation and Integration Assessment".
107. RDTL, *Strategic Development Plan*, p. 170; RDTL, *Strategic Concept for Defence and National Security* (Dili: Ministry of Defence, 2016).
108. RDTL, *Strategic Development Plan*, p. 173.
109. Norrie MacQueen, "A Community of Illusions? Portugal, The CPLP and Peacemaking in Guinē-Bissau", *International Peacekeeping* 10, no. 2 (June 2003): 1.
110. Sinfree Makoni and Cristine Severo, "Lusitanization and Bakhtinian Perspectives on the Role of Portuguese in Angola and East Timor", *Journal of Multilingual and Multicultural Development* 36, no. 2 (2014): 152. For a history of the CPLP, see Luís António Santos, "Portugal and the CPLP: Heightened Expectations, Unfounded Disillusions", in *The Last Empire: Thirty Years of Portuguese Decolonisation*, edited by Stewart Lloyd-Jones and António Costa Pinto, pp. 67–81 (Bristol: Intellect Books, 2003).
111. Rodrigo Tavares and Luís Brás Bernardino, "Speaking the Language of Security: The Commonwealth, the Francophonie and the CPLP in Conflict Management in Africa", *Conflict, Security and Development* 11, no. 5 (2011): 623.
112. Ibid.
113. Helena Sousa and Manuel Pinto, *Lusophony: Communication in the Portuguese Speaking World*, p. 2 (Washington D.C.: International Communication Association, July 1999).
114. Makoni and Severo, "Lusitanization and Bakhtinian Perspectives on the Role of Portuguese in Angola and East Timor", p. 161.
115. Community of Portuguese Language Countries (CPLP), *Estatutos da Comunidade dos Países de Língua Portuguesa (The Statutes)* (Lisbon: CPLP, 2007).
116. Including immigration, racism, discrimination, education, justice, sustainable development, rights of children, gender rights, culture and sport. See

CPLP, *Declaração Constitutiva da Comunidade dos Países de Língua Portuguesa (Constitutive Declaration of the CPLP)* (Lisbon: CPLP, 1996).
117. CPLP, *The Statutes*, article 3.
118. CPLP, *Constitutive Declaration of the CPLP*.
119. See Edalina Rodrigues Sanches, "The Community of Portuguese Language Speaking Countries: The Role of Language in a Globalizing World", *Atlantic Future Scientific Paper* 14 (June 2014).
120. Pereira, "The Challenges of Nation-State Building", p. 27; Gusmão, "Timor-Leste and ASEAN: Perspectives and Challenges".
121. Michael Leach, "Talking Portuguese: China and East Timor", *Arena* 92 (2007–8): 6.
122. A report into social and economic conditions in East Timor states "[e]xcept for the last decade of Portuguese rule in East Timor, education was, to a large extent, a neglected area during the colonial period from the mid-1500s to 1975. Most schools were run by the Catholic Church, teaching was in Portuguese, and only a small fraction of children had access to education." See Jon Pederson and Marie Arneberg, eds., *Social and Economic Conditions in East Timor*, pp. 84–85 (New York and Oslo: Columbia University's International Conflict Resolution Program and The Institute for Applied Social Science, 1999).
123. John Hajek, "Language Planning and the Sociolinguistic Environment in East Timor: Colonial Practice and Changing Language Ecologies", *Current Issues in Language Planning* 1 (2000): 400–13.
124. RDTL, *Census of Population and Housing 2004*, p. 66 (Dili: National Statistics Directorate, 2006).
125. Kerry Taylor-Leech, "Language and Identity in East Timor: The Discourses of Nation Building", *Language Problems and Language Planning* 32, no. 2 (2008): 160.
126. Leach, "Talking Portuguese", p. 8.
127. The 2010 reports less than 25 per cent of Timorese could read, write and speak in Portuguese, compared with 56 per cent literacy rates in Tetum and 45 per cent in Indonesian. RDTL, *Census of Population and Housing 2010: Suco Report*, p. xiv (Dili: National Statistics Directorate, 2011).
128. Lusa, "Cimeira CPLP: Declaração sobre Timor-Leste apoia independência", 18 July 2000.
129. Taylor-Leech, "Language and Identity in East Timor", pp. 157–58.
130. See Bruno Reis and Pedro Oliveria, "The Power and Limits of Cultural Myths in Portugal's Search for a Post-Imperial Role", *The International History Review* (2017): 19.
131. Agence France-Presse (AFP), "Portuguese to be East Timor's Official Language: Gusmão", *Agence France-Presse*, 11 February 2000; Associated Press

(AP), "East Timor Chooses Portuguese as Official Language", 14 February 2000.
132. Rui Araújo, "Speech by His Excellency the Prime Minister on the Occasion of the Swearing-In of the Sixth Constitutional Government", Lahane Palace, Dili, 6 February 2015.
133. Gusmão, "Timor-Leste and ASEAN: Perspectives and Challenges".
134. RDTL, "500th Anniversary of the Affirmation of the Timorese Identity", RDTL Press Release, Dili, 2016.
135. RDTL Presidency of the Republic, "H.E. the President of the Republic, Taur Matan Ruak, Unveils Monument in Lifau", RDTL Press Release, Dili, 3 December 2016.
136. Agio Pereira, "2015 Timor-Leste Update: Keynote Speech by His Excellency Agio Pereira, Minister of State and of the Presidency of the Council of Ministers, Government of Timor-Leste", Australian National University, Canberra, 19 November 2015.
137. John Taylor, *East Timor: The Price of Freedom*, p. 175 (Annandale, New South Wales: Zed Books, 1999).
138. Seabra, "The Need for a Reshaped Foreign Policy", p. 149.
139. Sahin, "Timor-Leste's Foreign Policy", p. 9.
140. Leach, "Talking Portuguese", p. 7.
141. CPLP, *Constitutive Declaration of the CPLP*.
142. CPLP, *The Statutes*, article 5; Sanches, "The Community of Portuguese Language Speaking Countries", p. 10.
143. See MacQueen, "A Community of Illusions?"; Tavares and Bernardino, "Speaking the Language of Security", pp. 609, 623.
144. Tavares and Bernardino, "Speaking the Language of Security", pp. 624, 627.
145. Ibid., p. 626; MacQueen, "A Community of Illusions?", p. 2.
146. MacQueen, "A Community of Illusions?", p. 1.
147. Tavares and Bernardino, "Speaking the Language of Security", p. 626.
148. RDTL, *Strategic Development Plan*, p. 173.
149. Ibid., p. 175.
150. ADB, "Regional Cooperation and Integration Assessment".
151. Gusmão, "Timor-Leste and ASEAN: Perspectives and Challenges".
152. East Timor Planning Commission, *National Development Plan*, p. 113 (Dili: Planning Commission, May 2002).
153. RDTL, "Program of the Sixth Constitutional Government 2015–2017".
154. RDTL, *Strategic Development Plan*, p. 175.
155. RDTL, "Program of the Sixth Constitutional Government 2015–2017".
156. Simon Fenby, "The g7+ Group of Fragile States: Towards Better International Engagement and Accountability in Aid Delivery to Fragile Nations", in *Critical Reflections on Development*, edited by Damien Kingsbury, p. 33 (London: Palgrave Macmillan, 2013).

157. Ibid., p. 35.
158. g7+, "A New Deal for Engagement in Fragile States".
159. Isabel Rocha de Siqueira, "Measuring and Managing 'State Fragility': The Production of Statistics by the World Bank, Timor-Leste and the g7+", *Third World Quarterly* 35, no. 2 (2014): 277.
160. g7+, "A New Deal for Engagement in Fragile States".
161. Ibid.
162. g7+, "Haiti Declaration: Port-au-Prince", 14 November 2012, available at <http://www.g7plus.org/en/resources/haiti-declaration-port-au-prince-14-november-2012> (accessed 15 May 2017).
163. Fenby, "The g7+ Group of Fragile States", p. 43.
164. Sahin, "Timor-Leste's Foreign Policy".
165. Pires was found guilty in December 2016 of economic crimes, sentenced to seven years imprisonment and was in hiding at the time of writing. It appears that Pires remains a "special envoy" to the g7+. See Anne Barker, "Australian Citizen, Former East Timorese Minister Fights Against 'Unfair' Seven-Year Jail Sentence for Corruption", *ABC News*, 10 February 2017.
166. g7+, "Annual Report", Lome, Togo, 2014, available at <http://www.g7plus.org/sites/default/files/resources/g7%2B-Annual-Report-2013.pdf> (accessed 15 May 2017).
167. See Sonja Grimm, Nicolas Lemay-Hebert, and Olivier Nay, "'Fragile States': Introducing a Political Concept", *Third World Quarterly* 35, no. 2 (2014): 197–209.
168. Siqueira, "Measuring and Managing 'State Fragility'", p. 268.
169. Simon Roughneen, "Aid and Independence", *The Diplomat*, 29 September 2011.
170. Gusmão, "Timor-Leste and ASEAN: Perspectives and Challenges".
171. See RDTL, *"Goodbye Conflict, Welcome Development": A Citizen's Guide to the 2012 State Budget of the Democratic Republic of Timor-Leste* (Dili: Democratic Republic of Timor Leste, 2012); Xanana Gusmão, "Goodbye Conflict, Welcome Development: The Timor-Leste Experience", Address by His Excellency the Prime Minister of the Democratic Republic of Timor-Leste Kay Rala Xanana Gusmão at John Hopkins University, Washington D.C., 24 February 2011.
172. Gusmão, "Goodbye Conflict, Welcome Development".
173. RDTL, "The Dili Consensus", Dili, 28 February 2012.
174. Ibid.
175. Pacific Institute of Public Policy, "The Dili Consensus Calls For a New Deal on Global Development", Press Release, 28 February 2013, available at <http://www.pacificpolicy.org/wp-content/uploads/2013/02/PRESS-RELEASE-Dili-Consensus1.pdf> (accessed 14 February 2017).

176. RDTL, "The Dili Consensus".
177. Xanana Gusmão, "g7+ Ministerial Meeting in Togo", Address by His Excellency the Prime Minister of the Democratic Republic of Timor-Leste Kay Rala Xanana Gusmão, Togo, 29 May 2013.
178. RDTL, "The Dili Consensus".
179. Ibid.
180. Ibid.
181. Ibid.
182. Ibid.
183. United Nations Economic and Social Commission for Asia and the Pacific (UNESCAP), "UNESCAP: 'Dili Consensus' Calls For Voices of Fragile and Conflict-Affected States to be Heard in Reshaping Global Development Agenda", Press Release G/07/2013, Bangkok, March 2013.
184. Gusmão, "g7+ Ministerial Meeting in Togo".
185. Siqueira, "Measuring and Managing 'State Fragility'", p. 276.
186. ADB, "Regional Cooperation and Integration Assessment", p. 2.
187. Tama Salim, "Timor-Leste Looks to Benefit from ASEAN Membership", *The Jakarta Post*, 26 May 2016.
188. Sahin, "Timor-Leste's Foreign Policy", p. 11.
189. Gusmão, "Timor-Leste's Role and Future in a Rising Asia Pacific".

7

Timor-Leste's National Security Agenda

While the previous chapter demonstrated the centrality of cooperation within diverse multilateral forums as part of Timor-Leste's foreign policy, political rhetoric and policies tend to straddle the line between contest and cooperation. This chapter identifies how Timor-Leste perceives its external security challenges and the steps it has taken to address them. Engaging with "security" requires considering *what* security and for *whom*. The conventional sovereignty-security nexus focuses on the defence capabilities of the state in protecting its territory and population from aggression by other states. This chapter argues that this conventional approach to "national security" is viewed by dominant political elites as integral to the independence of the Timorese state. This sovereignty-security conception is shaped by Timor-Leste's historical experiences with colonialism under Portugal and Indonesia, and the collusion of Western and ASEAN states in permitting illegal occupation. Timor-Leste's leaders have presented an image of the international environment as insecure and competitive in some contexts. They suggest Timor-Leste should devote more resources to building military capacities to guarantee its sovereignty. Like many states, however, defence self-reliance is an unattainable goal.

Small states have been viewed as particularly vulnerable to the power politics because their limited assets make it difficult to repel foreign combatants.[1] Timor-Leste's external security threats, however, are mostly low-level and non-traditional (e.g. non-military), including transnational crimes such as the illegal movement of goods and people across porous sections of the borders between Indonesia and Timor-Leste.[2] Maritime security has also been identified as a priority by multiple sources, with Timor-Leste government arguing that a naval force is required to protect against illegal fishing, destruction of maritime fauna, piracy and other violations of Timor-Leste's Exclusive Economic Zone (EEZ).[3] East Timorese leaders, such as Xanana Gusmão, have targeted global security issues such as terrorism, trafficking of people, humans and weapons and international crime as potential threats to Timor-Leste's national security.[4]

While realist approaches to external national security may be relevant for great power politics and material security interests among long-established, "Westphalian" states, they are generally less useful for explaining the post-colonial security dilemmas of new states in which threats generally emerge from within borders rather than beyond. Generally speaking, new states such as Timor-Leste are more likely to experience internal conflict and disorder than established, industrialized states. As the introduction outlined, the security dilemma for many developing states "arises in meeting internal rather than external threats".[5] Rather than being threatened by other states, since the 1999 referendum Timor-Leste's external sovereignty has been supported by *de jure* recognition, state-building and aid delivery.

Timor-Leste's biggest security challenges emerge from domestic security challenges. Similar to other fragile post-colonial states, a range of different issues emerged in Timor-Leste following its independence, including social divisions, elite rivalries, poverty and unemployment, economic underdevelopment, youth unemployment, a weak justice system, and unstable political institutions.[6] The dismissal of 591 army servicemen by the government in 2006 catalyzed a political crisis as the deep social, political, and economic challenges contributed to the escalating tensions in Timor-Leste.[7] One of the initial challenges for the new East Timorese state was legitimizing and consolidating democratic political structures because customary forms of governance retained their currency in local communities. Further, Timor-Leste's key security sectors, the FALINTIL-Defence Forces of Timor-Leste (F-FDTL) and the National Police Force, "were marked by internal rifts stemming from historical, regional and personal differences".[8] These issues threatened the capacities of Timor-Leste's fragile political institutions to provide internal security during the first years of its statehood. Internal security threats include clashes between community groups, assaults and presence of resistance groups, such as the Maubere Revolutionary Council, that challenge the legitimacy of the Timorese state and conduct violent operations against security forces.

As chapter four argued, states and intergovernmental agencies actively assisted in the creation of the political institutions necessary for internal sovereign capabilities. Since 1999, Timor-Leste has been the subject of five United Nations (UN) missions and two peacekeeping interventions that have sought to consolidate Timorese state institutions and building capacity in security sectors (see Table 4.1 in chapter four). From 2006–12, an international peacekeeping force and the United Nations Integrated Mission in Timor-Leste (UNMIT) assisted Timor-Leste in regaining and consolidating internal order and building capacity in security institutions such as the police and military. Despite this international support, the Parliamentary Majority Alliance (AMP) coalition, which formed government following Timor-Leste's 2007 parliamentary elections, began emphasizing the conventional sovereign-security concept in both its rhetoric and military build-up. One of Timor-Leste's aims has been to reduce the foreign military presence.[9] While necessary to establish social and political order, international assistance undermined the ability of elites to exercise "real" independence as the state was no longer in control of primary security institutions. After the election of the AMP government, Timor-Leste shifted its attention to external defence and sought to bolster defence capacities in line with traditional observations about security and "real" independence. The political rhetoric has reinforced the importance of territorial defence capacities as a core component of sovereignty, and Timor-Leste's leadership has sought to guarantee and protect Timor-Leste's newly attained political status.

In a speech delivered in 2010, Gusmão's explanation of Timor-Leste's security reflected his past as the commander-in-chief of the armed resistance movement.[10] He identified the key weaknesses of East Timor's independence movement in 1974–75, including: political immaturity; continuous misunderstandings between political parties; a lack of consensus on strategic interests; internal divisions; and unprotected seas.[11] Gusmão argued that learning the lessons of the past is necessary for Timor-Leste to protect its sovereignty, inferring that a key lesson from Indonesia's invasion was that the conflict between emergent political parties clouded their capacity to manage external threats (Indonesia).[12] For Gusmão, Timor-Leste's history demonstrates the dangers of concentrating solely on domestic security challenges and neglecting potential external threats. Although international assistance has been integral in preserving and protecting Timor-Leste's sovereignty, Gusmão argued that this is no excuse for Timor-Leste to be complacent regarding the possibility of invasion or attack from other states. Rather, Timor-Leste should adopt a "realist" vision of the international political community: defence, he argued, entails the armed forces being prepared for the eventuality of war.[13] Gusmão's argued that Timor-Leste "should never set aside the possibility of armed conflict, of whatever nature".[14] This reflects a sense of insecurity borne from Indonesia's occupation.

While leaders argue that Timor-Leste needs to protect its sovereignty in order to develop "real" independence, attack from another state is highly improbable. Security in Timor-Leste has been undermined by organizational gulfs between the police and the military.[15] After the 2006 crisis, international peacekeepers assisted Timor-Leste in Security Sector Reform (SSR) to build capacity in security institutions.[16] As Simonsen notes, the fundamental question of whether Timor-Leste requires an army was not addressed in the discussions on SSR.[17] The creation of Timor-Leste's armed forces was a result of domestic policy not the United Nations Transitional Administration. While some states may be able to survive without permanent standing armies, leaders Taur Matan Ruak and José Ramos-Horta have argued that this is not the case for Timor-Leste due to the "challenges that this country faces internally and externally".[18] Ideational factors motivate Timor-Leste's security policy, insofar as defence is viewed as a constitutive component of independent statehood. The domestic political context also motivates security policies as leaders draw upon popular narratives of historical struggle and national valour to justify the strengthening of Timor-Leste's military.

Building a Military

During the independence movement, leaders envisaged an independent Timor-Leste without a standing army, following the lead of other states such as Costa Rica.[19] Ramos-Horta presented the idea that Timor-Leste would rely on a "Treaty of Neutrality" guaranteed by the United Nations Security Council (UNSC). Not having a standing army would free up funds for social policies: "at least 40 per cent of our resources will be allocated to our best resources — our people — through massive investment in health, education and food production".[20] As chapter five examined, a Timorese state would also work towards the total demilitarization of East Asia and the Pacific, establishing a "Zone of Peace" around the island of Timor.[21] Following the 1999 referendum, the decision by leaders to only have a national gendarmerie was abandoned as Operation Clean Sweep precipitated fears that pro-autonomy militia presented security threats that a police force alone would not ameliorate. There was also the issue of what the resistance veterans would do after independence. It was thought that possessing a military would defuse dangers presented by disaffected soldiers from the resistance movement's military arm, FALINTIL.[22]

In 2000, the UNTAET and Timorese leaders requested the King's College London to write a defence study to support the development of a Timorese military.[23] The resultant report provided Timor-Leste with three options:

1. Compose a "national guard" force of 3,000–5,000 military by integrating FALINTIL combatants and conscripts, with a small air and naval arm.
2. Compose a force of 1,500 core troops in addition to 1,500 annual conscript drafts, with no air or naval arm.
3. Compose a force of 1,500 core troops and another 1,500 volunteer reservists, with initially no air or naval arm.[24]

The first model represented the most expensive choice. The report suggested that this was unrealistic relative to Timor-Leste's economic situation, and would inflate the risk of external threats to Timor-Leste's security and sovereignty. The most economically viable option was the third model. FALINTIL's leadership, on the other hand, wanted a defence force of 5,000.[25] Option three was adopted by Transitional Cabinet of East Timor (ETTA) in September 2000, and the Falintil-*Force de Defesa de Timor Leste* (F-FDTL) was established on 31 January 2001, becoming the smallest defence force in Southeast Asia.[26] The first 650 troops in the light infantry force were ex-resistance veterans. According to Feijo, Timor-Leste's armed resistance movement antecedents of the F-FTDL provided "revolutionary legitimacy" to the military.[27]

Initially, external threats included the pro-Indonesia militia, the movement of goods and weapons across borders, and "non-traditional" threats including organized crime and violations of maritime security.[28] During the FRETLIN government (2002–7), Timor-Leste's "two-pronged" approach to international relations was adopted to promote Timor-Leste's external security, and was awkwardly skewed towards placating Indonesia while shoring up support from Western states, especially Australia.[29] Many leaders continued to view Indonesia as a threat immediately following independence, and the violence surrounding the 1999 consultation reminded the East Timorese of their "vulnerable position".[30] Timor-Leste's leaders understood that a "volatile" Indonesia could also have added to Timor-Leste's economic, social, and political challenges.[31] As chapter nine argues, Timor-Leste's policy of appeasement reflects a "pragmatic realist" approach to foreign policy as it acknowledges both Indonesia's previous actions in Timor-Leste and its growing might in the twenty-first century.

Despite Australia's cooperation with Indonesia during the war of resistance from 1975–99, Timor-Leste's pursuit of "real" independence depended heavily upon Australia's assistance during and after the transition period. Timor-Leste required its security to be underwritten by its Western neighbour, and relied upon defence training from Australia and Portugal. However, as Indonesian analyst Hadi Soesastro points out, a formal defence relationship with Australia would have put Indonesia offside.[32] While emphasizing cooperation with Australia in its foreign affairs, it also appeared that many East Timorese had not forgotten Australia's role in denying their rights to political independence. Timor-Leste's pursuit of ASEAN membership also reflected a recognition that its future lay with other Southeast Asian states, despite the significant role of Australia in supporting the development of Timor-Leste's defence forces by providing technical and financial support and equipment.

There was a widespread perception among the East Timorese population that Australia was a "bully", driven mostly by Australia's aggressive negotiations over gas and oil reserves in the Timor Sea during and after Indonesia's occupation.[33] For example, Xanana Gusmão was vocal about Australia "stealing" Timor-Leste's oil, arguing that if maritime borders were drawn up according to international maritime law, Australia would have received a far smaller share of hydrocarbon resources (see chapter eight). Another concern about Timor-Leste's dependence on Australia emerged in 2010 when Australian Prime Minister Julia Gillard announced that the government was discussing a plan with Ramos-Horta for a regional refugee processing centre in Timor-Leste.[34] While Ramos-Horta reportedly advocated the centre, Gusmão opposed it, and the plan was also voted down by the Timorese parliament. Civil society activists argued that this was another example of Australian government "abuse" and "arrogance" towards the Timorese.[35] As a consequence, in 2011, Foreign Minister Zacarias da Costa refused to attend the Bali Process ministerial forum, preferring instead to attend talks in Suva. This was interpreted as a "direct diplomatic snub" to Australia because of its sour relationship at the time with Fiji's now Prime Minister Commodore Frank Bainimarama. [36]

The choice of building a military in the early years of independence had its critics. Smith observed that "the development of Timor-Leste military has not been welcomed by a number of commentators who point out that the F-FDTL is undisciplined... and that Timor-Leste cannot fund its long-term military ambitions".[37] Ball pointed out that fiscal constraints would limit the capacities of Timor-Leste to meet its military ambitions, particularly as oil revenue had yet to flow into the state.[38] Fundamentally, the idea of having a force for dealing with external threats did not solve the problems of internal security: as Wainwright puts it, the military had little to do while the police was underfunded and overstretched.[39] The lack of clear definition of the roles and responsibilities of the security apparatuses would come to a head in 2006.

Force 2020: A More Expansive Military

The 2002 National Development Plan viewed defence as closely aligned with internal security. It stated that Timor-Leste's "defence and security will be understood in the widest context of social, political and economic development, in the context of poverty reduction and a participatory and responsible citizenship".[40] However, following the achievement of independence, Timor-Leste's defence forces began shifting the security focus to possible external threats and pressing the government to increase military capacity. In 2005, a study of Timor-Leste's strategic defence called *Force 2020* was produced for the Timorese government with some international assistance and publically released in 2007.[41] While originally criticized by Xanana Gusmão's National Congress for Timorese Reconstruction (CNRT) during the 2007 election campaign, strong advocacy by then-army commander Taur Matan Ruak won government backing for the strategy.[42] *Force 2020* was the initial stage of Timor-Leste's development of its Strategic Concept of National Defence and Security. This is better known in international relations as "grand strategy", in which state actors articulate their imagined place in the world, the national interests that are informed by this strategic positioning, and the anticipated deployment of hard and soft power assets to guarantee those interests.[43] *Force 2020* shaped Timor-Leste's defence strategy, and thus provides an illuminating example of the aspirations for the military. *Force 2020* acknowledged the economic and material limitations facing Timor-Leste in establishing a larger defence force, however, viewed increased defence spending as important because it is "a public sector that deserves strategic investment that contributes to the country's sustainability".[44] While option three was initially chosen for Timor-Leste, *Force 2020* preferred the more expansive — and expensive — option one.[45] Instead, it outlined a plan to develop an armed force capable of exclusively confronting and preventing external threats.

Timor-Leste's defence force comprises "two active light infantry battalions and 1,500 reservists, with a unit of marines and small brown water naval capabilities".[46] *Force 2020* recommended an F-FDTL force of 3,600 by 2020, with a land force (45 per cent), a light naval fleet (35 per cent), a support and service unit (15 per cent) and a command unit (5 per cent). A piece written by Timor-Leste defence advisor, José Manuel Neto Simões, defended the idea that geopolitical and historical realities meant Timor-Leste required a larger, modernized armed forces for the defence of national sovereignty and security, in addition to assuming responsibilities in collective defence, including contributing to regional security and international peace.[47] The report revealed a number of key reasons why strategists move towards option three. First, it demonstrated concerns that King's College underemphasized external threats to Timor-Leste's national sovereignty. While the report paid lip service to internal threats such as "subversive actions against national identity", internal wars and organized crime, the document devoted considerable attention to external security threats.[48] The threats included maritime organized crime, border issues with ex-militias and militarized land borders. It focused on the dangers that Indonesia's political instability posed, its "fragile" democratization and "the possibility of a return to military rule and to the disintegration of the State".[49] Importantly, it warned of the "chance of external intervention that may arise at any moment, taking into account a threat of a global nature (terrorism, natural disasters, and others of a political-strategic character) that will engage the interest of the immediate and near neighbours, and surpass their capacities for management".[50] For example, the report stated that Timor-Leste "may suffer an imposition of foreign forces in the security domain if it becomes a concern to the pursuance of other States' own interests", and defence forces need to guard Timor-Leste against "potentially antagonistic powers".[51] *Force 2020* made a number of references to the fundamental objective of the state as defending the sovereignty of the country and territorial integrity.[52] The military would serve as a "constant affirmation of Timor-Leste in the world", reflecting the important idea that a military contributes to legitimatizing the sovereign identity of the Timorese state within the international community.

Force 2020 also criticized the King's College report for not paying sufficient attention to Timor-Leste's status as a maritime nation and the need to protect natural resources in the surrounding seas. It argued that Timor-Leste needed to focus on continental and maritime defence, with naval security a particular concern given the economic emphasis Timor-Leste places on energy resources in the Timor Sea, the fishing sector, maritime transport, tourism, ports and sea lanes.[53] Low-intensity maritime threats provided the rationale for a "sophisticated and modern" light naval force to ensure surveillance and protection of territorial waters.[54] Most donor countries considered a naval component as unnecessary as they viewed Australia as capable of patrolling East Timor's territorial waters.[55] However, *Force 2020* argued that Timor-Leste's geostrategic position between Indonesia and Australia constituted high vulnerability and subjected it to "constant attempts at strategic influence".[56] The rejection of option three was also linked to the fear of intervention in the military forces by other international actors, and the scepticism of being dependent upon Australia for maritime defence through its Pacific Patrol Boats Program. The report explicitly states that this situation would expose Timor-Leste sovereignty to risk, reflecting the perception that sovereignty entails "real" independence in security and defence.[57] Therefore, naval capabilities were viewed as "indispensable" to Timor-Leste's identity as a maritime state.[58]

Force 2020 is illustrative of the role of colonial history in Timor-Leste's perception of threat, particularly in the early years of statehood. In the first sentence, the document argues that the history and current "reality" of the world highlights how powerful states, "by excessive use and abuse of power, drag vulnerable countries into their economic dominion".[59] Threat perceptions based on historical events have been a driving force behind Timor-Leste's emergent national security policies. Additionally, *Force 2020* highlights the continuity from FALINTIL and F-FDTL, and the collective will to defend Timor-Leste's "sovereignty" during the Indonesian occupation.[60] The historical role of FALINTIL "functions as a guiding framework for the process of formulating the national defence strategy" and the aim was to establish a military institution that incorporated FALINTIL's "historic value" and "unique heritage", which has "immerasurable importance in providing experience and knowledge to defend the nation".[61] Here, the guerrilla forces form an important part of Timor-Leste's national identity.[62] The militarized culture that developed during the resistance appears to have shaped aspirations for a bigger F-FDTL and the belief that it is central to state survival. The report represented the armed forces as a "point of stability within national borders", a claim that would be undermined by the 2006 crisis (discussed below).[63] The idea of deploying armed forces throughout the territory "in order to maintain constant contact with the local populations" and incorporating citizens in the defence of the nation (e.g. through education) demonstrates a troubling emphasis on militarizing society.

Finally, *Force 2020* emphasized the importance of "real" independence, describing UN interventions as an "imposition of peace".[64] It criticized the role of the UN in the development of F-FDTL, arguing that the "imbalance" created by the prioritization of the PNTL reflected the UN's "lack of experience" and support in developing Timor-Leste's armed forces.[65] Later, the report obliquely referred to "analyses" that were "simplistic and indicative of underlying political and strategic interests" that shaped the initial formation of the armed forces and the choice of option three.[66] The initial plan, the report argued, aimed to turn the F-FDTL into a "symbolic force to guard or secure strategic points in order to consolidate the regional strategic defence of other countries, including world powers" and would "blackmail the future of the people of Timor-Leste, who fought, sacrificed and died for that future, for their own freedom and independence".⁶⁷ Consequently, the defence agenda would seek to move beyond "imported concepts" and find ways to bolster the role of the F-FDTL as an integral institution of the state.⁶⁸

The defence strategic blueprint referenced the legacy of Timor-Leste's experiences with intervention and resistance, and indicates that the past continues to shape perceptions of threat and the belief in defence preparedness even in times of peace. There is an acknowledgment that state fragility may provoke foreign intervention, especially by neighbours such as Australia.⁶⁹ In other places, *Force 2020* reflected on the tensions in the roles of the international community in denying and then securing Timor-Leste's statehood:

> The international community has systematically given Timor-Leste its support for development, has stimulated the strengthening of the systems of construction of the State, and the preservation of the values of liberty, fully attained by the supremacy of the national resistance struggle. A national resistance that, for 24 years, brandished its right to the independence that was denied to it and ignored by neighbouring states and by the international community.⁷⁰

By privileging external threats, *Force 2020* failed to anticipate the 2006 political crisis.

Internal security challenges came to the fore in 2006 as the "Petitioners Group", formed from 591 national army soldiers, were sacked for leaving their barracks during a strike in February.⁷¹ The petitioners were protesting against "perceived discrimination in favour of their ex-Falintil comrades, those traditionally connected to Fretilin, mostly drawn from the Eastern part of the island".⁷² After refusing to go back to their barracks, the petitioners were fired for desertion by the then-FRETILIN Government headed by Prime Minister Mari Alkatiri.⁷³ Over four hundred members of the East Timorese military took up arms in April 2006 to protest the firings and they demanded an investigation into claims of discrimination, leading to violent clashes with government troops and police in Dili.⁷⁴ On 28 March 2006, the riots were exacerbated when Alkatiri ordered troops to shoot at the protesters, and the police and army were unable to control the ensuing violence.⁷⁵ These riots could be understood as a resistance against the FRETILIN government and its increasingly authoritarian tendencies, highlighting the difficulties Timor-Leste's fragile democratic institutions faced in ensuring internal security and functional sovereignty in the new state.⁷⁶ The intervention in Timor-Leste internal security sector suggests that internal threats represented a greater security challenge for Timor-Leste than external threats presented by other states.

This crisis reflected the post-colonial security dilemma, characterized by pressing security challenges emerging from within state borders. Once again, Timor-Leste security relied upon external intervention, as a military force from Australia was deployed, along with smaller contingents from Malaysia, New Zealand and Portugal, to restore social and political order.⁷⁷ The United Nations Security Council Resolution 1704 of 25 August 2006 established the UNMIT, which was mandated to support Timor-Leste's Government in its efforts to consolidate stability and foster national cohesion.⁷⁸ The UNMIT was also responsible for restoring public security through interim law enforcement and assisting with the training, institutional development and strengthening of the police force (see Table 4.1 in chapter 4).⁷⁹ Timor-Leste was unable to make its independence "real" because it was unable to effectively exert empirical sovereign authority, and were ultimately forced to relinquish some control over key state functions such as the police and military to outside actors.

A New Approach to External Security in East Timor

By the 2007 elections, the political climate in Timor-Leste had mostly stabilized and the first FRETILIN government was replaced by the AMP coalition headed by former President, Xanana Gusmão. This government appeared determined to progress the state on many fronts; the IV Constitutional Programme, produced in September 2007, articulated a range of different governmental priorities mainly related to economic and political development and social cohesion.⁸⁰ The AMP government established a Ministry of Defence and Security, headed by Prime Minister Xanana Gusmão. On 11 February 2008, internal security was again challenged by assassination attempts on Ramos-Horta and Gusmão by a rebel group of assassins led by Alfredo Reinado.⁸¹

In September 2008, a Timor-Leste National Security Policy Workshop was held in which representatives of Timor-Leste parliament, government, civil society and security forces discussed national interests and priorities.⁸² The workshop found that while Timor-Leste security challenges were mostly domestic, external challenges, such as violations of territorial and maritime borders, were also identified. The workshop emphasized bilateral and multilateral security cooperation as a pathway to dealing with external threats. In 2009, the International Crisis Group criticized Timor-Leste's government for taking "few serious steps" to address SSR, and noted Timorese dissatisfaction with UN officials.[83] Following this conference, a new security focus emerged relating to external security and the survival of the East Timorese state, and in 2009 the government produced a Draft Law on National Security.[84] The 28/2011 Government Resolution adopted a new model for the F-FDTL based on the *Force 2020* study to prevent and respond to new threats such as terrorism and to support the integrated national security system outlined in the National Security Act (2/2010). The resolution confirmed F-FDTL's position as a national priority.

The Draft Law began with the statement: "[i]n the sovereign Democratic Republic of Timor-Leste, the State has the right and the duty to defend its essential elements; its territory, sovereignty and political power".[85] This corresponds with Timor-Leste's Constitution, which provides a vision of how Timor-Leste's political leaders perceived the constitutive components of sovereignty. Section 6 (Objectives of the State) of the Constitution states:

> the fundamental objectives of the State shall be: a) to defend and guarantee the sovereignty of the country; b) to guarantee and promote fundamental rights and freedoms of the citizens and the respect for the principles of the democratic States based on the rule of the law; c) to defend and guarantee political democracy and participation of the people in the resolution of national problems.[86]

The Constitution reflects the concerns of drafters for protecting Timor-Leste's hard-won rights to self-determination and sovereign independence. Defending the territorial integrity of the state is described as a central objective of sovereign states, corresponding to the absolute external sovereignty concept. In defining national security, Section 1 Article 2 of the Draft Law states:

> The State defends and ensures the independence and sovereignty of political power, the unity and integrity of the national territory and the freedom and safety of communities pursuant to the Constitution, this law and other legislation that is in force, through an integrated and coordinated array of State-led activities that make up National Defence, Internal Security and Civil Protection.[87]

The purpose of the national security law was to implement a programme of SSR by integrating and coordinating the activities of the military (FALINTIL-FDTL) and police force (PNTL) concerning national defence, internal security and civil protection.[88] Due to the complex nature of internal and external threats in the twenty-first century, Timor-Leste sought to reform its security sector by blurring the roles of the police and military in international and domestic spheres to negotiate the increasingly unclear divisions between internal and domestic threats.

The Draft Law permitted the state to "involve all resources" to address threats to national security (Article 3).[89] "National Security" referred specifically to guaranteeing national sovereignty and preventing and deterring threats (Article 4).[90] According to Gusmão, the FALINTIL-FDTL is responsible for preparing "for the eventuality of war in order to fulfil its constitutional responsibilities to guarantee national independence, territorial integrity and the freedom and security of the population against any aggression and external threat".[91] This indicated the concerns held by Timor-Leste leadership regarding the maintenance of its national security against external threats, despite the 2006 crisis highlighting the deep internal security challenges. In 2010, the National Security Law legislation was passed in order to clarify the roles of the police and military in East Timor.

On 11 June 2010, two 1960s Class Jaco Patrol Boats were purchased from China by the AMP government, who outlayed US$28 million over five instalments from 2008–10, adding to the two patrol boats donated by Portugal in 2001.[92] As Timor-Leste's 2009 State Budget totalled US$680.8 million, the money allocated to purchasing the patrol boats is relatively substantial, particularly given the various economic challenges facing Timor-Leste as the poorest state in the Southeast Asian region.[93] The two vessels were part of the National Defence Policy that the AMP government had been developing over several years.[94] According to Defence Minister Julio Tomas Pinto, "[t]he purpose of purchasing the vessels is firstly to provide resources to the F-FDTL, the Naval Component and other bodies. Secondly it seeks to enable control of the Timor Sea along with neighbouring countries, especially in the South Coast. Politically it seems positive for Timor-Leste to buy these two vessels."[95] Gusmão justified the spending by arguing that "the independence of a state entails possessing the necessary means to secure the territorial integrity and ongoing functioning of the institutions, and therefore, this also entails having the capacity to defend the peoples natural wealth".[96] The patrol boats were perceived as a means of securing "real" independence by bolstering external defence capacities in an attempt to reduce reliance upon other states such as Australia.

The purchase of these vessels drew criticism from neighbouring states, especially Australia which was not consulted in the process. At the handover ceremony of the two patrol boats, Gusmão responded by stating "we cannot consider ourselves a sovereign country if every time we are to make a fundamental decision, we have to consult our neighbours, friendly and partner countries".[97] This statement reflects Timor-Leste desire to reduce reliance on Australia and Indonesia for external and internal security, and reinforced the image of a traditional state, with sovereignty entailing the capacity to defend the territory from external threat. A radio broadcast in Australia suggested that Timor-Leste AMP government perceived China's involvement as a "counter-balance to dependence, particularly on Australia".[98] Murdoch suggested that the Chinese boats were a "slap in the face for Australian diplomacy" and strained relations between the AMP coalition and the Australian government (see chapter ten).[99]

Survival and protection of sovereign status became an integral component of Timor-Leste national security policy. In a lecture on defence and security in 2010, Prime Minister Xanana Gusmão declared:

> the same way that democratic and developed countries have been worrying about their defence and security for hundreds of years, investing in those areas, Timor-Leste cannot hesitate to invest in its defence of security so that it may PROTECT THE SOVEREIGNTY OF THE COUNTRY.[100]

Gusmão maintained that "in terms of security and defence, Timor-Leste, which is located both in Southeast Asia and in the greater Pacific region, is not immune to regional strategic manoeuvrings".[101] Timor-Leste is, like any state, vulnerable to threats, including non-state threats such as terrorism, piracy, organized crime, illegal immigration, weapons trade and so forth. While the purchase of the boats in 2010 was primarily motivated by illegal fishing, Timor-Leste's leadership was also concerned with national defence and survival through developing its military capabilities.

Gusmão argued that Timor-Leste could no longer rely so heavily upon Australia and Indonesia for security and offered a justification for moving towards friendlier relations with other states. He declared:

> Timor-Leste has to avoid falling into political naivety, thinking our constitution, on its own, can guarantee our national independence, territorial integrity and sovereignty over its resources.[102]

This declaration reveals several important thoughts on Timor-Leste's security and defence policy: first, that Indonesia and Australia have colluded in the past against Timor-Leste's interests and could do so again; second, that sovereignty is not guaranteed, even if it has been developed and supported by the international community; and third, that functional independence relies upon the capacities of Timor-Leste to be realistic (i.e. not "naïve") concerning its external security. The 2011 Strategic Development Plan (SDP) similarly contended that "the national 'spirit of defence' would be to prevent a climate of complacency that may be detrimental to our national strategic interests". This links "real" independence with the capacity to ensure territorial integrity and defence of the sovereign state.

Timor-Leste's security and defence policy is motivated by the protection of its territory and population from another invasion, reflecting a sense of insecurity grounded in past experiences with foreign rule and occupation. Gusmão stated:

> one should never cast aside the possibility of armed conflicts, whatever their nature should be. Our own history has shown us, as well as all the other wars that have been fought and that are still being fought, that wars can be caused for a great many reasons, including to take control over natural resources of other countries.[103]

The "realist" perspective underpinning the development of Timor-Leste's National Security Policy is contestable. Timor-Leste's political history includes collusion between Australia and Indonesia in opposing Timor-Leste's right to self-determination; however, its right to self-determination, and subsequent attainment of sovereignty, was ultimately permitted and supported by the international community through various state-building and peace-building activities.

On 15 November 2010, Lindsay Murdoch reported in *The Sydney Morning Herald* that Timor-Leste would acquire two patrol boats from South Korea and aimed to purchase an additional nine smaller patrol boats to add to its fleet.[104] These boats, delivered in June 2011, would be primarily responsible for intercepting asylum seeker boats.[105] According to Murdoch, this symbolized Timor-Leste's movement away from Australia's "sphere of military influence". East Timorese leaders criticized the Australian government for not supporting their efforts to build their navy. Timor-Leste Secretary of State for Defence, Julio Tomas Pinto, suggested the Australian government was reluctant to support a Timorese navy with boats and accused it of hindering Timor-Leste's efforts to tackle people smuggling by putting too many conditions on its eligibility for the "Pacific Patrol Boat Program" (Australia's maritime cooperation scheme in the South Pacific). He suggested that Australia's reluctance to assist Timor-Leste in developing its naval capacity was reflected in its unwillingness to provide patrol boats, unlike China.[106] However, in April 2008, the Australian Defence Department did send a maritime needs analysis team to Timor-Leste to examine maritime security cooperation, including the possibility that Timor-Leste could participate in the Pacific Patrol Boats Program.[107] The offer to join the programme was rejected by Timor-Leste on the grounds that the communication systems would run through Australia.

China, it seems, "got in first".[108] Pinto argued that China supported Timor-Leste "without conditions", unlike other states such as Australia and the United States.[109] The AMP government shifted its foreign security policy away from the two-pronged approach that had been pursued by the first FRETILIN government. The patrol boats, therefore, symbolized an effort by Timor-Leste to strengthen its independence by building defence capacities and reducing its heavy reliance upon Australia.[110] Consistent with its diversified approach to foreign policy, Dili's patrol boats purchase allowed it to show Canberra that it has "other choices when it comes to defence partners".[111] Even though Australia and Timor-Leste's bilateral relations have been challenged by a long-running dispute over Timor Sea resources, Australia remains a key security partner for Timor-Leste. In June 2014, a new $1.88 billion Pacific Patrol Boat Program was announced by Australia's foreign and defence ministers.[112] Timor-Leste was invited to participate in the Australian Pacific Maritime Security Program, and the Australian government offered Timor-Leste two new patrol boats, including sustainment, training for naval personnel, and advisory support.[113] The purchase of patrol boats from China was viewed by some defence experts as undermining Australia's maritime security interests. It is in Australia's interests to support small maritime states in the region such as Timor-Leste in patrolling their waters.[114] Defence experts also viewed it in Timor-Leste's interests to join the programme because the boats are the only ones capable of protecting the EEZs of island states such as Timor-Leste.[115] Timor-Leste ultimately joined the Pacific Patrol Boat Program, and in November 2017 it was announced that the company Austal would build two boats for Timor-Leste. Timorese security NGO Fundasaun Mahein wrote that this was a significant improvement on the "ineffective" vessels provided by South Korea and China that were unable to operate in the rough Timor Seas, leaving the National Police of Timor-Leste to rely upon a boat owned by an environmental NGO to arrest shark poachers.[116]

In November 2016, Timor-Leste's government approved the Ministry of Defence Strategic Concept for Defence and National Security, a defence and security white paper covering the future decade.[117] It confirmed the central mission of the defence forces to protect against threat and aggression, and drew on the history of Timor-Leste's struggle, although also focused on the importance of foreign policy and internal security for Timor-Leste's sovereignty.[118] In 2015, US$33.4 million was budgeted to defence, the second highest spending since 2006 (US$37.7 million was allocated in 2012).[119] This constituted approximately 2.5 per cent of the government spending, a 6.1 per cent real increase on the 2014 defence budget and the highest percentage since 2010.[120] In contrast, Singapore (a small state model for Timor-Leste in international relations) spends significantly more on defence capabilities to act as a deterrent as a result of vulnerability. A defence budget of around 5 per cent has enabled the acquisition of most modern defence equipment "beyond the capacity of its close neighbours".[121] This spending, however, corresponded with significant economic development. Increases in military spending appear unnecessary given the relatively low-level external security threats that it faces, particularly in contrast to internal challenges. Despite the increases, Timor-Leste has not significantly advanced its ambitious procurement plans outlined in *Force 2020*, highlighting the mismatch between aspirations and capabilities. Timor-Leste's armed forces could only offer minor resistance in the face of external attack regardless of increases in military spending.[122]

Security Beyond the State

Timor-Leste's strategic interests as a small state demands defence cooperation with other states. On 21 March 2012, at the second Jakarta International Defence Dialogue, Gusmão contended that "nowadays interdependence is critical. We are here with the assumption that states should work together and protect the interests, both national and global."[123] This followed the signing of a memorandum with Indonesia in August 2011 which covered training and military support.[124] The defence ministers of Australia, Indonesia and Timor-Leste have also held trilateral meetings.[125] These defence cooperation schemes highlighted Timor-Leste's willingness to engage with its neighbours on security — despite the history between the states — when it suited its perceived interests.[126] However, the SDP makes it clear that it pursues cooperation because it does "not want to become militarily dependent" on other states.[127] The *Force 2020* report presents a realist vision of the limitations of diplomacy when it argued that "it is unrealistic to consider it possible to overcome foreign controversies without the use of Armed Forces. The new strategic environment and developments... confirm that diplomacy without force is nothing more than an exercise in abstract and inconsequential rhetoric."[128] Defence and naval power was presented as important for supporting Timorese foreign policy and diplomacy and defence of national interests.

Force 2020 expressed a desire to take part in joint exercises and operations at regional and global levels.[129] The report also makes it clear that within the context of defence interdependence and collective security mechanisms, Timor-Leste was determined to move away from a dependent, "subordinate" position in collective defence mechanisms and would "fight to take a partner's role".[130] The capacity to engage in defence cooperation and global peace missions relies upon resources, such as professional personnel and interoperable capacities.[131] The key for Timor-Leste's perspective was to develop an independent approach to defence and security within the context of interdependence, whereby Timor-Leste would be an equal partner that could conduct combined military activities with increased interoperability with Indonesia and Australia. This is again linked back to Timor-Leste's history and the potential threat that it could be subject to colonialism in the future:

> In the case of Timor-Leste, if our country loses the capacity to defend itself and to participate equitably in collective defence efforts, it will consequently cease to have a voice in international organisations. Moreover, when a sudden conflict emerges in which Timor-Leste cannot remain neutral or participate with forces, its national sovereignty and independence will be put at risk. This situation will reduce Timor-Leste *to the condition of a "colony"* of the nation-State providing its defence [my emphasis].[132]

Timor-Leste's main security partners are Australia, the United States, Japan and Portugal. Australia has provided assistance to Timor-Leste through the Defence Cooperation Program since early 2001, which involves offering military training, advice and support (and is separate from the Australian Defence Force commitments in UN missions). In May 2008, Timor-Leste signed a military cooperation agreement with seven other Portuguese-speaking countries. Brazil and Portugal agreed to assist with military training of F-FDTL personnel.[133] A joint Australia–Timor-Leste bilateral agreement was signed in September 2013 to consolidate security cooperation.[134] The US Navy also conducts training exercises with Timor-Leste's defence force.[135] The sixth unity government views the departure of the International Stabilization Force and the United Nations Mission in 2012 as a sign that Timor-Leste has "learned from its weaknesses" in internal security and has achieved "an atmosphere of social and political peace".[136] The sixth government maintained its focus on modernizing and professionalizing the F-FDTL in order for it to defend the nation, "support internal security and contribute to efforts seeking to tackle threats against regional and global peace and stability".[137] The perceived success of Timor-Leste's post-2006 peacebuilding period has compelled successive governments to participate more actively in securing international peace and stability by sharing its "accomplishments" in international dialogues and aspiring to provide peacekeepers.[138]

Defence cooperation is viewed as supporting Timor-Leste's broader foreign policy agenda as it strengthens "trust" between states.[139] Underpinning this is a constructivist notion that dialogue and diplomacy work to alleviate traditional security dilemmas that arise from arms procurements. As chapter ten will discuss further, military modernization is one of the emergent threats shaping geopolitical security and order in the Asia-Pacific region. Like many states, Timor-Leste has developed a two-pronged strategy in response to this contemporary regional threat by building trust through dialogue and cooperation whilst simultaneously contributing to this dynamic by building up and modernizing its military.

Timor-Leste's contribution to international peacebuilding and peacekeeping reflects the aspirational foreign policy outlined in the previous chapter, and is shaped by a desire to be perceived as a leader among fragile states within the international community. *Force 2020* emphasized not just Timor-Leste's capacity to defend its territory and population, but to also contribute to global and regional security. It aspired for Timor-Leste to contribute during peacetime to peacekeeping missions as a "powerful instrument of support to the State's foreign policy".[140] The SDP presented an ambitious aim for the PNTL and the F-FDTL to possess the capability to be fully utilized by the United Nations in its peacekeeping activities.[141] Making contributions to peacekeeping is not necessarily unique among fragile and/or post-conflict states. The OECD Peacekeeping Database demonstrates that many fragile states provide peacekeepers to other fragile states, including Burundi, Chad, Côte d'Ivoire, Democratic Republic of Congo and Sierra Leone.[142] For fragile states such as Timor-Leste, peacekeeping can also provide a valuable income stream. One avenue is through the Melanesian Spearhead Group (MSG) which has ambitions to establish a regional peacekeeping force. According to Sousa-Santos, Timor-Leste's cooperation with the MSG and the Pacific Islands states more generally could be advantageous to mitigating traditional and non-traditional security threats in the region as it has "nascent special force capabilities and growing UN peacekeeping experience, as well as large, and well-trained and equipped policing and paramilitary units".[143] Additionally, Timor-Leste has experience dealing with the development-security nexus that can be shared with other fragile and conflict-affected states in the region.[144]

Timor-Leste's defensive strategic posture is supported by alliances, diplomacy and participation in defence forums.[145] This posture, however, "does not renounce the use of forces to guarantee… independence", indicating Timor-Leste's readiness to defend national interests when more peaceful options fail.[146] This indicates a realist vision of external security threats as Timor-Leste's independence requires the state being capable of defending territory from foreign forces despite the low likelihood of external military threats or being invaded by another state.[147] Yet, ideational motivations also underpin Timor-Leste's pursuit of absolute external sovereignty through military strengthening despite the improbability of external threats. Realistically, Timor-Leste armed forces could only offer minor resistance in the face of external attack regardless of increased military spending.[148] The SDP declared that the East Timorese state would support its national security agenda by ensuring that the F-FDTL has the capacity to both defend the nation and contribute to tackling "threats to regional and global peace and stability", reflecting a perception that national security is a "vital investment" in Timor-Leste's future.[149]

The Problems of Internal Security

In May 2012, Timor-Leste celebrated the tenth anniversary of its attainment of independent sovereign statehood. In the same month, President José Ramos-Horta was replaced by Taur Matan Ruak, who was endorsed by Prime Minister Xanana Gusmão (himself re-elected in July 2012).[150] Both leaders share similar sentiments about security and sovereignty, reflecting their roles as military chiefs during the resistance struggle. Taur Matan Ruak took over the armed-wing of resistance movement following the arrest of Xanana Gusmão in 1992, and became Timor-Leste's defence chief after independence. In 2008, Taur Matan Ruak submitted a proposed Law on Defence and Security to National Parliament which bizarrely featured references to Maharishi's "Absolute Theory of Defence, Sovereignty in Invincibility", an idea emerging from transcendental meditation that suggests national security relies upon an unconquerable military.[151] In June 2012, the new president was quoted as saying: "[m]y major concerns is security and good lives [sic] and both things will not be separated and they are bases [sic] of the independence and sovereignty for sustainable economic system and is the way of good lives [sic]."[152] This reflects a belief in a mutual relationship between security and providing citizens with the capacity to live a good life, and recognition that internal and external security are conducive to peace and stability.

The relatively free and fair elections in 2012 were particularly important as they demonstrated the consolidation of Timor-Leste democratic institutions, which are integral for ensuring domestic security and social and political order. The success of the elections enabled the withdrawal of international forces and UNMIT from the territory in November 2012, giving Timor-Leste greater independence by ensuring its internal security and continuing to develop its security forces. Similar to other Southeast Asian and South Pacific states, illegal fishing remains a challenge for Timor-Leste's maritime economy and sustainability, however persistent security challenges remain largely internal. Understanding Timor-Leste's management of internal security is important as it positions itself as a leader within the g7+ organization of fragile nations (see chapter six).

The SDP articulated plans for achieving a secure, stable Timorese society as a precondition for social and economic development.[153] It outlined three dimensions to East Timor's defence policy: human security, cooperative security, and homeland defence.[154] Key goals regarding internal security included "the development of a professional, respected defence force that is under democratic control and that has the capacity to defend our nation".[155] In terms of internal security, political violence has decreased in Timor-Leste since 2008, and it ranked 56th of 163 states according to the 2016 Global Peace Index.[156] However, in 2016, the Fund for Peace Failed State Index had Timor-Leste in the "alert" category indicating a high risk of failing institutions, using a methodology that overwhelmingly considers political and security conditions as causes of state fragility.[157] The report puts Timor-Leste's economy in the lowest quintile of the world's 141 weakest states. The Index of State Weakness in the Developing World report produced by the Brookings Institute positions Timor-Leste as one of the top five weakest states in East Asia and the Pacific, deemed marginally less fragile than Papua New Guinea.[158]

The legitimacy of the Timorese state continues to be challenged by a small number of ex-resistance rebel forces. In February 2008, Major Alfredo Reinado, the highest ranking officer of the Petitioner rebels, was killed during a "half baked" failed coup attempt against Ramos-Horta and Gusmão.[159] Mauk Moruk (Paulino Gama), regarded by elites as a symbol of resistance against the government, was also killed by security forces in 2015.[160] His Maubere Revolutionary Council (KRM) is a pro-poor paramilitary organization linked to the veteran organizations Sagrada Familia and the Committee for the Popular Defence of the Democratic Republic of Timor-Leste (CPD-RDTL). These groups have denied recognition of the constitution, questioned the legitimacy of Timor-Leste's government, conducted attacks on policy and marched in military uniforms.[161] These groups increasingly picked up on the discontent of the majority of Timorese who had been excluded from the economic benefits that oil wealth has provided for some in the country. As Powles and Sousa-Santos argue, the divisions between the KRM and Gusmão have their legacy in the resistance movement when Gama attempted a coup against Gusmão's leadership in 1984.[162] Compounding this dynamic is the public support offered to the Sagrada Familia by F-FDTL chief, General Lere Anan Timur during the resistance. In a worrying sign for human rights in the territory, Amnesty International reported dozens of arbitrary arrests and instances of torture and ill-treatment by security forces in response to the KRM attacks against police.[163] This example highlights the ways in which the legacies of the resistance movement continue to affect the internal security situation in Timor-Leste as the military became a source of alternative "cult" leaders and would-be revolutionaries. Informal security groups such as armed gangs, paramilitaries and martial arts groups also continue to present threats to the Timorese state's monopoly on the legitimate use of violence. While levels of conflict appear lower than in the 2006 crisis, martial arts groups remain a threat to peace.[164]

A study by Valters, Dewhurst and Catheu suggests that Timor-Leste's security situation has been underpinned by international peacekeeping, local responses to violence and SSR, and it relied upon the "national unity" consensus between political leaders and the charismatic legitimacy of Gusmão, in addition to the distribution of state revenues from finite oil and gas reserves.[165] One of the crucial factors to improved political stability has been the revenue from hydrocarbon resources in the Timor Sea.[166] Other cases of oil-rich developing states have largely demonstrated the negative impacts on stability and security.[167] According to Scambary, however, governments have used the oil revenue for major infrastructure projects and for buying peace at the expense of "other urgent socio-economic needs".[168] Of particular concern is the government spending on generous veterans pensions and cash transfers in order to "buy the peace" by limiting tensions within and between the military and police, in addition to the socio-economic inequalities that emerge when state benefits are directed towards "elites".[169] The OECD reports that several groups "have demanded and received payments by threatening violence".[170] Patronage systems also underpin the stability as the "allocation of contracts to influential elites is widely considered as a necessary evil".[171] The 2016 budget allocated more money to the ministry that oversees veteran pensions than the Ministries of Health and Education combined; far less than the 40 per cent promised by Ramos-Horta in 1996.[172]

While international intervention has made a positive contribution to Timor-Leste in terms of legitimizing the state and providing the conditions for basic security, in the interviews they conducted, Valters, Dewhurst and Catheu noted a clear narrative "that much of the security progress made in Timor-Leste has been due to a shift in decision-making away from donors towards the Timorese state".[173] This reflects a general distrust towards international donors, and Timor-Leste's political elite compounded this by condemning the UNMIT. Gusmão, for instance, accused UN staff of "mental colonialism" and disregarding Timor-Leste's sovereignty: "[i]n our constitution it says: do not alienate our sovereignty, do not sell our sovereignty to other people."[174] An overconfident Timor-Leste emerged after oil and gas revenues began to flow, and by the end of the UNMIT's term, elites were reported to feel that it was time for Timor-Leste "to run its own affairs, unbridled by foreigners poking their noses around and venturing opinions on how they are doing it", whilst reluctantly recognizing its ongoing dependence on foreign advice.[175] An article written by Pinto in 2009 in *Tempo Semanal* (translated into English, and presumably aimed at a foreign audience) indicates that the leadership wanted UNMIT to leave, and evoked Timor-Leste's sovereignty in his argument.[176]

One of the key challenges for Timor-Leste's security is the transfer of power from the resistance leaders to the "next generation". According to Timorese government spokesperson Agio Pereira, "voters believe that only Gusmão can guarantee national security".[177] This statement symbolizes the troubling authoritarian streak of "big man politics" that infects Timor-Leste's nascent democracy. While Gusmão quitted the Prime Ministership in 2015, and a new "national unity" government headed by Dr Rui Maria de Araújo was formed, Gusmão did not step aside completely from government. It is commonly understood that Gusmão continued to exert considerable authority within the new government, complicating the idea that a genuine transfer had occurred. The uncertainty following the 2017 parliamentary elections, wherein the Parliamentary Alliance Majority led by Gusmão prevented the FRETILIN government from passing its national programme through parliament, highlights his continuing influence, although what shape this will take beyond 2017 is unknown.[178] In any case, the reliance on Gusmão's charismatic legitimacy to underwrite stability suggests that peace may not be as sustainable as government officials represent.

Some measures that have decreased political violence may not continue to yield results in the longer term unless there are more sustainable economic and development policies instituted.[179] In other words, Timor-Leste's security requires policy not military solutions. As the next chapter examines in greater detail, Timor-Leste's state budget remains highly dependent upon oil and gas revenues from the Timor Sea. By the end of 2017, Australia, Timor-Leste and the commercial venture partners had yet to agree on a development plan for the contested Greater Sunrise gas field, which Timor-Leste depends upon for short- to mid-term economic viability. Even if a solution is found, it is unlikely to be a panacea for the long-term development challenges facing the small state, particularly in the absence of a substantive economic diversification plan. An economic collapse would likely have catastrophic effects on Timor-Leste's internal security and governance capacities.

Conclusion

Since becoming a sovereign state, Timor-Leste has sought to exert an independent and autonomous foreign policy, including establishing a defence policy that views the key national interest as protecting Timor-Leste's sovereignty and territory from external threat. According to Seabra, while "Timor-Leste clearly has the right to provide for its own national defence, these overly ambitious designs and the apparent political will to pursue them may, in the short-term, become counter-productive and complicate longer-term training and other military-to-military relationships."[180] This chapter has argued that internal security challenges are the dominant threats to Timor-Leste's "real" independence, as political instability, economic underdevelopment and the fragility of policing and military institutions have resulted in international intervention. Timor-Leste's history demonstrates that international intervention is more likely to occur due to internal disorder prompted by social, economic and political challenges. According to McDougall, "[a] strengthening of legitimacy is what is needed to enable Timor-Leste to facilitate 'development' in various substantive areas. Such development in the context of legitimacy would provide a basis for achieving 'security' on a long-term basis."[181] Social and economic development and the consolidation of political institutions are more likely to support Timor-Leste's goal of self-determination. "Security" should be associated with policy responses rather than the military domain, a theme that is picked up in chapter ten. International intervention can thus be avoided by developing internal security, which itself is supported by the consolidation of democracy and human development, and the presence of a robust civil society.

Successive East Timorese governments have sought to make it "as difficult as possible for an external power ... to invade" by establishing a standing army.[182] While both the FRETILIN and AMP coalition governments emphasize these external threats, consolidating military capacity has been a prominent feature of East Timor's foreign policy agenda since 2005. The rhetoric of leaders such as Xanana Gusmão and the military build-up indicate East Timor's desire to ensure conventional sovereignty by enhancing its capacities to guarantee its own sovereignty, reflecting ideational motivations and a sustained distrust of foreign actors. As Ball and others have argued, military threats against East Timor from foreign sources are the least probable.[183] While East Timor was denied independence for twenty-four years, the international community was crucial in permitting and supporting its legal and domestic sovereignty through recognition of its sovereign rights and the international state-building and peacekeeping missions. Since World War Two, the principle of self-determination has rendered political colonization an illegitimate action and it is unlikely that Timor-Leste will be invaded now that its sovereignty is guaranteed and supported by international law. This renders East Timor's pursuit of "real" independence through military build-up (at the expense of other priorities) somewhat irrelevant.

While emphasizing cooperation with Indonesia and Australia in official policy documents, Timor-Leste has also sought to develop relations with other states, particularly in Asia. The next chapters examine Timor-Leste's relationships with its powerful neighbours in more detail. In its relations with Australia, the defining foreign policy issue has been the Timor Sea dispute. Chapter eight examines how this has the capacity to affect Timor-Leste's future socio-economic prospects, thereby having likely flow-on effects on the government's capacity to "buy" internal peace and stability. Chapter nine, meanwhile, demonstrates that Timor-Leste's post-colonial security dilemmas continue to be driven by its relationship with Indonesia. Timor-Leste's pragmatic foreign policy approach of appeasement is examined in relation to international reconciliation, which is in a sense an insurance policy that simultaneously undermines principles of international justice and efforts to establish democratic rule of law. This reflects a trade-off between normative values and building an international image as a state that conforms to liberal principles of human rights, and the pragmatic realism driven by fears stemming from a history of Indonesian colonialism. Finally, the concluding chapter discusses broader regional security and changing balance of power dynamics that might threaten Timor-Leste's security in the future, as well as non-traditional security threats relating to sustainability and climate change.

NOTES

1. Alyson Bailes, Jean-Marc Rickli, and Baldur Thorhallsson, "Small States, Survival and Strategy", in *Small States and International Security: Europe and Beyond*, edited by Clive Archer, Alyson Bailes and Anders Wivel, pp. 26–45 (Oxon: Routledge, 2014).
2. See International Crisis Group, "Timor Leste: Oecusse and the Indonesian Border", *Asia Briefing* No. 104 (Dili/Brussels: International Crisis Group, 20 May 2010); Alexandra Retno Wulan, "Border Incident a Test Case for Jakarta–Dili Ties", *The Jakarta Post*, 14 January 2006; Warren Wright, "The Complexities of Timor-Leste–Indonesia Border Control", *East Timor Law and Justice Bulletin*, 25 February 2013.
3. See República Democrática de Timor-Leste (RDTL), *Strategic Development Plan*, p. 166 (Dili: Government of Timor-Leste, 2011); Xanana Gusmão, "Military Operations Other than War: Regional and National Perspectives", Address by His Excellency the Prime Minister and Minister of Defence and Security, Kay Rala Xanana Gusmão, on the Occasion of the Second Jakarta International Defence Dialogue, Jakarta, 21 March 2012; Asia Pacific Center for Security Studies, "Timor-Leste National Security Policy Workshop", Honolulu, 8–12 September 2008.
4. Gusmão, "Military Operations Other than War".
5. See Brian Job, "Introduction", in *The Insecurity Dilemma: National Security of Third World States*, edited by Brian Job, p. 12 (Boulder: Lynne Rienner Publishers, 1992).

6. Ben Dolven, Rhoda Margesson and Bruce Vaughn, *Timor-Leste: Political Dynamics, Development, and International Involvement* (Congressional Research Service, 3 July 2012).
7. Sven Gunnar Simonsen, "The Role of East Timor's Security Institutions in National Integration – and Disintegration", *The Pacific Review* 22, no. 5 (2009): 576.
8. Ibid.
9. Selver Sahin, "Timor-Leste: A More Confident or Overconfident Foreign Policy Actor?", in *Southeast Asian Affairs 2012*, edited by Daljit Singh and Pushpa Thambipillai, p. 341 (Singapore: Institute of Southeast Asian Studies, 2012).
10. Xanana Gusmão, "Reviewing Resistance and Understanding the Present", Lecture by His Excellency the Prime Minister and Minister for Defence and Security Kay Rala Xanana Gusmão on the Strategic Framework Module for Timor-Leste Within the Pilot Course on Defence and Security, Dili, 9 November 2010.
11. Ibid.
12. Ibid.
13. Ibid.
14. Lindsay Murdoch, "Timor's Boats Buy Real Independence", *The Age*, 15 November 2010.
15. See Selver Sahin and Donald Feaver, "The Politics of Security Sector Reform in 'Fragile' or 'Post-Conflict' Settings: A Crucial Review of the Experience in Timor-Leste", *Democratization* 20, no. 6 (2012): 1056–80.
16. The last Australian Defence Force Troops left Timor-Leste on 28 March 2013. Australian Broadcasting Commission, "Last ADF Troops Leave East Timor", *ABC News*, 28 March 2013.
17. Simonsen, "The Role of Timor-Leste Security Institutions in National Integration", p. 586.
18. Ibid., p. 586.
19. See the National Council of Maubere Resistance, "East Timor Peace Plan", available at <http://www.ci.uc.pt/timor/cnrm.htm> (accessed 11 February 2017).
20. José Ramos-Horta, *Towards a Peaceful Solution in East Timor*, 2nd ed., p. 23 (Sydney: ETRA, 1997).
21. Ibid., p. 21.
22. Elsina Wainwright with Alan Dupont, James J. Fox, Ross Thomas and Hugh White, *New Neighbour, New Challenge: Australia and the Security of East Timor*, p. 23 (Canberra: Australian Strategic Policy Institute, 20 May 2002). For a history of F-FDTL development, see Edward Rees, *Under Pressure: Falintil – Forças de Defesa de Timor-Leste. Three Decades of Defence*

Force Development in Timor-Leste 1975–2004 (Geneva: Centre for the Democratic Control of Armed Forces, 2005).
23. Rees, *Under Pressure*, pp. 12–13.
24. Centre for Defence Studies, *Independent Study on Security Force Options for East Timor* (London: The Centre for Defence Studies, King's College, 2000).
25. Desmond Ball, "The Defence of East Timor: A Recipe for Disaster?" *Pacifica Review Global Change, Peace and Security* 14, no. 3 (2002): 176.
26. Ibid., pp. 175, 178.
27. Rui Graça Feijó, "Challenges to the Consolidation of Democracy", in *A New Era? Timor-Leste After the UN*, edited by Sue Ingram, Lia Kent and Andrew McWilliam, pp. 62–63 (Canberra: ANU Press, 2015).
28. Rizal Sukma, "Securing East Timor: Military and External Relations", in *Peace Building and State Building in Timor-Leste*, edited by Hadi Soesastro and Landry Haryo Subianto, p. 97 (Jakarta: Centre for Strategic and International Studies, 2002).
29. Anthony Smith, "Constraints and Choices: East Timor as a Foreign Policy Actor", *New Zealand Journal of Asian Studies* 7, no. 1 (June 2005): 15.
30. Sukma, "Securing East Timor", pp. 95–97.
31. RDTL, *Strategic Development Plan*, p. 166; Gusmão, "Military Operations Other than War".
32. Smith, "Constraints and Choices", p. 29.
33. Ibid., p. 25.
34. Julia Gillard, "Moving Australia Forward", Lowy Institute, Sydney, 6 July 2010.
35. Refworld, "Timor-Leste (East Timor): Activists Say No to Proposed New Refugee Centre", 23 July 2010, available at <http://reliefweb.int/report/timor-leste/timor-leste-activists-say-no-proposed-new-refugee-centre> (accessed 11 February 2017).
36. Tom Allard and Kirsty Needham, "No Refugee Centre For Us: East Timor", *The Age*, 29 March 2011.
37. Smith, "Constraints and Choices", p. 31.
38. Ball, "The Defence of East Timor", p. 179.
39. Wainwright, "New Neighbour, New Challenge", p. 23.
40. East Timor Planning Commission, *National Development Plan*, p. 106 (Dili: Planning Commission, May 2002).
41. RDTL, *Force 2020*, 2007, available at <https://www.locjkt.or.id/Timor_E/pdf/Forca202007.pdf> (accessed 11 February 2017).
42. International Crisis Group, "Timor-Leste: No Time for Complacency", *Asia Briefing* No. 87, p. 6 (Dili/Brussels: International Crisis Group, 9 February 2009).
43. Peter Edwards, "Two Cheers for Forward Defence", *The Strategist* (Canberra: Australian Strategic Policy Institute, 29 May 2015).

44. *Force 2020*, pp. 46, 47, 72, 76, 77.
45. Centre for Defence Studies, *Independent Study on Security*.
46. José Kei Lekke Sousa-Santos, "Acting West, Looking East: Timor-Leste's Growing Engagement with the Pacific Islands Region", in *Regionalism, Security and Cooperation in Oceania*, edited by Rouben Azizian and Carleton Cramer, p. 110 (Honolulu: Asia-Pacific Centre for Security Studies, 2015).
47. José Manuel Neto Simões, "Novo modelo das Forças Armadas de Timor-Leste (FALINTIL-FDTL)", *Jornal de Defesa e Relaçôes Internacionals* (2012).
48. *Force 2020*, p. 13.
49. Ibid., p. 19.
50. Ibid., p. 20.
51. Ibid., pp. 6, 93.
52. Ibid., pp. 33, 34 .
53. Ibid., p. 17. For a comprehensive account of maritime challenges in the Asia-Pacific, see Sam Bateman, "Managing Good Order at Sea in the Asia-Pacific", in *Maritime Challenges and Priorities in Asia: Implications for Regional Security*, edited by Sam Bateman and Joshua Ho, pp. 21–33 (London and New York: Routledge, 2013).
54. *Force 2020*, pp. 7, 24, 77.
55. Ibid., p. 91.
56. Ibid., pp. 7, 35.
57. Ibid., p. 92.
58. Ibid., p. 94.
59. Ibid., p. 3.
60. Ibid., p. 41.
61. Ibid., pp. 45, 70, 85.
62. Ibid., p. 133.
63. Ibid., p. 85.
64. Ibid., p. 4.
65. Ibid., pp. 62, 132, 133.
66. Ibid., p. 72.
67. Ibid., p. 70.
68. Ibid., p. 66.
69. Ibid., p. 22.
70. Ibid., p. 14.
71. Damien Kingsbury, "Political Developments", in *East Timor: Beyond Independence*, edited by Damien Kingsbury and Michael Leach, p. 21 (Clayton: Monash University Press, 2007); Damien Kingsbury and Michael Leach, "Introduction", in *East Timor: Beyond Independence*, edited by Damien Kingsbury and Michael Leach, p. 5 (Clayton: Monash University Press, 2007); Selver Sahin, "Building the State in Timor-Leste", *Asian Survey* 47, no. 2 (2007): 266.

72. Matsuno, "Analysing Timor-Leste Electoral Politics from a Socio-Economic Perspective", p. 334.
73. Kingsbury, "Political Developments", p. 21.
74. Sahin, "Building the State in Timor-Leste", p. 266.
75. Kingsbury, "Political Developments", p. 21.
76. Jacqueline Siapno, "Timor-Leste: On a Path of Authoritarianism?" *Southeast Asian Affairs* (2006): 325–40; Sven Gunnar Simonsen, "The Authoritarian Temptation in East Timor: Nationbuilding and the Need for Inclusive Governance", *Asian Survey* 46, no. 4 (July/August 2006): 575–96.
77. Derek McDougall, "The Security-Development Nexus: Comparing External Interventions and Development Strategies in Timor-Leste and Solomon Islands", *Asian Security* 6, no. 2 (2012): 177; Doven, Margesson and Vaughn, *Timor-Leste*.
78. UNSC, "Resolution 1704", S/RES/1704, 25 August 2006.
79. Ibid.
80. RDTL, *Fourth Constitutional Government Program 2007–2012*.
81. Ben Dolven, Rhoda Margesson and Bruce Vaughn, *Timor-Leste: Political Dynamics, Development, and International Involvement*, p. 8 (Congressional Research Service, 3 July 2012).
82. Asia Pacific Center for Security Studies, "Timor-Leste National Security Policy Workshop".
83. International Crisis Group, "No Time for Complacency", pp. 1, 6.
84. RDTL, *Law on National Security* (Dili: Government of Democratic Republic of Timor-Leste, 2009).
85. Ibid.
86. Constituent Assembly, *Constitution of the Democratic Republic of Timor-Leste* (Dili: Democratic Republic of Timor-Leste, 2002).
87. RDTL, *Law on National Security*.
88. Ibid.
89. Ibid.
90. Ibid.
91. Gusmão, "Reviewing Resistance and Understanding the Present".
92. Linda Mottram, "Timor-Leste Navy Buys Chinese Boats", *ABC Radio National*, 7 June 2010.
93. United Nations Mission in Timor-Leste, "Socio Economic Affairs", 20 August 2009, available at <https://unmit.unmissions.org/socio-economic-affairs> (accessed 16 July 2012).
94. Lindsay Murdoch, "Relations Strained as Timor-Leste Buys Chinese Navy Boats", *The Age*, 7 June 2010.
95. Julio Tomas Pinto, "Reforming the Security Sector: Facing Challenges, Achieving Progress in Timor-Leste", *Tempo Semanal*, 18 August 2009.

96. Xanana Gusmão, Speech by His Excellency the Prime Minister and Minister for Defence and Security Kay Rala Xanana Gusmão at the Handover Ceremony of the Two Patrol Boats Class Jaco, Dili, 11 June 2010.
97. Ibid.
98. Mottram, "Timor-Leste Na vy Buys Chinese Boats".
99. Murdoch, "Relations Strained as Timor-Leste Buys Chinese Navy Boats".
100. Gusmão, "Reviewing Resistance and Understanding the Present".
101. Ibid.
102. Lindsay Murdoch, "Timorese Tweak Canberra with Patrol Boat Buys", *The Age*, 15 November 2010.
103. Gusmão, "Reviewing Resistance and Understanding the Present".
104. Murdoch, "Timorese Tweak Canberra with Patrol Boat Buys".
105. Mark Dodd, "Timor-Leste Blasts Australia for Failing to Help with Patrol Boats", *The Australian*, 10 February 2011.
106. Ibid.
107. Mottram, "Timor-Leste Navy Buys Chinese Boats".
108. Ibid.
109. Pinto cited in Rebecca Strating, "East Timor's Emerging National Security Agenda: Establishing 'Real' Independence", *Asian Security* 9, no. 3 (2013): 199 .
110. Dolven, Margesson and Vaughn, *Timor-Leste*, p. 14.
111. Murdoch, "Relations Strained as Timor-Leste Buys Chinese Navy Boats".
112. Shahryar Pasandideh, "Australia Launches New Pacific Patrol Boat Program", *The Diplomat*, 1 July 2014.
113. Commonwealth of Australia, *2016 Defence White Paper*, p. 128 (Canberra: Department of Defence, 2016); Australian Embassy in Timor-Leste, "Australia Offers Timor-Leste New Patrol Boats", 27 April 2016, available at <http://timorleste.embassy.gov.au/dili/Defence.html> (accessed 11 February 2017).
114. Linda McCann, *The Future of Australia's Pacific Patrol Boat Program*, p. 21 (Canberra: Centre for Defence and Strategic Studies, Australian Defence College, August 2013).
115. Anthony Bergin, "Pacific Maritime Security—From Quad to Hexagon", *The Strategist* (Canberra: Australian Strategic Policy Institute, 22 July 2014).
116. Fundasaun Mahein, "Timor-Leste Must Prepare for New Patrol Boats", 8 November 2017.
117. RDTL, *Strategic Concept for Defence and National Security* (Dili: Ministry of Defence, 2016); RDTL, "Launching of the Strategic Concept for Defence and National Security", Democratic Republic of Timor-Leste, Dili, 8 September 2015; RDTL, "Council of Ministers Meeting on November 22nd, 2016", Democratic Republic of Timor-Leste, Dili, 22 November 2016.

118. RDTL, *Strategic Concept for Defence and National Security*.
119. Prior to 2010, higher percentages on defence reflect much lower government spending. Government of Australia, *2016 Defence Economic Trends in the Asia-Pacific*, DIO Reference Aid 16–512, pp. 26–27 (Canberra: Department of Defence, Government of Australia, August 2016).
120. Ibid.
121. Michael Leifer, *Singapore's Foreign Policy: Coping with Vulnerability*, p. 3 (London: Routledge, 2000).
122. Simonsen, "The Role of East Timor's Security Institutions in National Integration", p. 585.
123. Gusmão, "Military Operations Other than War".
124. Republic of Indonesia Defence Ministry, *Indonesia Defence White Paper 2015*, p. 82 (Jakarta: Ministry of Defence of the Republic of Indonesia, 2015).
125. Xanana Gusmão, "Timor-Leste's Role and Future in a Rising Asia Pacific", Singapore, 4 June 2013.
126. Mark Dodd, "Forgive and Forget as Dili Signs Jakarta Defence Pact", *The Australian* (Sydney: News Limited, 29 August 2011).
127. Pinto, "Reforming the Security Sector".
128. *Force 2020*, p. 91.
129. Ibid., p. 69.
130. Ibid., pp. 36, 43.
131. See for example Bailes, Rickli and Thorhallsson, "Small States, Survival and Strategy".
132. Ibid., p. 91.
133. Global Security, "Armed Forces of Timor-Leste (F-FDTL)", available at <http://www.globalsecurity.org/military/world/timor/f-fdtl-htm> (accessed 11 February 2017).
134. Ibid.
135. Government of Australia, *2016 Defence Economic Trends in the Asia-Pacific*, pp. 26–27.
136. RDTL, "Program of the Sixth Constitutional Government 2015–2017" (Dili: Government of the Democratic Republic of Timor-Leste, 6 March 2015).
137. Ibid.
138. Ibid.
139. Ibid.
140. *Force 2020*, pp. 54, 69, 70.
141. RDTL, *Strategic Development Plan*, p. 174.
142. The OECD 2014 fragile states report states that "a country contributing 100 troops for one year would receive at least USD 1.3 million in reimbursement from the UN". OECD, *Fragile States 2014: Domestic Revenue Mobilisation in Fragile States*, p. 40, available at <https://www.oecd.org/dac/conflict-fragility-resilience/docs/FSR-2014.pdf> (accessed 11 February 2017).

143. Sousa-Santos, "Acting West, Looking East", pp. 110, 117–18.
144. Ibid., p. 120.
145. RDTL, *Strategic Development Plan*, p. 165.
146. Ibid., p. 165.
147. Ball, "The Defence of East Timor", p. 18.
148. Simonsen, "The Role of Timor-Leste Security Institutions in National Integration", p. 585.
149. RDTL, *Strategic Development Plan*, p. 165.
150. Dolven, Margesson and Vaughn, *Timor-Leste*, p. 4.
151. Bu V.E. Wilson, "The Exception Becomes the Norm in Timor-Leste: The Draft National Security Laws and the Continuing Role of the Joint Command", *Centre for International Governance and Justice Issues Paper* 11, p. 11 (Canberra: Australian National University, September 2009).
152. Author unknown, *Guide Post Magazine* 70 (June 2012): 54.
153. RDTL, *Strategic Development Plan*, p. 160.
154. Ibid., p. 160.
155. Ibid., p. 160.
156. Institute for Economics and Peace, "Global Peace Index 2016", available at <www.economicsandpeace.org> (accessed 11 February 2017).
157. The Fund for Peace, *Fragile States Index 2016* (Washington: Fund for Peace, 2016).
158. Susan Rice and Stewart Patrick, *Index of State Weakness* (Washington: Brookings Institution, 2008).
159. Jill Jolliffe, "Ramos-Horta Shot Twice", *The Sydney Morning Herald*, 11 February 2008.
160. Australian Broadcasting Commission, "Former East Timor Guerrilla Leader and Opposition Figure Mauk Moruk Killed in Security Operation, Government Says", *ABC News*, 10 August 2015.
161. Anna Powles and José Sousa-Santos, "Xanana Gusmão – Mauk Moruk: Timor Struggles with Its Past and Future", *Lowy Interpreter*, 5 December 2013; Michael Leach, "The Politics of History in Timor-Leste", in *A New Era? Timor-Leste After the UN*, edited by Sue Ingram, Lia Kent and Andrew McWilliam, p. 45 (Canberra: Australian National University Press, 2015).
162. Powles and Sousa-Santos, "Xanana Gusmão – Mauk Moruk".
163. Amnesty International, *Timor-Leste 2015/2016 Annual Report*, available at <https://www.amnesty.org/en/countries/asia-and-the-pacific/timor-leste/report-timor-leste/> (accessed 11 February 2017).
164. James Scambary, "Informal Security Groups and Social Movements", in *Politics of Timor-Leste: Democratic Consolidation After Intervention*, edited by Michael Leach and Damien Kingsbury, pp. 203–13 (New York: Cornell University Press, 2013); Janina Pawelz, "Security, Violence, and Outlawed

Martial Arts Groups in Timor-Leste", *Asian Journal of Peacebuilding* 3, no. 1 (2015): 121.
165. Craig Valters, Sarah Dewhurst and Juana de Catheu, *After the Buffaloes Clash: Moving from Political Violence to Personal Security in Timor-Leste*, Development Progress Case Study Report, p. 7 (London: Overseas Development Institute, 2015).
166. Doven, Margesson and Vaughn, *Timor-Leste*.
167. John Braithwaite, Hilary Charlesworth and Aderito Soares, *Networked Governance of Freedom and Tyranny: Peace in Timor-Leste*, p. 248 (Canberra: ANU Press, 2012).
168. James Scambary, "In Search of White Elephants: The Political Economy of Resource Income Expenditure in East Timor", *Critical Asian Studies* 47, no. 2 (2015): 283–308.
169. Valters, Dewhurst and Catheu, *After the Buffaloes Clash*, pp. 13, 22.
170. OECD, *Fragile States 2014*, p. 79.
171. Valters, Dewhurst and Catheu, *After the Buffaloes Clash*, p. 27.
172. RDTL Ministry of Finance, *State Budget 2016: Book One* (Dili: Democratic Republic of Timor-Leste, 2016).
173. Valters, Dewhurst and Catheu, *After the Buffaloes Clash*, pp. 21–22.
174. Author unknown, "Gusmão Accuses UN of Trampling on Timor", *Sydney Morning Herald*, 20 May 2011.
175. Gordon Peake, "Timor-Leste Declares Open Season on the UN", *Lowy Institute*, 7 July 2011.
176. Pinto, "Reforming the Security Sector".
177. Agio Pereira, "Timor-Leste Transforming Belligerent Democracy into Consensus Democracy", *Tempo Semanal*, 26 January 2014.
178. Rebecca Strating, "Timor-Leste in 2017: A State of Uncertainty", in *Southeast Asian Affairs 2018*, edited by Malcolm Cook and Daljit Singh (Singapore: ISEAS – Yusof Ishak Institute, 2018).
179. Valters, Dewhurst and Catheu, *After the Buffaloes Clash*, p. 7.
180. Pedro Seabra, "The Need for a Reshaped Foreign Policy", in *The Politics of Timor-Leste: Democratic Consolidation After Intervention*, edited by Michael Leach and Damien Kingsbury, p. 156 (Ithaca, NY: Cornell University, 2014).
181. McDougall, "The Security-Development Nexus", p. 180.
182. Smith, "Constraints and Choices", p. 33.
183. Ibid.; Ball, "The Defence of East Timor", p. 18.

8

Securing Economic Sovereignty

The central contention of this book is that Timor-Leste's leaders promote an absolute external sovereignty concept that views self-determination and a lack of reliance upon other actors in the international community as central to effective statehood. As the previous chapter examined, the "security-development nexus" reflects the mutually-reinforcing relationship between conflict management, and economic and institutional development. According to José Ramos-Horta, Timor-Leste is "keenly aware of the link between security, stability and poverty reduction".[1] The capacities of state governments to deliver key services to citizens are "essential" for managing conflict, and internal security conditions influence the capacities of states to promote economic development.[2] While the previous chapter highlighted the security dimensions of effective statehood, this chapter examines the use of foreign policy by Timorese governments to advance their economic ambitions to secure empirical sovereignty by consolidating their governmental capacities.

As a self-identified fragile state, Timor-Leste's ability to enact its vision of sovereignty relies upon its medium- and long-term development and resource allocation plans, and its economic relations with other actors in the global economy. Timor-Leste's leaders recognized during the independence movement that Timor-Leste's economic independence would rely upon the oil and gas reserves in the Timor Sea, a body of water separating the coastlines of the island of Timor and Australia by less than 400 nautical miles. Since 2007, Timor-Leste has experienced high rates of economic growth and associated gains in socio-economic development indicators due to joint oil and gas development with Australia.[3] This has enabled Timor-Leste's political leaders to present the state as a fragile state "success story" (see chapter four). Timor-Leste's representatives, including Xanana Gusmão, promote these finite resources as the centrepiece of its ambitious economic plans. The 2011 Strategic Development Plan (SDP) articulated aspirations of turning Timor-Leste into an upper-middle income state by 2030. This goal forms an important part of its aspirational foreign policy.

Timor-Leste's biggest economic challenge has also constituted its biggest foreign policy challenge: since 2002, the issue of who "owns" the resources in the Timor Sea has complicated bilateral relations between Timor-Leste and Australia. Maritime resources are inherently tied up with Timor-Leste's economic viability and internal sovereign capabilities as oil revenues have provided over 90 per cent of government revenue, rendering the state as central to wealth production and the allocation of scarce economic resources. However, its foreign policy approach became increasingly defined by *symbolic* sovereign narratives, based on the idea that permanent maritime boundaries are central to completing full sovereignty. Timor-Leste shifted towards an "activist" foreign policy approach to pursue its Timor Sea aims.

While oil revenues from joint production with Australia have reduced Timor-Leste's dependence on the international community, the scope and depth of Timor-Leste's economic development challenges remain daunting. Although oil revenues have flowed through the country, and the poverty rate has declined since 2007, the national poverty rate in 2014 was higher than in 2001.[4] By 2014, approximately 41 per cent of the population lived on an income of less than US$0.88 per day.[5] Over recent years, Timorese leaders prioritized spending on ambitious industrialization plans at the expense of investment in health, education and agriculture. The lack of economic diversification and unequal balance of trade arrangements create vulnerabilities that may adversely affect Timor-Leste's international relations and threaten the achievement of its upper middle income aspirations, particularly after the hydrocarbon revenues disappear.

Timor-Leste's Constitution promotes a vision of a social democratic state that provides social, cultural and economic rights to citizens.[6] However, as Hey notes, small states are often caught between the neoliberal policies of intergovernmental organizations and demands from citizens for government spending.[7] Since the 1980s, multilateral economic forums engaged in the global development agenda, such as the World Bank and the International Monetary Fund (IMF), have inculcated neoliberal discourses that promote economic structural reform in favour of the market over state intervention. Through advice or loan conditionalities, these institutions privilege neo-classical economic ideas such as fiscal consolidation, enhancing the private sector and promoting foreign direct investment (FDI). Timor-Leste has sought to conform to orthodox neoliberal policies in areas of trade and FDI, but has struggled to advance diversification, invest substantially in human capital, strengthen institutions or engage in sustainable spending. This creates challenges for the future of Timor-Leste's independence and democratic consolidation.

The Problems of Aid Dependence

The sovereignty of "fragile" states is underwritten by the international community, a dynamic which itself constitutes a form of dependence, particularly for those states who rely upon aid or loans in order to deliver basic services to citizens. There are well-noted tensions between self-determination and international assistance as the donor-recipient relationship constitutes a power hierarchy that means sovereignty can be "held hostage" by the demands of an ideologically-driven international development agenda.[8] The reliance upon international loans and/or foreign aid is anathema to ideals of self-determination at the heart of the absolute external sovereignty concept. Upon achieving sovereign independence, Timor-Leste became one of the poorest and most underdeveloped states in Southeast Asia and the world.[9] Timor-Leste initially relied upon a range of international aid donors, experts and advisors for the provision of essential services, resources and programmes.[10] In May 2002, for instance, the World Bank and partners established a Transition Support Program to provide bridging finance for Timor-Leste's first government in the absence of revenue, contributing over US$70 million a year from 2003–5.[11] It is difficult to get a clear picture of the foreign aid directed to Timor-Leste, including where it came from and where it was spent.[12] It is estimated that Timor-Leste received $6 billion to $9 billion in foreign assistance between 1999 and 2011.[13] Its biggest aid donor, Australia, contributed around US$930 million in foreign aid from 1999–2010.[14] According to Brant, in the period of 2006 until 2014, Australia provided significantly more aid than other foreign donors, donating US$789.19 million.[15] In comparison, the second largest donor, the United States, contributed US$238.65 million, followed by the European Union, Japan, New Zealand and China.[16]

Many in the development sphere criticized the assistance in Timor-Leste as "top-down", western-centric and hubristic, more likely to reinforce patterns of dependency than build capacity. The period of state-building under the United Nations Transitional Administration in East Timor (UNTAET) was described by some as an "invasion" of foreign donors, UN agencies, and international non-governmental organizations (INGOs).[17] Others have questioned the efficacy of the aid in supporting Timorese citizens. *La'o Hamutuk*, for instance, estimates that only around 10 per cent of foreign assistance stayed in Timor-Leste, as the vast bulk of the money has been spent on foreign staff wages, consultancies and administration.[18] These interventions paradoxically compromised and supported Timor-Leste's political independence. According to Sousa-Santos, these experiences of foreign intervention "shaped Timorese perspectives of their own political agency".[19] As previous chapters have argued, that "non-interference" features as a constitutive component of Timor-Leste's vision of sovereign independence reflects these experiences of foreign intervention.

There is considerable scholarship on the ways in which assistance can disempower local decision-makers and compromise self-determination. Some critics have viewed aid assistance as a form of neo-colonialism in which development "partners" exert forms of power on aid dependent states.[20] Dependence is created and reified as aid recipients are required to conform to donor demands. According to this narrative, one such way that donors, experts and advisors exert power is through the dissemination and inculcation of dominant global development norms around concepts such as "good governance", which relates to the management of public resources, the presence of rule of law, civic rights and a lack of corruption and transparency.[21] Processes of socialization have seen international development culture and norms become increasingly prominent within recipient communities.[22] These norms may differ from the social, cultural or traditional norms within individual states, which can establish cognitive dissonances between the international development community and the states they seek to assist. This has led some observers to comment on the ways the development agenda imposes values upon dependent states as international actors become increasingly important for determining governance in domestic politics.[23]

International actors can exert power through assessment tools they use to allocate aid. Hughes defines "aid dependence" as "the pressing and continuous orientation of local political practices towards a monitoring, evaluating and decision-making international audience".[24] One such example is the World Bank Country Policy and Institutional Assessment (CPIA), which provides a measure of state economic fragility by assessing "the extent to which a country's policy and institutional framework supports sustainable growth and poverty reduction".[25] It is used by decision-making agencies to allocate aid resources, and highlights the kinds of uniform demands that international institutions make on developing states.[26]

International actors can also exert power through the use of conditions and incentives in aid provision.[27] Some argue that aid conditionalities are important for improving good governance in recipient states, however, the effectiveness of such conditions are debated within the literature.[28] Indeed, Hughes points out that national political elites can also "promote" aid dependence "as a means to exercise power".[29] The U.S. foreign policy, for example, tends to link aid with good governance. The United States Agency for International Development (USAID) reports that the United States provided $272 million to Timor-Leste between 2000 and 2008, mostly on fostering economic growth (via a free market economy), human development, democracy, governance and institutional development, media and civil society.[30] The 2005 Paris Declaration recognized the importance of local ownership and self-determination in development strategies, which has led to a downplaying of aid conditionalities.[31] Nevertheless, the "imposition" of standards of good governance has been a part of the critique of donors in Timor-Leste.

Aid dependencies can undermine the capacities of governments to act free of foreign constraints as recipients must meet the demands of donors, advisors and experts. Being reliant on aid is presented as antithetical to the vision of "real" independence promoted by Timor-Leste's representatives. In 2012, Sahin noted the tendency of Timorese representatives to dismiss or resent international criticisms or advice about policies or activities as a "product of biased approach and inaccurate knowledge".[32] Xanana Gusmão went as far as to accuse foreigners of wishing Timor-Leste to be classified as unstable because they prefer to work in Timor-Leste than other conflict-affected states.[33] At the 2013 Bali Democracy Forum, Gusmão stated that, "[i]n the current world juncture, western nations or the developed democracies demand the integral accomplishment of all the standards, imposed on us under the guise of all sorts of conventions, regardless of whether we are able or not to implement them."[34] Even Ramos-Horta criticized UN bureaucrats for "pseudo-analysis" and their remote attitudes towards local culture and society.[35]

Aid can increase dependency, however dependence can also stimulate demands for greater self-determination and autonomy, presenting a binary within the political rhetoric between local actors ("us") and foreign actors ("them") that drives nationalism.[36] The Timorese Director of the g7+, Helder da Costa, described the "influx" of aid, donors and INGOs in 2002 — each with different theories and approaches to development — as a cause of the political instability from 2002 until the crisis in 2006.[37] According to da Costa, "peace" was only re-established following the election of the Gusmão-led National Congress for Timorese Reconstruction (CNRT) government in 2007. He praised the "Goodbye Conflict, Welcome Development" policy platform for enabling Timor-Leste to reach "considerable key performance indicators", including reducing poverty rates and increases in gross domestic product (GDP). What was noticeably absent from the analysis is that the CNRT-government's election coincided with the flow of revenues from the exportation of Timor Sea oil and gas. It also neglected to note that internal stability was underwritten by the international stabilization force from 2006–12.

However, overly structuralist explanations of international aid tend to neglect local agency: the Timorese were not "passive recipients" or "victims" of development.[38] Aid recipients can appropriate and exploit state fragility "for their own purposes, in order to delay political reforms or to convince donors to invest more aid money in 'situations of fragility'".[39] As chapter five argued, the g7+, along with other development forums, have offered Timor-Leste's representatives a mechanism for shaping the global development agenda. The "fragile state" identity is used as a way to develop its international image as a leader within the development space. It is hence important to recognize that Timor-Leste is not simply a passive recipient of aid and subject to values and structures imposed by the international community, but uses international forums and leadership as a means to pursue interests.

Timor-Leste's Economic Ambitions

Timor-Leste's economic ambitions are outlined in the SDP. It aspired for Timor-Leste to transform its subsistence economy into a "modern diversified economy" and become a significant regional economic player in ASEAN.[40] Former Finance Minister Emilia Pires stated in 2010, "if the first decade of the twenty-first century was dominated by China, then I feel the second decade will be for Timor-Leste".[41] The SDP makes it clear that Timor-Leste's future is "bound up with the sea".[42] On the day of Timor-Leste's independence, Australia and Timor-Leste's Prime Ministers signed the Timor Sea Treaty (TST), which established the Joint Petroleum Development Area (JPDA) and placed a moratorium on boundary delimitation. Timor-Leste's achievement of lower-middle income status in 2011 was largely a result of Timor Sea revenues, increased state spending and high global oil prices.[43] The Timor Sea oil revenues have been crucial for Timor-Leste's independence and economic viability as they have furnished around 90 per cent of state budgets, and enabled Timor-Leste to build a Petroleum Wealth Fund worth US$16 billion.[44] As a consequence, Timor-Leste's formal economy is almost entirely dependent upon petroleum exports. The flow of oil and gas revenues, and the corresponding decrease in aid dependence, increased the power of political leaders over the allocation of resources.[45]

Successive Timorese governments viewed Timor Sea oil and gas reserves as providing the basis for developing local petrochemical refining industries. The SDP presented the case for oil industrialization as allowing Timor-Leste to extend its economy "beyond the simple selling of oil and gas".[46] Timor-Leste's political leaders claimed that an oil industry would help establish and strengthen infrastructure, create employment opportunities and provide an industrial base to the economy. Although the SDP committed the state to developing three key pillars — agriculture, tourism and petroleum — Timor-Leste's narrow and undiversified economic base has led leaders to prioritize oil and gas resources in the formation of economic policy. The oil mega-project, *Tasi Mane*, has been promoted as one of the Timorese government's highest priorities.[47] The development comprises three industrial clusters — the Suai Supply Base, the Betano Refinery and Petrochemical Industry Cluster, and the Beaco Liquified Natural Gas (LNG) Plant — an airport and a 155-kilometre highway.[48]

The key to Timor-Leste's petroleum refining ambitions is the lucrative but contested Greater Sunrise gas field, a 5.1 trillion cubic foot gas field estimated to be worth US$40 billion. Encompassing the Sunrise and Troubadour deposits, Greater Sunrise straddled the interim eastern lateral boundary of the Timor Gap. Ownership of the field was contested between Australia and Timor-Leste. Under principles of "natural prolongation", Australia argued that the Timor Trough — a 3,500 metre trench 40 nautical miles from the coastline of Timor-Leste — divides two continental shelves. Australia claimed sovereign rights over territory that extends under the sea to the edge of the continental shelf. However, contemporary international law through the United Nations Convention on the Law of the Sea (UNCLOS) tended to support Timor-Leste's claims that the principle of equidistance should see a median boundary drawn between the two states.[49]

While the median line arguments are relatively straightforward, the boundary that mattered for determining ownership was the eastern lateral boundary that splits Greater Sunrise. The legal arguments around where the lateral boundary should be located was much more complex and legally ambiguous than the median line (i.e. the horizontal line between Australia and Timor-Leste).[50] Australia supported the eastern lateral interim line, which was originally drawn according to legal principles of simplified equidistance. In March 2003, Timor-Leste and Australia finalized the Sunrise International Unitization Agreement (Sunrise IUA) in March 2003, and the states agreed that 20.1 per cent of Greater Sunrise was located in the shared JPDA and 79.9 per cent within Australia's jurisdiction. Under the terms of the Sunrise IUA, based on the principle of equidistance, Timor-Leste would only receive an 18.1 per cent share of the revenue derived from its 90 per cent share of the JDPA. Timor-Leste's leadership, however, argued that a permanent boundary should be shifted to the east (i.e. adjusted equidistance).

Timor-Leste relied upon the *Opinion in the Matter of East Timor's Maritime Boundaries* (the "Lowe opinion") commissioned in 2002 by Petrotimor, an oil and gas company with a vested interest in shifting the line eastward.[51] This legal opinion was challenged by other legal and maritime boundary experts.[52] The UNCLOS provides little guidance beyond the requirement of equity, "making it difficult to precisely determine where the boundaries in the Timor Sea may be drawn".[53] The point is that, unlike the JPDA area, the ownership of Greater Sunrise was unclear under the UNCLOS regime.[54]

The technical aspects of maritime boundary law was rendered somewhat irrelevant by Australia's withdrawal from the relevant UNCLOS and the International Tribunal for the Law of the Sea (ITLOS) arbitration instruments in 2002. This denied Timor-Leste the ability to test its boundary claims in an international court. The 2006 Treaty on Certain Maritime Arrangements in the Timor Sea (CMATS), signed and ratified by both states, established a framework for developing Sunrise by setting aside these contests about boundaries. It was Ramos-Horta who suggested a moratorium on maritime boundary delimitation to circumvent contested territorial claims.[55] While the terms of the previous Sunrise IUA had allocated less than 20 per cent of Greater Sunrise to Timor-Leste, Ramos-Horta secured a 50 per cent revenue share.[56] Crucially, however, the CMATS put aside questions of how the gas field would be developed. Following the 2007 elections, Xanana Gusmão's administration sought to develop an export pipeline from Greater Sunrise to the south coast of Timor-Leste on the basis that onshore processing would allow Timor-Leste to develop its economy through petroleum industrialization. In April 2010, the licensee Woodside informed the Australian stock exchange (ASX) that a floating LNG platform was the best commercial option for processing the gas.[57] Australia supported Woodside, putting at risk Timor-Leste's export pipeline and oil industrialization plans. As a consequence of Timor-Leste's failure to achieve downstream processing, Timor-Leste reactivated its pursuit of maritime boundaries. Rather than abandon industrialization plans in the absence of an agreement with Australia, Timor-Leste's leaders invested resources from the Petroleum Wealth Fund into developing *Tasi Mane*. In essence, Timor-Leste's economic development plans depended upon its capacities, as a small state, to change the foreign policy of a powerful state.

By the end of 2017, it had appeared that Timor-Leste's strategy was successful in altering important aspects of Australia's policies, although it remained unable to secure the pipeline necessary for its oil industrialization plans. There are two key pillars to Timor-Leste's "activist" strategy.[58] Since 2012, the strategy has been firstly characterized by a concerted public relations campaign designed to bring about social and political change. There are reports that Timor-Leste's government allocated over US$600,000 to an Australian public relations company to assist with the activist campaign.[59] The central narratives emphasize normative considerations and principles, such as justice, and are disseminated through networks and structures of international solidarity. It resembles a traditional "activist campaign", and its objective is to change Australia's foreign policy in relation to the Timor Sea. The activist approach is driven by the aspirational foreign policy outlined in chapter four; the government has co-opted long-running civil society narratives to serve its economic ambitions and draws upon solidarity networks developed through the independence movement. The public diplomacy campaign sought to persuade Australia to negotiate permanent maritime boundaries in a way that would give Timor-Leste a larger proportion of Greater Sunrise. Failing this, Timor-Leste argued that Australia should submit to the International Court of Justice (ICJ) to arbitrate the dispute. For a number of years, Australia's responses to public diplomacy efforts was to steadfastly support CMATS and refuse to re-enter boundary negotiations.

The second pillar was using international legal proceedings to place pressure on Australia, and to prosecute the case that Australia was acting outside the acceptable boundaries of the "rules-based order". By 2016, Timor-Leste had initiated four international legal proceedings against Australia relating to the Timor Sea dispute. In 2013, Dili initiated a proceeding aimed at invalidating the CMATS on the grounds that Australia allegedly spied on East Timorese negotiators in 2004, which contravened the Vienna Convention of the Law of Treaties.[60] Australia's intelligence apparatuses retaliated by seizing legal documents and property from the offices of Timor-Leste's Australian legal representative. This culminated in a second proceeding initiated in the ICJ against Australia. In 2014, this case was abandoned following Australia's return of Timor-Leste's documents. The third proceeding initiated under the TST related to the taxation of the petroleum exported from the JPDA.[61] These traditional strategies were also ineffective in changing Australia's approach.

A series of breakthroughs in the maritime boundary dispute arrived through the use of unprecedented United Nations Compulsory Conciliation (UNCC) proceedings under Annex V of UNCLOS, initiated by Timor-Leste in 2016. The UNCC is not a court or an arbitral tribunal: its purpose was to assist states to reach an amicable settlement of maritime disputes. A commission of five conciliators was due to produce a report by October 2017 for Australia and Timor-Leste as a basis of future bilateral negotiations, however, the highly confidential talks remained ongoing at the end of 2017.

In January 2017, as part of the UNCC proceedings, Timor-Leste notified Australia of its wish to terminate the CMATS, a move that Australia accepted without threatening the terms of the TST. As a *quid pro quo*, Timor-Leste abandoned the spying and taxation legal proceedings.[62] This revived Australia's obligation to negotiate permanent maritime boundaries, but also exposed Timor-Leste to the risk of receiving less than the 50 per cent revenue share in the CMATS. On 30 August 2017, a press release revealed details of progress in the negotiations that would become known as the "Copenhagen Agreement".[63] Both states agreed to the central elements of a maritime boundary delimitation and addressed "the legal status of the Greater Sunrise gas field, the establishment of a Special Regime for Greater Sunrise, a pathway to the development of the resource, and the sharing of the resulting revenue". It was possible to glean from the "Copenhagen Agreement" that while Timor-Leste was able to negotiate a maritime boundary with Australia, it had to compromise on its claims to the entire Greater Sunrise gas field.[64] A commitment was undertaken in December 2017 for the states to sign the treaty text by March 2018.[65] A plan for joint development, however, had not been reached between Timor-Leste and the venture commercial partners, highlighting again that one of the most stubborn disagreements has been how to develop the field.

The UNCC process appears to have been useful for Timor-Leste pursuing maritime boundaries under the rules of UNCLOS, although how it may ultimately contribute to its oil industrialization goals remains to be seen. While Australian representatives initially emphasized the non-binding nature of the conciliation, and argued that it was under no obligation to reach a settlement based on the final report, the UNCC process forced Australia to come to the negotiating table in a way that it had previously been avoiding. The conciliation structures alleviated some of the power imbalances within the typically asymmetrical relationship. Yet, without a development plan for Greater Sunrise, the deal on maritime boundaries provides a symbolic rather than a material victory.

In part, the evolution of Timor-Leste's foreign policy strategy since 2004 reflects the importance of particular leaders in shaping Timor-Leste's ambitions. The turn to an activist strategy reflects a shift away from the pragmatic realism of Ramos-Horta, who was principally concerned with expediting the development of the Sunrise gas field, given its centrality to Timor-Leste's economy. In contrast, Timor-Leste's then-President, Xanana Gusmão, threatened to veto the treaty because he was not persuaded that Timor-Leste should compromise its (perceived) sovereignty over the gas fields.[66] While Ramos-Horta was viewed as "conciliatory and forgiving" of Australia's stance, nationalist Gusmão has been a "passionate advocate" for boundaries and onshore oil development.[67] Gusmão's rise to the Prime Ministership in 2007 corresponded with an increasingly nationalist tone regarding the importance of sovereign boundaries and Timor-Leste's perceived ownership of petroleum reserves.

Another way of understanding Timor-Leste's activist strategy is based on the historical success of the independence movement, which relied considerably on international solidarity. Understanding why this has become the foci of Timor-Leste's public diplomacy campaign requires acknowledging that "shared" (albeit contested) narratives of the national past links this dispute to the independence movement. Timor-Leste's narratives draw significantly upon past and current perceptions of Timor-Leste's "struggle for recognition". There is a belief that Timor-Leste has beaten "Goliath" before and can do so again.[68] However, as chapter two suggests, Australia's policy on the question of East Timor's self-determination did not shift as a result of civil society pressure, but because Indonesia permitted the popular consultation.

Timorese political representatives have presented the contest as the next phase of Timor-Leste's independence movement, a narrative that evokes the idea that Timor-Leste's sovereignty remained incomplete without permanent maritime boundaries. For example, in a speech in February 2016, Prime Minister Dr Rui Maria de Araújo argued that permanent maritime boundaries was:

> the final step in realising our full sovereignty as an independent State. From our perspective, this is the second and last phase of our pursuit of the liberation of Timor-Leste. It has been almost fourteen years since the restoration of our independence. We have made tremendous progress. We have made great socio-economic development — we have constructed the foundations of the State, and the construction of the nation. We have moved from a fragile country towards strong development in different areas. But, our struggle for sovereignty will not be over until we have claimed our maritime sovereignty.[69]

Similarly, Timor-Leste's Ambassador to Australia, Abel Guterres, publically declared that "for Timor-Leste this is another struggle for our full independence and sovereignty over land and sea".[70] As such, Timorese leaders have promoted the idea that Timor-Leste's struggle for sovereign recognition is not actually complete after the attainment of political independence. The struggle for recognition narrative was designed to generate support from within Australia civil society, sectors of which showed considerable support to Timor-Leste's independence movement during Indonesia's occupation.[71]

Timor-Leste's activist foreign policy strategy has also been motivated by domestic political factors. The anti-colonial nationalism that developed through resistance against Indonesia's occupation continues to be integral to Timorese national identity, and roles in the resistance movement continue to be a potent source of political legitimacy. Domestically, the "struggle for recognition" narrative serves multiple political purposes: they unify and mobilize Timor-Leste's public against a common enemy, they provide a distraction from significant socio-economic challenges facing the nation and from criticism about its allocation of resources, and assist in consolidating the power of those in the Timorese government.

Personal motivations of Timor-Leste's leaders should also be factored into the formation of the Timor Sea activist strategy. Political economy experts, such as James Scambary, have questioned the rationale for the *Tasi Mane* project, suggesting that it appears to be motivated by personal rather than economic motivations.[72] Any cost-benefit analysis of *Tasi Mane* has not been conducted transparently.

A study commissioned by the government put the socio-economic benefits of oil processing plant in Timor-Leste at about US$155 million over five years, which is minimal compared with the costs of the investment.[73] Developing Greater Sunrise would cost Timor-Leste around US$24 billion, more if the project hits technical problems. Evans cites independent oil and gas analysts who calculate that the project would lose $28 billion over a 30-year production life if the gas is processed in Timor-Leste.[74] In contrast, reusing the Bayu-Undan facilities could commercialize Greater Sunrise for US$4 billion.[75] This is not to mention the risks involved in building the pipeline due in part to the depths of the Timor Trench. The pipeline would be 75 per cent deeper and thicker than the heaviest pipeline ever built, and would require supports "that no present underwater tool could handle at such depths".[76] Piping the gas to Darwin appears to make greater economic sense, particularly as a LNG glut pushes down gas prices.[77] In contrast with mainstream thinking that small state foreign policy is driven predominantly by external factors, this foreign policy strategy demonstrates the ways in which leaders of small, fragile states can use foreign policy to advance domestic and personal agendas.

Timor-Leste's activist strategy sought to overcome power asymmetries *vis-à-vis* Australia by drawing upon solidarity networks, advancing narratives through public diplomacy and using international legal mechanisms. Yet, its oil dependence will impact its talks with the venture partners on the joint development plans. Without an agreement on developing Greater Sunrise, Timor-Leste would be left with very few sources of revenue outside of the $16 billion petroleum sovereign wealth fund. Over 2006–12, production from the JPDA contributed, on average, 80 per cent of total GDP.[78] Timor-Leste's GDP growth rates ranged from 2.9 per cent to 9.5 per cent between 2011 and 2015, and has relied upon oil and gas revenues and state spending. According to independent economic monitoring organization, *La'o Hamutuk*, the oil from the JDPA will be depleted by 2020–22.[79] On current spending, Timor-Leste's Petroleum Wealth Fund is projected to last until 2026–28.[80] Unlike Australia or the commercial venture partners, it cannot afford a prolonged contest over the Greater Sunrise development plan.

Timor-Leste's narratives privilege territorial and symbolic concepts of sovereignty as concerning borders, and symbolic concepts of sovereignty that compare the struggle for permanent boundaries with the resistance against Indonesia's occupation. While Timorese governments have employed the *territorial* and *symbolic* visions of sovereignty in its pursuit of the export pipeline, the foreign policy could have consequences for its *empirical* sovereignty, and its capacities to provide internal security and public goods to its population if a joint development deal is not forthcoming. This would also put into doubt its sovereign independence: on current spending, if Greater Sunrise development does not begin within the next decade, Timor-Leste risks again becoming heavily dependent on aid and external support to avoid state failure. There are concerns that foreign investors will not view commercializing Greater Sunrise as a stable investment prospect.[81] A return to aid dependence would undermine political independence and the capacity of Timorese governments to implement its long-term economic development plans.

The Resource Curse

It is not difficult to understand why Timor-Leste's leaders would seek to pursue the value-added benefits of developing oil refining industries and leveraging its competitive advantage. Industrialization is commonly understood as vital for economic development. The East Asian Tigers — Singapore, Hong Kong, South Korea, Taiwan — offer instructive models of export-led industrialization for Timor-Leste.[82] Since the 1960s, development literature has been preoccupied with the roles of the state versus the market in producing the "economic miracles" of these Newly Industrializing Economies (NIEs). As an attractive example of an economically successful small, new state with a large oil refining sector, Singapore presents a development prototype for Timor-Leste. Indeed, in 2013, Xanana Gusmão declared that Singapore inspires Timor-Leste and "is a model for what can be achieved with a clear vision, good governance and outstanding public leadership".[83] In the 1970s, Singapore developed a deliberate strategy of moving away from low-skilled, labour intensive industries to those requiring higher labour skills and more capital. Four years before it became fully independent in 1965, Singapore begun establishing an oil refining industry. Some have argued that this early oil industrialization was the driver of Singapore's economic success story. Singaporean policymakers were able to embark on an "export-oriented, foreign investment driven industrialisation" and Singapore subsequently became one of the world's top three oil export refining centres.[84] It also became a regional oil refining hub.

There are, however, risks in following Singapore's lead. In the absence of Greater Sunrise gas to process, Timor-Leste's petrochemical refining industries would be left to compete in the global market for oil processing with Singapore (and Malaysia) in the Southeast Asian region. Singapore's development also relied upon attracting FDI. Singapore's colonialism by British provided favourable conditions for its development. Upon independence, Singapore was already a trading entrepôt in a geographically privileged location with robust institutions. In contrast with the underdevelopment and neglect experienced by East Timor under dual colonization, Singapore "prospered" prior to independence.[85] The differences in these conditions mean that Singapore is likely to be an unrealistic model for Timor-Leste.

While Timor-Leste disseminates narratives of fragile state exceptionalism, economic experts have expressed concerns that Timor-Leste is, in fact, following a common development trajectory known as the "resource curse".[86] The term "resource curse" attempts to encapsulate the "paradox" of resource rich developing states performing economically worse than comparable states with few natural resources.[87] The popular narratives supporting Timor-Leste's claim to Greater Sunrise often implicitly or explicitly carry the belief that gas revenues would improve the developmental prospects of Timor-Leste.[88] Yet, the experiences of many resource-rich fragile states with weak institutions and poor governance run counter to this idea. Studies have demonstrated across a diverse range of oil-rich states that oil and gas can actually be a hindrance rather than a benefit for institutionally weak states as they experience lower rates of economic and human development. In many cases, oil and gas wealth has been accompanied by "poor rates of economic growth, high levels of poverty, a higher than average risk of conflict and a higher than average risk of authoritarian rule".[89] The resource curse arises due to a confluence of social, economic and political factors: the state's dependence upon income from natural resources; the ease of access to wealth from non-productive and non-renewable resources; the temptation of governments to spend revenues on short-term rather than long-term projects; and, the presence of weak institutions that stifle transparency and increase the likelihood of corruption. The states most susceptible to the resource curse are those most dependent upon extractive industries and the least diversified.[90]

One of the major economic challenges for Timor-Leste was avoiding dependence on oil and gas exports. States that rely on oil exports are vulnerable to fluctuations in global oil prices.[91] Since 2014, state revenues have decreased due to a plunge in world oil prices. In the first quarter of 2015, for instance, state revenues fell over 46 per cent. In 2015, while government expenditure reportedly increased by over 33 per cent in the first five months of 2015 (compared with the same period in 2014), total revenues fell 46.4 per cent in the first three months.[92] Heavy reliance on non-renewable resources for export also does little to contribute to employment, can discourage economic diversification and stunt the growth of industries such as agriculture and manufacturing.[93] According to *La'o Hamutuk*, industries that produce goods for consumption, such as agriculture and manufacturing, contribute less than 5 per cent of GDP, despite the large majority of Timorese being involved in agricultural industries.[94] Timor-Leste faces a number of interconnected social and economic challenges, including rapid population growth combined with high rates of youth unemployment. Around 70 per cent of Timor-Leste's population is under 30,[95] and over 60 per cent of youth under 25 are unemployed.[96] Per year, 27,000 youths enter the job market but "only a handful of job opportunities" are created annually.[97] As Nixon points out, population growth could place pressure on both subsistence agricultural systems and on the state to deliver "post-subsistence material expectations".[98]

A decade of economic growth from oil revenues has done little to alter Timor-Leste's mostly informal agrarian subsistence economy, or lift people out of poverty.[99] According to the Asian Development Bank, "[a]pproximately 70 per cent of Timorese live in rural areas and continue to rely on farming for survival."[100] Rural Timor-Leste, in particular, has experienced minimal economic development over its history and the majority of rural farmers depend upon subsistence crops.[101] Problematically, subsistence economy does not prevent common food shortages and agricultural yields are typically low compared to other Asian states.[102] In Timor-Leste, around 64–70 per cent of households are classified as severely food insecure, and around 50 per cent of children suffer from chronic and severe malnutrition.[103] Compounding the problems of agriculture is the flood of cheap imported rice, much of which comes from Indonesia.¹⁰⁴ These imports are subsidized by the government, which has the dual effect of deterring farmers from producing rice for sale, as well as increasing Timor-Leste's dependence on its neighbour.

Former Timor-Leste government advisor, Guteriano Neves, argues that Timor-Leste's oil dependency has transformed it into a "rentier" state as the economy is dominated by government spending on infrastructure and social security schemes.¹⁰⁵ A rentier state is one that collects its income from natural resources (i.e. "rent") rather than taxes, "breaking the link between taxation, representation and accountability".¹⁰⁶ The state generates rent and distributes it to the community, a situation that has led to the potential for corruption and mismanagement as rents are often decided through political and personal connections. Elites in rentier states can become "addicted" to petroleum revenues and pursue "oil profits over the public good".¹⁰⁷ Heavy reliance on oil exports increases the likelihood of "rent-seeking" activities, which are those that "yield income or profits to private interests but do not produce goods or services that add to societal outputs".¹⁰⁸ The state-owned Timor GAP company, intended to partner with international firms for development of petroleum resources, has been allocated millions in resources, and resembles the type of rent-seeking activities that political economists warn against.¹⁰⁹

The reliance on oil exports is also a problem because oil and gas are exhaustible, non-renewable resources. Timor-Leste's Petroleum Wealth Fund was established to assist Timor-Leste avert the resource curse, and was designed to replace oil and gas revenues once the deposits were depleted.¹¹⁰ Circumventing the resource curse required Timor-Leste's government to avoid "the trap of overspending".¹¹¹ While the design of the Petroleum Fund was lauded by the World Bank and meets the guidelines set by the Extractive Industries Transparency Initiative, good practice in managing petroleum rents has unravelled as governments made off-budget resource allocations enabled by inadequate public investment procurement procedures.¹¹² *La'o Hamutuk* and other international organizations, such as the Asian Development Bank (ADB) and IMF, have criticized governments for repeatedly spending in excess of the Estimated Sustainable Income (ESI), which is calculated as 3 per cent of the total value of the Petroleum Fund.¹¹³ These drawdowns have lowered the amount of money in the fund.¹¹⁴ Rosser and Blunt both point to the Timorese government's ignoring advice to draw down slowly on the Petroleum Fund as a problem for the resource curse.[115] An ongoing challenge is to ensure that the Petroleum Fund will enable the economy to move beyond subsistence and create a broader tax base for state revenues.[116] In a report on Timor-Leste's non-oil economy in 2014, the ADB argued that declining petroleum income and increasing deficits in goods and services trade would lower "prospects for future surpluses".[117] The *Pacific Economic Monitor* also notes that government expenditure is the biggest driver of the non-petroleum economy: government expenditure increased by 33.4 per cent from 2014 levels which is ultimately unsustainable.[118]

The Timorese government talks about the importance of economic diversification for avoiding the resource curse, however, governments have clearly prioritized oil refining industrialization at the expense of other policy areas, such as health and education.[119] The United Nations Development Programme (UNDP) recommends that developing states spend at least 28 per cent of budgets on national services.[120] Only 14 per cent of Timor-Leste's 2014 budget was spent on health and education.[121] While *Tasi Mane* has been allocated at least US$1.4 billion from 2015 until 2020 (not including all components), budget figures from 2016 show that US$161,634,883 was allocated to the Ministry of Social Solidarity for spending on pensions for veterans, and only US$100,613,356 and US$43,887,000 were allocated to the Ministries of Education and Health respectively.[122] Budgets have also significantly prioritized petroleum industrialization ahead of agriculture and tourism. The ministries representing agriculture and tourism were allocated only US$22,343,000 and US$5,590,000 respectively.[123] The tourism sector, for instance, has played a minimal role in Timor-Leste's economic plans. In 2017, it was reported that the Timorese government actively worked against Timor-Leste's only air carrier, Air Timor, by giving Indonesian airline, Sriwijaya, a monopoly on routes to Indonesia.[124] In the meantime, *Tasi Mane* has raised concerns that representatives are "deluding" citizens about winning Sunrise, and wasting resources on "white elephants" and "fantasy" projects.[125]

Timor-Leste appears to be following a similar resource-cursed path as other poor but resource-rich new states.[126] In 2016, Timor-Leste ranked 101th out of 176 states on Transparency International's global corruption perceptions index.[127] Timor-Leste scored low on the World Bank 2015 CPIA ranking, which includes the indicators property rights and rules based government, budget and financial management, quality of public administration and transparency, accountability and corruption in the public sector.[128] Its ranking placed it in the second lowest group of states globally, on par with its pacific neighbours Papua New Guinea and Solomon Islands, but ranking lower than Myanmar, Vietnam and Vanuatu.[129] According to political economy experts, political and business elites and their families and associates have benefited from capturing major rent distribution streams, which has been enabled by the fact that poor governance and weak institutions are easily subverted by ruling elites.[130] Timor-Leste's transparency reputation has also been tarnished by high profile corruption cases involving government ministers, including former ministers Lucia Lobato and Emilia Pires.

Transparency International indicates public financial management as the most significant concern as Timor-Leste's over-dependence on oil export has "created new opportunities for corruption and administrative malpractice".[131] Scambary argues that Timor-Leste's political economy resembles a "patronage" system characterized by "disbursement of state funds through questionable development projects, allocated as illicit income to figures with the right political connections".[132] Structures of patronage and clientelism are legacies of Indonesian rule.[133] Blunt argues that the training of Timor-Leste's politicians and civil servants in the Indonesian civil service shaped bureaucratic practices and processes in the new state.[134] These legacies reveal themselves with the influx in oil revenue, which in turn exacerbated patronage as ruling elites use state spending to generate political support. Political-economy research suggests that patronage-based governance systems in Timor-Leste are likely to be strongly defended by ruling elites.[135]

The extent to which the benefits of Timor Sea oil has been extended to all citizens is questionable. In 2015, the UNDP ranked Timor-Leste as 133th in the world according to its Human Development Index.[136] As a "medium human development" state, Timor-Leste is ranked below fellow Southeast Asian states Indonesia, the Philippines and Vietnam but above Cambodia, Laos and Myanmar.[137] While the Gross National Income has increased due to oil wealth, there are concerns about rising inequality and the concentration of wealth in Dili. A UN Special Rapporteur, Magdelina Sepúlveda Carmona, reported that rural citizens are disproportionally affected by poverty, food insecurity and unemployment.[138] The Timorese state has struggled to meet the basic needs of all of its citizens by providing public goods and services, which is recognized as a central feature of empirical sovereignty. Unless economic and foreign policy shifts on oil industrialization and diversification, Timor-Leste looks likely to follow the path of other resource-rich, resource-cursed states.

Beyond Oil: Timor-Leste's Development in the Global Economic Context

While neoclassical political economy perspectives are sceptical about government intervention in markets, state-led theories of development emphasize the role of the state in economic planning. Given the weak non-oil GDP, it would be virtually impossible for Timor-Leste to have minimal government intervention. Nevertheless, the IMF diagnoses the main sources of medium- to long-term risk as "higher fiscal spending, public investments not yielding adequate returns and enhanced growth, and inadequate mobilization of domestic revenues".[139] Consequently, economic multilateral institutions tend to offer Timor-Leste relatively generic neoliberal policy prescriptions, including the need for "fiscal consolidation" in the medium term, reduced spending from the Petroleum Fund, increasing foreign investment, reducing import reliance and developing the non-oil private sector.[140] The ADB recommends diversification towards agriculture and tourism, increasing productivity through improving training, workforce skills, infrastructure, and improving rural livelihoods, particularly by increasing food security.[141] The extent to which the Timorese government has implemented policy reforms to reduce dependence upon oil and state spending is mixed. This final section considers Timor-Leste's prospects in the international economy beyond oil, focusing on trade relations and pursuit of FDI.

Trade

Although its economy is reliant upon oil exports, Timor-Leste depends heavily upon imports for basic necessities such as food and clothing.[142] Timor-Leste's second largest export, coffee, comprises 90 per cent of non-oil merchandise exports but yields only US$16 million a year.[143] According to the Massachusetts Institute of Technology Observatory of Economic Complexity, Timor-Leste is the 184th largest export economy in the world.[144] In 2014, Timor-Leste's exports valued US$119 million and imports valued US$627 million, with petroleum accounting for over 80 per cent of Timor-Leste's exports.[145] This import dependence has consequences for Timor-Leste's capacities to secure economic sovereignty. Its largest trading partner is Indonesia, but the terms of trade flow heavily in favour of Indonesia as Timor-Leste's exports are minimal.[146] This renders Timor-Leste highly dependent upon imported products from Indonesia, a situation that has prompted Timor-Leste to adopt a pragmatic realist approach to its nearest neighbour (see chapter nine). There is also a significant trade imbalance between Timor-Leste and its other neighbour, Australia. In 2013, Australian exports to Timor-Leste were valued at A$27.4 million, whereas Timor-Leste's exported merchandise was worth a mere A$1.45 million to Australia, mostly coffee.[147]

In its international relations, Timor-Leste has pursued bilateral and multilateral trade agreements, including the trilateral agreement towards subregional triangular development area encompassing Indonesia's East Nusa Tenggara province and Australia's Northern Territory.[148] In 2016, Timor-Leste became a member of the World Trade Organization. If Timor-Leste's application into ASEAN is approved, Timor-Leste will enter one of the world's largest free trade blocs. For Timor-Leste, ASEAN membership would provide "ongoing investments and reforms paving the way for a closer integration in the coming years".[149] The ADB also anticipates a modest economic benefit from ASEAN accession in the short-term, however, it also notes that Timor-Leste already has a relatively open and liberal trade policy, so ASEAN membership rules are unlikely to substantially alter Timor-Leste's approach to trade. As chapter six highlighted, Timor-Leste's membership into ASEAN has been delayed because of economic and institutional weaknesses. The ADB argues that any longer term benefits of joining ASEAN will be contingent upon the government's ability or willingness to address the serious shortcomings in doing business in Timor-Leste.[150]

Timor-Leste's leaders have expounded the economic benefits of joining ASEAN in public speeches and declaratory policy. For example, in 2014, Gusmão argued that ASEAN membership would allow Timor-Leste to "strengthen trade and investment relations with our Southeast Asian brothers and sisters".[151] While most leaders appear sold on the economic benefits, Taur Matan Ruak has been more publically cautious in considering "the questions of mobility, competitiveness and our effective participation in the full agenda" of ASEAN.[152] Given Timor-Leste's import dependence, ASEAN's free trade arrangements may disadvantage Timor-Leste. Timor-Leste's export markets — with the exception of Indonesia — are largely non-ASEAN states.[153] In 2014, Timor-Leste's top imports came from ASEAN states: Indonesia provided 36 per cent of imports (US$226 million), Singapore 15 per cent, Thailand 11 per cent and Malaysia 9.9 per cent.[154] In contrast, ASEAN states barely featured among Timor-Leste's top export destinations: Singapore was 1.5 per cent, and Malaysia and Indonesia both less than 1 per cent. Timor-Leste's exports were more heavily directed to South Korea, Japan, Germany, Australia and Canada.[155] Percival-Wood argues that membership into the ASEAN Economic Community (AEC) could result in Timor-Leste being "flooded with cheap goods from ASEAN countries", a situation that could further stifle the development of Timorese industries.[156]

Critics have argued that Timor-Leste's economy would be better served by abandoning or delaying its plans for ASEAN accession. Percival Wood, for example, suggests that Timor-Leste would be best to cultivate bilateral and multilateral trade relations given its heavy dependence on imports, and ongoing aid dependency.[157] *La'o Hamutuk* promotes Import Substitution Industrialisation (ISI), which is based on the logic that substituting imports with domestically produced goods bolsters domestic manufacturing capacity and provides employment, reduced reliance on imports and isolates states from the vagaries of international trade and globalization.[158] However, global development history suggests ISI might not be a panacea for Timor-Leste's economic problems. Paradoxically, states that followed ISI in the past not only continued to rely upon imports, but the pursuit of industrialization *weakened* the agriculture sector rather than strengthened it. Domestic markets were too small to realize economies of scale. ISI led to the Latin American debt crisis of the early 1980s, and the introduction of Structural Adjustment Programs as loan conditionalities that imposed neoliberal reforms on these states and compromised the economic self-determination of indebted states. In small states, such as Singapore, economic growth was associated with manufactured *export* goods. Ultimately, it seems that protectionism and free trade both present risks to small economies. Expansion in trade relations will need to be accompanied by economic diversification and FDI for it to be beneficial to economic development over the long-term.

Foreign Direct Investment (FDI)

According to neoliberal orthodoxy, FDI is viewed as a key driver of self-sustaining economic growth in developing economies.[159] The Singapore Model, for example, highlights the importance of FDI for establishing oil refining industries. Timor-Leste's leaders have been actively courting FDI internationally in overseas speeches. In Singapore in 2013, for example, Gusmão declared: "Timor-Leste is also open to foreign capital and investment, with some of the world's lowest tax rates, which are helping to power our positive economic growth."[160] Timor-Leste's Trade Invest website, established in 2015 as a "one-stop shop" for foreign investment inquiries, declares that "Timor-Leste is establishing itself as a preferred destination for foreign investment, characterized by a fair and favorable business environment and one of the most attractive tax systems for business in the world."[161] This reflects the neoliberal orthodoxy that has driven Timor-Leste's approach to FDI, and the ways that Timor-Leste's leaders have sought to promote its image as a desirable location for foreign investment.

Timor-Leste has provided investors a number of tax-based incentives to encourage FDI. One reform that Timor-Leste initiated was cutting the corporate tax rate from 30 per cent to 10 per cent, touted by the government as the lowest corporate tax rate in Southeast Asia.[162] Timor-Leste's government also offered generous investment incentives, including five, eight, or 10 years of tax exemptions depending on the location of the investment.[163] Timor-Leste's government has invested significantly in free trade zones, including the Special Zone for Social Market Economy (ZEESM) in the Oecusse exclave. In 2009, the World Bank lauded Timor-Leste's neoliberal tax reforms, yet its "Doing Business" report of 2016 ranked Timor-Leste a lowly 173rd out of 189 countries for ease of doing business.[164]

While the government of Timor-Leste has been optimistic regarding prospects of FDI, the private sector has remained cautious as the structural and regulatory conditions remain largely unfavourable. One of the significant problems outlined by the ADB is the emphasis by Timor-Leste's government on tax incentives which overlooked the key market, governance and infrastructural weaknesses that continue to deter foreign investors.[165] A 2016 U.S. State Department Investment Climate Statement noted that Timor-Leste continues to struggle with incomplete and inadequate legislation and regulatory mechanisms governing investment, a lack of personnel, "deficient" infrastructure and remaining issues with corruption.[166] Key issues in economic development include limited human capital and high labour costs, poor quality of public investments including electricity and transportation, a poor regulatory environment, weak investment facilitation and limited access to finance.[167] According to investment certificates issued, in the period between 2006 and 2016, 97 certificates were issued to foreign investors. From January 2010 to March 2015, a mere 36 were issued. The source countries included Indonesia (10), Australia (7), Singapore (3), China (2), Fiji (2) and South Korea (2).[168] The biggest foreign investors have been oil companies with a stake in the oil and gas fields located in the JPDA, such as ConocoPhillips, the largest investor in Timor-Leste.[169]

In spite of concerns, Timor-Leste has had some limited success in attracting FDI. In 2014 it was announced that Dutch beer producer Heineken would be the first "world renowned" manufacturer to set up in Timor-Leste, committing US$40 million to produce beer, soft drinks and water for import and export.[170] A US$520 cement project funded by TL Cement, a largely Australian-backed company, promises thousands of jobs for Timorese during the construction phase and 600 permanent jobs when the mine is operational.[171] However, concerns have been raised about the environmental impacts of the cement mine, particularly as it is expected to be in close proximity to subsistence communities. This example raises questions about the potential environmental and social costs of underegulated FDI. *La'o Hamutuk* has argued that Timor-Leste's government has too heavily favoured investors over the public interests, and could invite "illegitimate" investors to take advantage of the weaknesses of Timor-Leste's institutional and regulatory frameworks. Critics of a draft investment law in 2016, for instance, argued that it would allow investors to "bypass normal systems" or receive favours not available to citizens.[172] It also argued that the lack of regulation could consolidate the rent-seeking attitude that has developed with "easy" oil money.[173] Ultimately, Timor-Leste's attempts to attract greater trade and FDI in the international economy will require the strengthening of institutions and good governance.

Conclusion

Timor-Leste's capacities to secure the state is intricately linked with economic development, foreign policy and internal security. Timor-Leste's economic ambitions depend heavily on the oil and gas reserves in the Timor Sea and its capacity to successfully establish an oil refining industry depends upon the piping of gas from the disputed Greater Sunrise to the south coast. This plan was prioritized despite the absence of an agreement with Australia about developing Greater Sunrise. The oil industrialization ambitions drove its foreign policy approach to the Timor Sea. However, it was highly risky, and the price for not succeeding was potentially receiving less than what was negotiated under the CMATS. Timor-Leste's activist foreign policy strategy reflected idealistic belief in its diplomatic capacities to shift Australia's position, which contrasts against the pragmatic realism that defines Timor-Leste's approach to Indonesia, examined in the next chapter. Ultimately, the UNCC processes initiated by Timor-Leste appear to have contributed to resolving the maritime boundary dispute, however, the development of Greater Sunrise continues to be discussed.

In the short- to mid-term, if Timor-Leste's energy diplomacy on the Timor Sea fails to provide a quick development agreement on Greater Sunrise, future Timor-Leste governments may have little revenue with which to maintain empirical sovereignty through the provision of political order, internal security and public goods that support human development. Timor-Leste's ambitious policy of pursuing the pipeline and *Tasi Mane* was designed to prevent future intervention, but may ultimately be what precipitates it if an agreement cannot be struck with the commercial venture partners. This would have implications for its capacity to be an independent and autonomous actor in the international realm, as aid or loans would be necessary to fill the budgetary hole left by the expired hydrocarbon revenues. As chapter seven argued, governments have used oil and gas revenues to contribute to internal security by providing cash payments to veterans in order to "buy peace". A break down in Timor-Leste's fragile peace due to a lack of revenue would likely invite foreign intervention, a situation Timor-Leste's political leaders are attempting to avoid.[174]

Over the longer term, the "resource curse" presents economic and security related challenges that Timor-Leste is unlikely to cope well with.¹⁷⁵ Some political leaders appear to recognize the danger of relying upon Timor Sea oil and gas revenues for medium- and long-term economic policy. In an incendiary speech to National Parliament in 2016, the former-President Taur Matan Ruak criticized the 2012–17 legislature under the leadership of Xanana Gusmão for the "paralysis" that had stalled Timor-Leste's development progress.¹⁷⁶ He condemned the lack of diversification and ongoing dependence on oil, and said that the government policies had failed to substantially achieve "a sustainable and inclusive economy".¹⁷⁷ Governments cannot rely on the "trickle down" effect of petroleum wealth to alleviate poverty, they need to implement policies to ensure inclusive growth.¹⁷⁸ Ensuring human development across the population is necessary for developing political legitimacy and internal security. This theme is considered further in the context of sustainable development in chapter ten.

NOTES

1. Cited in Vandra Harris and Andrew Goldsmith, "The Struggle for Independence was Just the Beginning", in *Security, Development and Nation-Building in Timor-Leste*, edited by Vandra Harris and Andrew Goldsmith, p. 4 (Oxon: Routledge, 2011).
2. International Peace Academy, "The Security-Development Nexus: Conflict, Peace and Development in the 21st Century", pp. 1–2 (New York: International Peace Academy, 2004).
3. United Nations Development Programme (UNDP), *Timor-Leste Human Development Report 2011: Managing Natural Resources for Human Development: Developing the Non-Oil Economy to Achieve the MGDs*, 2011, p. 17, available at <https://www.laohamutuk.org/econ/HDI10/TLHDR2011En.pdf> (accessed 20 February 2017).
4. World Bank, "Timor-Leste", available at <http://data.worldbank.org/country/timor-leste> (accessed 20 February 2017).
5. República Democrática de Timor-Leste (RDTL), *Timor-Leste's Initial National Communication under United Nations Framework Convention on Climate Change*, p. iii (Dili: Timor-Leste's State Secretariat for Environment, 2014); UNDP, *Timor-Leste Human Development Report 2011*, p. 40.
6. Rebecca Strating, *Social Democracy in East Timor*, chapter 6 (Oxon: Routledge, 2015).
7. Jeanne Hey, "Introducing Small State Foreign Policy", in *Small States in World Politics: Explaining Foreign Policy Behaviour*, edited by Jeanne Hey, p. 1 (Boulder: Lynne Rienner Publishers, 2003).

8. Caroline Hughes, *Dependent Communities: Aid and Politics in Cambodia and East Timor*, p. 1 (Ithaca: Cornell Southeast Asia Program, 2009).
9. Harris and Goldsmith, "The Struggle for Independence was Just the Beginning", p. 3.
10. Andrew Rosser, "The Transition Support Program in Timor-Leste", in *Making Aid Work in Fragile States*, edited by James Manor, pp. 61–62 (Washington: World Bank, 2007). For an overview of development challenges East Timor faces upon independence, see Hal Hill and Joao M. Saldanha, eds, *East Timor: Development Challenges for the World's Newest Nation* (Singapore: Institute of Southeast Asian Studies, 2001).
11. Ibid.
12. Simon Roughneen, "Aid and Independence", *The Diplomat*, 29 September 2011.
13. Ibid.
14. Pedro Seabra, "The Need for a Reshaped Foreign Policy", in *The Politics of Timor-Leste: Democratic Consolidation after Intervention*, edited by Michael Leach and Damien Kingsbury, p. 149 (Ithaca, NY: Cornell University, 2014). Portugal contributed US$525 million in the period 1999–2006.
15. Philippa Brant, "Chinese Aid in the Pacific" (Australia: Lowy Institute for International Policy, 2015), available at <https://www.lowyinstitute.org/chinese-aid-map/> (accessed 20 February 2017).
16. Ibid.
17. Cecilia Brunnstrom, "Another Invasion: Lessons from International Support to East Timorese NGOs", *Development in Practice* 13, no. 4 (2003): 310, 314; Andrew McGregor, "Development, Foreign Aid and Post-development in Timor-Leste", *Third World Quarterly* 28, no. 1 (2007): 160.
18. Roughneen, "Aid and Independence".
19. José Kei Lekke Sousa-Santos, "Acting West, Looking East: Timor-Leste's Growing Engagement with the Pacific Islands Region", in *Regionalism, Security and Cooperation in Oceania*, edited by Rouben Azizian and Carleton Cramer, p. 119 (Honolulu: Asia-Pacific Centre for Security Studies, 2015).
20. For example Arturo Escobar, Encountering Development: The Making and Unmaking of the Third World (Princeton: Princeton University Press, 2011).
21. See for example United Nations Human Rights Office of the High Commissioner (OHCHR), "Good Governance and Human Rights", available at <http://www.ohchr.org/EN/Issues/Development/GoodGovernance/Pages/GoodGovernanceIndex.aspx> (accessed 20 February 2017); McGregor, "Development, Foreign Aid and Post-development in Timor-Leste", p. 168.
22. McGregor, "Development, Foreign Aid and Post-development in Timor-Leste", p. 168.
23. Hughes, *Dependent Communities*, p. 11.

24. Ibid., p. 7.
25. World Bank, "2016 Country Policy and Institutional Assessments", available at <http://pubdocs.worldbank.org/en/449561467141303352/Cpia15finalIDAxlsx.pdf> (accessed 26 February 2017).
26. Isabel Rocha de Siqueira, "Measuring and Managing 'State Fragility': The Production of Statistics by the World Bank, Timor-Leste and the g7+", *Third World Quarterly* 35, no. 2 (2014): 271.
27. For example Paul Collier, Patrick Guillaumont, Sylviane Guillaumont and Jan Willem Gunning, "Redesigning Conditionality", *World Development* 25, no. 9 (1997): 1399.
28. For a literature review, see World Bank, "Review of World Bank Conditionality: The Theory and Practice of Conditionality, a Literature Review" (Development Economics World Bank, 6 July 2005).
29. Hughes, *Dependent Communities*, p. 7.
30. United States Agency for International Development (USAID), "Our Work (Timor-Leste)", available at <https://www.usaid.gov/timor-leste/our-work> (accessed 20 February 2017).
31. See Organisation for Economic Cooperation and Development (OECD), *The Paris Declaration on Aid Effectiveness and the Accra Agenda for Action*, 2005 and 2008, available at <http://www.oecd.org/dac/effectiveness/34428351.pdf> (accessed 20 February 2017).
32. Selver Sahin, "Timor-Leste: A More Confident or Overconfident Foreign Policy Actor?", in *Southeast Asian Affairs 2012*, edited by Daljit Singh and Pushpa Thambipillai, p. 348 (Singapore: Institute of Southeast Asian Studies, 2012).
33. Ibid., p. 348.
34. Xanana Gusmão, "Consolidating Democracy in a Pluralist Society", Address by His Excellency the Prime Minister Kay Rala Xanana Gusmão on the Occasion of the Bali Democracy Forum, Bali, 7 November 2013.
35. Cited in Sahin, "Timor-Leste", p. 328.
36. Sousa-Santos, "Acting West, Looking East", p. 119.
37. Helder Da Costa, "g7+ and the New Deal: Country-Led and Country-Owned Initiatives: A Perspective from Timor-Leste", *International Journal of Peacebuilding & Development* 7, no. 2 (2012): 96–97.
38. McGregor, "Development, Foreign Aid and Post-development in Timor-Leste", p. 168.
39. Sonja Grimm, Nicolas Lemay-Hebert, and Olivier Nay, "'Fragile States': Introducing a Political Concept", *Third World Quarterly* 35, no. 2 (2014): 198.
40. RDTL, *Strategic Development Plan*, p. 9 (Dili: Government of Timor-Leste, 2011); RDTL, "Program of the Sixth Constitutional Government 2015–2017" (Dili: Government of the Democratic Republic of Timor-Leste, 6 March 2015).

41. James Scambary, "In Search of White Elephants: The Political Economy of Resource Income Expenditure in East Timor", *Critical Asian Studies* 47, no. 2 (2015): 284.
42. RDTL, *Strategic Development Plan*, p. 166.
43. World Bank, "Timor-Leste Overview", available at <http://www.worldbank.org/en/country/timorleste/overview> (accessed 24 April 2017).
44. La'o Hamutuk, "La'o Hamutuk: Oil Running Out is Reality, Not Propaganda", Dili, 15 June 2015, available at <http://www.laohamutuk.org/econ/model/RespostaMina15Jun2015en.pdf> (accessed 26 February 2017).
45. Andrew Rosser, "Timor-Leste and the Resource Curse: An Assessment", in *Security, Development and Nation-Building in Timor-Leste*, edited by Vandra Harris and Andrew Goldsmith, p. 188 (Oxon: Routledge, 2011).
46. RDTL, *Strategic Development Plan*, p. 139; RDTL, "Program of the Sixth Constitutional Government 2015–2017".
47. Timor Gap E.P., *Annual Report & Accounts 2015*, available at <https://timorgap.com/databases/website.nsf/vwAll/Resource-Full_TIMOR%20GAP%202015%20Annual%20Report_EN_Final/$File/TIMOR%20GAP%202015%20Annual%20Report_EN_Final.pdf?openelement> (accessed 26 February 2017).
48. RDTL, "Program of the Sixth Constitutional Government 2015–2017"; Timor Gap E.P., *Timor Gap E.P. Annual Report 2014*, available at <http://www.timorgap.com/databases/website.nsf/vwAllNew/Resource-AnnualReport_TIMORGAP_PubVer_English/$File/AnnualReport_TIMORGAP_PubVer_English.pdf?openelement> (accessed 26 February 2017).
49. RDTL, "Maritime Boundary Office", available at <http://www.gfm.tl/> (accessed 24 February 2017).
50. Stephen Grenville, "East Timor, Australia and the 'Timor Gap'", *Lowy Interpreter*, 25 November 2014.
51. See Vaughan Lowe, Christopher Carelton and Christopher Ward, "In the Matter of East Timor", *Legal Opinion on East Timor Maritime Boundaries provided to Petrotimor*, 11 April 2002.
52. See for example Pat Brazil, "Critique of the Lowe Opinion", Submission No. 22.1 Delivered to the Joint Standing Committee on Treaties, 11 April 2002; Clive Schofield, "Minding the Gap: The Australia–East Timor Treaty on Certain Maritime Arrangements in the Timor Sea (CMATS)", *The International Journal of Marine and Coastal Law* 22 (2007): 199; Victor Prescott, "East Timor's Potential Maritime Boundaries", in *The Maritime Dimensions of Independent East Timor*, edited by Donald R. Rothwell and Martin Tsamenyi, pp. 90, 105 (Wollongong: Centre for Maritime Policy, University of Wollongong, 2000).

53. Anthony Heiser, "East Timor and the Joint Petroleum Development Area", *Australian and New Zealand Maritime Law Journal* 17 (2003): 69; Clive Schofield and I. Made Andi Arsana, "The Delimitation of Maritime Boundaries: A Matter of Life or Death for East Timor?" in *East Timor: Beyond Independence*, edited by Damien Kingsbury and Michael Leach, p. 68 (Clayton: Monash University Press, 2007).
54. Bovensiepen, as one example, accepts the idea that Timor Sea oil and gas belongs to Timor-Leste. See Judith Bovensiepen, "Visions of Prosperity and Conspiracy in Timor-Leste", *Focaal — Journal of Global and Historical Anthropology* 75 (2016): 75.
55. José Ramos-Horta, "Address by the Hon. José Ramos Horta to the Lowy Institute for International Policy", Sydney, 29 November 2004.
56. Schofield, "Minding the Gap", 197.
57. Woodside, *Woodside Annual Report 2010*, p. 35, available at <http://www.woodside.com.au/Investors-Media/announcements/Documents/21.02.2011%20Annual%20Report%202010.pdf> (accessed 26 February 2017).
58. For an examination of the public diplomacy strategy, see Rebecca Strating, "Timor-Leste's Foreign Policy Approach to the Timor Sea Disputes", *Australian Journal of International Affairs* (2017).
59. Damon Evans, "East Timor's Gas Dream is Doomed, ConocoPhillips and Woodside have Failed", *Forbes*, 12 December 2016.
60. Permanent Court of Arbitration (PCA), "Arbitration under the Timor Sea Treaty (Timor-Leste v Australia)", PCA Case Repository, 2016, available at <https://www.pcacases.com/web/view/37> (accessed 27 February 2017).
61. International Court of Justice, "Questions Relating to the Seizure and Detention of Certain Documents and Data (Timor-Leste v. Australia): Case Removed from the Court's List at the Request of Timor-Leste", Press Release, 12 June 2015, available at <http://www.icjcij.org/docket/files/156/18692.pdf> (accessed 27 February 2017).
62. Rebecca Strating, "A Sunset for Greater Sunrise?", *New Mandala*, 7 February 2017.
63. PCA, "Conciliation between the Democratic Republic of Timor-Leste and the Commonwealth of Australia", PCA Press Release, The Hague, 2 September 2017.
64. Rebecca Strating, "Timor-Leste in 2017: A State of Uncertainty", in *Southeast Asian Affairs 2018*, edited by Malcolm Cook and Daljit Singh (Singapore: ISEAS – Yusof Ishak Institute, 2018).
65. PCA, "Conciliation between the Democratic Republic of Timor-Leste and the Commonwealth of Australia", PCA Press Release, The Hague, 26 December 2017.

66. Lydia Beuman, "Cohabitation in New Post-Conflict States: The Case of Timor-Leste", [Invited Oral Presentation] *Reordering Power, Shifting Boundaries, AISP/IPSA 22nd World Congress of Political Science*, Madrid, Spain, 8–12 July 2012.
67. Frank Brennan, "Time to Draw the Line between Australia and Timor-Leste", *Eureka Street*, 13 May 2013.
68. Strating, "Timor-Leste's Foreign Policy Approach to the Timor Sea".
69. Rui Araújo, "Speech by His Excellency the Prime Minister Dr Rui Maria de Araújo on the Occasion of the Launch of the Maritime Boundary Office Website", Dili Government Palace, 29 February 2016.
70. Ben Weir, "Interview: Ambassador Abel Guterres", *The Diplomat*, 20 April 2016, available at <http://thediplomat.com/2016/04/interview-ambassador-abel-guterres/> (accessed 1 July 2016).
71. Clinton Fernandes, *Reluctant Saviours: Australia, Indonesia and the Independence of East Timor* (Melbourne: Scribe Publications, 2004).
72. Scambary, "In Search of White Elephants".
73. Evans, "East Timor's Gas Dream is Doomed".
74. Ibid.
75. Ibid.
76. Hamish McDonald, "Boundary Row Escalates as Finances Deteriorate", *Nikkei Asian Review*, 20 November 2015.
77. Babs McHugh, "Development of Greater Sunrise Gas Field in East Timor Could Be Decades Away", *Australian Broadcasting Commission*, 12 June 2017.
78. Asian Development Bank (ADB), *Growing the Non-Oil Economy: A Private Sector Assessment for Timor-Leste*, pp. 1–2 (Manila: ADB, 2015).
79. La'o Hamutuk, "Oil Running Out is Reality, Not Propaganda".
80. La'o Hamutuk, "Timor-Leste's Oil and Gas are Going Fast", Dili, 15 April 2015, available at <http://laohamutuk.blogspot.com.au/2015/04/timor-lestes-oil-and-gas-are-going-fast.html> (accessed 26 February 2017).
81. Evans, "East Timor's Gas Dream is Doomed".
82. See, for example, International Monetary Fund (IMF), "Democratic Republic of Timor-Leste: Selected Issues and Statistical Appendix", Country Report No. 07/86 (Washington D.C.: IMF, February 2007).
83. Xanana Gusmão, Address by His Excellency the Prime Minister, Kay Rala Xanana Gusmão on the Occasion of the Lunch Hosted by International Enterprise Singapore, Singapore, 3 June 2013; Xanana Gusmão, "Timor-Leste's Role and Future in a Rising Asia Pacific", Singapore, 4 June 2013.
84. Anis Chowdhury and Iyanatul Islam, *The Newly Industrialising Economies of East Asia*, p. 31 (London: Routledge, 1993).

85. Ibid., p. 35.
86. See, for example, Jennifer Drysdale, *Sustainable Development or Resource Cursed? An Exploration of Timor-Leste's Institutional Choices?* (Mannheim: VDM Verlag, 2009); Rosser, "Timor-Leste and the Resource Curse"; Charles Scheiner, "Can the Petroleum Fund Exorcise the Resource Curse from Timor-Leste?", in *A New Era? Timor-Leste After the UN Intervention*, edited by Sue Ingram, Lia Kent and Andrew McWilliam, pp. 73–102 (Canberra: ANU Press, 2015).
87. Terry Lynn Karl, "The Perils of the Petro-State: Reflections on the Paradox of Plenty", *Journal of International Affairs* 53, no. 1 (1999): 32; Mats Lundahl and Fredrik Sjöholm, "The Oil Resources of Timor-Leste: Curse or Blessing?" *The Pacific Review* 21, no. 1 (2008): 72.
88. See, for example, Tony Clifton, "Field of Dreams: The Battle for the Timor Sea, Home of Oil, Gas, Hot Air and Hope", *The Monthly*, July 2005.
89. UNDP, *Timor-Leste Human Development Report 2011*, p. 57; see also Lundahl and Sjöholm, "The Oil Resources of Timor-Leste", pp. 68, 72; Benjamin Sovacool, "The Political Economy of Oil and Gas in Southeast Asia: Heading Towards the Natural Resource Curse?" *The Pacific Review* 23, no. 2 (2010): 226; Naazneen Barma, "The Rentier State at Work: Comparative Experiences of the Resource Curse in East Asia and the Pacific", *Asia and the Pacific Policy Studies* 1, no. 2 (2014): 257.
90. Sovacool, "The Political Economy of Oil and Gas in Southeast Asia", p. 230.
91. Scheiner, "Can the Petroleum Fund Exorcise the Resource Curse from Timor-Leste?", p. 85.
92. ADB, *Pacific Economic Monitor Midyear Review*, July 2015, p. 14, available at <http://reliefweb.int/sites/reliefweb.int/files/resources/Pacific%20Economic%20Monitor_July%202015%20Midyear%20Review.pdf> (accessed 26 February 2017).
93. Drysdale, *Sustainable Development or Resource Cursed?*, p. 13.
94. Scheiner, "Can the Petroleum Fund Exorcise the Resource Curse from Timor-Leste?", p. 75.
95. Fidelis Magalhães, "Past, Present and Future", in *A New Era? Timor-Leste After the UN Intervention*, edited by Sue Ingram, Lia Kent and Andrew McWilliam, p. 38 (Canberra: ANU Press, 2015).
96. Susan Marx, "Timor-Leste's Non-Oil Economy Must Look to Tourism", *Asia Foundation*, 22 July 2016.
97. Magalhães, "Past, Present and Future", p. 38.
98. Rod Nixon, *Justice and Governance in East Timor: Indigenous Approaches and the 'New Subsistence State'*, p. 152 (Oxon: Routledge, 2013).
99. Anna Powles and José Sousa-Santos, "Xanana Gusmão – Mauk Moruk: Timor Struggles with Its Past and Future", *Lowy Interpreter*, 5 December 2013.

100. ADB, *Growing the Non-Oil Economy*, pp. 1–2; USAID, "Timor-Leste Country Profile", p. 2, available at <https://www.usaid.gov/sites/default/files/documents/1861/TIMOR-LESTE_Country_Profile_2016.pdf> (accessed 20 February 2017).
101. Nixon, *Justice and Governance in East Timor*, pp. 151–52.
102. Ibid.; ADB, *Growing the Non-Oil Economy*, p. 56.
103. Nicholas Molyneux, Gil Rangel da Cruz, Robert Williams, Rebecca Andersen and Neil Turner, "Climate Change and Population Growth in Timor-Leste: Implications for Food Security", *AMBIO* 41, no. 8 (2012): 823, 826.
104. ADB, *Growing the Non-Oil Economy*, p. 58.
105. Guteriano Neves, "The Political Economy of Petroleum Dependency", *State, Society & Governance in Melanesia*, p. 2, available at <http://dpa.bellschool.anu.edu.au/sites/default/files/publications/attachments/2016-04/ib-2016-6-neves.pdf> (accessed 20 February 2017).
106. Sovacool, "Political Economy of Oil and Gas in Southeast Asia", p. 231; Barma, "The Rentier State at Work", p. 258; Drysdale, *Sustainable Development or Resource Cursed?*, p. 13; Peter Blunt, "The Personal Economy of Accountability in Timor-Leste: Implication for Public Policy", *Public Administration and Development* 29 (2009): 93.
107. Karl cited in Sovacool, "Political Economy of Oil and Gas in Southeast Asia", p. 233.
108. Chowdhury and Islam, *The Newly Industrialising Economies of East Asia*, p. 45; Drysdale, *Sustainable Development or Resource Cursed?*, p. 20.
109. Scheiner, "Can the Petroleum Fund Exorcise the Resource Curse from Timor-Leste?", p. 84.
110. Drysdale, *Sustainable Development or Resource Cursed?*, p. 2; ibid., p. 79.
111. Lundahl and Sjöholm, "The Oil Resources of Timor-Leste: Curse or Blessing?", p. 77.
112. Nixon, *Justice and Governance in East Timor*, p. 151; Barma, "The Rentier State at Work", pp. 263–65.
113. Ibid., pp. 150–51.
114. Scheiner, "Can the Petroleum Fund Exorcise the Resource Curse from Timor-Leste?", p. 80.
115. Rosser, "Timor-Leste and the Resource Curse", p. 189; Blunt, "The Political Economy of Accountability in Timor-Leste", p. 92.
116. Nixon, *Justice and Governance in East Timor*, p. 151.
117. ADB, "Timor-Leste: Economy", available at <https://www.adb.org/countries/timor-leste/economy> (accessed 26 February 2017).
118. Mong Palatino, "Is East Timor Now a Rich Country", *The Diplomat*, 22 August 2015.
119. Drysdale, *Sustainable Development or Resource Cursed?*, p. 2.

120. Sahin, "Timor-Leste", p. 346.
121. Scheiner, "Can the Petroleum Fund Exorcise the Resource Curse from Timor-Leste?", p. 83.
122. RDTL Ministry of Finance, *State Budget 2016: Book One* (Dili: Democratic Republic of Timor-Leste, 2016); La'o Hamutuk, "2016 Budget Proposal Puts Fantasies Before People's Needs", 8 November 2015, available at <http://laohamutuk.blogspot.com.au/2015/11/2016-budget-proposal-puts-fantasies.html> (accessed 26 February 2017).
123. RDTL, *State Budget 2016: Book One*.
124. Anne Barker, "Air Timor: Government Policy, Suspected Corruption 'Destroying' East Timor's Only Airline", *ABC News*, 13 January 2017.
125. Strating, "Timor-Leste's Foreign Policy Approach to the Timor Sea Disputes"; Scambary, "In Search of White Elephants".
126. Barma, "The Rentier State at Work", p. 263. See also Nixon, *Justice and Governance in East Timor*, p. 160; Lundahl and Sjöholm, "The Oil Resources of Timor-Leste: Curse or Blessing?", p. 75.
127. Transparency International, "Timor-Leste", available at <http://www.transparency.org/country/TLS> (accessed 26 February 2017).
128. World Bank, "2016 Country Policy and Institutional Assessments".
129. Ibid.
130. Barma, "The Rentier State at Work", pp. 265, 269; Blunt, "The Political Economy of Accountability in Timor-Leste", p. 90.
131. Transparency International, "Timor-Leste: Overview of Corruption and Anti-Corruption", available at <http://www.transparency.org/files/content/corruptionqas/Country_profile_Timor_Leste_2015.pdf> (accessed 26 February 2017).
132. Scambary, "In Search of White Elephants", p. 287.
133. Scambary defines patronage as "the politically motivated distribution of favors or goods not to individuals, but to larger groups". Clientelism refers to the ways brokers "mediate the exchange between the 'little man' and the 'big man'". See ibid., p. 287.
134. Blunt, "The Political Economy of Accountability in Timor-Leste", pp. 90–91.
135. Ibid., p. 90.
136. UNDP, *Human Development Report 2015*, p. 49 (New York: UNDP, 2015).
137. Ibid.
138. Magdalena Sepulveda Carmona, "Report of the Special Rapporteur on Extreme Poverty and Human Rights Mission to Timor-Leste", 10 September 2014, p. 5, available at <https://ssrn.com/abstract=2494404> (accessed 26 February 2017).
139. IMF, "Republic of Timor-Leste: Article IV Consultation – Press Release; Staff Report; and Statement by the Executive Director for Timor-Leste",

International Monetary Fund Country Report No. 16/183, p. 2 (Washington D.C.: IMF, June 2016).
140. Ibid.
141. ADB, *Growing the Non-Oil Economy*, p. ix.
142. Ibid., p. 5
143. Roughneen, "Aid and Independence"; U.S. Department of State, "U.S. Relations with Timor-Leste", available at <https://www.state.gov/r/pa/ei/bgn/35878.htm> (accessed 27 February 2017).
144. Observatory of Economic Complexity, "Timor-Leste", available at <http://atlas.media.mit.edu/en/profile/country/tls/> (accessed 27 February 2017).
145. Ibid.
146. ADB. "Timor-Leste: Country Partnership Strategy (2016–2020)", April 2016, available at <https://www.adb.org/documents/timor-leste-country-partnership-strategy-2016-2020> (accessed 14 February 2017); RDTL, *Force 2020*, 2007, p. 18, available at <https://www.locjkt.or.id/Timor_E/pdf/Forca202007.pdf> (accessed 11 February 2017).
147. Australian Trade and Investment Commission, "Market Profile Export Markets – East Timor", available at <https://www.austrade.gov.au/Australian/Export/Export-markets/Countries/East-Timor/Market-profile> (accessed 27 February 2017).
148. Agio Pereira, "Challenges and Opportunities: The View from Timor-Leste", *The Diplomat*, 19 January 2016.
149. RDTL, "TradeInvest Timor-Leste", available at <http://www.investtimor-leste.com/?q=node/1> (accessed 27 February 2017).
150. ADB, *Country Partnership Strategy: Timor-Leste 2016–2020*, p. 3.
151. Xanana Gusmão, Address by His Excellency the Prime Minister of the Democratic Republic of Timor-Leste Kay Rala Xanana Gusmão at the Forum on Trade and Investment Opportunities in Timor-Leste, Kuala Lumpur, Malaysia, 1 April 2014.
152. Taur Matan Ruak, "State of the Nation", Speech by His Excellency Taur Matan Ruak to the National Parliament, Dili, 20 September 2016.
153. Department of Foreign Affairs and Trade, Australian Government, "Timor-Leste", available at <https://dfat.gov.au/geo/timor-leste/pages/timor-leste.aspx> (accessed 27 June 2018).
154. Observatory of Economic Complexity, "Timor-Leste".
155. Ibid.
156. Sally Percival-Wood, "Timor-Leste's ASEAN Aspirations Can Benefit From Pragmatic Indecision", *Australian Outlook*, 29 May 2015.
157. Ibid.
158. La'o Hamutuk, "La'o Hamutuk Submission on the Proposed Private Investment Policy", 29 March 2016, p. 4, available at <https://www.

laohamutuk.org/econ/invest/LHSubMECAEInvestLaw29Mar2016en.pdf> (accessed 27 February 2017). See also Thomas Oatley, *International Political Economy*. 5th ed., p. 121 (Oxon: Routledge, 2012).
159. ADB, *Growing the Non-Oil Economy*, p. 51.
160. Gusmao, "Timor-Leste's Role and Future in a Rising Asia-Pacific".
161. TradeInvest replaced the Specialized Investment Agency (AEI). See U.S. Department of State, "Timor-Leste Investment Climate Statement 2015", p. 4, available at <https://www.state.gov/documents/organization/241976.pdf> (accessed 27 February 2017).
162. RDTL, "TradeInvest Timor-Leste".
163. See U.S. Department of State, "Timor-Leste Investment Climate Statement 2015". p. 7.
164. World Bank, "Ease of Doing Business Index", available at <http://data.worldbank.org/indicator/IC.BUS.EASE.XQ> (accessed 10 March 2017). For comprehensive data see World Bank, *Doing Business 2016: Measuring Regulatory Quality and Efficiency. 2016 Economy Profile Timor-Leste*, 13th ed. (Washington: World Bank, 2016); La'o Hamutuk, "Summary of New Tax Laws", 14 July 2008, available at <https://www.laohamutuk.org/misc/AMPGovt/tax/NewTaxLaw08.htm> (accessed 10 March 2017).
165. ADB, *Growing the Non-Oil Economy*, pp. 52–53.
166. U.S. Department of State, "Timor-Leste Investment Climate Statement 2015".
167. ADB, *Country Partnership Strategy: Timor-Leste, 2016–2020*.
168. ADB *Growing the Non-Oil Economy*, p. 52.
169. Ibid., p. 51.
170. Sadachika Watanabe, "Heineken Entry Could Open Taps on Foreign Investment", *Asia Nikkei*, 1 December 2015.
171. James Norman, "Environmental Concerns for Timor-Leste Cement Project", *The Saturday Paper*, 11 February 2017.
172. La'o Hamutuk, "Timor-Leste's Private Investment Law and Policy", 30 March 2016, available at <https://www.laohamutuk.org/econ/invest/16InvestPolicy.htm> (accessed 10 March 2017).
173. Ibid.
174. Rosser, "Timor-Leste and the Resource Curse", p. 192.
175. Ibid., p. 190.
176. Taur Matan Ruak, "State of the Nation".
177. Ibid.
178. UNDP, *Timor-Leste Human Development Report 2011*, p. 6.

9

International Reconciliation and Transitional Justice

As previous chapters have argued, the two most significant bilateral relationships for guaranteeing Timor-Leste's sovereign independence are Australia and Indonesia. Timor-Leste's "post-colonial security dilemma" reflects its attempts as a new state to achieve and sustain "real" independence while grappling with its ongoing dependence upon other states in the international community. The emphasis on its bilateral relationship with Indonesia reflects dependence upon Indonesia's assistance in achieving socio-economic development and foreign affairs objectives, including gaining membership into ASEAN. It also highlights Timor-Leste's post-colonial insecurities arising from its limited military and defence capabilities and past experiences of resistance against Indonesian rule. As chapter seven outlined, the key military planning document, *Forcas 2020*, saw key external threats emerging from Indonesia in terms of boundary security and the perceived fragility of its democratization processes. Timor-Leste's foreign policy has recognized the need for a pragmatic realist orientation when it comes to its foreign policy towards Indonesia. Successive Timorese governments have privileged good relations with Indonesia ahead of international norms and values relating to transitional justice. This pragmatic realist approach sits in contrast with the "activist foreign policy" displayed in its negotiations with Australia over Timor Sea oil and gas detailed in the previous chapter.

Timor-Leste has sought to address security fears arising from its close proximity to Indonesia through a process of "international reconciliation". Timor-Leste's national identity was largely formed through the independence movement, and was driven by an anti-colonial nationalism, with Indonesia positioned as the "common enemy". The movement from enemy to friend through the processes of political reconciliation required reorienting Indonesia's relationship with the East Timorese and *vice versa* following Timor-Leste's attainment of sovereignty. This entailed developing new relationships between Timorese and Indonesian political leaders, and recasting the relationship between the two states within Timor-Leste's foreign policy narrative. Timor-Leste has sought international reconciliation with Indonesia to benefit border security, trade relations and development projects across a range of sectors.

Timor-Leste's political reconciliation with Indonesia is most prevalent when examining issues of transitional justice. Since attaining sovereignty in 2002 Timor-Leste has been responsible for establishing legitimate democratic institutions that possess widespread public support and encourage socio-political order through respect for rule of law. Following the independence referendum, Timor-Leste faced a number of divergent challenges in implementing post-conflict, transitional justice mechanisms to promote democratization, rule of law and a human rights culture.[1] The first challenge involved achieving "substantive justice", including punishing major human rights crimes during Indonesia's twenty-five-year *de facto* administration. Civic trust in Timor-Leste's judiciary depended upon the capacities of the new legal system to prosecute crimes from 1999.[2] In 2001, the Commission of Reception, Truth and Reconciliation (CAVR) was established to encourage community reconciliation by recording human rights abuses and promoting non-judicial ways of dealing with low-level offences.[3] Internal reconciliation was a priority as the state needed to integrate pro-autonomy supporters back into their communities.

Timor-Leste, however, struggled to achieve substantive justice for these human rights violations. Transitional justice efforts focused on the violations committed prior to and following the referendum, including during the "scorched earth" campaign that was actively encouraged by the Indonesian military (see chapter four). However, many of the alleged perpetrators of human rights violations escaped prosecution with the assistance of the Indonesian state. As part of the international reconciliation process, Timor-Leste and Indonesia established the world's first bilateral Truth and Reconciliation Commission, the Indonesia-Timor-Leste Commission of Truth and Friendship (CTF), established in 2005. This chapter analyses the Commission's recommendations and their implementation by Indonesia and Timor-Leste. Little has been done to press Indonesia on its responsibilities to provide compensation for victims of human rights abuses in 1999. Consequently, this chapter argues that the Commission was primarily a political mechanism designed to support Timor-Leste's priortization of reconciliation and friendship with Indonesia.

Internationally, states are viewed as having obligations to respect norms of international justice. International justice is characterized by the global articulation of basic human rights and peremptory norms outlawing crimes against humanity. In the twenty-first century, an international obligation of states to pursue individuals who bear responsibility for gross violations of human rights has formalized. International human rights instruments, such as the Rome Statute, are designed to limit the extent to which political leaders and military personnel can escape prosecution by using the norm of sovereignty as a protective shield.[4] The appeasement of Indonesia, however, effectively required Timor-Leste to sideline the pursuit of transitional justice in accordance with international norms. This highlights a realist approach insofar as Timor-Leste chose bilateral relations with Indonesia ahead of international values of rights and justice.

Timor-Leste's prioritization of reconciliation with Indonesia was evident in the ways it permitted Indonesia's avoidance of responsibility for human rights violations committed by senior military and civilian figures in 1999.[5] The CTF was responsible for finding a "conclusive truth" about "the perpetration of gross human rights violations and institutional responsibility" by conducting an inquiry and "arriving at recommendations and lessons learned".[6] The Commission employed a definition of crimes against humanity that accorded with international law under the Rome Statute, including torture, rape and murder.[7] In addressing past crimes, the Commission made recommendations regarding institutional reform, the development of joint policies, the creation of new human rights institutions and the provision of material and symbolic reparations. However, following the release of the CTF report in 2008, both Indonesia and Timor-Leste demonstrated a lack of political will in implementing many of the Commission's recommendations. This suggests that the core aim of the CTF was to promote cooperation between Timor-Leste and Indonesia through a unique form of international reconciliation designed to set aside past conflicts at the expense of transitional justice.[8]

Indonesia in Timor-Leste's Foreign Policy

The 2011 Strategic Development Plan (SDP) outlines the importance that the state places on bilateral relations with Indonesia in foreign policy. It states the need for Timor-Leste to have a positive relationship with Indonesia — its "nearest neighbour, friend and largest trading partner".[9] It argues that they are two nations undertaking a process of democratic consolidation and indicated an intention to "face the challenges of this process together".[10] It articulated a vision of strengthening the relationship through "reconciliation and a profound spirit of friendship and solidarity".[11] This is generally reflective of the effusive rhetoric that Timor-Leste's foreign policymakers tend to employ in declaratory policy and public declarations regarding Indonesia. The need for good relations with Indonesia is a consequence of Timor-Leste's geopolitical reality.

There is an awareness among East Timor's leaders that good relations with Indonesia were vital for a number of security issues, such as border control, cross-border trade, sea lane transport, access to Oecussi and managing the movement of people.[12] There has also been an acknowledgment in defence planning that a "volatile" Indonesia could contribute to East Timor's economic, social and political challenges.[13] As chapter six outlined, Timor-Leste has become increasingly responsible for its own internal and external security and has sought to build up its limited defence capabilities. Since independence, it has only faced relatively low-level external security threats, including the illegal movement of goods and people, and various maritime violations, such as illegal fishing, destruction of fauna and piracy.[14] Mitigating these external threats requires cooperation with Indonesia, for instance, in improving security across the porous sections of the border between East and West Timor. Both states have taken steps to improve security and defence relations. Memorandums of understanding covering defence and security issues were signed by Indonesian and Timorese representatives in August 2011 and February 2014 (see chapter seven).[15] Timor-Leste's emerging reliance on Indonesia for supplying military equipment has also highlighted cooperation on defence and security issues.[16]

Political leaders present Indonesia as one of Timor-Leste's main development partners.[17] As chapter eight noted, Indonesia is Timor-Leste's largest trading partner. Timor-Leste is dependent upon Indonesia, its primary supplier of imports, for foodstuffs, daily necessities and clothing. By contrast, exports to Indonesia are inconsequential because of Timor-Leste's limited productive capacity and relatively high labour costs.[18] Timor-Leste is hence dependent upon Indonesia for assistance with socio-economic development and citizenry welfare. According to Timor-Leste's former Home Affairs Minister Jorge da Conceição Teme, "the economic dependence of Timor-Leste on Indonesia is high because all our foodstuffs are bought from Indonesia".[19] Timor-Leste relies upon rice exports from Indonesia to survive periods of food insecurity known as the "hungry season".[20] Timor-Leste's prioritization of international reconciliation reflects a belief that a friendly relationship with Indonesia will support its development objectives.

As previous chapters have noted, Timor-Leste also depends upon Indonesia's support for its political and economic objectives in the broader Southeast Asian region, most notably its desire to become a member of ASEAN. Its membership prospects continue to hinge upon Indonesia's support. When Timor-Leste's bid for ASEAN membership in 2011 failed, Indonesian President Susilo Bambang Yudhoyono reiterated his support and Foreign Affairs Minister Marty Natalegawa promised to "work hard to realize Timor-Leste's vision to be a member of ASEAN".[21] As a major regional player, Indonesia's advocacy of Timor-Leste's bid for ASEAN membership is crucial.

Smith argued that a cooperative approach with Indonesia was evident in the decisions of East Timorese leaders such as Gusmão "to normalise ties with Indonesia... [and ignore] the burden of history" in order to ensure state survival.[22] This policy, however, was less concerned with ignoring history and more a matter of recognizing the power of Indonesia as East Timor's closest neighbour. Indeed, history looms large in shaping policy: Timor-Leste's policy of appeasement reflects a realistic approach to foreign policy as it acknowledged both Indonesia's previous actions in East Timor and its growing might in the twenty-first century. There is a continuing awareness among Timorese leaders that Indonesia has violated the security of its people in the past and it cannot be naïve when it comes to national security (see chapter six). Timor-Leste has sought to mitigate any potential threat posed by Indonesia by promoting friendship and cooperation, which assists in explaining the unwillingness of Timor-Leste's leaders to press Indonesia on the issue of substantive justice for past human rights violations.

Timor-Leste's emphasis on reconciliation with Indonesia needs to be assessed in the context of vulnerability and dependence. Timor-Leste's leaders have sought to promote good relations with Indonesia as a way of achieving key security objectives. At the same time, Timor-Leste's ongoing insecurity arising from past experiences with Indonesian rule has continued to shape the leadership's view that Indonesia remains a potential security threat. In 2010, Gusmão argued that "[o]ur own history has shown us... that wars can be caused for a great many reasons, including to take control over natural resources".[23] Timor-Leste has hence advanced reconciliation with Indonesia in order to bolster its national security interests as a small state.

This has required Timorese leaders to recast the narrative of Timor-Leste and Indonesia's relationship to focus on solidarity, shared values and common challenges. In doing so, Timorese leaders have emphasized the common experiences of Timor-Leste and Indonesia of "colonialization and oppression", which glosses over Indonesia's colonizing role in East Timor.[24] The narrative suggests that the states have bridged the "chasm" and built "bonds of trust and cooperation" despite the "difficult history": the Timorese and Indonesian "brothers and sisters" now purportedly enjoy "deep bonds of solidarity".[25] The foreign policy narrative also positions Timor-Leste and Indonesia as holding a mutual commitment to their shared transition to democracy and to the rights of its people: "while our nations have had a difficult past — a past shaped by colonialism, and the global politics of the Cold War — we now share the values of democracy, tolerance, peace and human dignity."[26] These public statements praise Indonesia's "amazing" transition from the authoritarian Suharto regime that occupied Timor-Leste to a democracy. This is despite the fact that many of the political and military elites that were active in the Suharto era — and in the occupation of East Timor — continue to have roles in Indonesia's new democratic system. Nevertheless, Timorese representatives publically praise Indonesia's politics and society and describe it as inspiring:

> [w]ith its pluralistic and tolerant society, Indonesia is more than a close neighbour. Indeed, it is an inspiration for Timor-Leste. Under the wise leadership of His Excellency President Susilo Bambang Yudhoyono we have witnessed the establishment of a modern democracy that harmonises progress with the promotion of national, regional and international peace.[27]

This praise is reminiscent of the rhetoric of Timorese leaders *vis-à-vis* its close friendship with its other former colonizer, Portugal.

The International Dimensions of Transitional Justice

As noted in chapter four, unlike many other former colonies, Timor-Leste was provided significant international support in establishing democratic institutions, including an independent judiciary. The United Nations (UN) Security Council Resolution 1272 that created the United Nations Transitional Administration in East Timor (UNTAET) obliged it to ensure that "those [persons] responsible for such violence be brought to justice" and "bear individual responsibility" for their past crimes.[28] This was a significant challenge: the scorched earth campaign — "Operation Clean Sweep" — destroyed what little judicial infrastructure existed in Timor-Leste. Working in the UN Legal Office, Hans Strohmeyer reported that "not a single judge, prosecutor or attorney was left, the court buildings were destroyed or stripped of any useful materials, including the electrical wiring, legal libraries were removed or dislocated, the prisons were emptied".[29] By the time the UNTAET arrived in Timor-Leste, less than ten lawyers were left in the territory, all inexperienced.[30] By early 2000, it was clear the UN Legal Office would be responsible for providing justice in domestic courts.[31]

In January 2000, a UN-sponsored International Commission of Inquiry was instituted to gather and compile information on acts that took place in 1999 which may have breached international humanitarian law and to examine possibilities for pursuing justice.[32] United Nations Secretary-General Kofi Annan emphasized the responsibilities of the international community in investigating and punishing those responsible for rights violations and to "help safeguard the rights of the people of East Timor, promote reconciliation, [and] ensure future social and political stability".[33] The Commission of Inquiry ultimately recommended the creation of an international tribunal partly due to the likely implication of senior TNI members.[34] Timor-Leste did not have the necessary resources to operate such an extensive tribunal, and it could not be certain that convictions would be secured in Indonesian courts.

Indonesia rejected the idea of establishing an international tribunal, and instead sought to reassure the international community of its commitment to justice by signing a Memorandum of Understanding with the UNTAET in April 2000, which included provisions for sharing evidence, facilitating the participation of witnesses and extraditing accused perpetrators.[35] Indonesia was committed to establishing its own human rights tribunal to investigate and prosecute crimes committed in Timor-Leste. These assurances in part contributed to the decision of the UN to ignore the advice of its own inquiry and abandon the establishment of an international tribunal.[36]

Instead, the UNTAET established a "hybrid" tribunal composed of international and domestic personnel. The UNTAET Regulation 2000/11, promulgated on 6 March 2000, mandated the creation of the judiciary, comprising District Courts and one Court of Appeal.[37] The District Court of Dili held exclusive jurisdiction over serious crimes committed in the period between 1 January 1999 and 25 October 1999, defined as genocide, war crimes, crimes against humanity, murder, sexual offences and torture.[38] Three months later, on 6 June 2000, the UNTAET Regulation 2000/15 established the Special Panels in the District Court of Dili to hear serious crimes, comprising one Timorese and two international judges.[39] The panels held universal jurisdiction with regard to serious criminal offences committed in the mandated timeframe, regardless of whether they were committed by citizens of Timor-Leste.[40] It ambitiously adopted a "slightly modified" version of the Rome Statute (designed for the International Criminal Court), which determined that the panels should, where appropriate, defer to the principle and norms of international law.[41]

The Indonesian National Human Rights Commission (*Komisi Nasional Hak Asasi Manusia*, Komnas HAM), meanwhile, established the Commission for Human Rights Violations in East Timor (KPP-HAM) on 22 September 1999.[42] The ensuing report, released only as an executive summary on the same day as the UN Commission of Inquiry, 31 January 2000, found "widespread collaboration between Indonesian military and police and pro-autonomy militia", and identified high-ranking officials, including Commander-in-Chief General Wiranto, as responsible for crimes against humanity.[43] It made the same recommendation as the UN Commission of Inquiry that an international tribunal was necessary for trying crimes committed in 1999.[44] Amid substantial international pressure, in November 2000, the Indonesian Parliament passed legislation to create an *ad hoc* Human Rights Court in Jakarta, which was established in August 2001.[45]

Neither of these justice mechanisms satisfactorily addressed the human rights violations committed in 1999. Significant criticism of Indonesia's *ad hoc* courts emerged from international institutions and civil society organizations, including the High Commissioner of the Human Rights Commission, Mary Robinson.[46] By the end of 2002, only two individuals had been convicted in the *ad hoc* courts, both Timorese.[47] The influence of the TNI in judicial processes and the lack of political will in prosecuting senior TNI officials contributed to a 2005 UN Commission of Experts report describing the *ad hoc* courts as "manifestly inadequate".[48] Indonesia's assurances to the international community that it would prosecute those responsible for the human rights violations in Timor-Leste were not fulfilled.[49] While the Special Courts in East Timor were widely considered a genuine attempt at providing justice, they were unable to hold to account those most responsible. While this was partly due to Timor-Leste's lack of institutional and resource capacity, Indonesia's refusal to comply with the Memorandum of Understanding and extradite alleged perpetrators was a significant limitation. By January 2008, 76 per cent of indictees continued to enjoy sanctuary in Indonesia.[50]

Timor-Leste's leadership was unwilling to press Indonesia on the issue. Indonesian officials charged with crimes against humanity by the Special Courts, such as General Wiranto, had their arrest warrants "disavowed by the UN and subsequently by the government of

East Timor".[51] The privileging of good relations with Indonesia was confirmed in June 2004, when President Xanana Gusmão met with his "dear friend" General Wiranto less than two weeks after the former TNI chief's indictment by the serious crimes unit.[52] Timor-Leste's leaders obstructed the achievement of retributive justice in order to advance its foreign affairs interests, presenting problems for Timor-Leste in developing political order through rule of law.[53] The departure of the UNTAET in 2002 further limited the capacities of Timor-Leste's fledgling judiciary to prosecute past crimes and presented issues for institutionalizing its newly established democratic institutions. In 2001, the UNTAET mandated the establishment of the CAVR.[54] Beginning its work in 2002, the Commission shifted the focus from substantive justice to reconciliation involving widespread community participation. The CAVR's final report, titled *Chega!* (Portuguese for "enough"), was released in 2005, and made a series of recommendations regarding the responsibilities of Timor-Leste and Indonesia.

International Reconciliation and the Commission of Truth and Friendship

On 21 December 2004, Indonesia and Timor-Leste jointly announced their intention to establish a Commission of Truth and Friendship (CTF) to investigate the 1999 violence. On 18 February 2005, it was announced that the UN Secretary-General had established a Commission of Experts to review and assess the Indonesian *ad hoc* Human Rights Courts and the Special Panels for Serious Crimes in Dili, and to make appropriate recommendations.[55] Having predicted the Commission of Experts would recommend the creation of an international tribunal, both Timor-Leste and Indonesia admitted that the CTF was designed to block progress on such a recommendation.[56] They were correct: the Commission of Experts report, released 26 May 2005, recommended that if Timor-Leste and Indonesia did not commit to prosecuting perpetrators within six months, an international tribunal should be established with the power to investigate human rights violations.[57] This style of diplomatic pressure from the UN reflected an attempt to ensure that both states abided by their international obligations regarding justice.

However, the efforts of the Commission of Experts failed to compel Timor-Leste and Indonesia to prosecute perpetrators. Instead, the CTF was borne from Timor-Leste's efforts to secure beneficial relations with Indonesia by preventing the establishment of the tribunal that Indonesia was desperate to avoid. The influential role of the military in Indonesia's democratic transition is important for understanding its reluctance to pursue substantive justice for past human rights violations. As Crouch points out, democratization in Indonesia relied in part upon the willingness of the TNI to disentangle itself from the "doomed" Suharto regime.[58] Reform-minded members of the TNI were convinced that removing the military from the political sphere was necessary to ensure their own political survival and avoid renewals of the mass riots that had contributed to the collapse of the Suharto regime.[59] The negotiated resetting of the relationship between the military and democratically-elected government was pivotal for the success of Indonesia's democratic transition, however, this fragile and uncertain political context also made Indonesian political leaders reluctant to pursue crimes committed by TNI officers in 1999.

For Timor-Leste, the CTF was created as a political mechanism driven by its international interests and advanced at the expense of domestic justice imperatives and rule of law. Many civil society organizations raised concerns about the establishment of the CTF, warning that it would fail to provide justice for Timorese victims. For instance, the Judicial System Monitoring Program predicted that individuals responsible for human rights violations in East Timor would "be neither identified nor held to account".[60] The *Chega!* report also criticized the CTF, suggesting that while further research may be necessary, the work of the CAVR and the Serious Crime Unit should be "respected and protected from denial".[61] There was a fear among transitional justice and human rights advocates that the CTF would work to prevent the achievement of substantive justice and ultimately undermine democratization processes in both states.

On 9 March 2005, the Terms of Reference for the CTF were settled.[62] The Commission was positioned as integral to democratization and would consist of half Indonesian and half East Timorese Commissioners.[63] The Terms of Reference stated:

> our peoples endeavor [sic] to build a solid foundation for a future of peace; a future where human dignity and social justice are the guiding force of transformation. Peace, however, is a process and has to be built. The pillars of peace are democracy, sustainable development and respect for human rights.[64]

The key objective of the CTF, according to the Terms of Reference, was to establish "the conclusive truth" of the events of 1999 and present "factual and objective information".[65] Whether a "conclusive truth" even exists is contentious: one challenge for the Commission was balancing the multiple versions of truth conveyed by participants.[66] The Terms of Reference also emphasized the "forward-looking and reconciliatory" approach taken by Timor-Leste and Indonesia in their aim of creating a "shared historical record".[67] Timor-Leste leaders were openly enthusiastic about this aspect of the CTF: Gusmão declared "[w]hen building a State and Nation there is no room for nurturing past hatreds".[68] Similarly, José Ramos Horta predicted that the CTF would "finally close this chapter" on past conflict between the two states.[69]

The Commission viewed its role as supporting diplomatic relations between Timor-Leste and Indonesia. This was made clear in the CTF report, released in 2008, which stated:

> as nations and democratic states that are still undergoing transformation towards a better life, each nation faces its respective domestic problems and priorities, especially in strengthening the social, political and economic order. To this end, the two nations desire conducive circumstances for peace and development, including harmonious mutual relations.[70]

Through the establishment of the CTF, both states committed to developing "dynamic, friendly and mutually beneficial" relations to promote domestic and international interests and contribute to regional stability, development and democratization.[71] However, this was not a commitment made by two states possessing relatively equal material power capacities. The context of power asymmetry is significant for understanding Timor-Leste's motivations in promoting international reconciliation: Timor-Leste's vulnerabilities as a small state means that leaders recognized the importance of its relations with Indonesia even if this means sacrificing the pursuit of substantive justice. Lipscomb suggested that Timor-Leste actively exploited its "geopolitical vulnerability" to justify inaction on substantive justice for past crimes.[72]

In contrast to Timorese political leaders, civil society organizations continued to question the relevance of the CTF, with the East Timor and Indonesia Action Network arguing that the "truth-telling" focus would prevent actual closure, which requires the achievement of "genuine justice".[73] Indeed, the CTF did not have any prosecutorial powers, which reflected the political rather than judicial objectives underpinning its creation. The CTF could "recommend amnesty for those involved in human rights violations who cooperate fully in revealing the truth", and, confusingly, "recommend rehabilitation measures for those wrongly accused of human rights violations". The controversial amnesty provisions compelled Indonesia's Constitutional Court to declare the CTF "unconstitutional".[74] They also undermined article 160 of Timor-Leste's Constitution, which states that crimes against humanity committed between 1974 and 1999 "shall be liable to criminal proceedings with the national or international courts".[75] Many international, Timorese and Indonesian civil society organizations considered the establishment of the CTF as "farcical", lacking transparency and a clear procedure, and designed to prematurely close the question of accountability.[76] Ultimately, the Commission would not be able to fulfil the demands of the Commission of Experts that both states commit to the prosecution of past human rights violations.[77] The prioritization of bilateral relations in the establishment of the CTF compromised the capacities of both states to fulfil their international justice obligations.

While permitting impunity assisted Timor-Leste's friendship with Indonesia, it simultaneously threatened its capacities to institute rule of law. As chapter seven highlighted, while internal and external security issues are interrelated, Timor-Leste's most serious security threats have emanated from inside the state rather than outside. Weaknesses in state security institutions also threatened Timor-Leste's capacities to govern effectively. Challenges in inculcating and institutionalizing new political structures present an ongoing risk to Timor-Leste's sovereignty and independence. An editorial in the *Jakarta Post* prior to the release of the CTF report argued that Timorese citizens "were resentful of their leaders' pragmatic decision to seek a solution through the set-up of the commission".[78] Timor-Leste's emphasis on reconciliation with Indonesia undervalued the expectations held by citizens that human rights violations would be punished and victims appropriately compensated. As democratization literature recognizes, a strong independent judiciary is necessary for providing "horizontal" legal accountability and engendering key democratic institutions and procedures with political legitimacy derived from "an intrinsic value commitment rooted in the political culture at all levels of society".[79]

The privileging of bilateral relations with Indonesia simultaneously threatened Timor-Leste's aspirational self-image of a democratic state that abides by international norms.

Per Memoriam ad Spem: The Final Report of the Commission of Truth and Friendship and the Implementation of Recommendations

At the end of 2005, the Commission began working on three key tasks: research; making findings on violations and "institutional responsibility"; and, making recommendations in consultation with various community groups. The completed report *Per Memoriam ad Spem* (From Memory to Hope) was completed in March 2008.[80] While civil society organizations had routinely advocated the end of the CTF during its investigations, the final report, submitted to Timor-Leste's parliament in October 2008 by Ramos-Horta, was not what many were expecting.[81] While the report sought to shift Indonesia away from Suharto's regime, the findings largely corroborated the reports from both the KPP-HAM and the CAVR.[82] It found crimes against humanity had been committed in East Timor by Indonesian military, police and civilians and it condemned the *ad hoc* Jakarta trials as having serious shortcomings.[83] While it did not get to the heart of the widespread nature of the violations, it acknowledged the institutional responsibilities of Indonesia. The report stated that the combination of a large military influence and weak controls in civilian administration "opened the way to perpetration of violence by involved institutions".[84] The Commission also found the violence was not random or spontaneous but systematic and organized.[85] Indonesian President Susilo Bambang Yudhoyono's endorsement of the report was Indonesia's first official recognition of the systematic nature of human rights violations in Timor-Leste.[86]

However, if the core aim was to develop a conclusive truth, the Commission did not attempt to develop a fact-finding mission much beyond what other commissions had conducted. It relied heavily upon documentary evidence and testimony compiled by other commissions, such as the CAVR, which had interviewed thousands of community members. The Commission only interviewed 85 people and took statements of 62 witnesses, a number of whom, according to Hirst, provided "self-serving evidence" and were "never seriously cross-examined".⁸⁷ The report avoided questions regarding the complicity and active roles of Indonesian senior military in perpetrating and encouraging violence, and the desire to "share blame" between Indonesia and Timor-Leste led to flawed analysis of responsibilities of pro-independence groups.⁸⁸

Part of the CTF's mandate was to make recommendations for the purposes of strengthening the human rights culture of each state and prevent systemic rights abuses in the future. The Commission sought to make forward-looking recommendations in the form of "collective reparations" requiring material and other forms of support from Timor-Leste and Indonesia.⁸⁹ The Commission found that both states held "a political and moral obligation to accept responsibility for gross human rights violations committed by groups to which they have an historical connection, even when those institutions no longer exist or have undergone significant transformation".⁹⁰ The recommendations were vague on how the cost of providing reparations and establishing new institutions should be distributed amongst the states.⁹¹ The CTF also made a number of recommendations aimed at preventing future systemic failures through institutional reforms, including human rights training and engaging in further security sector reform.⁹² The report noted that "remedying systemic and institutional failures through institutional reform is… necessary to prevent future reoccurrences of violence and to ensure the foundation for peace and friendship between the two countries".⁹³ The Commission itself was relatively consistent in its recommendations to support democratization and the development of a human rights culture.

To support the consolidation of democratic institutions, the CTF recommended the two governments engage in further Security Sector Reform (SSR) through the "transformation of military doctrine and institutional practices".⁹⁴ Several programmes in Timor-Leste have sought to assist in SSR, in particular decoupling the police and military in a way that supports democratization (see chapter seven). Reform was supported by bilateral agreements with donor states, such as Australia, Portugal and China, as well as international operations such as the United Nations Integrated Mission in Timor-Leste.⁹⁵ However, it was the security breakdown in 2006 that was the catalyst for SSR in Timor-Leste, two years prior to the release of the CTF report.⁹⁶ Indonesia also engaged in SSR following the fall of the Suharto regime in 1998.⁹⁷

Security Sector Reform and substantive justice are mutually supportive goals. In both Indonesia and Timor-Leste, SSR has not been adequately supported by the pursuit of substantive justice, and *vice versa*. The International Center for Transitional Justice reports that for SSR to be successful in Timor-Leste:

> the government must address the culture of impunity and strengthen the rule of law. It must move away from short sighted attempts to encourage reconciliation through impunity for security sector and government personnel implicated in violent crimes and human rights abuses, and look to the long-term goal of establishing trust in the state and security forces.[98]

Timor-Leste's prioritization of international reconciliation and avoidance of pursuing those most responsible for past human rights abuses undermine SSR and hinder the states' ability to inculcate a culture of human rights. By focusing on international reconciliation, successive Timor-Leste governments and officials have been complicit in the failure to deal with gross human rights violations, and many accused perpetrators retain their freedom in Indonesia.[99]

The CTF also recommended that Timor-Leste and Indonesia develop joint security and border policies in order to strengthen their bilateral friendship. This recommendation aligns with the broader national objectives of both states and would have occurred with or without the CTF recommendations. A number of small border disputes have occurred since Timor-Leste's independence. Both states have publically committed to resolving land and maritime boundary issues, although land boundaries are yet to be fully resolved. One recommendation focused on establishing "peace zones" on the border and "safe crossings", increasing border security through cooperation, coordination and training, and resolving "private asset claims" asserted by citizens.[100] The Indonesian delegation representing the Ministry for Foreign Affairs at the Fourth Senior Officials Meeting in 2010 identified short and long-term goals for establishing "zones of peace" on shared borders.[101] Timor-Leste also emphasized cooperation in the area of security, including holding joint training in a third state.[102] In 2013, a Memorandum of Understanding was signed to maintain border entry crossings in three areas and enable free movement by using frontier crossings.[103] Yudhoyono emphasized "trust" between Indonesia and Timor-Leste, and said that "a number of sensitive issues that were recommended by the Commission of Truth and Friendship" were resolved.[104] While making progress on a number of important issues supporting bilateral relations and regional stability, these agreements are relatively uncontentious and provided little by way of addressing the human rights abuses of 1999.

Another key set of recommendations of the CTF related to the establishment of new institutions, including a Documentation and Conflict Resolution Centre and a Commission of Disappeared Persons. The CTF report suggested that preventing future violence requires an understanding of past conflict.[105] A Documentation and Conflict Resolution Centre would be located in Dili with a partner centre in Jakarta and would be charged with "[p]romoting friendship between the two peoples".[106] At the Fourth Senior Officials Meeting in 2010, Timor-Leste's delegation from the Ministry of Foreign Affairs noted its intention to begin deliberations on the Centre for Documentation and Conflict Resolution.[107] In June 2010, two bills were submitted to the National Parliament of Timor-Leste, one to establish a Framework for a National Reparations Programme and the other to establish a Public Memory Institute.[108] Debates on these bills were delayed indefinitely in February 2011.[109]

Some civil society activist groups have emphasized the failures of Timor-Leste and Indonesia in establishing the recommended Commission on Disappeared Persons. The CTF found Indonesian security forces "responsible for the majority of conflict-related disappearances" in Timor-Leste, estimated to number in the tens of thousands.[110] It advised the Indonesian and Timor-Leste governments to "work together to acquire information about the fate of disappeared people and cooperate to gather data and provide information to their families".[111] Timor-Leste's representatives have attempted to raise the issue of the Commission on Disappeared Persons in international forums. For instance, the Timor-Leste delegation at the second session of Universal Periodic Review on 23 May 2011 "warned Indonesia to end impunity by accelerating the establishment of the Commission for the Disappeared".[112] However, the attempts of Timor-Leste's Ministry of Foreign Affairs and Cooperation to engage its Indonesian counterparts on the Commission on Disappeared Persons have elicited only "lukewarm responses, confirming the Indonesian government's lack of political will to address this issue".[113]

In 2015/16, Amnesty International reported that no progress had been made on implementing recommendations of the CAVR and CTF.[114]

Despite extended agreements between Indonesia and Timor-Leste's national human rights institutions, a Commission for Disappeared Persons had yet to be established. Several civil society organizations have pressured both governments to take action, including the Timor-Leste National Alliance for an International Tribunal (ANTI), which argued that "the Indonesian government has shown no interest, commitment or goodwill to encourage or accelerate the process of establishing this Commission on Disappeared Persons."[115] One human rights NGO coalition questioned the commitment of Indonesia and Timor-Leste and argued that the two governments instead chose to strengthen bilateral ties.[116] This reflects the tensions for Timor-Leste between implementing the CTF's recommendations and advancing pragmatic foreign affairs aims.

The lack of follow up on a number of CTF recommendations indicates that the exercise was not designed to assist with the pursuit of transitional justice of those who committed serious crimes in Timor-Leste in 1999, but were designed rather to improve Timor-Leste and Indonesia's bilateral relationship behind a veneer of meeting international obligations regarding accountability and justice. Four Senior Officials Meetings between representatives of each states' Ministry of Foreign Affairs were held between 2008 and 2010 to discuss a "Joint Plan of Action" for the implementation of the CTF's recommendations.[117] On 6 October 2011, Yudhoyono issued Decree No. 72/2011 on the Action Plan for the Implementation of the Recommendations of the CTF and established a working group to monitor the "Joint Plan of Action".[118] However, little progress was made.[119] As Pampalk suggests, the plan was "focused on programme delivery in Timor-Leste rather than in Indonesia, which reflects how Indonesia apprehends its role in the process".[120] Executive Director of Timor-Leste's Judicial System Monitoring Programme, Luis de Oliveira Sampaio, argued that the lack of follow-up showed "the Governments of Indonesia and Timor-Leste are not serious in addressing the issue of past crimes to respond to the suffering of the victims".[121] The broad recommendations relating to Security Sector Reform have been more successful than those directly related to the 1999 conflict, such as the Public Memory Institute and Commission for Disappeared Persons.[122] The Senior Officials Meetings produced agreement only on "relatively uncontroversial issues" such as the Temporary Stay Permit Card and Visa on Arrival for Timorese citizens.[123]

The CTF report recommended that both states acknowledge institutional responsibility for rights abuses in the form of an apology.[124] While issues of complicity complicate the question of who should pay reparations, both states are responsible for meeting international humanitarian law requirements that culpable governments remedy gross human rights violations and restore dignity to victims.[125] Numerous Timorese leaders have offered apologies as a symbolic reparations gesture despite the various truth commissions emphasizing the roles of Indonesian military and civilian personnel in the 1999 human rights abuses committed.[126] While former Indonesian President Abdurrahman Wahid apologized to Timor-Leste when he visited in 2000, successive Indonesian governments have only expressed regret and Yudhoyono refused to issue an apology upon presentation of the CTF report.[127] Instead, in July 2008, he made a statement of "deep regret" that was "accepted by the government of Timor-Leste as an apology".[128] Civil society organizations pressed Indonesia to offer an apology and hold military leaders such as General Wiranto to account, and, in 2010, Ramos-Horta argued that "the only thing still missing is an apology... by those who were directing all the suffering."[129] However, in 2012, Ramos-Horta seemed to change his mind, arguing that there was "pragmatic state interests at stake" and he was "sympathetic to post-Suharto Indonesia".[130] This recognizes that both Timor-Leste and Indonesia have undergone considerable political transformations since the fall of the Suharto regime, but also reflects the political compromises made by Timor-Leste on the issue of institutional responsibility dictated by a realist approach.

Attempts to implement the recommendations of reparations were weak.[131] In Timor-Leste, there has been little forthcoming in the way of material reparations for the crimes of 1999, in contrast with the reparations offered by the government following the 2006 crisis.[132] Neither state demonstrated the political will to provide funding for a reparations fund. In December 2009, Timor-Leste's parliament passed a resolution asking its Human Rights Committee A to "provide a basis for the first public governmental debate on a national reparations policy".[133] In June 2010, parliamentary debates on a draft bill to establish a Framework for a National Reparations Programme were delayed indefinitely in February 2011 after opposition.[134] According to Amnesty International, the bill did not provide "for Indonesia to contribute to the funding or implementation of the Reparations Programme, despite the fact that both the CAVR report and the CTF concluded that the Indonesian government and its forces bear responsibility for many of the human rights violations committed in Timor-Leste."[135]

While there appears to be an absence of meaningful action in regards to the recommendations, Timor-Leste's leaders have publically praised the CTF as a success. According to Gusmão, the report:

> put an end to the painful past, with a solemn agreement that the Timorese and Indonesian people will never again be harmed. Both Timor-Leste and Indonesia wanted to clear the way for true and genuine reconciliation and tolerance amongst communities and people, rather than feed hatred and revenge that would only destroy the country and impede the efforts of the population to improve their living conditions. As a result of this forward looking policy, Indonesia and Timor-Leste now enjoy a solid relationship between people and between States, based on cooperation, friendship and a collective vision for the future.[136]

A number of public declarations in the international sphere have presented Timor-Leste and Indonesia's political reconciliation as a unique success story and a global model of goodwill and leadership in overcoming conflict.[137] In 2013, Gusmão declared that Timor-Leste "now enjoys the friendliest of relationships with Indonesia. Rather than being enslaved by the trauma of our history, we are instead honouring our struggle by working towards a better future for our people. We know that Indonesia and Timor-Leste not only share an island, we share a future."[138] In a 2014 speech honouring former Indonesian President Susilo Bambang Yudhoyono, he argued that Timor-Leste and Indonesia ended the conflict between them and:

> what remains today is the memory of the heroic deeds of the people of Timor-Leste... without precedent, the two governments and the two peoples knew how to show to today's world not only extraordinary courage but, above all, a particular understanding of each of our own processes. The policy of reconciliation between our two peoples will be, for many regions of the globe, a reference to reduce tensions and to end conflicts plaguing less developed countries.[139]

This again highlights the fragile state exceptionalism of Timor-Leste as leaders present it as a model for others to emulate.

Timor-Leste's reluctance to follow through with recommendations of the CAVR and the CTF is linked to its unwillingness to displease Indonesia.[140] Timor-Leste's acceptance of impunity highlights the importance it places on its relationship with Indonesia and its vulnerability as a small state. Many high-level Indonesian military officials, such as

General Wiranto, have not faced trial for the atrocities committed in Timor-Leste in 1999. The CTF report offered protection to allegedly complicit officials by promoting a façade of closure on the issue of impunity.[141] This is reflected in the words of General Wiranto who stated that "the case of disturbances in Timor-Leste has now been resolved."[142] According to the transitional justice literature, one of the key purposes of establishing a truth and reconciliation commission is to encourage governments to take responsibility for past injustices and to prevent systemic human rights abuses in the future. Reconciliation commissions are viewed as especially beneficial for states undergoing democratic political transition in post-conflict contexts. However, the CTF was not designed to achieve justice for past human rights violations: its primary goal was to promote friendship between Indonesia and Timor-Leste by moving relations beyond past conflicts without adequately dealing with human rights violations.

The decision of both states to sideline the pursuit of justice has meant the CTF became a shield for those senior TNI officials responsible for human rights abuses in 1999. Former members of Suharto's military have become influential and high-profile political figures in the post-transition phase, including former President Susilo Bambang Yudhoyono and 2014 presidential candidate Prabowo Subianto, who played a considerable military role in Indonesia's occupation in East Timor. General Wiranto is a minister in Indonesian President Joko Widodo's administration. Relations between Indonesia and Timor-Leste have continued to be close under the new administration, with Timor-Leste even bestowing upon Widodo the highest decoration available — the *Grande Colar de Ordem de Timor Leste* — in January 2016.[143] Timor-Leste's leaders actively sought good relations with Indonesian leaders even though it has been unwilling to pursue former members of the TNI who continue to actively participate in Indonesian politics. Timor-Leste's pragmatic realism on the issue has meant that it has actively colluded with Indonesia to allow impunity.

Conclusion

As the *Force 2020* notes, Timor-Leste has "been extremely cautious" in seeking cooperation with its more powerful neighbour.[144] Since independence, successive East Timorese governments have faced tough decisions in negotiating competing agendas in domestic policy and foreign affairs. While avoiding prosecution for past human rights abuses risks the processes of democratization and consolidating internal sovereignty through rule of law, not pursuing friendship with Indonesia would also threaten other political, economic and security objectives. The need to appease Indonesia reflects the insecurities that arise from Timor-Leste's historical experiences with colonialism as well as its ongoing dependence upon its former colonizer. As a consequence, Timor-Leste has sought to pragmatically pursue good relations with Indonesia. This sits in contrast with its approach to its bilateral relationship with Australia, which has been fraught since Timor-Leste's achievement of independence. Timor-Leste's Timor Sea "activist" diplomacy lacked the realism that inflects its approach to relations with Indonesia, even though Timor-Leste's short- to mid-term economic viability rests upon a resolution regarding Greater Sunrise.

The other realist aspect of Timor-Leste's foreign policy approach in relation to Indonesia is its willingness to subordinate international norms of transitional justice. Timor-Leste has sought to project its image as a "good international citizen" that abides by international law, and criticized Australia for ostensibly failing to respect the rules-based order on maritime boundary delimitation. However, Indonesia and Timor-Leste have prioritized bilateral ties and international reconciliation ahead of fulfilling their international obligations to bring perpetrators of gross human rights violations to justice. The CTF was designed to support international reconciliation at the expense of domestic justice and reconciliation priorities, which is problematic for both states as they seek to consolidate democracy and institute rule of law. Both states failed to take seriously the commission's recommendations because the CTF was a political mechanism designed to enhance foreign relations between Indonesia and Timor-Leste rather than a serious effort to pursue substantive and reparative forms of justice.

NOTES

1. Sanam Naraghi Anderlini, Camille Conaway and Lisa Kays, "Transitional Justice and Reconciliation", in *Inclusive Security, Sustainable Peace: A Toolkit for Advocacy and Action*, p. 1 (International Alert: Women Waging Peace, November 2004).

2. Suzanne Katzenstein, "Hybrid Tribunals: Searching for Justice in East Timor", *Harvard Human Rights Journal* 16 (2003): 250.
3. Commission for Reception, Truth and Reconciliation (CAVR), *Chega! Final Report of the Commission for Reception, Truth and Reconciliation Timor-Leste*, chapter 3, p. 10 (Dili: CAVR, 2005).
4. International Criminal Court, "Rome Statute of the International Criminal Court", United Nations Document A/CONF. 183/9, 17 July 1998.
5. Indria Fernida, "Four Years of Final Report of Indonesia–Timor-Leste Commission of Truth and Friendship (CTF): Recommendation without any Implementation", *East Timor Law and Justice Bulletin* (16 July 2012).
6. Commission of Truth and Friendship (CTF), *From Memory to Hope: Final Report of the Commission of Truth and Friendship (CTF) Indonesia–Timor-Leste*, pp. x, 17 (Denpasar: CTF, 31 March 2008).
7. Megan Hirst, *An Unfinished Truth: An Analysis of the Commission of Truth and Friendship's Final Report on the 1999 Atrocities in East Timor*, p. 8 (New York: International Center for Transitional Justice, January 2009).
8. Samuel Huntington, *The Third Wave: Democratization in the Late Twentieth Century*, pp. 213–14 (Oklahoma: University of Oklahoma Press, 1991).
9. República Democrática de Timor-Leste (RDTL), *Strategic Development Plan*, p. 173 (Dili: Government of Timor-Leste, 2011).
10. Ibid.
11. Ibid.
12. Anthony Smith, "Constraints and Choices: East Timor as a Foreign Policy Actor", *New Zealand Journal of Asian Studies* 7, no. 1 (June 2005): 15–36. See also Damien Kingsbury, "East Timor Border Security", in *Violence in Between: Conflict and Security in Archipelagic Southeast Asia*, edited by Damien Kingsbury, pp. 277–97 (Clayton: Monash University Press, 2005).
13. Rizal Sukma, "Securing East Timor: Military and External Relations", in *Peace Building and State Building in Timor-Leste*, edited by Hadi Soesastro and Landry Haryo Subianto, p. 101 (Jakarta: Centre for Strategic and International Studies, 2002); RDTL, *Force 2020*, 2007, available at <https://www.locjkt.or.id/Timor_E/pdf/Forca202007.pdf> (accessed 11 February 2017).
14. Smith, "Constraints and Choices", p. 15; International Crisis Group, "Timor Leste: Oecusse and the Indonesian Border", *Asia Briefing* No. 104 (Dili/Brussels: International Crisis Group, 20 May 2010); Alexandra Retno Wulan, "Border Incident a Test Case for Jakarta–Dili Ties", *The Jakarta Post*, 14 January 2006; Warren Wright, "The Complexities of Timor-Leste–Indonesia Border Control", *Timor-Leste Law and Justice Bulletin* (25 February 2013), available at <http://easttimorlegal.blogspot.com/2013/02/thecomplexities-of-timor-leste.html> (accessed 4 April 2013).

15. Mark Dodd, "Forgive and Forget as Dili Signs Jakarta Defence Pact", *The Australian*, 29 August 2011.
16. *East Timor Law and Justice Bulletin*, "Timor-Leste Strikes Troubling New Weapon Deal with Indonesia, says Fundasaun Mahein", 13 March 2014, available at <http://www.easttimorlawandjusticebulletin.com/2014/03/timor-leste-strikes-troubling-new.html> (accessed 19 June 2014).
17. Xanana Gusmão, "Peace, Security and Human Development", Address by His Excellency the Prime Minister Kay Rala Xanana Gusmão on the Occasion of the World Summit 2014, Seoul, 10 August 2014.
18. Bob Lowry, "After the 2006 Crisis: Australian Interests in Timor-Leste", *Strategic Insights* 38, p. 4 (Canberra: Australian Strategic Policy Institute, November 2007).
19. Author unknown, "Timor Leste–Indonesia Bilateral Relations Improve", *Antara News*, 27 September 2013.
20. Marcelino dJ. Da Costa, Modesto Lopes, Anita Ximenes, Adelfredo do Rosario Ferreira, Luc Spyckerelle, Rob Williams, Harry Nesbitt and William Erskine, "Household Food Insecurity in Timor-Leste", *Food Security* 5 (2013): 83–94.
21. Bagus BT. Saragih, "Marty Reiterates Support for Timor-Leste's ASEAN Bid", *The Jakarta Post*, 12 September 2012.
22. Smith, "Constraints and Choices", p. 20.
23. Xanana Gusmão, "Reviewing Resistance and Understanding the Present", Lecture by His Excellency the Prime Minister and Minister for Defence and Security Kay Rala Xanana Gusmão on the Strategic Framework Module for Timor-Leste Within the Pilot Course on Defence and Security, Dili, 9 November 2010.
24. Agio Pereira, "The Challenges of Nation-State Building", in *A New Era? Timor-Leste After the UN*, edited by Sue Ingram, Lia Kent and Andrew McWilliam, pp. 25–26 (Canberra: ANU Press, 2015).
25. Xanana Gusmão, "Alliance of Civilizations", Address by His Excellency the Prime Minister of the Democratic Republic of Timor-Leste Kay Rala Xanana Gusmão to the Sixth Global Forum United Nations Alliance of Civilizations, Bali, 29 August 2014; Xanana Gusmão, "Consolidating Democracy in a Pluralist Society", Address by His Excellency the Prime Minister Kay Rala Xanana Gusmão on the Occasion of the Bali Democracy Forum, Bali, 7 November 2013.
26. Xanana Gusmão, Speech by His Excellency the Prime Minister of the Democratic Republic of Timor-Leste Kay Rala Xanana Gusmão at the Farewell Dinner for their Excellencies Dr H. Susilo Bambang Yudhoyono and Madam HJ. Ani Bambang Yudhoyono, President and First Lady of the Republic of Indonesia, Dili, 26 August 2014. See also Rui Araújo,

"Remarks by the Prime Minister of the Democratic Republic of Timor-Leste His Excellency Dr Rui Maria de Araújo, on the Occasion of the Official Luncheon Hosted by the President of the Republic of Indonesia, His Excellency IR. Joko Widodo", Jakarta, 26 August 2015; Gusmão, "Consolidating Democracy in a Pluralistic Society".
27. Xanana Gusmão, Address by His Excellency The Prime Minister Kay Rala Xanana Gusmão at the 69th Session of the United Nations General Assembly, New York, 25 September 2014.
28. United Nations Security Council (UNSC), "Resolution 1272", S/RES/1272, 25 October 1999.
29. Hansjoerg Strohmeyer, "Building a New Judiciary for East Timor: Challenges of a Fledgling Nation", *Criminal Law Forum* 11 (2000): 266.
30. Ibid., p. 263.
31. Katzenstein, "Hybrid Tribunals", p. 250.
32. United Nations Office of the Commissioner of Human Rights, "Report of the Commission for Inquiry on East Timor to Secretary-General", section 4 (United Nations General Assembly, A/54/726, S/2000/59, January 2000); CAVR, *Chega!*, chapter 1, p. 3.
33. Ibid., p. 1.
34. Ibid., section 4.
35. Human Rights Watch, "Justice Denied in East Timor", 20 December 2002, available at <http://www.hrw.org/legacy/backgrounder/asia/timor/etimor1202bg.htm> (accessed 24 March 2015); TAPOL, "International Tribunal Proposal for East Timor Welcomed", TAPOL Press Release, 29 June 2005.
36. Katzenstein, "Hybrid Tribunals", p. 247.
37. United Nations Transitional Administration in East Timor (UNTAET), "On the Organization of Courts in East Timor", UNTAET/REG/1999/1, 27 November 1999, p. 1.
38. Ibid., p. 4.
39. UNTAET, "On the Establishment of Panels with Exclusive Jurisdiction over Serious Criminal Offences", UNTAET/REG/2000/15, 6 June 2000, p. 1; Suzannah Linton, "Cambodia, East Timor and Sierra Leone: Experiments in International Justice", *Criminal Law Forum* 12 (2001): 203–4.
40. UNTAET, "On the Establishment of Panels with Exclusive Jurisdiction over Serious Criminal Offences", p. 2.
41. David Cohen, "'Hybrid' Justice in East Timor, Sierra Leone, and Cambodia: 'Lessons Learned' and Prospects for the Future", *Stanford Journal of International Law* 43 (2007): 8.
42. Commission for Human Rights Violations in East Timor (KPP-HAM), *Executive Summary on the Investigation of Human Rights Violations in East Timor* (Jakarta: KPP-HAM, 31 January 2000).

43. Ibid.; Caitlin Reiger and Marieke Wierda, *The Serious Crimes Process in Timor-Leste: In Retrospect*, pp. 8–9 (New York: International Center for Transitional Justice, March 2006).
44. Herbert Bowman, "Letting the Big Fish Get Away: The United Nations Justice Effort in East Timor", *Emory International Law Review* 18 (2004): 380.
45. Hamish McDonald and Richard Tanter, "Introduction", in *Masters of Terror: Indonesia's Military and Violence in Timor-Leste*, edited by Richard Tanter, Desmond Ball and Geert Arend Van Klinken, pp. 7–9 (Lanham, Maryland: Rowman and Littlefield Publishers, 2006).
46. Human Rights Watch, "Justice Denied in East Timor", 20 December 2002, available at <http://www.hrw.org/legacy/backgrounder/asia/timor/etimor1202bg.htm> (accessed 24 March 2015).
47. See Jemma Purdey, "Legal Responses to Violence in Post-Soeharto Indonesia", in *Indonesia: Law and Society*, 2nd ed., edited by Timothy Lindsay, pp. 521–22 (Annandale: The Federation Press, 2008).
48. United Nations Commission of Experts, "Report to the Secretary-General of the Commission of Experts to Review the Prosecution of Serious Violations of Human Rights in Timor-Leste (then East Timor) in 1999", S/2005/458, 26 May 2005.
49. Jeffrey Kingston, "Balancing Justice and Reconciliation in East Timor", *Critical Asian Studies* 38, no. 3 (2006): 273.
50. East Timor and Indonesia Action Network, "ETAN Renews Call for Meaningful Justice for Victims of Indonesian Occupation", East Timor and Indonesia Action Network Press Release, 14 July 2008.
51. Kingston, "Balancing Justice and Reconciliation", p. 291.
52. Reiger and Wierda, *The Serious Crimes Process in Timor-Leste*, p. 32; Cohen, "'Hybrid' Justice in East Timor, Sierra Leone, and Cambodia", p. 10.
53. Reiger and Wierda, *The Serious Crimes Process in Timor-Leste*, p. 32.
54. UNTAET, "On the Establishment of a Commission for Reception, Truth and Reconciliation in East Timor", UNTAET/REG/2001/10, 13 July 2001.
55. United Nations Commission of Experts, "Report to the Secretary-General of the Commission of Experts".
56. Robin Perry, "Asia-Pacific: The Commission of Truth and Friendship and Justice for East Timor", *Alternative Law Journal* 34, no. 3 (2009): 199.
57. United Nations Commission of Experts, "Report to the Secretary-General of the Commission of Experts".
58. Harold Crouch, *Political Reform in Indonesia After Soeharto*, p. 3 (Singapore: Institute of Southeast Asian Studies, 2010).
59. Ibid., p. 131.
60. Judicial System Monitoring Program (JSMP), "'Truth and Friendship Commission': More Friendship, Less Truth, Impunity from the Law", JSMP Press Release, 14 January 2005.

61. CAVR, *Chega!*, chapter 11, p. 27.
62. Judicial System Monitoring Program, "Truth and Friendship Commission".
63. Madalena Pampalk, "Accountability for Serious Crime and National Reconciliation in Timor-Leste: Progress or Wishful Thinking?", *Austrian Journal of Southeast Asian Studies* 3, no. 1 (2010): 18.
64. Republic of Indonesia and Democratic Republic of Timor-Leste, "Terms of Reference for The Commission of Truth and Friendship", Jakarta, 10 March 2005, available at <http://www.etan.org/et2005/march/06/10tor.htm> (accessed 24 March 2015).
65. Ibid.; CTF, *From Memory to Hope*, p. i.
66. John Roosa, "How Does a Truth Commission Find Out What the Truth Is? The Case of East Timor's CAVR", *Pacific Affairs* 18, no. 4 (2007/8): 569.
67. CTF, *From Memory to Hope*, pp. i–ii.
68. RDTL, "Joint Conference on Peace and Reconciliation between ICAP-CAPDI", RDTL Press Release, Dili, 4 May 2012.
69. Judicial System Monitoring Program, "Truth and Friendship Commission".
70. CTF, *From Memory to Hope*, p. 2.
71. Ibid.
72. Leigh-Ashley Lipscomb, "Beyond the Truth: Can Reparations Move Peace and Justice Forward in Timor-Leste?" *Asia Pacific* 93, p. 9 (Honolulu: East-West Centre, March 2010).
73. East Timor and Indonesia Action Network, "Truth Known, East Timorese Need Justice", East Timor and Indonesia Action Network Press Release, 9 March 2005.
74. TAPOL, "Submission to 2008 Universal Periodic Review of Indonesia by UN HRC", 27 November 2007.
75. Constituent Assembly, *Constitution of the Democratic Republic of Timor-Leste*, section 160 (Dili: Democratic Republic of Timor-Leste, 2002).
76. East Timor and Indonesia Action Network, La'o Hamutuk, Human Rights Working Group, Australian Coalition for Transitional Justice in East Timor, and TAPOL, "Rights Groups Call for End to Farcical Joint Timor-Indonesia Commission", Media Release, 24 May 2007.
77. Republic of Indonesia and Democratic Republic of Timor-Leste, "Terms of Reference".
78. *The Jakarta Post*, "Truth at Last?", 2 April 2008.
79. Larry Diamond, Juan Linz and Seymour Lipset, "Introduction: What Makes for Democracy", in *Politics in Developing Countries*, 2nd ed., edited by Larry Diamond, Juan Linz and Seymour Lipset, p. 10 (Boulder, Colorado: Lynne Rienner Publisher, 1995).
80. CTF, *From Memory to Hope*, pp. x, 289.
81. Megan Hirst, *Too Much Friendship Too Little Truth*, p. 8 (New York: International Center for Transitional Justice, January 2008).

82. CTF, *From Memory to Hope,* xii; ibid., p. 6.
83. Hirst, *An Unfinished Truth,* p. 6.
84. CTF, *From Memory to Hope,* p. xii.
85. Ibid., p. xiii.
86. Hirst, *An Unfinished Truth,* p. 5.
87. Ibid., pp. 14, 21.
88. Ibid., pp. 7, 24.
89. CTF, *From Memory to Hope,* pp. 288–89.
90. Ibid., p. xvii.
91. Hirst, *An Unfinished Truth,* p. 7.
92. CTF, *From Memory to Hope,* p. 290.
93. Ibid., p. 290.
94. Ibid., p. 292.
95. International Center for Transitional Justice, *Security Sector Reform in Timor-Leste,* p. 11 (Brussels: Initiative for Peacebuilding Security Cluster, June 2009).
96. Fernida, "Four Years of Final Report of Indonesia-Timor-Leste Commission of Truth and Friendship".
97. Rizal Sukma and Edy Prasetyono, *Security Sector Reform in Indonesia: The Military and the Police,* p. 9 (The Hague: Conflict Research Unit, Netherlands Institute of International Relations Clingendael, February 2003); Leonard C. Sebastian and Isingdarsah, *Assessing 12-Year Military Reform in Indonesia,* RSIS Working Paper (Singapore: S. Rajaratnam School of International Studies, April 2011).
98. International Center for Transitional Justice, *Security Sector Reform in Timor-Leste,* p. 7.
99. Amnesty International, *'We Cry for Justice': Impunity Persists 10 Years on in Timor-Leste,* ASA 57/001/2009, 27 August 2009.
100. CTF, *From Memory to Hope,* pp. 293–94.
101. Republic of Indonesia and Democratic Republic of Timor-Leste, "Fourth Senior Officials' Meeting between Indonesia and Timor-Leste", Joint Press Statement of the Republic of Indonesia and the Democratic Republic of Timor-Leste, Bali, 21–22 January 2010.
102. Ibid.
103. RDTL, "Timor-Leste and Indonesia Sign a Memorandum on Border Crossings", RDTL Press Release, Dili, 24 June 2013.
104. Republic of Indonesia, "Indonesia-Timor Leste Relation Grows Because of Trust: President Yudhoyono", Republic of Indonesia Press Release, Jakarta, 20 March 2013.
105. CTF, *From Memory to Hope,* pp. 294–95.
106. Ibid., p. 294.

107. Republic of Indonesia and Democratic Republic of Timor-Leste, "Fourth Senior Officials' Meeting between Indonesia and Timor-Leste".
108. Amnesty International, *Timor-Leste: Annual Report 2012*, ASA 57/001/2012, 2012, p. 5; International Center for Transitional Justice, *Unfulfilled Expectations: Victims Perception of Justice and Reparations in Timor-Leste*, p. 3 (Brussels: International Center for Transitional Justice, 2 December 2010).
109. United Nations General Assembly (UNGA), *Report of the Working Group on Enforced on Involuntary Disappearances: Mission to Timor-Leste*, A/HRC/19/58/Add.1, 26 December 2011.
110. CTF, *From Memory to Hope*, p. 3; Naomi Kinsella and Soren Blau, "Searching for Conflict Related Missing Persons in Timor-Leste: Technical, Politics and Cultural Considerations", *Stability: International Journal of Security and Development* 2, no. 1 (2013): 2.
111. CTF, *From Memory to Hope*, p. 297.
112. Fernida, "Four Years of Final Report of Indonesia-Timor-Leste Commission of Truth and Friendship".
113. Kinsella and Blau, "Searching for Conflict Related Missing Persons in Timor-Leste", p. 14.
114. Amnesty International, *Annual Report Timor-Leste 2015/2016*, available at <https://www.amnesty.org/en/countries/asia-and-the-pacific/timor-leste/report-timor-leste/> (accessed 11 February 2017).
115. Sisto Dos Santos, *Timor-Leste National Alliance for an International Tribunal Report*, pp. 4–5 (Dili: Timor-Leste National Alliance for an International Tribunal, 1 March 2014).
116. KontraS, Timor-Leste National Alliance for an International Tribunal, and Amnesty International, "Timor-Leste/Indonesia: Calls on Truth and Reparation made by Bilateral Truth Commission 'Ignored'", ASA 57/002/2013, 7 July 2013.
117. Republic of Indonesia and Democratic Republic of Timor-Leste, "Fourth Senior Officials' Meeting between Indonesia and Timor-Leste".
118. Judicial System Monitoring Program, "JSMP Appeals to Indonesian Government to Implement Keppres 71/2011 on Forced Disappearances", *East Timor Law and Justice Bulletin* (6 November 2012).
119. Santos, *Timor-Leste National Alliance for an International Tribunal Report*, p. 5.
120. Pampalk, "Accountability for Serious Crime and National Reconciliation in Timor-Leste", p. 20.
121. Judicial System Monitoring Program, "JSMP Appeals to Indonesian Government to Implement Keppres 71/2011 on Forced Disappearances".
122. Ibid.

123. International Center for Transitional Justice, *Unfulfilled Expectations*, p. 7; Republic of Indonesia and Democratic Republic of Timor-Leste, "Fourth Senior Officials' Meeting between Indonesia and Timor-Leste".
124. CTF, *From Memory to Hope*, p. xx.
125. Amnesty International, *Timor-Leste: Annual Report 2012*, pp. 17, 24; CAVR, *Chega!*, chapter 11, p. 42.
126. Working Group on Reparations, "Concept Paper on a National Reparations Program for Timor-Leste", Prepared by the Working Group on Reparations for Parliamentary Committee A, July 2008, p. 1.
127. International Center for Transitional Justice, *Unfulfilled Expectations*, p. 6. See also AAP, "Timor Violence: Regret But No Apology", *Sydney Morning Herald*, 15 July 2008.
128. Lipscomb, *Beyond the Truth*, p. 4.
129. Agence France-Presse (AFP), "E Timor 'Still Needs Indonesia Apology", *Sydney Morning Herald*, 16 March 2010.
130. Author unknown, "Former East Timor President Still Sees Value in Indonesian Relationship", *Jakarta Globe*, 19 July 2012.
131. Amnesty International, *Remembering the Past: Recommendations to Effectively Establish the "National Reparations Programme" and "Public Memory Institute"*, p. 5 (London: Amnesty International Publications, February 2012).
132. Working Group on Reparations, "Concept Paper on a National Reparations Program for Timor-Leste",, p. 1.
133. Lipscomb, *Beyond the Truth*, p. 2.
134. UNGA, *Report of the Working Group on Enforced on Involuntary Disappearances*, p. 14.
135. Amnesty International, *Timor-Leste: Annual Report 2012*, p. 17.
136. Xanana Gusmão, "Peace, Security and Human Development", Address by His Excellency the Prime Minister Kay Rala Xanana Gusmão on the Occasion of the World Summit 2014, Seoul, 10 August 2014.
137. Gusmao, "Consolidating Democracy in a Pluralist Society"; Araujo, "Remarks"; Pereira, "The Challenges of Nation-State Building", pp. 25–26.
138. Xanana Gusmão, "State Building: The Timor-Leste Experience in a Southeast Asian Context", Address by His Excellency the Prime Minister Kay Rala Xanana Gusmão at the Vietnam University, Hanoi, Vietnam, 3 September 2013.
139. Gusmão, Speech by His Excellency the Prime Minister of the Democratic Republic of Timor-Leste Kay Rala Xanana Gusmão at the Farewell Dinner for their Excellencies Dr H. Susilo Bambang Yudhoyono and Madam HJ. Ani Bambang Yudhoyono, President and First Lady of the Republic of Indonesia, Dili, 26 August 2014. See also Xanana Gusmão, "Timor-Leste and ASEAN: Perspectives and Challenges", Address by His Excellency the

Prime Minister and Minister of Defence and Security, Kay Rala Xanana Gusmão, Sabah, Malaysia, 2 April 2014.
140. Andrew Marriott, "The Justice Sector: Achievements, Challenges and Comparisons", in *Politics of Timor-Leste: Democratic Consolidation After Intervention*, edited by Michael Leach and Damien Kingsbury, pp. 103–4 (Ithaca, NY: Cornell University Press, 2013).
141. Judicial System Monitoring Program, "Justice Not Served by Truth and Friendship Commission". Justice Update, July 2008.
142. TAPOL, "Though Limited by its Mandate, the CTF Revealed a Great Deal", TAPOL Press Release, 21 July 2008.
143. Faiz Nashrillah, "Jokowi Receives Highest Decoration from Timor-Leste President", *Tempo*, 26 January 2016.
144. RDTL, *Force 2020*, p. 19.

10

Conclusion: Timor-Leste in the Changing Regional Order

> Now into its second decade as a sovereign state, Timor-Leste is ready to take its place in the community of nations.
>
> – Agio Pereira[1]

This book has argued that Timor-Leste's security interests have been shaped by conceptions of sovereignty, self-determination and independence that reflect its historical and ongoing struggle for recognition. In its international relations, Timor-Leste's leaders have progressively pursued a more confident and outward-looking foreign policy as it defines and asserts its place within the community of states. This book has employed the term "aspirational foreign policy" to encapsulate Timor-Leste's ambitious and expansive approach to bilateral and multilateral relations, its desire to transform into an upper-middle income country by 2030 and the narrative of fragile state exceptionalism. Its approach to international affairs is syncretic: realist and idealist orientations have been observed across a range of different issue areas that affect national security as perspectives on the international political environment oscillate between conflictual and cooperative. Timor-Leste's leaders abandoned pragmatism in the Timor Sea dispute in favour of an "activist" strategy, however, realism remains central to understanding the ways in which international normative principles of justice were sacrificed in favour of good relations with Indonesia. The theories of international relations provide useful tools for understanding how states work to secure the state, however, not one theory alone can help us understand the range of policy options, behaviours and interactions that a small state such as Timor-Leste draws upon in its international relations.

This complexity of how states perceive and address security threats is thrown into sharp relief when considering the future challenges of small states such as Timor-Leste in the Asia-Pacific region. This final chapter looks forward to the two most pressing security challenges for Timor-Leste in the twenty-first century: one that reflects conventional geopolitical thinking in International Relations, and the other that undermines it. The first section examines Timor-Leste's position in the Asia-Pacific region, currently the epicentre of great power competition between the United States and China. Power dynamics in Southeast Asia and the South Pacific are relevant to Timor-Leste as it is located in the "transition zone" between these regions. Liberal outlooks on a rising China tend to reject bipolar Cold War prisms for assessing U.S. and China in Asia-Pacific, instead focusing on the complex mix of policy contestation, appeasement and convergence and the ways that global economic interdependencies mitigate tensions.[2] Realist visions, on the other hand, are concerned about the possibilities of conflict as a rising China seeks to remake the world order in its favour.[3] There are risks of the United States falling victim to the "Thucydides Trap", whereby existing superpowers perceive themselves as threatened by emerging powers and seek to defend the state using security apparatuses. The great power competition has the potential to precipitate a negative security spiral that is conventionally referred to as the security dilemma.

The shifting regional balance of power dynamics between the United States and China — and others, such as Russia — presents both risks and opportunities for small states in the region. The mainstream balance of power literature assumes that the limited defence capacities of small states, such as Timor-Leste, leads them to either balance against a powerful state or bandwagon with it.[4] Yet, as this book has examined, smaller states can have "choices rather than imperatives".[5] Changing balance of power dynamics can influence the actions of small states, but are not necessarily deterministic in the ways that neorealism suggest. The choices of states are influenced by geopolitical factors insofar as they depend upon the "constellation" of power dynamics within the salient security environment of the small state.[6] Yet, the behaviours and interactions of small states also affect the constellations of power they sit within. For Timor-Leste, the immediate security environment is defined by two great powers (U.S. and China), but its critical relations have been with neighbouring middle powers, Australia and Indonesia. Timor-Leste's immediate security environment — the Asia-Pacific region — is not defined solely by great powers, but by the complex, interrelated networks of relations between great, middle and small power states.

In terms of its relations with more powerful states in the region, Timor-Leste has chosen to hedge against dependence upon any one state as a way of asserting its autonomy, eschewing formal alliances with great or neighbouring powers. Hedging is a method of conflict avoidance, as states use mixed strategies to assure great powers of their desire to cooperate.[7] It has avoided a formal alliance with Australia, preferring instead to establish and maintain its independence within an interdependent international community. This chapter contends that Timor-Leste will have to re-evaluate its hedging strategy if a Cold War-style bipolar structure emerges in Asia-Pacific as the current flexibility and freedom offered to small states on the international stage is at least partly contingent upon the permission of great powers.[8] If competition continues to increase, the "having the cake and eating it too" hedging strategy may become increasingly untenable for Timor-Leste. In the context of a more dynamic, fluid and contested regional order, Timor-Leste will also have to negotiate the policies and preferences of its more powerful neighbours, Australia and Indonesia.

The second part of this chapter examines the challenges presented by climate change and the importance of sustainable development in securing the empirical sovereignty of small island states. Climate change promises to dramatically undermine taken-for-granted assumptions about geopolitics by complicating territorial sovereignty and the notion that there are distinct "inside" (domestic) and "outside" (international) political realms.⁹ Climate change is a "threat multiplier", one that is predicted to add more stress to the fragile institutions and developmental prospects of small island countries like Timor-Leste. This issue highlights the need for international cooperation, and Timor-Leste has increasingly participated in multilateral forums and monitoring mechanisms. Timor-Leste's leaders also enthusiastically employ the key terms of the international development zeitgeist, including "sustainable development" and "inclusive growth". However, Timor-Leste's policies and budget priorities do not often conform to the rhetoric of sustainability. As chapter eight demonstrated, Timor-Leste's economic plans rely almost solely upon accessing and refining unsustainable and non-renewable fossil fuels. In the long term, Timor-Leste's security is more likely to be ensured by developing genuinely sustainable and diversified economic policies.

Timor-Leste's Hedging: Relations with China

Since Timor-Leste became independent, the United States as the world's preponderant superpower has been increasingly challenged by the rise of China. These shifting power dynamics have provoked questions about what type of regional order might replace the "hub-and-spokes" alliance network crafted by the United States in the post-World War Two era, whether a rising China will be a benign or aggressive power, and the extent to which the United States might permit a greater leadership role for China in the global order.[10] According to hegemonic transition theory, a shifting balance of power can provoke conflict, particularly if powers hold divergent views on international rules and leadership. This depends upon the satisfaction levels of rising powers towards the existing rules-based order. According to Schweller, status quo powers are generally content with the existing international order, whereas revisionist powers seek to undermine it.[11] Offensive realists such as Mearsheimer argue that conflict between the United States and China is inevitable as China is a revisionist power that will subvert the established liberal order.[12] In contrast, proponents of liberal interdependence argue that mutual economic reliance means that conflict between U.S. and China is not inevitable.[13] As Ikenberry and Tsuchiyama contend, security relationships in Southeast Asia are not necessarily organized around a balance of power, nor are they fully embedded in multilateral institutions.[14] The Southeast Asian context is defined by "unsettled relations" between states with "divergent interests and cultural identities".[15] It remains unclear what type of order will supplant U.S. preponderance, but it is evident that such uncertainty contributes to shaping the threat perceptions of national leaders.

Walt argues that in a unipolar world, states have three alliance possibilities: balancing (countering the preponderant power), bandwagoning (joining the preponderant power) or hedging.[16] Small states, however, rarely engage in "true" balancing because it is costly, instead preferring to "hedge" to avoid antagonizing powerful states.[17] In Southeast Asia, hedgers engage both the United States and China. Hedgers include Indonesia, Malaysia, Singapore and Brunei, while the Philippines and Thailand are formal U.S. allies. The states most developmentally similar to Timor-Leste — Cambodia, Laos and Myanmar, plus Vietnam — gravitate towards China due to a "lack of strategic opportunities *vis-à-vis* other great powers".[18] In contrast, the South Pacific has long been considered part of Australia's sphere of influence as a U.S. proxy, as the United States and United Kingdom have gradually withdrawn their presence.[19] In particular, Australia views the South Pacific as a buffer protecting it from potential northern adversaries.[20] China has become more "aggressive" in its soft power diplomacy in the South Pacific, a development that Australian policymakers tend to view as in competition with its regional leadership, particularly as states such as Papua New Guinea have moved closer to China.

Hedging is a strategy adopted by many Asian-Pacific states as they seek to enjoy strong economic relations with China while maintaining or strengthening security ties with the United States. Timor-Leste uses hedging as a way of managing uncertainty by avoiding a formal alliance with the relevant powerful or influential states, including the United States, China, Australia and Indonesia.[21] For weaker states, hedging can assist in negotiating difficult situations by promoting cooperation, avoiding tensions and seeking absolute gains (i.e. win-win outcomes).[22] Hedging can also alleviate uncertainty by offsetting risks as states "bet" on multiple alternative futures.[23] Yet, as Chong points out, it will become more difficult for weaker states to balance the need to mollify great powers with developing and modernizing the defence capabilities required to respond to growing competition and uncertainty.[24] Hedging can invite mistrust and suspicions of duplicity, which may render states less secure if their policies alarm rather than reassure other states.

Hedging supports Timor-Leste's efforts to establish a diversified and independent foreign policy that maximizes its range of strategic options. In particular, Timor-Leste's engagements with China over the last decade reflect its growing confidence and willingness to offset its reliance on Indonesia and Australia.[25] However, China's attractiveness to Timor-Leste is also partly based on its history; China initially provided support for East Timor's independence movement, and was the first state to recognize the Democratic Republic of Timor-Leste in 2002. Like other states, however, China's initial support for the independence movement waned and it ultimately recognized Indonesia's *de facto* sovereignty (see chapter three).

Successive Timorese governments have used Chinese aid diplomacy as a way of expanding its international relations in line with its aspirational foreign policy. Through its soft power diplomacy, China has sought to become an alternative source of international development assistance within and beyond the Pacific region. Timor-Leste accepted China's offer to finance several important and prominent government buildings, which have provided China maximum exposure for minimum outlay.[26] China financed the Palace of the President at a cost of US$6 million and provided US$7 million for the Ministry of Foreign Affairs and Cooperation in Dili.[27] It also contributed US$9 million to establish offices for Timor-Leste Defence Force.[28] In April 2012, Gusmão declared that "this gesture of friendship is even more significant as there are no strings attached".[29] Gusmão argued that bilateral cooperation between China and Timor-Leste had been "extremely advantageous and results from an unquestionable willingness by both peoples to establish stronger ties of friendship".[30] China has also provided extensive training for Timorese civil servants.[31]

China is an attractive donor for Timor-Leste because it promotes the illusion that they are "equal" development partners. One of China's soft power strategies in the development arena is to reject aid conditionalities in favour of non-conditional grants and investment arrangements that are ostensibly mutually beneficial. This plays against the dominant Western development paradigm — the

"Washington Consensus" — which for a long time made loans and aid assistance contingent upon developing states meeting particular market and governance benchmarks. The "Beijing Consensus" involves constructing an international environment that challenges U.S. preponderance and supports China's growing international power and influence in development through south-south cooperation.[32] As argued previously, small states are strong defenders of international law and norms, because they help protect weak states from the strong and guarantee principles of sovereignty, non-intervention and self-determination. The Beijing Consensus reflects the ways that China's diplomacy is challenging conventional concepts of legitimacy in development and reinforces — in theory at least — the absolute external sovereignty concept.

The Beijing Consensus ostensibly offers a pragmatic and flexible approach to development, guided by three ideals: innovation; rejection of per capita Gross Domestic Product (GDP) as a central development goal (instead focusing on quality of life) and; self-determination.[33] This final feature emphasizes the imperatives of developing states in becoming independent from outside forces. As Ramo puts it, the Beijing Consensus provides "hope that every nation can be a power in its own right. Perhaps not powerful enough for domination, but at least strong enough for self-determination."[34] China itself has marked a path for developing states as they figure out "how to fit into the international order in a way that allows them to be truly independent, to protect their way of life and political choices in a world with a single massively powerful centre of gravity".[35] In the era of globalization and interdependence, the Beijing Consensus appeals to the concept of self-reliance, which has been a consistent feature of Timor-Leste's approach to international relations.

As chapter seven demonstrated, part of Timor-Leste's efforts to secure "real" independence in the form of self-determination has involved increasing resistance to foreign interference in the economic realm. Yet Timor-Leste's ongoing dependence on assistance continues to render it vulnerable to influence by external donors. China provides soft loans and investment in infrastructure and construction projects without forcing states to change their preferences, unlike Australia and other Western donors.[36] On the other hand, there have been criticisms of the reliability of Chinese assistance, including the debt incurred by developing states through soft loans, inferior quality of work and the flouting of national laws.³⁷ As the discussion below reveals, Timor-Leste's experiences with Chinese assistance present a cautionary tale of accepting China's attractive, "no-strings-attached" aid.

There are myriad reasons why China would be interested in developing its relationship with Timor-Leste. China's activities in the developing world have been motivated by its need for energy resources and raw materials for development. Some observers, such as Storey and Reid-Smith, argue that China's interests lay in gaining access to Timor-Leste's oil and gas reserves.³⁸ In 2005, PetroChina paid US$1.6 million for a study to assess Timor-Leste's offshore oil and gas reserves, although nothing much appears to have materialized.³⁹ Other economic motivations include China's interests in securing commercial contracts for developing infrastructure, and in strengthening other opportunities for Chinese companies and citizens in Timor-Leste.⁴⁰ In 2014, China became Timor-Leste's third largest provider of imports behind Indonesia and Singapore, which was worth $41 million.⁴¹ The economic benefits flow largely towards China. While China has donated a relatively small amount of aid to Timor-Leste, its companies have received hundreds of millions of dollars in construction contracts since 2009.⁴² Timor-Leste also participates in the Macau Forum Ministerial Conference that brings together China and Portuguese-speaking countries to promote trade relations.⁴³

The future of the Asia-Pacific region will be defined by the type of role that China will seek to play, and how it will attempt to influence the "rules-based order". One of the most important sites of contestation is in the arena of multilateral economic institutions. Since the end of World War Two, the global market order has been governed by the liberal-oriented Bretton Woods institutions: the International Monetary Fund, the World Bank and the World Trade Organization. China has challenged liberal economic multilateral organizations by developing new institutions in the global economic architecture, focused on influencing developing states and succeeding the Bretton Woods institutions. Beijing has been instrumental in establishing the Asia Infrastructure Investment Bank (AIIB), the Regional Comprehensive Economic Partnership (RCEP), the BRICS New Development Bank and the "Belt and Road" (BRI) initiative. In September 2016, Timor-Leste began the path to joining the Beijing-based AIIB.⁴⁴ The BRI comprises the Silk Road Economic Belt (SREB) and the twenty-first century Maritime Silk Road (MSR), the latter of which includes states in the Pacific Ocean. The Timorese government has offered its support for BRI, and cooperation under the MSR auspices can be expected.[45]

Timor-Leste's geostrategic position is important for China's interest in developing military-security ties, particularly gaining access to the Ombai-Wetar Strait, which motivated U.S. policy during the Cold War (see chapters three and seven).[46] China has also sought to avoid Timorese recognition of Taiwan's sovereignty, as South Pacific states, such as Vanuatu, Kiribati, Nauru, Solomon Islands and Tonga, have switched (or attempted to switch) their allegiances.[47] In return, Beijing recognizes and supports Dili's ambition to join ASEAN to reinforce Timor-Leste's credibility as an independent sovereign state.[48] As Storey argues, Timor-Leste's predicted membership of ASEAN renders it "another friendly government within the organization" for China to lobby.[49] China's soft power diplomacy in Timor-Leste is driven by its interests in expanding its influence and balancing the power of the United States in Southeast Asia.[50] There are diverse views about the rising influence of China across the ASEAN states, particularly pertaining to the tensions arising from territorial claims in the South China Sea.[51] The Philippines initiated proceedings against China in the Permanent Court of Arbitration (PCA), which found that China's claims to historic title are contrary to United Nations Convention on the Law of the Sea (UNCLOS) and without lawful effect.[52] China argued that the PCA lacked jurisdiction to hear the case and refused to heed the decision.[53] Scholars have predicted that the maritime boundary and sovereignty disputes in the South China Sea will create regional instability that is likely to continue in the foreseeable future.[54] Timor-Leste's own national interests lie in supporting the current maritime rules-based order governed by UNCLOS as it searched for a "better deal" in its Timor Sea dispute with Australia (see chapter eight).

Timor-Leste's strategic choices are likely to have ripple effects on its relations with its two neighbours. China's influence in Timor-Leste could be perceived as inimical to Australia's national interests. The naval boats donated to East Timor by China in 2010 were initially manned by a Chinese crew, and this was interpreted by some in Australia as a potential security risk (see chapter seven). The boats were ultimately found to be unseaworthy.[55] In 2011, leaked diplomatic cables revealed that China proposed to build and operate a surveillance radar facility in Timor-Leste in 2007, ostensibly to monitor shipping in the strategic Wetar Strait. Suspicious Timor-Leste leaders consulted with U.S. and Australian officials before rejecting the plan on the basis of concerns raised about the security implications of having a Chinese radar on Timor.[56] Any expansion of Chinese intelligence in Timor-Leste would be viewed by Australia as a threat to its national security.

Australia's key security interest is that no foreign military bases be established on the island of Timor.[57] Australia's 2009 Defence White Paper states that what matters most is that neighbouring states are not a source of threat to Australia and "no major military power that could challenge our control of the sea and air approaches to Australia has access to bases in our neighbourhood".[58] As chapter eight argued, Timor-Leste may again become dependent upon foreign sources of assistance if the contested Greater Sunrise gas field is not developed within the next decade. A more vulnerable Timor-Leste would provide Beijing greater leverage through its soft power diplomacy, and Australia's 2016 Defence White Paper makes it clear that it is in its national interest to support a secure and stable Timor-Leste.[59]

While there are security concerns about rising influence of China in the future, the prospect of China's putting military bases on Timor-Leste remains highly unlikely. First, the Timorese are unlikely to antagonize both Indonesia and Australia by permitting bases. Geostrategically, Timor-Leste remains in a position of vulnerability as it is surrounded by two more powerful states that could jointly block sea access to Timor-Leste. Second, Lowry points out that Indonesia's geostrategic location "straddles the choke points for oil and gas shipments", which means China is also unlikely to offend Indonesia by inserting a base into the archipelago.[60] As the surveillance radar example attests to, Timor-Leste's leadership has been sensitive of Australia's security concerns, particularly as its southern neighbour is a U.S. ally and remains Timor-Leste's primary development donor. In the past, Timor-Leste's leaders have also sought to assure Australian officials of its desire to cooperate with democratic partners including Australia, the United States, Portugal and Japan.[61] This in part reflects the reality that these partners have been dominant in providing aid to Timor-Leste.

Timor-Leste's aim of developing relations with China while maintaining friendly relations with Indonesia could prove problematic in the future. Like Australia, Indonesia has a historically close strategic relationship with the United States, although they are not formal allies.[62] Relations between China and Indonesia have been historically tense; diplomatic engagement froze for decades during the Cold War, only to be re-established in 1990.[63] The Widodo and Jinping administrations have experienced some hostility over maritime security issues as Indonesia's 200 nautical mile Exclusive Economic Zone (EEZ) overlaps with China's ambiguous "nine-dash line" based on its historic waters claim, putting Indonesia's sovereignty of the Natuna islands to the north of the archipelago under threat. In 2015, reports surfaced of Indonesia sinking illegal Chinese fishing vessels, and in 2016, a Chinese Coast Guard rammed an Indonesian patrol boat in order to free a Chinese trawler in Indonesia's EEZ. While Widodo has sought greater Chinese investment and joined the AIIB, like Australia, it would be sensitive to Timor-Leste becoming militarily closer to China.

Indonesia, along with other ASEAN states, has sought to push back against China's growing power in the region. As Sukma notes, coping with the rise of China has become one of Indonesia's "most elusive foreign policy challenges".[64] While they aim for a "strategic partnership", Indonesian politicians and policymakers are suspicious of Chinese ambitions in the region. Indonesia regards itself as a leader in Southeast Asia, and would find "a China-centric regional order with itself subordinate to Beijing a deeply unpalatable prospect".[65] Like Timor-Leste, Indonesia itself has sought to both counterbalance and engage China.[66] These regional power dynamics are likely to matter more for Timor-Leste's foreign policy decisions once its membership of ASEAN is official.

Indeed, Indonesia's support for Timor-Leste's ascension to ASEAN also appears to be influenced by perceptions of China's growing influence in Timor-Leste. Timor-Leste's former Deputy Prime Minister, Estanislau da Silva, told Radio Australia that "[o]f course, we have neighbours, like Indonesia and Australia, but we also want to have a very close relationship with other continents, and particularly, China. China has been very, very supportive."[67] In 2015, Timor-Leste Defence Minister Cirilo Cristóvão was reported by Chinese media as saying that Timor-Leste appreciates China's support and assistance and that "Timor-Leste is willing to strengthen military-to-military exchanges and cooperation with China."[68] China and Timor-Leste have agreed to strengthen cooperation in political, economic, trade, energy, agricultural, defence and security areas.[69] A press release from the Chinese Ministry of National Defence described military relations between the two states as "moving forward with great momentum, China is willing to strengthen group exchange, personnel training and cooperation in other fields with East Timor, so as to tighten the mil-to-mil [military-to-military] relations and boost the all-round development of bilateral relations".[70] As China has sought to play a bigger role in assisting East Timor develop its military capacities, Timor-Leste has been willing to expand its relationship with China.

In some areas, China has persuaded Timor-Leste to implement policies that appear contrary to its interests. In one report by Dan Flitton, Chinese fishermen have been forced south to the seas surrounding Timor as tensions in the South China Sea increase and its fish stocks decline. This has constituted a form of "state-sponsored illegal fishing" by the so-called Chinese "maritime militia".[71] Timor-Leste granted a fleet of fifteen Chinese vessels a twelve-month permit to fish inside its sovereign waters for US$312,450. While they were permitted to fish for tuna, inspections by Timorese and Australian officials found an estimated 40 tonnes of sharks and rays. The Chinese company granted the permit, Hong Long Fisheries, was owned by the same owners as Pintang Marine Enterprises, which was banned from Indonesian waters after accusations of theft.[72] Pintang has claimed that the licence could reap annual revenue of US$3 million, raising concerns about the reasoning behind granting the company such a cheap licence. It is difficult to see how such a permit protects its nascent local fishing industry or assist with the sustainability of fishing stocks. This is an alarming development in a country that struggles to feed a significant proportion of its population, and highlights the vulnerabilities faced by Timor-Leste in protecting its maritime resources (see chapter seven).

On the other hand, it is important not to overstate the closeness of China and Timor-Leste: Timor-Leste receives more aid from Australia, the United States, European Union, Japan, New Zealand and Portugal.[73] Additionally, Chinese aid to Timor-Leste pales in comparison to its South Pacific neighbours. While Timor-Leste received US$52 million from 2006–14, Papua New Guinea received US$630 million (far less than the US$3,435 million donated by Australia), and Samoa, Vanuatu and Fiji all received in excess of US$200 million in Chinese loans and grants in the same time period.[74] Taur Matan Ruak voiced critical remarks of China's unilateralism in the South China Sea in a joint statement with Japan's Prime Minister Shinzo Abe, earning a rebuke by the Chinese Foreign Ministry.[75] The policy of hedging has thus far allowed Timor-Leste to pursue a range of relations to support its independence. It is questionable, however, whether Timor-Leste will be able to continue strategic hedging after the oil and gas revenues have evaporated, and any energy leverage that might have induced China to seek closer relations is exhausted. An aid dependent Timor-Leste would almost certainly have to rely upon its existing donors, which means that Timor-Leste's access to Greater Sunrise will continue to have security and economic implications for Australia.

Disputed Orders: Timor-Leste and the Future of Regional Security

Small states are vulnerable to the impacts of global shifts in power balance, particularly if this results in regional insecurity and instability. During the first decade of the twenty-first century in Southeast Asia, the international distribution of power rendered pure-bandwagoning and pure-balancing strategies irrelevant.[76] However, a rising China could result in a bipolar balance of power in the future, which would provide advantages and disadvantages for small states. On the one hand, bipolarity during the Cold War provided manoeuvrability as superpowers sought to extend their global influence and power through building alliances. Great power rivalry may enable small states in Asia-Pacific, such as Timor-Leste, to take advantage of attempts to win influence and provide greater flexibility for small states in their international relations. In a liberal scenario, Timor-Leste could continue to hedge because it would not have to choose between China, the United States or any other emergent powers, or even attempt to play off the great powers against each other. On the other hand, it could offer weak new states in particular less security as great powers expand their empires and engage in proxy wars, including in smaller powers in Southeast Asia, as they did during the Cold War.

Timor-Leste's security could be threatened by increased aggression between the great powers, and the space for foreign policy manoeuvring may become more constrained. Realist visions suggest that small states will ultimately have to abandon hedging in preference for a balancing or bandwagoning alliance strategy. Timor-Leste's hedging strategy needs to be increasingly sensitive to emerging balance of power dynamics and the national interests of Australia, Indonesia, the United States and China.

Of concern is the emergence of a traditional security dilemma in Asia. Competition in the Asia-Pacific region has intensified amid maritime disputes, and states have increased militarization and arms modernization programmes. In 2014, military spending in Asia increased by 5 per cent and is now larger than Europe's.[77] Military modernization tends to increase strategic competition and can result in an arms race. The "tragedy" of the security dilemma is that states' misperceptions of the motives of others *vis-à-vis* their military build-up can precipitate conflict. The increased defence spending and military modernizations of neighbouring states affects the regional security environment that Timor-Leste inhabits, but has negligible capacity to influence. While increased spending does not inevitably lead to arms races, and arms races do not inevitably lead to conflict, possible miscalculation regarding intent could spiral into conflict. It might be unlikely, but there is little doubt that a major conflict between the United States and China would be disastrous: it would create massive problems for the global economy, would escalate the risk of nuclear warfare, would divert attention and resources of Timor-Leste's donors away from developing states and potentially see Timorese territory become included in the conflict zone, as it was in World War Two.

In Timor-Leste's immediate neighbourhood, Indonesia's military modernization focuses on naval capabilities as it asserts itself as a maritime power, while Australia aims to bolster its defence capabilities via the ambitious procurement agenda outlined in the 2016 Defence White Paper, including doubling the size of its submarine force.[78] The security spiral of the traditional security dilemma is a self-fulfilling prophecy as it encourages a feedback loop based on perceptions that arise under conditions of anarchy. Realist thinking encourages fears about rising competition, which contributes to activities, such as growing the defence sector, that in turn heighten tensions and suspicion in the region. This dynamic could work to limit the scope of Timor-Leste's interactions with other rising powers, as it seeks to avoid contributing to the fears of the states that surround it. In 2014, for example, there were concerns about a Chinese naval presence in Sunda, Lombok and Malacca Straits.[79] The five-day official visit by a Chinese navy taskforce early in 2016 signals that China remains an important influence in Timor-Leste, although the Task Force 152 also visited Indonesia and Australia. Cristóvão said that the visit would promote bilateral relationship and defence cooperation between the two states.[80] In the future of great power competition, Timor-Leste's diplomacy will need to walk an increasingly skilful line if it continues to hedge. Escalating tensions will require Timor-Leste to be more sensitive to the security concerns of its major partners and neighbours, Australia and Indonesia, and make a choice as to whether defence cooperation with China is in its national interests given its geopolitical vulnerabilities. This will entail ensuring that its powerful neighbours are assured that potential aggressors do not become the pre-eminent foreign influence in Timor-Leste. For Timor-Leste, the "post-colonial security dilemma" is reflected in the ways that small, fragile states such as Timor-Leste have little influence in shaping regional security dynamics, but must react prudently to them to ensure ongoing support for their sovereignty.

The South China Sea dispute is considered a key theatre of contestation in the region. Official statements by the Timorese government reaffirmed its "commitment to the rules based order" under UNCLOS, and Australia publically declared that China should abide by the PCA's ruling on the Scarborough Shoal.[81] Australia, however, faced a public image problem as criticisms of China as acting outside of the rules were viewed as hypocritical given Australia's refusal to submit to third-party arbitration on maritime boundary disputes. While the exclusion is within UNCLOS rules, Timor-Leste's leaders and advocates cast this decision as contrary to the international rules-based order. While the Certain Maritime Arrangements in the Timor Sea (CMATS) was in place, Australia defended its support for the binding treaty as an expression of its respect for international law.[82] The termination of the CMATS made it difficult for Australia to avoid boundary discussions while defending the primacy of the "rules-based order" in maritime dispute resolution.

Some reports have argued that China is more effectively spreading its influence in Southeast Asia via soft power diplomacy in ways that might influence the stance of other claimant states on the South China Sea. Changes in domestic leadership in the Philippines, for example, have led to a softened stance on the rules-based order governing maritime boundary delimitation and related maritime activities. Philippines' President, Rodrigo Duturte, has repeatedly suggested cutting the ties that bind the Philippines and the United States, stating a preference for China and Russia leading a "new world order".[83] This raises particular concerns for Timor-Leste in dealing with its own maritime issues which rely upon the "old" rules governed by UNCLOS. The decline of the United States may threaten the future viability of treaty regimes formed during the period of U.S. hegemony, such as UNCLOS. The UNCLOS may now be the "constitution of the sea" as Timor-Leste's government spokesperson suggests, however, its capacity to govern maritime relations will depend upon whether states believe it offers utility in solving maritime disputes. For small states, such as Timor-Leste, rules created by regimes such as UNCLOS provide some certainty and protection in the anarchical international environment. Contests about the legitimate "rules of the game" will likely have flow-on effects for the maritime security environment of the Asia-Pacific, with potential consequences for Timor-Leste's security, relationships and claims in the maritime realm.

Climate Change, Sustainability and "Inclusive Growth"

It is not just structural balance of power dynamics that are contributing to a changing international order. The problems arising from climate change and the demands of sustainable development also challenge the international order based on territorial sovereignty. While small developing states, such as Timor-Leste, seek to consolidate "real" independence, environmental degradation reinforces the myth of impermeable state boundaries that is embedded in expressions of absolute external sovereignty. Furthermore, maintaining order in a climate-changed world will present ecological and political challenges including, inter alia, wars over resources, environmental refugee flows, increasing "natural" disasters and transboundary pollution.[84] Maintaining self-determination in a climate-changed global order will require states to ensure the long-term well-being of its citizens while protecting and guaranteeing the ecological system within which they are nested. This final section posits that climate change and sustainability — in political, economic, environmental and social realms — will constitute the most significant challenge for Timor-Leste's pursuit of "absolute", territorial sovereignty in the future. Climate change has undermined traditional ways of thinking about security in international relations. As a global issue, it transgresses state boundaries and highlights the ecological interdependencies and mutual vulnerabilities between international actors and societies.

In terms of security, climate change is a "threat multiplier" as it interacts with other risk factors in complex and multi-dimensional ways. Traditional state-focused visions of national security view climate change as potentially exacerbating interstate tensions, disrupting the geopolitical environment and compelling self-interested states to maximize power through traditional (military) means.[85] In this conception, resource wars in the Asia-Pacific would compound the power asymmetries between developed and developing states, rendering fragile states increasingly vulnerable to incursions by more powerful states and contributing to the erosion of the "rules-based order" that ostensibly protects the weak from the strong. Yet, the challenges of climate change require the adoption of lenses that look beyond the state as the locus of security. For developing states such as Timor-Leste, climate change deepens the already considerable challenges to social, economic and political development, and the linked resources insecurities, including the availability of food, energy and water. Climate change is hence inextricably tied to human security as the livelihoods of people, their access to nutrition and water, health outcomes and social cohesion depend upon adaptation and the capacity to prevent — or at least manage — natural disasters that are predicted to rise in incidence due to climate change.[86] It is not necessarily inevitable that conflict will emerge as a result of environmental pressures, however, the combination of climate change, environmental degradation and sustained population growth is likely to progressively curtail the already limited capacity of Timor-Leste's governments to respond.[87] Timor-Leste will be more vulnerable to the interrelated effects of climate change, such as reduced agricultural production, economic decline and widespread displacement, which are key drivers of internal insecurity (see chapters seven and eight).[88] A key dilemma for Timor-Leste is balancing the imperative of sustainable development with its oil industrialization aspirations that depend upon the sale and use of fossil fuels.

Nevertheless, Timor-Leste's responses to the internationalization of environmental politics have emphasized the need for sustainable development. "Sustainability" is not new: according to the landmark 1987 Brundtland Commission Report, "sustainable development is development that meets the needs of the present without compromising the ability of future generations to meet their own needs."[89] The Sustainable Development Goals (SDG) are the latest iteration of the global development agenda that replaced the Millennium Development Goals (MDGs) after the conclusion of their cycle in 2015.[90] The SDGs are a wide-ranging set of development aspirations comprising 169 targets that focus on "inclusive" and "sustainable" growth. Sustainable development is, at its heart, a development paradigm based on "limits to growth".[91] However, Timor-Leste's economic plans, like most states, continue to emphasize the importance of economic growth. According to the Strategic Development Plan (SDP), "[i]n the Asian century, and close to emerging economic giants, Timor-Leste is well positioned to trade and partner with our neighbours to achieve rapid and unprecedented economic growth."[92] As Boothe suggests, while "growth is the essence of the environmental problem", an alternative vision is of an economy that satisfies human needs while preserving the global environment.[93] This sustainable alternative to the growth paradigm stands in tension with Timor-Leste's industrialization aspirations.

The discourses of "inclusive growth" and "sustainability" that underpin the SDGs have been skilfully adopted by Timorese representatives in their public diplomacy. In December 2013, Gusmão stated, "[w]e have before us a unique opportunity to make development truly inclusive and sustainable and to lead the world's post-2015 development agenda."[94] He promised that "[i]t is absolutely our intention — and our unrelenting focus — to wisely use our natural resource wealth to develop a diversified economy and build our beloved nation for all our people."[95] In December 2013, he argued that states must make sure their "economies work to support people rather than operate in the interests of a privileged multinational elite and a corrupt global financial system".[96] These narratives construct a story about why "fragile states" continue to "suffer" that attributes blame to powerful global elites and the economic experts and advisors working within a flawed global development space. Gusmão's rhetoric has rejected development expertise, arguing that Timor-Leste had difficulty "finding a common understanding with the experts on the poverty of others".[97] The rhetoric establishes an effective binary between the developing and developed world in which the latter is characterized by corrupt systems, unfair financial and governance rules and self-interested elites. Upon these bases, a "fragile state" identity is reified in opposition to the global economic order created by developed countries at the expense of developing states.

Timor-Leste's SDP identifies climate change as its greatest environment challenge and commits Timor-Leste to a National Adaptation Programmes of Action (NAPA) to identify key national challenges and implement and monitor adaptation strategies.[98] Timor-Leste ratified the United Nations Framework Convention on Climate Change (UNFCCC) in 2006 and the Kyoto Protocol in 2008, and has engaged in a number of annual Conference of Parties (COP) in the UNFCCC negotiating process.[99] Timor-Leste also participates in smaller multilateral forums based on collective interests and identities, for example the Small Island Developing States (SIDS) and Alliance of Small Island States (AOSIS) that share similar vulnerabilities to climate change. Organizations such as SIDS and AOSIS see growth prospects of member states like Timor-Leste as threatened by environmental factors, for example "climate change, the impact of natural disasters, the high cost of imported energy and the degradation of coastal and marine ecosystems and sea-level rise".[100] Timor-Leste's Pacific Islands Development Forum (PIDF) membership is also based on a sustainable development agenda that reflects "the Pacific way" of sustaining livelihoods.[101] According to a government statement, "Timor-Leste always attaches great importance to the promotion of genuine and enduring partnerships to safeguard transparency and good governance, confidence, support and trust in the leadership of the Pacific Islands States in bringing forward the PIDF to be able to realize the theme of green economic growth in the Pacific."[102] In November 2016, Timor-Leste sent a twenty-member delegation to the 22nd Session of the COP (COP22), and participated in key developing state groupings such as AOSIS, Least Developed Countries (LDC), and the Group of 77 (G77). The delegation advocated major polluters increase their emission reduction targets and contribute to climate finance funds aimed at assisting developing states. As chapter six has discussed, shaping the SDGs and influencing international development dialogues is an important component of Timor-Leste's leadership of the g7+ grouping of fragile states.

Timor-Leste's economic growth and poverty eradication are predicted to be severely affected by climate change. The key implications of climate change, according to Timor-Leste's *Initial National Communication* to the UNFCCC, are:

1. Decreasing area for new agricultural expansion;
2. Further reductions in cropping intensity, particularly in the north;
3. Scarcity of water, with implications for irrigation;
4. More extreme climate events leading to economic loss — including damage to "offshore oil and gas infrastructure";
5. Increasing incidence of certain diseases (but decreasing after 2040).[103]

Like other small developing island states, Timor-Leste faces warming ocean temperatures and rising sea levels caused by El Niño: sea levels have risen about 9 mm per year since 1993, which is larger than the global average of 2.8–3.6 mm per year.[104] El Niño weather events are projected to become more frequent.[105] Coastal areas, including Dili, are likely to be damaged from sea-level rise.[106] Ocean acidification in the seas around Timor-Leste has been slowly increasing, impacting the growth of coral and maritime diversity.[107] Annual mean temperatures are expected to rise and the intensity of rain events will increase while drier areas in the north will expand.[108] Timor-Leste has also been increasingly affected by strong winds and storms, drought, floods and landslides.[109]

Climate change is likely to increase the incidence of natural disasters, which compounds pre-existing human security challenges.[110] Chapter seven argued that Timor-Leste's build-up of military and naval capacities neglects the reality that threats to Timor-Leste's sovereignty are more likely to emerge from internal rather than external sources. According to its *Initial National Communication*, Timor-Leste ranks ninth in the world among countries most at risk of natural disasters, due to its geographic location, topography and socio-economic conditions.[111] This vulnerability is compounded by "a significant lack of coping capacity and adaptive capacity".[112] Climate change exacerbates Timor-Leste's security dilemmas, as conflict and instability are more likely in places "where physical safety and secure access to food, water, housing, employment and health care are not available".[113] Benjamin Habib argues that military establishments as traditional implements of national security are not necessarily suited to climate change mitigation and adaptation because threats tend to present as human security problems. As the central security challenge of the twenty-first century, climate change responses "lie in the realm of public policy".[114] In its international declaratory policy and diplomacy, Timor-Leste's leaders demonstrate a commitment to low-emission development policies focusing on climate resilient infrastructure.[115] Attention has been devoted to adaptation strategies such as improving water management, development of adaptive technologies for agriculture and maritime sectors, strengthening institutional capacities for addressing climate change and rehabilitation of damaged ecosystems.[116] However, the main economic and energy policies of Timor-Leste do little to support sustainable livelihoods or community resilience in practice.

Agriculture, Food Security and Water

The livelihoods of the majority of Timorese people are heavily dependent upon agriculture. Climate change will adversely impact on agricultural production and food insecurity. The almost tripling of the population by 2040 is likely to further stretch the states' capacity to feed its citizens.[117] As chapter eight has pointed out, Timor-Leste has a largely subsistence economy with around 70–80 per cent of the population working outside of the formal economy, and 80 per cent of the population living in rural areas. Traditional agricultural systems have barely changed since the early twentieth century.[118] While the majority of people depend on subsistence agriculture, 30–40 per cent of food needs are imported, and — with the exception of coffee — its farmers do not produce enough quantities to ensure marketable surpluses.[119] Nearly 60 per cent of *suco* (village) chiefs reported food shortages in their community, and around 50 per cent of children are underweight and malnourished.[120] Changes in rainfall patterns and sea level rises are predicted to strain the groundwater resources and the availability of water for irrigation that crops rely upon.[121]

Timor-Leste has large areas of soil that is fragile and unproductive.[122] Warmer conditions can reduce livestock productivity and crop yields, which are already far lower than in other Southeast Asian states and are the primary cause of food insecurity.[123]

Water scarcity will increase problems of land degradation as sloped areas (around 44 per cent of Timor-Leste) are already susceptible to erosion due to "deforestation, unsustainable farming practices, recurring wildfires and overgrazing".[124] This will continue to impact on the livelihoods of rural constituents, yet Timor-Leste's government has done little to prioritize agriculture (see chapter eight). Climate change is also likely to exacerbate existing health challenges as the incidence of diseases that prosper due to unsafe drinking water and poor sanitation, such as diarrheal disease, malaria and dengue fever, increases.[125] While Timor-Leste's government is clearly aware of the challenges presented in the area of health, as chapter eight has pointed out, only around 3 per cent of the budget is allocated to health, even though access to health facilities remains problematic, especially in rural areas.

To be food secure in the future, significant increases in agricultural output is necessary, requiring much higher levels of government investment. If the status quo is maintained, population rises will continue to deepen Timor-Leste's dependence upon other states for imports as the climate changes, leading to further imbalances in terms of trade. As the second most valuable commodity exported by Timor-Leste after oil, coffee production will also become increasingly vulnerable to climate shocks. Coffee yields have already been problematic: in 2012, yields were 25 per cent less than in 2007.[126] Timorese smallholders are likely to struggle to adapt with changing climate conditions, a situation which will disadvantage Timor-Leste's biggest non-oil export. Timor-Leste receives support from donors, such as AusAid and United Nations Development Programme, to assist with climate change.[127] The "Seeds for Life" programme, an Australian agricultural aid programme, addressed food shortages by promoting farming practices to increase crop yields and varieties. The programme moved to Timor-Leste's Ministry of Agriculture in June 2016.[128] WithOneSeed is an Australian-based civil society forestry initiative designed to help subsistence farmers generate income through their land, rehabilitate soil to improve nutritional outcomes and plant trees to help combat climate change.[129] As its website notes, the WithOneSeed organization is necessary because Timor-Leste's dependence on oil is unsustainable.[130] Timor-Leste has largely relied upon foreign actors to assist with climate change mitigation and adaptation and environmental rehabilitation, while leaders advanced ambitious oil industrialization plans. Its dependence on food imports has increased while hydrocarbon income declines, which is reflective of the fragility of Timor-Leste's economic sovereignty and long-term developmental capacities.

Energy

At its heart, the 2016 Paris Agreement on Climate Change is about the use of energy resources, and as such, the multilateral commitments to lowering carbon emissions complement the SDGs.[131] The "post-carbon" international economy denotes the transition away from fossil fuels and an increased demand for renewables in the global energy sector. Natural gas is forecast to fare best among the fossil fuels with an anticipated 50 per cent rise in consumption, however, this growth is less than renewable energy.[132] Unlike coal, gas is likely to remain a transitional energy resource, however, oil and gas that is difficult to access — such as that in the Timor Sea — are vulnerable to price fluctuations. Timor-Leste has already experienced the consequences of decreasing global oil prices on state revenue since 2014.

In Timor-Leste's largely subsistence economy, many citizens have limited energy purchasing capacity and tend to use traditional services and fuels, such as kerosene or batteries for lighting and biomass fuels for cooking and heating.[133] The national electricity grid has been a priority of Timor-Leste government. The primary power supply facilities run on heavy fuel oil, which have been subject to volatile petrol prices. In 2011, the electrification rate was approximately 80 per cent in Dili and 10 per cent in rural areas, with limited hours of electricity access in the regions and power outages frequent, even in Dili.[134] *Electricidade de Timor-Leste* (EDTL) is the state-owned monopoly electricity generator, and most electricity is produced by diesel generators.[135] Even though Timor-Leste is an oil exporter, fossil fuels are imported from neighbouring states, mostly Indonesia, with 75 per cent used for electricity production and 25 per cent used in the transport sector.[136] Problematically, only about 40 per cent of commercial and governmental customers located in Dili pay their electricity bills.[137] The EDTL's extensive losses due to chronic non-payment has been subsidized by donor countries such as Australia and Japan.[138]

The SDP envisages that by 2020 at least half of Timor-Leste energy needs will be met by renewable energy sources.[139] Timor-Leste has committed to "focusing on a low-carbon development path through the promotion of renewable energy".[140] While Timor-Leste's government has made noise about having a plan to reduce dependence on imported fossil fuels and focus on renewable energy, it lacks a comprehensive energy policy.[141] Various multilateral and bilateral agencies assisting Timor-Leste in energy have focused primarily on securing conventional energy supplies, with limited efforts to enhance renewable energy to reduce poverty and enhance sustainability.[142] Vitor reports that 9,000 solar panels were distributed to households by the government;[143] however, without proper maintenance many of these have become inoperative.[144] In addition, some of the isolated electricity grids in rural Timor-Leste were also rendered dysfunctional due to a lack of maintenance.

China has managed to exert some influence in Timor-Leste's government energy policies. Timor-Leste's government has been criticized for buying twenty-year-old power plants from China, thus committing the state to around three decades of heavy oil energy production using outdated technology that is banned in many states.[145] Timor-Leste's government signed a deal with the Chinese Nuclear Industry 22nd Construction Company to provide electricity across the country, which was budgeted to cost US$375 million. The opaque tendering processes and dubious legality of the contract were controversial, as payments would come from the Petroleum Fund and acquisitions processes consulted with just one supplier.[146] An independent report revealed deteriorating quality of work, lax safety practices and environmental negligence, and the 20,000 jobs for Timorese touted by Timor-Leste's government never eventuated as Chinese workers were imported.[147] The Government decided to "secretly" procure power plants from an Indonesian company instead for a contracted amount of US$350 million.[148] This has come at the expense of the majority who live in un-electrified rural areas in which citizens — often women and girls — are required to spend considerable time hunting for biomass fuels, the burning of which carries adverse health risks from indoor air pollution.[149] Ultimately, Timorese governments have demonstrated limited inclination or capacity to enact its commitments on renewable energy in practice, which will affect the abilities of future governments to provide sustainable, long-term solutions to energy problems and to fulfil the promises of economic development.

Responsibility and Vulnerability

Arguably, the burden of climate change mitigation should not fall on fragile new states such as Timor-Leste. The "common and differentiated responsibilities" narrative features in Timor-Leste's foreign policy discourse on the subject, promoting the idea that developed states must take on a greater share of the burden than developing states. At the April signing of the Paris Agreement, Timor-Leste's representative argued that like other LDC and SIDS, Timor-Leste "has not contributed to the cause of climate change. However, its impacts amplify our existing and future development challenges… We urge developed countries to take the lead in reducing their emissions and in fulfilling long-standing pledges on means of implementation."[150] Timor-Leste's NAPA report makes it clear that Timor-Leste's climate change vulnerabilities "will be intensified by its extremely high dependency on the natural resource base, inadequate infrastructure and lack of institutional capacity".[151] Contemporary climate change politics has moved away from the idea that smaller developing states can continue to industrialize in the same ways as developed states. The responsibilities of wealthier states, for example, are demonstrated by the Green Climate Fund, in which billions of dollars are allocated to assist developing states with climate change mitigation and adaptation.[152] There is tension between the actions and rhetoric of Timorese leaders in their economic and environmental policies. Timor-Leste's public commitments to sustainable and inclusive development stands in tension with its dependence upon the production and export of non-renewable, finite fossil fuels. While it may not be possible to wean developing states off fossil fuels entirely, it will be essential for Timor-Leste's long-term viability to diversify its economy, consolidate its institutions and ensure the safety and security of its people.

Conclusion

Both the rise of great power competition in the region and the security threats arising from climate change are likely to challenge Timor-Leste's efforts to adopt an independent, autonomous foreign policy that support its goal of absolute external sovereignty. Donald Trump's election to the U.S. Presidency provides further difficulties in predicting how contested orders in the Asia-Pacific will affect Timor-Leste's external security environment in the future. Managing these structural uncertainties through a hedging strategy reflects Timor-Leste's incapacity to influence the regional security picture. If Timor-Leste's Timor Sea tactics work, then its geopolitical security dilemma will be whether to bandwagon or balance against China or the United States. Like many small and middle powers, it is seems increasingly unlikely that Timor-Leste's hedging will be sustainable over the longer term as competition and suspicion between the great powers increases. However, the linchpin moment for Timor-Leste in terms of security may be the end of hydrocarbon revenues from the Timor Sea. As a relatively stable small state it is largely inconsequential but as a failed state it would become a tangible security problem for surrounding powers, and would be again at risk of foreign intervention.

State-centric balance of power politics is the dominant lens for examining security in the Asia-Pacific, and this book has taken a largely state-based focus to the question of security as it examined how leaders have defined and defended national security interests in the fields of foreign policy, security and defence, development and justice. Climate change is likely to be a significant challenge for democratic consolidation, national security and economic and human development in Timor-Leste's future. Yet the politics and political-economy of climate change in Timor-Leste is alarmingly under-researched. More research is required to map the complex interdependencies between national, environmental and human concepts of security, and how this impacts on the international relations of Timor-Leste. Climate change may prompt Timor-Leste to redefine its security and economic interests in the future, however, at the time of writing, Timor-Leste's leaders continue to prioritize industrialization models of economic development at the expense of sustainable development and inclusive growth.

The analysis of the defence, development and diplomacy sectors in this book has highlighted how Timor-Leste has pursued a concept of absolute external sovereignty and self-determination as a cornerstone of its aspirational foreign policy. This vision has emerged from a long history of colonialism and denial of rights to self-determination, in addition to invasive periods of United Nations state-building that have compromised the decision-making capacities of Timorese leaders. Previous chapters have highlighted the importance of legitimate identity projection, multilateralism, internal security and economic development to Timor-Leste's capacities to secure the state. Overall, the book highlights the agency of Timor-Leste in defining and pursuing national goals through foreign policy, challenging some of the core assumptions about the imperatives of small states in International Relations literature. However, Timor-Leste's vision of independence — defined by the lack of dependence and foreign intervention — relies most upon empirical sovereignty: that is, the capacity to enact internal security and political order, good governance and strong institutions, and provide public goods such as infrastructure, health and education.

Timor-Leste's aspirational foreign policy is reflected most clearly in Timor-Leste's energy diplomacy. Leaders staked the economic viability of the state on oil industrialization and their capacities to negotiate a beneficial deal with commercial venture partners on the development of the Greater Sunrise gas field. In the future, the consequences of failure could be dire for internal security as resource revenues have been used by governments to "buy the peace". Even if Timor-Leste's oil refining plans come to fruition, this does little to solve its longer-term sustainability challenges as the Timor Sea provides limited and finite hydrocarbon resources. The pre-occupation with "white elephants" challenges political, social, economic and environmental sustainability, which in the long term could present a significant internal security threat. Securing the state requires thinking locally rather than relying on grand industrial ambitions, and devoting greater resources to health, education, food security, agricultural capacities, environmental regeneration and renewable energy. As the "post-colonial security dilemma" suggests, the biggest risks for Timor-Leste's independence are internally generated: securing the Timorese state depends not on military responses, but on democratic, sustainable and inclusive structures that protect the livelihoods of Timorese citizens.

NOTES

1. Agio Pereira, "Challenges and Opportunities: The View from Timor-Leste", *The Diplomat*, 19 January 2016.
2. Steven Ratuva, "A New Regional Cold War? American and Chinese Posturing in the Pacific", *Asia and the Pacific Policy Studies* 1, no. 2 (2014): 410, 419.
3. For example, see John Mearsheimer, *The Tragedy of Great Power Politics* (New York: W.W. Norton, 2001).
4. Anthony Smith, "Constraints and Choices: East Timor as a Foreign Policy Actor", *New Zealand Journal of Asian Studies* 7, no. 1 (June 2005): 16.
5. JC Sharman, "Sovereignty at the Extremes: Micro-States in World Politics", *Political Studies* 65, no. 3 (2016): 559–75.
6. Hans Mouritzen, "Testing Weak-Power Theory: Three Nordic Reactions to the Soviet Coup", in *European Foreign Policy: The EC and Changing Perspectives in Europe*, edited by Walter Carlsnaes and Steve Smith, pp. 156–76 (London: Sage, 1994).
7. Ja Ian Chong, "America's Asia-Pacific Rebalance and the Hazards of Hedging: A Review of Evidence from Southeast Asia", in *Asia Pacific Countries and the US Rebalancing Strategy*, edited by David W.F. Huang, p. 155 (New York: Palgrave, 2016).
8. Christopher Browning, *Constructivism, Narrative and Foreign Policy Analysis: A Case Study of Finland*, p. 27 (Bern: Peter Lang, 2008).
9. Simon Dalby, "Environmental Geopolitics in the Twenty-First Century", *Alternatives: Global, Local, Political* 39, no. 1 (2014): 4–5.
10. The U.S. "hub-and spokes" system refers to the bilateral alliance between the United States and states in the Asia-Pacific, including South Korea, Japan, Taiwan in Northeast Asia, Thailand and the Philippines in Southeast Asia, and Australia and New Zealand in the South Pacific.
11. Randall Schweller, *Deadly Imbalances: Tripolarity and Hitler's Strategy of World Conquest*, p. 24 (New York: Columbia University Press, 1998).
12. Mearsheimer, *The Tragedy of Great Power Politics*.
13. For example, see G. John Ikenberry, *After Victory: Institutions, Strategic Restraint, and the Rebuilding of Order after Major Wars* (New Jersey: Princeton University Press, 2001).
14. G. John Ikenberry and Jitsuo Tsuchiyama, "Between Balance of Power and Community: The Future of Multilateral Security Co-operation in the Asia-Pacific", *International Relations of the Asia-Pacific* 2 (2002): 70.
15. Ibid., p. 69.
16. Stephen Walt, "Alliances in a Unipolar World", *World Politics* 61, no. 1 (2009): 86.
17. Evelyn Goh, "Understanding 'Hedging' in Asia-Pacific Security", *Pacnet* 43 (2006): 1.

18. Bates Gill, Evelyn Goh and Chin-Hao Huang, *The Dynamics of US–China–Southeast Asia Relations*, p. 7 (Sydney: The United States Studies Centre at the University of Sydney, 2006).
19. Yongjin Zhang, "China and the Emerging Regional Order in the South Pacific", *Australian Journal of International Affairs* 61, no. 3 (2007): 375–76.
20. Matt Hegarty, *China's Growing Influence in South-West Pacific: Australian Policies that Could Respond to China's Intentions and Objectives*, p. 8 (Canberra: Australian Defence College, March 2015).
21. Rizal Sukma, "Indonesia's Response to the Rise of China: Growing Comfort amid Uncertainties", in *The Rise of China: Responses for Southeast Asia and Japan*, edited by Jun Tsunekawa, pp. 152–54 (Japan: National Institute of Defense Studies Joint Researches Services No. 4, 2009).
22. Chong, "America's Asia-Pacific Rebalance and the Hazards of Hedging", p. 159.
23. Evelyn Goh, "Meeting the China Challenge: The U.S. in Southeast Asian Regional Security Strategies", *Policy Studies* 16 (2005): 2.
24. Chong, "America's Asia-Pacific Rebalance and the Hazards of Hedging", p. 160.
25. Selver Sahin, "Timor-Leste's Foreign Policy: Securing State Identity in the Post-Independent Period", *Journal of Current Southeast Asian Affairs* 33, no. 2 (2014): 13.
26. Ian Storey, "China's Inroads into East Timor", *China Brief* 9, no. 6 (2009).
27. Ian Storey, *Southeast Asia and the Rise of China: The Search for Security*, p. 278 (New York: Routledge, 2011).
28. Loro Horta, "Timor-Leste: The Dragon's Newest Friend", *Irasec Discussion Papers* 4 (May 2009).
29. Xanana Gusmão, *Address by His Excellency the Prime Minister and Minister of Defence and Security Kay Rala Xanana Gusmão at the Inauguration of the Building of the Ministry of Defence and F-FDTL Headquarters* (Fatuhada, Dili: Democratic Republic of Timor-Leste Office of the Prime Minister, 3 April 2012).
30. Ibid.
31. John Copper, *China's Foreign Aid and Investment Diplomacy Volume II*, p. 36 (New York: Palgrave Macmillan, 2016).
32. For criticism of the Beijing Consensus see Scott Kennedy, "The Myth of the Beijing Consensus", *Journal of Contemporary China* 19, no. 65 (2010): 462, 468–73.
33. Joshua Cooper Ramo, *The Beijing Consensus: Notes on the New Physics of Chinese Power* (London: The Foreign Policy Centre, 2004).
34. Ibid., p. 38.
35. Ibid., p. 3.
36. See Stefan Halper, *The Beijing Consensus: How China's Authoritarian Model Will Dominate the Twenty-First Century*, pp. 15–22 (New York: Basic Books, 2010).

37. Ratuva, "A New Regional Cold War", p. 412.
38. Storey, *Southeast Asia and the Rise of China*; Kate Reid-Smith, "Crocodile Oil: Dragon's Treasure – a Possible Future Southeast Asian Geopolitical Diaspora?" in *The Crisis in Timor-Leste: Understanding the Past, Imagining the Future*, edited by Dennis Shoesmith, pp. 65–72 (Darwin: Charles Darwin University Press, 2007).
39. Copper, *China's Foreign Aid and Investment Diplomacy Volume II*, p. 36.
40. Storey covers these issues thoroughly in his chapter on Timor-Leste and China. See Storey, *Southeast Asia and the Rise of China*, p. 279.
41. David Hutt, "Is China's Influence in Timor-Leste Rising?", *The Diplomat*, 19 November 2016.
42. Ibid.
43. Ibid.
44. Ibid.
45. República Democrática de Timor-Leste (RDTL), "Joint Statement between the People's Republic of China and the Democratic Republic of Timor-Leste on Establishing Comprehensive Partnership of Good-Neighbourly Friendship, Mutual Trust and Mutual Benefit", Minister of State and of the Presidency of the Council of Ministers and Official Spokesperson for the Government of Timor-Leste Press Release, Dili, 14 April 2014.
46. Storey, *Southeast Asia and the Rise of China*, p. 282.
47. Zhang, "China and the Emerging Regional Order in the South Pacific", p. 370.
48. Rizal Sukma, "Securing East Timor: Military and External Relations", in *Peace Building and State Building in Timor-Leste*, edited by Hadi Soesastro and Landry Haryo Subianto, p. 102 (Jakarta: Centre for Strategic and International Studies, 2002); RDTL, *Joint Statement between the People's Republic of China and the Democratic Republic of Timor-Leste*.
49. Storey, *Southeast Asia and the Rise of China*, p. 279.
50. Horta, "Timor-Leste".
51. For example, in 2012, ASEAN failed to produce a joint communiqué because there was no consensus on what to say regarding China and the South China Sea. Author unknown, "ASEAN in Crisis: Divided We Stagger", *The Economist*, 18 August 2012.
52. Permanent Court of Arbitration (PCA), "The South China Sea Arbitration", PCA Case Number 2013–19, In the matter of an arbitration before an arbitral tribunal constituted under annex VII to the 1982 United Nations Convention on the Law of the Sea between the Republic of the Philippines and the People's Republic of China: Award on Jurisdiction and Admissibility, The Hague, 12 July 2016, pp. 471–72.
53. Ibid., p. 4; Tom Phillips, Oliver Holmes and Owen Bowcott, "Beijing Rejects Tribunal's Ruling in South China Sea Case", *The Guardian*, 13 July 2016.

54. Liselotte Odgaard, "The South China Sea: ASEAN's Security Concerns about China". *Security Dialogue* 34, no. 11 (2003): 12.
55. Damien Kingsbury, "China's Interest in East Timor", *Deakin Speaking*, 10 August 2012, available at <https://blogs.deakin.edu.au/deakin-speaking/2012/08/10/chinas-interests-in-east-timor/> (accessed 19 February 2017).
56. Phillip Dorling, "Chinese Bid to Set Up East Timor Spy Base", *Sydney Morning Herald*, 10 May 2011.
57. Bob Lowry, "After the 2006 Crisis: Australian Interests in Timor-Leste", *Strategic Insights* 38, pp. 1–2 (Barton, ACT: Australian Strategic Policy Institute, November 2007).
58. Commonwealth of Australia, *2009 Defence White Paper*, p. 42 (Canberra: Department of Defence, 2009).
59. Ibid., p. 128.
60. Lowry, "After the 2006 Crisis", p. 2.
61. Dorling, "Chinese Bid to Set Up East Timor Spy Base".
62. Walt, "Alliances in a Unipolar World", p. 112.
63. For a history, see Rizal Sukma, *Indonesia and China: The Politics of a Troubled Relationship* (New York: Routledge, 1999).
64. Sukma, "Indonesia's Response to the Rise of China", p. 140.
65. Storey, *Southeast Asia and the Rise of China*, pp. 204, 211; Sukma, "Indonesia's Response to the Rise of China", pp. 152–54; Odgaard, "The South China Sea", p. 15.
66. Dewi Fortuna Anwar, "The Impact of Domestic and Asian Regional Changes on Indonesian Foreign Policy", *Southeast Asian Affairs* (2010): 137–39.
67. Radio Australia, "East Timor and China Move Closer", Australian Broadcasting Corporation, 16 April 2014.
68. *Xinhua*, "Chinese Defense Minister Holds Talks with Timor-Leste Counterpart", 19 October 2015.
69. RDTL, *Joint Statement between the People's Republic of China and the Democratic Republic of Timor-Leste*.
70. People's Republic of China Ministry of National Defence, "Defense Minister meets with Guests from Sri Lanka, East Timor, Nepal and Thailand", Press Release, The People's Republic of China, Beijing, 13 October 2016.
71. Daniel Flitton, "Economies of Scales: Depleted Stocks Force Asian Fishermen into Australian Waters", *The Age*, 25 February 2017; James Kraska, "China's Maritime Militia Upends Rules on Naval Warfare", *The Diplomat*, 10 August 2015.
72. Timor-Leste's officials naively sought assurances that these companies were not related.
73. Storey, "China's Inroads"; Philippa Brant, *Chinese Aid in the Pacific*. Lowy Institute for International Policy, 2015, available at <https://www.lowyinstitute.org/chinese-aid-map/> (accessed 20 February 2017).

74. Brant, *Chinese Aid in the Pacific*.
75. Kyodo, "Japan, East Timor Serve Up Veiled Criticism of China Over Maritime Rows", *Japan Times*, 15 March 2016.
76. Hidetaka Yoshimatsu, "ASEAN and Evolving Power Relations in East Asia: Strategies and Constraints", *Contemporary Politics* 18, no. 4 (2012): 401. See also Vibhanshu Shekhar, "ASEAN's Response to the Rise of China: Deploying a Hedging Strategy", *China Report* 48 (2012): 253–68.
77. Commonwealth of Australia, *2016 Defence White Paper*, pp. 49–51 (Canberra: Department of Defence, 2016).
78. Ibid., pp. 177–84.
79. Hegarty, *China's Growing Influence in South-West Pacific*, p. 9.
80. Xinhua, "China's Navy Warships Pay First Visit to Timor-Leste", *China Daily*, 16 January 2016.
81. Agio Pereira, "Government Reaffirms Commitment to UNCLOS as the 'Constitution of the Sea'", Government of Timor-Leste Media Release, Dili, 15 July 2016; Julie Bishop, "Australia Supports Peaceful Dispute Resolution in the South China Sea", Ministry for Foreign Affairs and Trade Press Release, Canberra, 12 July 2016.
82. Allaster Cox, "DFAT on China and Timor-Leste: No 'Two-Step' But One Considered Approach", *Lowy Interpreter*, 19 February 2017.
83. Michael Peel, "Philippines' Duterte Backs 'New Order' Led by China and Russia", *Financial Times*, 17 November 2016.
84. Beth Edmondson and Stuart Levy, *Climate Change and Order: The End of Prosperity and Democracy*, pp. 7–9 (New York: Palgrave, 2013).
85. See, for example, Michael Klare, *Resource Wars: The New Landscape of Global Conflict* (New York: Holt, 2001).
86. Benjamin Habib, "Climate Change, Security and Regime Formation in East Asia", in *Non-Traditional Security in East Asia*, edited by Ramon Racheco Pardo and Jeffrey Reeves, p. 49 (London: Imperial College Press, 2016).
87. Thomas Homer-Dixon, "On the Threshold: Environmental Changes as Causes of Acute Conflict", *International Security* 16, no. 2 (1991): 78.
88. Ibid.
89. United Nations World Commission on Environment and Development, "Our Common Future", Brundtland Commission Report, 1987, p. 43.
90. Jane Briant Carant, "Unheard Voices: A Critical Discourse Analysis of the Millennium Development Goals' Evolution into the Sustainable Development Goals", *Third World Quarterly* 38, no. 1 (2017): 19, 28–33.
91. Susan Baker, *Sustainable Development*, 2nd ed., p. 61 (Oxon: Routledge, 2016); Herman Daly, *Ecological Economics and Sustainable Development: Selected Essays of Herman Daly*, pp. 9, 39–40, 55 (Cheltenham and Northampton: Edward Elgar, 2007).

92. RDTL, *Strategic Development Plan*, p. 9 (Dili: Government of Timor-Leste, 2011).
93. Douglas Boothe, *The Environmental Consequences of Growth: Steady-State Economics as an Alternative to Ecological Decline*, p. 1 (New York: Routledge, 1998).
94. Xanana Gusmão, *Address by His Excellency the Prime Minister of the Democratic Republic of Timor-Leste Kay Rala Xanana Gusmão to the United Nations Economic and Social Commission of Asia and the Pacific Ministerial Conference on Regional Economic Cooperation and Integration in Asia and the Pacific*, Bangkok, 19 December 2013.
95. Xanana Gusmão, "Harnessing Natural Resource Wealth for Inclusive Growth and Economic Development", Keynote Address by His Excellency the Prime Minister Kay Rala Xanana Gusmão, Dili, 4 June 2013.
96. Ibid.
97. Xanana Gusmão, "Timor-Leste and ASEAN: Perspectives and Challenges", Address by His Excellency the Prime Minister and Minister of Defence and Security, Kay Rala Xanana Gusmão, Sabah, Malaysia, 2 April 2014.
98. RDTL, *Strategic Development Plan*, p. 53.
99. RDTL, *National Adaptation Programme of Action (NAPA) to Climate Change*, p. 13 (Dili: Ministry for Economy and Development Secretary of State for Environment, December 2010).
100. Alliance of Small Island States (AOSIS), *25 Years of Leadership at the United Nations*, 2015, available at <http://aosis.org/wp-content/uploads/2015/12/AOSIS-BOOKLET-FINAL-11-19-151.pdf> (accessed 14 February 2017).
101. RDTL, "Timor-Leste Participates in the Second Summit of the Pacific Islands Development Forum (PIDF) in Fiji", Press Release, 23 June 2014.
102. Ibid.
103. RDTL, *Timor-Leste's Initial National Communication under United Nations Framework Convention on Climate Change*, p. vii (Dili: Timor-Leste's State Secretariat for Environment, 2014).
104. Pacific-Australia Climate Change Science and Adaptation Planning Program, *Current and Future Climate of Timor-Leste*, p. 4 (Canberra: Australian Government, 2015).
105. RDTL, *Timor-Leste's Initial National Communication*, p. vi.
106. Jon Barnett, Suraje Dessai and Roger N. Jones, "Vulnerability to Climate Variability and Change in East Timor", *AMBIO: A Journal of the Human Environment* 36, no. 5 (2007): 372.
107. Pacific-Australia Climate Change Science and Adaptation Planning Program, *Current and Future Climate of Timor-Leste*, p. 4; RDTL, *National Adaptation Programme of Action (NAPA) to Climate Change*, p. 26; RDTL, *Timor-Leste's Initial National Communication*, p. vi.

108. Pacific-Australia Climate Change Science and Adaptation Planning Program, *Current and Future Climate of Timor-Leste*, pp. 5–7; RDTL, *Timor-Leste's Initial National Communication*, pp. vi–vii.
109. RDTL, *Timor-Leste's Initial National Communication*, p. 54.
110. RDTL, *National Adaptation Programme of Action (NAPA) to Climate Change*, pp. 34–35.
111. RDTL, *Timor-Leste's Initial National Communication*, p. v.
112. Ibid.
113. Habib, "Climate Change, Security and Regime Formation in East Asia", p. 57.
114. Ibid.
115. See RDTL, *National Adaptation Programme of Action (NAPA) to Climate Change*.
116. RDTL, *Timor-Leste's Initial National Communication*, pp. vii, 50.
117. Nicholas Molyneux, Gil Rangel da Cruz, Robert Williams, Rebecca Andersen and Neil Turner, "Climate Change and Population Growth in Timor-Leste: Implications for Food Security", *AMBIO* 41, no. 8 (2012): 837; Barnett, Dessai and Jones, "Vulnerability to Climate Variability and Change in East Timor", p. 372.
118. Molyneux et al., "Climate Change and Population Growth in Timor-Leste", p. 825.
119. RDTL, *National Adaptation Programme of Action (NAPA) to Climate Change*, p. 16.
120. Ibid., p. 28; Food and Agricultural Organisation (FAO), *Global Watch GIEWS: Timor Leste* (The Food and Agriculture Organisation of the United Nations, 2010); Secretariat of the Pacific Community in conjunction with CSIRO, *Food Security in the Pacific and East Timor and its Vulnerability to Climate Change*, p. 3 (Canberra: Australian Government, 2011).
121. Luke Wallace, Baskaran Sundaram, Ross S. Brodie, Sarah Marshall, Samantha Dawson, John Jaycock, Gerard Stewart and Lindsay Furness, *Vulnerability Assessment of Climate Change Impacts on Groundwater Resources in Timor-Leste*, Record 2012/55, p. iii (Canberra: Geoscience Australia, July 2012).
122. RDTL, *First National Report Land Degradation in Timor-Leste*, p. 8 (Dili: Timor-Leste Ministry of Agriculture, Forestry and Fisheries, February 2007).
123. RDTL, *National Adaptation Programme of Action (NAPA) to Climate Change*, p. 27; Molyneux et al., "Climate Change and Population Growth in Timor-Leste", p. 823.
124. RDTL, "Timor-Leste National Action Programme to Combat Land Degradation First Draft", Dili, November 2008, pp. 4, 7.
125. RDTL, *National Adaptation Programme of Action (NAPA) to Climate Change*, pp. 16, 32–33.

126. Asian Development Bank (ADB), *Growing the Non-Oil Economy: A Private Sector Assessment for Timor-Leste*, p. 58 (Manila: ADB, 2015).
127. RDTL, *Timor-Leste's Initial National Communication*.
128. Seeds for Life, "Seeds for Life Program Closing", June 2016, available at <http://seedsoflifetimor.org/> (accessed 16 February 2017); Sarina Locke, "Australian Agricultural Researchers Help Lift Timorese Farmers Out of Dire Poverty", Australian Broadcasting Corporation, 2 May 2016.
129. WithOneSeed, available at <http://withoneseed.org.au/> (accessed 8 March 2017).
130. Ibid.
131. International Energy Agency, *World Energy Outlook 2016: Executive Summary*, p. 1 (France: OECD, 2016).
132. Ibid.
133. United Nations Development Programme (UNDP), *New Solutions for a New Country: Timor-Leste's Future in Renewable Energy*, Case Study 16, September 2011, pp. v, 3; World Bank, *Timor-Leste: Key Issues in Rural Energy Policy*, p. xi (Washington: World Bank, December 2010).
134. UNDP, *New Solutions for a New Country*, p. 3.
135. Ibid.
136. Ibid.
137. Deloitte, "Review of Electricity of Timor-Leste (EDTL)", Commissioned by the Government of Democratic Republic of Timor-Leste, April 2011, p. 6, available at <https://www.laohamutuk.org/Oil/Power/2011/DeloitteEDTLApril2011En.pdf> (accessed 8 March 2017).
138. Walter Heiser, "The Future of Hydropower Development in Timor Leste", *International Journal of Hydropower and Dams* 22, no. 2 (2015): 78.
139. RDTL, *Strategic Development Plan*, pp. 85–92.
140. Constâncio da Conceição Pinto, Statement by Constâncio da Conceição Pinto Minister of Commerce, Industry and Environment of the Democratic Republic of Timor-Leste to the High-level Signature Ceremony for the Paris Agreement, New York, 22 April 2016.
141. UNDP, *New Solutions for a New Country*, p. 3.
142. Ibid., pp. 1–2.
143. Antonio Vitor, "Progress and Challenges of Infrastructure Spending in Timor-Leste", in *A New Era? Timor-Leste after the UN Intervention*, edited by Sue Ingram, Lia Kent and Andrew McWilliam, p. 110 (Canberra: ANU Press, 2015).
144. UNDP, *New Solutions for a New Country*, p. 3.
145. Lindsay Murdoch, "E. Timor Counts Cost of Chinese Power Plants", *Sydney Morning Herald*, 15 December 2010.
146. Deloitte, *Review of Electricity of Timor-Leste (EDTL)*, p. 5.
147. Copper, *China's Foreign Aid and Investment Diplomacy Volume II*, p. 36; Murdoch, "E. Timor Counts Cost of Chinese Power Plants".

148. Deloitte, *Review of Electricity of Timor-Leste (EDTL)*, p. 5; Murdoch, "E. Timor Counts Cost of Chinese Power Plants".
149. UNDP, *New Solutions for a New Country*, pp. v, 3; World Bank, *Timor-Leste: Key Issues in Rural Energy Policy*, p. xi.
150. Pinto, "Statement to the High-level Signatory Ceremony for the Paris Agreement".
151. RDTL, *National Adaptation Programme of Action (NAPA) to Climate Change*, p. 11.
152. See United Nations, *Paris Agreement*, article 9 (Paris: United Nations, 2015).

Postscript

Australia and Timor-Leste signed the Timor Sea Maritime Boundary Treaty on 6 March 2018 in New York City. While the treaty resolved the symbolic issue of maritime boundary delimitation, no agreement was reached on a development concept for the shared resource, Greater Sunrise. In February, a leaked letter from Timor-Leste's lead negotiator Xanana Gusmão signalled his discontent with these negotiations as he blasted the independent oil and gas expert who had raised significant concerns around the commercial viability of Timor-Leste's pipeline plan and the assumptions built into Timor-Leste's economic modelling. Gusmão publicly declared that the pipeline was "non-negotiable". The United Nations Compulsory Conciliation report released in April also confirmed that it had been unable to facilitate an agreement on the development concept for Greater Sunrise. The report outlined that Timor-Leste's proposal could only occur with a direct subsidy of US$5.6 billion by the government of Timor-Leste (or another funder), and it would only provide a mere 7 per cent return on a capital investment of US$15.6 billion.

By August 2018, a development deal for Greater Sunrise — the most critical resource for Timor-Leste's mid-term economic viability and functional sovereignty, and the centrepiece of its development agenda — remained elusive.

Bibliography

AAP. "Timor Violence: Regret But No Apology". *Sydney Morning Herald*, 15 July 2008.

Abuza, Zachary. "Laos: Maintaining Power in a Highly Charged Region". In *Small States in World Politics: Explaining Foreign Policy Behaviour*, edited by Jeanne Hey, pp. 157–84. Boulder: Lynne Rienner Publishers, 2003.

Acharya, Amitav. "After Liberal Hegemony: The Advent of a Multiplex World Order". *Ethics and International Affairs*, 8 September 2017. Available at <https://www.ethicsandinternationalaffairs.org/2017/multiplex-world-order/> (accessed 5 January 2018).

———. *Constructing a Security Community in Southeast Asia: ASEAN and the Problem of Regional Order*. 3rd ed. London and New York: Routledge, 2014.

———. *Whose Ideas Matter? Agency and Power in Asian Regionalism*. Ithaca and London: Cornell University Press, 2009.

———. *Singapore's Foreign Policy: The Search for Regional Order*. Singapore: World Scientific Publishing/Institute of Policy Studies, 2008.

———. "Regionalism and Regime Security in the Third World: Comparing the Origins of the ASEAN and the GCC". In *The Insecurity Dilemma: National Security of Third World States*, pp. 143–89. Boulder: Lynne Rienner, 1992.

Agence France-Presse (AFP). "E Timor 'Still Needs Indonesia Apology'". *Sydney Morning Herald*, 16 March 2010.

———. "Portuguese to be East Timor's Official Language: Gusmão". *Agence France-Presse*, 11 February 2000.

Agné, Hans. "The Politics of International Recognition: Symposium Introduction". *International Theory* 5, no. 1 (2013): 94–106.

Alagappa, Muthiah. "Introduction". In *Political Legitimacy in Southeast Asia: The Quest for Moral Authority*, edited by Muthiah Alagappa, pp. 1–10. Stanford: Stanford University Press, 1995.

———. "International Security in Southeast Asia: Growing Salience of Regional and Domestic Dynamics". In *Security of Third World Countries*, edited by Jasjit

Singh and Thomas Bernauer, pp. 109–49. Aldershot: United Nations Institute for Disarmament Research, 1993.

Alexandrov, Maxym. "The Concept of State Identity in International Relations: A Theoretical Analysis". *Journal of International Development and Cooperation* 10, no. 1 (2003): 33–46.

Allard, Tom and Kirsty Needham. "No Refugee Centre For Us: East Timor". *The Age*, 29 March 2011.

Alliance of Small Island States (AOSIS). *25 Years of Leadership at the United Nations*, 2015. Available at <http://aosis.org/wp-content/uploads/2015/12/AOSIS-BOOKLET-FINAL-11-19-151.pdf> (accessed 14 February 2017).

Ambrosio, Thomas. "East Timor Independence: The Changing Nature of International Independence". In *Transforming East Asian Domestic and International Politics: The Impact of Economy and Globalization*, edited by R. Compton. Aldershot: Burlington, 2002.

Amnesty International. *Annual Report Timor-Leste 2015/2016*. Available at <http://www.asia-pacific-solidarity.net/southeastasia/easttimor/reports/ai_annualreport_2015-16.htm> (accessed 11 February 2017).

———. *Remembering the Past: Recommendations to Effectively Establish the "National Reparations Programme" and "Public Memory Institute"*. London: Amnesty International Publications, February 2012.

———. *Timor-Leste: Annual Report 2012*. ASA 57/001/2012, 2012.

———. *'We Cry for Justice': Impunity Persists 10 Years On in Timor-Leste*. ASA 57/001/2009, 27 August 2009.

Anderlini, Sanam Naraghi, Camille Conaway and Lisa Kays. "Transitional Justice and Reconciliation". In *Inclusive Security, Sustainable Peace: A Toolkit for Advocacy and Action*. International Alert: Women Waging Peace, November 2004.

Anderson, Benedict. "Imagining East Timor". *Arena* 4 (April–May 1993).

Anwar, Dewi Fortuna. "The Impact of Domestic and Asian Regional Changes on Indonesian Foreign Policy". *Southeast Asian Affairs* (2010): 126–41.

Araújo, Rui. "Speech by His Excellency the Prime Minister of the Democratic Republic of Timor-Leste Dr Rui de Araújo at the Side Event for Pathfinders for Peaceful, Justice and Inclusive Societies". United Nations Headquarters, 20 September 2016.

———. "Remarks by His Excellency the Prime Minister of the Democratic Republic of Timor-Leste Dr Rui de Araújo at the Atlantic Council". Washington D.C., 21 June 2016.

———. "Speech by His Excellency the Prime Minister Dr Rui Maria de Araújo on the Occasion of the Launch of the Maritime Boundary Office Website". Dili Government Palace, 29 February 2016.

———. "Speech by His Excellency the Prime Minister of the Democratic Republic of Timor-Leste at the Dinner Celebrating the 40th Anniversary of the

Proclamation of Independence and the 500 Years of the Interaction between Two Civilisations: Timor-Leste and Portugal and the Affirmation of the Timorese Identity". Oecusse, Timor-Leste, 27 November 2015.

———. "Remarks by the Prime Minister of the Democratic Republic of Timor-Leste, His Excellency Dr Rui Maria de Araújo, on the Occasion of the Official Luncheon Hosted by the President of the Republic of Indonesia, His Excellency IR. Joko Widodo". Jakarta, 26 August 2015.

———. "Keynote Speech by His Excellency the Prime Minister Dr Rui Maria de Araújo at the Inaugural Meeting of the Pacific Island Regional Initiative of the Alliance for Financial Inclusion". Dili, 7 May 2015.

———. "Speech by His Excellency the Prime Minister on the Occasion of the Swearing-In of the Sixth Constitutional Government". Lahane Palace, Dili, 6 February 2015.

Archibugi, Daniele. "A Critical Analysis of the Self-Determination of Peoples: A Cosmopolitan Perspective". *Constellations* 10, no. 2 (2003): 488–505.

Asia Pacific Center for Security Studies. "Timor-Leste National Security Policy Workshop". Honolulu: Asia Pacific Center for Security Studies, 8–12 September 2008.

Asian-African Conference of Bandung. "Final Communiqué of the Asian-African Conference of Bandung". Indonesia, 24 April 1955.

Asian Development Bank (ADB). "Timor-Leste: Economy". Available at <https://www.adb.org/countries/timor-leste/economy> (accessed 26 February 2017).

———. "Timor-Leste: Country Partnership Strategy (2016–2020)", April 2016. Available at <https://www.adb.org/documents/timor-leste-country-partnership-strategy-2016-2020> (accessed 14 February 2017).

———. *Growing the Non-Oil Economy: A Private Sector Assessment for Timor-Leste*. Manila: Asian Development Bank, 2015.

———. *Pacific Economic Monitor Midyear Review*, July 2015. Available at <http://reliefweb.int/sites/reliefweb.int/files/resources/Pacific%20Economic%20Monitor_July%202015%20Midyear%20Review.pdf> (accessed 26 February 2017).

Asian Football Confederation. "Federacao Futebol Timor-Leste Expelled From AFC Asian Cup 2023". Available at <http://www.the-afc.com/media/federacao-futebol-timor-leste-expelled-from-afc-asian-cup-2023-34508> (accessed 22 March 2017).

Associated Press (AP). "East Timor Chooses Portuguese as Official Language", 14 February 2000.

Association of Southeast Asian Nations (ASEAN). "Partnering for Change, Engaging the World". Joint Communiqué of the 50th ASEAN Foreign Ministers' Meeting, Manila, Philippines, 5 August 2017.

———. "Turning Vision into Reality for a Dynamic ASEAN Community". Joint Communiqué of the 49th ASEAN Foreign Ministers' Meeting, Vientiane, 24 July 2016.

———. *ASEAN Charter*. Jakarta: ASEAN Secretariat, 2015.

———. "Treaty of Amity and Cooperation in Southeast Asia". Denpasar, 1976.

———. "The ASEAN Declaration (Bangkok Declaration)". Bangkok, 8 August 1967.

Aubrey, Jim. "Viva Timor L'este: Beyond Silence Betrayal, Cowardice and Murder". *Arena* 40 (1999).

Australian Broadcasting Corporation (ABC). "Former East Timor Guerrilla Leader and Opposition Figure Mauk Moruk Killed in Security Operation, Government Says". *ABC News*, 10 August 2015.

———. "East Timor's Former President José Ramos Horta says West Papua 'part of Indonesia'". *ABC News*, 23 July 2015.

———. "Last ADF Troops Leave East Timor". *ABC News*, 28 March 2013.

Australian Embassy in Timor-Leste. "Australia Offers Timor-Leste New Patrol Boats", 27 April 2016. Available at <http://timorleste.embassy.gov.au/dili/Defence.html> (accessed 11 February 2017).

Australian Trade and Investment Commission. "Market Profile Export Markets – East Timor". Available at <https://www.austrade.gov.au/Australian/Export/Export-markets/Countries/East-Timor/Market-profile> (accessed 27 February 2017).

Author unknown. "Timor Leste-Indonesia Bilateral Relations Improve". *Antara News*, 27 September 2013.

———. "ASEAN in Crisis: Divided We Stagger". *The Economist*, 18 August 2012.

———. "Former East Timor President Still Sees Value in Indonesian Relationship". *Jakarta Globe*, 19 July 2012.

———. *Guide Post Magazine* 70 (June 2012).

———. "Gusmão Accuses UN of Trampling on Timor". *Sydney Morning Herald*, 20 May 2011.

Ayoob, Mohammad. *The Third World Security Predicament: State-Making, Regional Conflict, and the International System*. Boulder: Lynne Rienner, 1995.

Ba, Alice. *(Re)Negotiating East and Southeast Asia: Region, Regionalism and the Association of Southeast Asian Nations*. California: Stanford University Press, 2009.

Babo-Soares, Dionisio. "The Future of Timor-Leste's Foreign Policy". In *A Reliable Partner: Strengthening Australia-Timor-Leste Relations*. ASPI Special Report 39, pp. 21–29. Canberra: Australian Strategic Policy Institute, April 2011.

———. "Political Developments Leading to the Referendum". In *Out of the Ashes: Deconstruction and Reconstruction of East Timor*, edited by James Fox and Dionisio Babo-Soares, pp. 57–78. Hindmarsh. South Australia: Crawford House Publishing, November 2003.

Bailes, Alyson, Jean-Marc Rickli, and Baldur Thorhallsson. "Small States, Survival and Strategy". In *Small States and International Security: Europe and Beyond*, edited by Clive Archer, Alyson Bailes and Anders Wivel, pp. 26–45. Oxon: Routledge, 2014.

Baker, Susan. *Sustainable Development*. 2nd ed. Oxon: Routledge, 2016.

Ball, Desmond. "The Defence of East Timor: A Recipe for Disaster?" *Pacifica Review Global Change, Peace and Security* 14, no. 3 (2002): 175–89.

Ballard, John. *Triumph of Self-Determination: Operation Stabilise and United Nations Peacemaking in East Timor*. Connecticut: Praeger Security International, 2004.

Barbara, Julien, John Cox and Michael Leach. "Emerging Middle Classes in Timor-Leste and Melanesia: Implications for Development and Democracy". *In Brief* 57. Canberra: Australian National University, 2014.

Barker, Anne. "Australian Citizen, Former East Timorese Minister Fights Against 'Unfair' Seven-year Jail Sentence for Corruption". *ABC News*, 10 February 2017.

———. "Air Timor: Government Policy, Suspected Corruption 'Destroying' East Timor's Only Airline". *ABC News*, 13 January 2017.

Barma, Naazneen. "The Rentier State at Work: Comparative Experiences of the Resource Curse in East Asia and the Pacific". *Asia and the Pacific Policy Studies* 1, no. 2 (2014): 257–72.

Barnett, Jon, Suraje Dessai and Roger N. Jones. "Vulnerability to Climate Variability and Change in East Timor". *AMBIO: A Journal of the Human Environment* 36, no. 5 (2007): 372–78.

Bartelson, Jens. "Three Concepts of Recognition". *International Theory* 5 (2013): 107–29.

Bateman, Sam. "Managing Good Order at Sea in the Asia-Pacific". In *Maritime Challenges and Priorities in Asia: Implications for Regional Security*, edited by Sam Bateman and Joshua Ho, pp. 21–33. London and New York: Routlesdge, 2013.

Beauvais, Joel. "Benevolent Despotism: A Critique of UN State-building in East Timor". *New York University Journal of International Law and Politics* 33 (2001–2): 1101–78.

Beeson, Mark. "ASEAN's Ways: Still Fit for Purpose?" *Cambridge Review of International Affairs* 22, no. 3 (2009): 333–43.

Bellamy, Alex. "Kosovo and the Advent of Sovereignty as Responsibility". In *Kosovo, Intervention and Statebuilding: The International Community and the Transition to Independence*, edited by Aidan Hehir, pp. 38–59. Oxon: Routledge, 2010.

———. "The Responsibility to Protect—Five Years On". *Ethics and International Affairs* 24, no. 2 (2010): 143–69.

Bellamy, Alex and Mark Beeson. "The Responsibility to Protect in Southeast Asia: Can ASEAN Reconcile Humanitarianism and Sovereignty?" *Asian Security* 6, no. 3 (2010): 262–79.

Bellamy, Alex, Paul Williams and Stuart Griffin. *Understanding Peacekeeping*. 2nd ed. Cambridge: Polity Press, 2010.

Belo, Jose. "East Timor Elites Try to Muzzle Media". *Crikey*, 23 June 2014.

Benzing, Markus. "Midwifing a New State: The United Nations in East Timor". *Max Planck Yearbook of United Nations Law* 9 (2005): 295–372.

Bergin, Anthony. "Pacific Maritime Security—From Quad to Hexagon". *The Strategist*. Canberra: Australian Strategic Policy Institute, 22 July 2014.

Beuman, Lydia. *Political Institutions in Timor-Leste: Semi-Presidentialism and Democratization*. London: Routledge, 2015.

———. "Cohabitation in New Post-Conflict States: The Case of Timor-Leste". [Invited Oral Presentation]. *Reordering Power, Shifting Boundaries, AISP/IPSA 22nd World Congress of Political Science*, Madrid, Spain, 8–12 July 2012.

Bickerton, Chris. "State-Building: Exporting State Failure". *Arena Journal* 32 (2009): 101–23.

Bishop, Julie. "Australia supports peaceful dispute resolution in the South China Sea". Ministry for Foreign Affairs and Trade Press Release, Canberra, 12 July 2016.

Blunt, Peter. "The Political Economy of Accountability in Timor-Leste: Implication for Public Policy". *Public Administration and Development* 29 (2009): 89–100.

Boothe, Douglas. *The Environmental Consequences of Growth: Steady-State Economics as an Alternative to Ecological Decline*. New York: Routledge, 1998.

Bovensiepen, Judith. "Visions of Prosperity and Conspiracy in Timor-Leste". *Focaal—Journal of Global and Historical Anthropology* 75 (2016): 75–88.

Bowman, Herbert. "Letting the Big Fish Get Away: The United Nations Justice Effort in East Timor". *Emory International Law Review* 18 (2004): 371–400.

Braithwaite, John, Hilary Charlesworth and Aderito Soares. *Networked Governance of Freedom and Tyranny: Peace in Timor-Leste*. Canberra: ANU Press, 2012.

Brant, Philippa. "Chinese Aid in the Pacific". Australia: Lowy Institute for International Policy, 2015. Available at <https://www.lowyinstitute.org/chinese-aid-map/> (accessed 20 February 2017).

Brazil, Pat. "Critique of the Lowe Opinion". Submission No. 22.1 Delivered to the Joint Standing Committee on Treaties, 11 April 2002.

Brennan, Frank. "Time to Draw the Line between Australia and Timor-Leste". *Eureka Street*, 13 May 2013.

Breuilly, John. *Nationalism and the State*. Manchester: Manchester University Press, 1982.

Brown, William and Sophie Harman. "African Agency in International Politics". In *African Agency in International Politics*, edited by William Brown and Sophie Harman, pp. 1–16. Oxon: Routledge, 2013.

Browning, Christopher. *Constructivism, Narrative and Foreign Policy Analysis: A Case Study of Finland*. Bern: Peter Lang, 2008.

Brunnstrom, Cecilia. "Another Invasion: Lessons from International Support to East Timorese NGOs". *Development in Practice* 13, no. 4 (2003): 310–21.

Bull, Hedley. *The Anarchical Society: A Study of Order in World Politics*. London: Macmillan, 1977.

Burchill, Scott. "East Timor, Australia and Indonesia". In *Guns and Ballot Boxes: East Timor's Vote for Independence*, edited by Damien Kingsbury, pp. 169–84. Clayton: Monash Asia Institute, 2000.

Burke, Roland. *Decolonization and the Evolution of International Human Rights*. Philadelphia: University of Pennsylvania, 2010.

Butler, Michael. "Ten Years After: (Re) Assessing Neo-Trusteeship and UN State-building in Timor-Leste". *International Studies Perspectives* 13 (2012): 85–104.

Buzan, Barry. *From International to World Society? English School Theory and the Social Structure of Globalisation*. Cambridge: Cambridge University Press, 2004.

———. *People, States, and Fear: The National Security Problem in International Relations*. Chapel Hill: North Carolina, University of North Carolina Press, 1983.

Cabellero-Anthony, Mely. *Regional Security in Southeast Asia: Beyond the ASEAN Way*. Singapore: Institute of Southeast Asian Studies, 2005.

Call, Charles T. "The Fallacy of the 'Failed State'". *Third World Quarterly* 29, no. 8 (2008): 1491–1507.

Camilleri, Joséph and Jim Falk. *The End of Sovereignty? The Politics of Shrinking and Fragmenting World*. Aldershot, UK: Edward Elgar, 2002.

Campbell, David. *Writing Security: United States Foreign Policy and the Politics of Identity*. Minnesota: University of Minnesota Press, 1998.

Caplan, Richard. *Europe and the Recognition of New States in Yugoslavia*. Cambridge: Cambridge University Press, 2005.

Carant, Jane Briant. "Unheard Voices: A Critical Discourse Analysis of the Millennium Development Goals' Evolution into the Sustainable Development Goals". *Third World Quarterly* 38, no. 1 (2017): 16–41.

Carmona, Magdalena Sepulveda. "Report of the Special Rapporteur on Extreme Poverty and Human Rights Mission to Timor-Leste", 10 September 2014, p. 5. Available at <https://ssrn.com/abstract=2494404> (accessed 26 February 2017).

Central Intelligence Agency. "The World Factbook Country Comparison: Area". Available at <https://www.cia.gov/Library/publications/the-world-factbook/rankorder/2147rank.html> (accessed 30 January 2017).

Centre for Defence Studies. *Independent Study on Security Force Options for East Timor*. London: The Centre for Defence Studies, King's College, 2000.

Chacko, Priya. "A New 'Special Relationship'? Power Transitions, Ontological Security and India–US Relations". *International Studies Perspectives* 15 (2014): 329–46.

———. *Indian Foreign Policy: The Politics of Post-Colonial Identity from 1947–2004*. Oxon: Routledge, 2012.

Chandler, David. *Empire in Denial: The Politics of Statebuilding*. London: Pluto Press, 2006.

Channel NewsAsia. "EXCLUSIVE: 'We are Friends with Everyone', says Timor Leste's new Prime Minister". *Channel NewsAsia*, 21 March 2015.

Charlesworth, Hilary. "The Constitution of East Timor". *International Journal of Constitutional Law* 1, no. 2 (2003): 325–34.

Chesterman, Simon. *You, the People: The United Nations, Transitional Administration, and State-Building*. Oxford: Oxford University Press, 2005.

———. "East Timor in Transition: Self-determination, State-building and the United Nations". *International Peacekeeping* 9, no. 1 (Spring 2002): 45–76.

Chesterman, Simon, Michael Ignatieff, and Ramesh Thakur, eds. *Making States Work: State Failure and the Crisis of Governance*. Tokyo and New York: United Nations University, 2005.

Chong, Ja Ian. "America's Asia-Pacific Rebalance and the Hazards of Hedging: A Review of Evidence from Southeast Asia". In *Asia Pacific Countries and the US Rebalancing Strategy*, edited by David W.F. Huang, pp. 155–14. New York: Palgrave Macmillan, 2016.

Chongkittavorn, Kavi. "Will Timor-Leste Finally Join ASEAN in 2017?". *Reporting ASEAN*. Available at <http://www.aseannews.net/will-timor-leste-finally-join-asean-2017a/> (accessed 12 February 2017).

Chopra, Jarat. "The UN's Kingdom of East Timor". *Survival* 42, no. 3 (Autumn 2000): 27–39.

Chopra, Jarat and Tanja Hohe. "Participatory Intervention". *Global Governance* 10 (2004): 289–305.

Chopra, Jarat and Thomas Weiss. "Sovereignty is No Longer Sacrosanct: Codifying Humanitarian Intervention". *Ethics and International Affairs* 6, no. 1 (1992): 95–117.

Chowdhury, Anis and Iyanatul Islam. *The Newly Industrialising Economies of East Asia*, p. 31. London: Routledge, 1993.

Chwaszcza, Christine. "'Recognition': Some Analytical Remarks". *International Theory* 5 (2013): 160–65.

Clamagirand, Brigette. "The Social Organization of the Ema of Timor". In *The Flow of Life: Essays on Eastern Indonesia*, edited by James J. Fox, pp. 134–51. Cambridge, Mass: Harvard University Press, 1982.

Clapham, Christopher. *Africa and the International System: The Politics of State Survival*. Cambridge: Cambridge University Press, October 2009.
———. "Degrees of Statehood". *Review of International Studies* 24 (1998): 143–57.
Cleary, Paul. "E Timor Civil Society on Skid Row: President". *The Australian*, 12 March 2016.
Clifton, Tony. "Field of Dreams: The Battle for the Timor Sea, Home of Oil, Gas, Hot Air and Hope". *The Monthly*, July 2005.
Clunan, Anne. *The Social Construction of Russia's Resurgence*. Baltimore: The Johns Hopkins University Press, 2009.
Cohen, David. "'Hybrid' Justice in East Timor, Sierra Leone, and Cambodia: 'Lessons Learned' and Prospects for the Future". *Stanford Journal of International Law* 43 (2007): 1–38.
Collier, Paul, Patrick Guillaumont, Sylviane Guillaumont and Jan Willem Gunning. "Redesigning Conditionality". *World Development* 25, no. 9 (1997): 1399–1407.
Collins, Alan. *The Security Dilemmas of Southeast Asia*. Hampshire: Palgrave Macmillan, 2000.
Commission for Human Rights Violations in East Timor (KPP-HAM). *Executive Summary on the Investigation of Human Rights Violations in East Timor*. Jakarta: KPP-HAM, 31 January 2000.
Commission for Reception, Truth and Reconciliation (CAVR). *Timor-Leste Self-Determination and the International Community: National Public Hearing 15–17 March 2004*. Dili: Commission of Reception, Truth and Reconciliation Production Team and Translation Unit, 2009.
———. *Chega! Final Report of the Commission for Reception, Truth and Reconciliation Timor-Leste*. Dili: CAVR, 2005.
Commission of Truth and Friendship (CTF). *From Memory to Hope: Final Report of the Commission of Truth and Friendship (CTF) Indonesia-Timor-Leste*. Denpasar: CTF, 31 March 2008.
Commonwealth of Australia. *2016 Defence White Paper*. Canberra: Department of Defence, 2016.
———. *2009 Defence White Paper*. Canberra: Department of Defence, 2009.
Commonwealth of Australia House of Representatives. *Debates* 76, 26 August 1975.
Constituent Assembly. *Constitution of the Democratic Republic of Timor-Leste*. Dili: Democratic Republic of Timor-Leste, 2002.
Cooper, Robert. *The Breaking of Nations: Order and Chaos in the Twenty-First Century*. London: Atlantic Monthly Press, 2003.
Copper, John. *China's Foreign Aid and Investment Diplomacy Volume II*. New York: Palgrave Macmillan, 2016.
Cotton, James. "Timor-Leste and the Discourse of State Failure". *Australian Journal of International Affairs* 61, no. 4 (2007): 455–70.

———. *East Timor, Australia and Regional Order: Intervention and its Aftermath in Southeast Asia*. London: RoutledgeCurzon, 2004.

Cox, Allaster. "DFAT on China and Timor-Leste: No 'Two-Step' But One Considered Approach". *Lowy Interpreter*, 19 February 2017.

Community of Portuguese Language Countries (CPLP). *Estatutos da Comunidade dos Países de Língua Portuguesa (The Statutes)*. Lisbon: CPLP, 2007.

———. *Declaração Constitutiva da Comunidade dos Países de Língua Portuguesa (Constitutive Declaration of the CPLP)*. Lisbon: CPLP, 1996.

Crawford, James. *The Creation of States in International Law*. 2nd ed. Oxford: Clarendon Press, 2006.

Cristóvão, Cirilo José. "Emerging Challenges to Small State Security in the Asia-Pacific". 14th Asia Security Summit, The IISS Shangri-La Dialogue, Singapore, 30 May 2015.

Croissant, Aurel. "Perils and Promises of Democratization Through United Nations Transitional Authority: Lessons from Cambodia and East Timor". *Democratization* 15, no. 3 (2008): 649–48.

Crouch, Harold. *Political Reform In Indonesia After Soeharto*. Singapore: Institute of Southeast Asian Studies, 2010.

Da Costa, Helder. "g7+ and the New Deal: Country-Led and Country-Owned Initiatives: A Perspective from Timor-Leste". *International Journal of Peacebuilding & Development* 7, no. 2 (2012): 96–102.

Da Costa, Marcelino dJ., Modesto Lopes, Anita Ximenes, Adelfredo do Rosario Ferreira, Luc Spyckerelle, Rob Williams, Harry Nesbitt and William Erskine. "Household Food Insecurity in Timor-Leste". *Food Security* 5 (2013): 83–94.

Dalby, Simon. "Environmental Geopolitics in the Twenty-First Century". *Alternatives: Global, Local, Political* 39, no. 1 (2014): 3–16.

Daly, Herman. *Ecological Economics and Sustainable Development: Selected Essays of Herman Daly*. Cheltenham and Northampton: Edward Elgar, 2007.

Deacon, Bob. "Assessing the SDGs from the Point of View of Global Social Governance". *Journal of International and Comparative Social Policy* 32, no. 2 (2016): 116–30.

Della-Giacoma, Jim. *Timor Loro Sa'e is Our Nation: A Report on Focus Group Discussions in East Timor*. Dili: National Democratic Institute for International Affairs and East Timor NGO Forum's Working Group on Electoral Education, March 2001.

Deloitte. *Review of Electricity of Timor-Leste (EDTL)*. Commissioned by the Government of Democratic Republic of Timor-Leste, April 2011. Available at <https://www.laohamutuk.org/Oil/Power/2011/DeloitteEDTLApril2011En.pdf> (accessed 8 March 2017).

Department of Foreign Affairs and Trade, Australian Government. "Timor-Leste". Available at <https://dfat.gov.au/geo/timor-leste/pages/timor-leste.aspx> (accessed 27 June 2018).

———. "ASEAN Regional Forum (ARF)". Available at <http://dfat.gov.au/international-relations/regional-architecture/Pages/asean-regional-forum-arf.aspx> (accessed 12 February 2017).

———. "East Asia Summit". Available at <http://dfat.gov.au/international-relations/regional-architecture/eas/pages/east-asia-summit-eas.aspx> (accessed 12 February 2017).

———. *Australia and the Indonesian Incorporation of Portuguese Timor, 1974-1976*, edited by Wendy Way, Damien Browne and Vivianne Johnson. Carlton: Melbourne University Press, 2000.

Diamond, Larry, Juan Linz and Seymour Lipset. "Introduction: What Makes for Democracy". In *Politics in Developing Countries*, 2nd ed., edited by Larry Diamond, Juan Linz and Seymour Lipset, pp. 1–16. Boulder, Colorado: Lynne Rienner Publisher, 1995.

Dodd, Mark. "Forgive and Forget as Dili Signs Jakarta Defence Pact". *The Australian*, 29 August 2011.

———. "Timor-Leste Blasts Australia for Failing to Help with Patrol Boats". *The Australian*, 10 February 2011.

———. "Gusmão Gives UN Team a Serve: 'We Don't Want a Legacy of Cars'". *Sydney Morning Herald*, 10 October 2000.

Dolven, Ben, Rhoda Margesson and Bruce Vaughn. *Timor-Leste: Political Dynamics, Development, and International Involvement*. Congressional Research Service, 3 July 2012.

Dorling, Phillip. "Chinese Bid to Set Up East Timor Spy Base". *Sydney Morning Herald*, 10 May 2011.

Downie, Sue. "UNTAET: State-building and Peace-Building". In *East Timor: Beyond Independence*, edited by Damien Kingsbury and Michael Leach, pp. 29–42. Clayton: Monash University Press, 2007.

Drysdale, Jennifer. *Sustainable Development or Resource Cursed? An Exploration of Timor-Leste's Institutional Choices?* Mannheim: VDM Verlag, 2009.

Dunn, James. *Timor: A People Betrayed*. Milton, Queensland: The Jacaranda Press, 1983.

———. *The Timor Story*. Canberra: The Parliamentary Library Legislature Research Service, 1976.

Dupont, Alan. "ASEAN's Response to the East Timor Crisis". *Australian Journal of International Affairs* 45, no. 2 (2000): 163–70.

Durand, Frédéric. *East Timor: A Country at the Crossroads of Asia and the Pacific, A Geo-Historical Atlas*. Chiang Mai: Silkworm Books and Bangkok: IRASEC, 2006.

East Timor and Indonesia Action Network. "ETAN Renews Call for Meaningful Justice for Victims of Indonesian Occupation". East Timor and Indonesia Action Network Press Release, 14 July 2008.

———. "Truth Known, East Timorese Need Justice". East Timor and Indonesia Action Network Press Release, 9 March 2005.

East Timor and Indonesia Action Network, La'o Hamutuk, Human Rights Working Group, Australian Coalition for Transitional Justice in East Timor, and TAPOL. "Rights Groups Call for End to Farcical Joint Timor-Indonesia Commission". Media Release, 24 May 2007.

East Timor Law and Justice Bulletin. "Timor-Leste Strikes Troubling New Weapon Deal with Indonesia, says Fundasaun Mahein", 13 March 2014. Available at <http://www.easttimorlawandjusticebulletin.com/2014/03/timor-leste-strikes-troubling-new.html> (accessed 19 June 2014).

East Timor Planning Commission. *National Development Plan.* Dili: Planning Commission, May 2002.

Edelstein, David. "Foreign Ministries, Sustainable Institutions". In *The Dilemmas of Statebuilding: Confronting the Contradictions of Postwar Peace Operations*, edited by Roland Paris and Timothy D. Sisk, pp. 81–103. Oxon: Routledge, 2009.

Edmondson, Beth and Stuart Levy. *Climate Change and Order: The End of Prosperity and Democracy.* New York: Palgrave Macmillan, 2013.

———. *International Relations: Nurturing Reality.* Frenchs Forest, NSW: Pearson, 2008.

Edwards, Peter. "Two Cheers for Forward Defence". *The Strategist*. Canberra: Australian Strategic Policy Institute, 29 May 2015.

Elman, Miriam Fendius. "The Foreign Policy of Small States: Challenging Neorealism in its Own Backyard". *British Journal of Political Science* 25, no. 2 (1995): 171–217.

Emmers, Ralf. "The Influence of the Balance of Power Factor within the ASEAN Regional Forum". *Contemporary Southeast Asia* 23, no. 2 (2000): 275–91.

Emmerson, Donald. "Challenging ASEAN: A Topological View". *Contemporary Southeast Asia* 29, no. 3 (2007): 424–46.

———. "'Southeast Asia': What's in a Name?" *Journal of Southeast Asian Studies* 15, no. 1 (March 1984): 1–21.

Erman, Eva. "The Recognitive Practices of Declaring and Constituting Statehood". *International Theory* 5 (2013): 129–50.

Escobar, Arturo. *Encountering Development: The Making and Unmaking of the Third World.* Princeton: Princeton University Press, 2011.

Evans, Damon. "East Timor's Gas Dream is Doomed, ConocoPhillips and Woodside have Failed". *Forbes*, 12 December 2016.

Evans, Gareth. "Indonesia and East Timor: Looking Back and Looking Forward", 27 September 1999. Available at <http://www.gevans.org/speeches/speech442I&ET1999.html> (accessed 4 February 2017).

———. "Foreign Policy and Good International Citizenship", 6 March 1990. Available at <http://www.gevans.org/speeches/old/1990/060390_fm_fpandgoodinternationalcitizen.pdf> (accessed 26 March 2017).

Ewin, Robert. "Peoples and Political Obligation". *Macquarie Law Journal* 3 (2003): 13–28.
Fabry, Mikulas. "Theorizing State Recognition". *International Theory* 5 (2013): 165–70.
———. *Recognizing States: International Society and the Establishment of New States since 1776*. Oxford: Oxford University Press, 2010.
Falk, Richard. "The East Timor Ordeal: International Law and its Limits". In *Bitter Flowers, Sweet Flowers: East Timor, Indonesia and the World Community*, edited by Richard Tanter, Mark Selden and Stephen R. Shalom, pp. 149–61. Annandale, New South Wales: Pluto Press Australia, 2001.
Fan, Hua. "The Missing Link between Self-Determination and Democracy: The Case of East Timor". *Northwestern Journal of International Human Rights* 6, no. 1 (2007): 176–95.
Farram, Steven. "The Two Timors: The Partitioning of Timor by the Portuguese and Dutch". *Studies in Languages and Culture of East Timor* 2 (1999): 38–54.
Fearon, James and David Laitin. "Neo-Trusteeship and the Problem of Weak States". *International Security* 28, no. 4 (2004): 5–43.
Federer, Juan. *The UN in East Timor: Building Timor-Leste, a Fragile State*. Darwin: Charles Darwin University Press, 2005.
Feijó, Rui Graça. *Dynamics of Democracy in Timor-Leste, 1999–2012*. Amsterdam: Amsterdam University Press, 2016.
———. "Challenges to the Consolidation of Democracy". In *A New Era? Timor-Leste After the UN*, edited by Sue Ingram, Lia Kent and Andrew McWilliam, pp. 59–70. Canberra: ANU Press, 2015.
Fenby, Simon. "The g7+ Group of Fragile States: Towards Better International Engagement and Accountability in Aid Delivery to Fragile Nations". In *Critical Reflections on Development*, edited by Damien Kingsbury, pp. 33–49. London: Palgrave Macmillan, 2013.
Fernandes, Clinton. *The Independence of East Timor: Multi-Dimensional Perspectives – Occupation, Resistance, and International Political Activism*. Brighton: Sussex Academic Press, 2011.
———. *Reluctant Saviours: Australia, Indonesia and the Independence of East Timor*. Melbourne: Scribe Publications, 2004.
Fernida, Indria. "Four Years of Final Report of Indonesia–Timor-Leste Commission of Truth and Friendship (CTF): Recommendation Without Any Implementation". *East Timor Law and Justice Bulletin* (16 July 2012).
Flitton, Daniel. "Economies of Scales: Depleted Stocks Force Asian Fishermen into Australian Waters". *The Age*, 25 February 2017.
Food and Agricultural Organization (FAO). *Global Watch GIEWS: Timor Leste*. The Food and Agriculture Organization of the United Nations, 2010.

Foreign Policy. "Fragile States Index 2015". Available at <http://foreignpolicy.com/fragile-states-index-2016-brexit-syria-refugee-europe-anti-migrant-boko-haram/> (accessed 20 February 2017).

Fox, James. "Tracing the Path, Recounting the Past: Historical Perspectives on Timor". In *Out of the Ashes*, edited by James J. Fox and Dionisio Babo-Soares, pp. 1–27. Canberra: ANU E Press, 2000.

Franck, Thomas M. "The Emerging Right of Democratic Governance". *The American Journal of International Law* 86, no. 1 (January 1992): 46–91.

Franck, Thomas M. and Paul Hoffman. "The Right of Self-Determination in Very Small Places". *New York University Journal of International Law and Politics* 8 (1975/76): 332–86.

Fukuyama, Francis. *State-Building: Governance and World Order in the Twenty-First Century*. Ithaca: Cornell University Press, 2004.

Fund for Peace, The. *Fragile States Index 2016*. Washington: Fund for Peace, 2016.

Fundasaun Mahein. "Timor-Leste Must Prepare for New Patrol Boats", 8 November 2017.

g7+. "Annual Report". Lome, Togo, 2014. Available at <http://www.g7plus.org/sites/default/files/resources/g7%2B-Annual-Report-2013.pdf> (accessed 15 May 2017).

———. "Haiti Declaration: Port-au-Prince", 14 November 2012. Available at <http://www.g7plus.org/en/resources/haiti-declaration-port-au-prince-14-november-2012> (accessed 15 May 2017).

———. "A New Deal for Engagement in Fragile States", 2011. Available at <http://www.g7plus.org/en/new-deal/document> (accessed 15 February 2017).

Ganesan. "Singapore: Realist cum Trading State". In *Asian Security Practice: Material and Ideational Influences*, edited by Muthiah Alagappa, pp. 579–607. California: Stanford University Press, 1998.

Garrison, Randall. *The Role of Constitution-Building Processes in Democratization Case Study: East Timor*. Stockholm: International Institute for Democracy and Electoral Assistance, 2005.

Ghani, Ashraf and Clare Lockhart. *Fixing Failed States: A Framework for Rebuilding a Fractured World*. Oxford: Oxford University Press, 2009.

Gill, Bates, Evelyn Goh and Chin-Hao Huang. *The Dynamics of US–China–Southeast Asia Relations*. Sydney: The United States Studies Centre at the University of Sydney, 2006.

Gillard, Julia. "Moving Australia Forward". Lowy Institute, Sydney, 6 July 2010.

Global Security. "Armed Forces of Timor-Leste (F-FDTL)". Available at <http://www.globalsecurity.org/military/world/timor/f-fdtl.htm> (accessed 11 February 2017).

Goh, Evelyn. "Understanding 'Hedging' in Asia-Pacific Security". *Pacnet* 43 (2006).
———. "Meeting the China Challenge: The U.S. in Southeast Asian Regional Security Strategies". *Policy Studies* 16 (2005).
Goncalves, Ivo Mateus. "Portugal in East Timor: Civilization at What Cost?". *Life at Aitarak Laran*, 24 November 2015. Available at <https://aitaraklaranlive.wordpress.com/2015/11/24/portugal-in-east-timor-civilization-at-what-cost/> (accessed 15 February 2017).
Gorjão, Paulo. "The Legacy and Lessons of the United Nations Transitional Administration in East Timor". *Contemporary Southeast Asia* 24, no. 2 (2002): 313–36.
Government of Australia. *2016 Defence Economic Trends in the Asia-Pacific*. DIO Reference Aid 16–512. Canberra: Department of Defence, Government of Australia, August 2016.
———. "Minutes: Decision No. 116". Canberra, 29 March 1983.
Graham, L. Bennett. "No to an International Blasphemy Law". *The Guardian*, 26 March 2010.
Gray, Andrew. "The People of East Timor and Their Struggle for Survival". In *East Timor: The Struggle Continues*, edited by Torben Retboll. Copenhagen: IWGIA International Work Group for Indigenous Affairs, 1984.
Greenhill, Brian. "Recognition and Collective Identity Formation in International Relations". *European Journal of International Relations* 14, no. 2 (2008): 343–68.
Grenfell, Damien. "Governance, Violence and Crises in Timor-Leste: Estadu Seidauk Mai". In *Democratic Governance in Timor-Leste: Reconciling the Local and the National*, edited by David Mearns and Stevens Farram, pp. 85–97. Darwin: Charles Darwin University Press, 2008.
Grenville, Stephen. "East Timor Maritime Boundary: The 'Equidistance' Principle". *Lowy Interpreter*, 24 February 2016.
———. "East Timor, Australia and the 'Timor Gap'". *Lowy Interpreter*, 25 November 2014.
Griffths, Ryan. "Admission to the Sovereignty Club: The Past, Present and Future of the International Recognition Regime". *Territory, Politics, Governance* 5, no. 2 (2016): 1–13. Grimm, Sonja, Nicolas Lemay-Hebert, and Olivier Nay. "'Fragile States': Introducing a Political Concept". *Third World Quarterly* 35, no. 2 (2014): 197–209.
Grimm, Sonja, Nicolas Lemay-Hebert, and Olivier Nay. "'Fragile States': Introducing a Political Concept". *Third World Quarterly* 35, no. 2 (2014): 197–209.
Guedes, Armando Marques. "Thinking East Timor, Indonesia and Southeast Asia". *Lusotopie* (2001): 315–25.
Gunn, Geoffrey. "The Five Hundred Year Timorese Funu". In *Bitter Flowers, Sweet Flowers: East Timor, Indonesia and the World Community*, edited by Richard

Tanter, Mark Selden and Steven Shalom, pp. 3–14. Annandale: Pluto Press Australia, 2001.

———. *Timor Loro Sae: 500 Years*. Hong Kong: Livros do Oriente, 1999.

Gusmão, Xanana. Address by His Excellency The Prime Minister Kay Rala Xanana Gusmão at the 69th Session of the United Nations General Assembly. New York, 25 September 2014.

———. "Peace and Capable Institutions as Stand-alone Goals in the post-2015 Development Agenda". Keynote Address by His Excellency the Prime Minister Kay Rala Xanana Gusmão at the High-Level Ministerial Lunch Meeting. New York, 22 September 2014.

———. "Alliance of Civilizations". Address by His Excellency the Prime Minister of the Democratic Republic of Timor-Leste Kay Rala Xanana Gusmão to the Sixth Global Forum United Nations Alliance of Civilizations. Bali, 29 August 2014.

———. Speech by His Excellency the Prime Minister of the Democratic Republic of Timor-Leste Kay Rala Xanana Gusmão at the Farewell Dinner for their Excellencies Dr H. Susilo Bambang Yudhoyono and Madam HJ. Ani Bambang Yudhoyono, President and First Lady of the Republic of Indonesia. Dili, 26 August 2014.

———. "Peace, Security and Human Development". Address by His Excellency the Prime Minister Kay Rala Xanana Gusmão on the Occasion of the World Summit 2014. Seoul, 10 August 2014.

———. Address by His Excellency the Prime Minister Kay Rala Xanana Gusmão to the 2014 Timor-Leste Development Partners' Meeting. Dili, 25 July 2014.

———. "Timor-Leste and ASEAN: Perspectives and Challenges". Address by His Excellency the Prime Minister and Minister of Defence and Security, Kay Rala Xanana Gusmão. Sabah, Malaysia, 2 April 2014.

———. Address by His Excellency the Prime Minister of the Democratic Republic of Timor-Leste Kay Rala Xanana Gusmão at the Forum on Trade and Investment Opportunities in Timor-Leste. Kuala Lumpur, Malaysia, 1 April 2014.

———. Address by His Excellency the Prime Minister of the Democratic Republic of Timor-Leste Kay Rala Xanana Gusmão to the United Nations Economic and Social Commission of Asia and the Pacific Ministerial Conference on Regional Economic Cooperation and Integration in Asia and the Pacific. Bangkok, 19 December 2013.

———. "Sharing Experiences". Lecture by His Excellency the Prime Minister of the Democratic Republic of Timor-Leste Kay Rala Xanana Gusmão. Juba, South Sudan, 2 December 2013.

———. "Consolidating Democracy in a Pluralist Society". Address by His Excellency the Prime Minister Kay Rala Xanana Gusmão on the Occasion of the Bali Democracy Forum. Bali, 7 November 2013.

———. "Peace Building and State Building: From Fragility to Resilience". Lecture by His Excellency the Prime Minister of the Democratic Republic of Timor-Leste Kay Rala Xanana Gusmão at the Lee Kuan Yew School of Public Policy at the National University of Singapore. Dili, 18 September 2013.

———. "State Building: The Timor-Leste Experience in a Southeast Asian Context". Address by His Excellency the Prime Minister Kay Rala Xanana Gusmão at the Vietnam University. Hanoi, Vietnam, 3 September 2013.

———. "Harnessing Natural Resource Wealth for Inclusive Growth and Economic Development". Keynote Address by His Excellency the Prime Minister Kay Rala Xanana Gusmão. Dili, 4 June 2013.

———. "Timor-Leste's Role and Future in a Rising Asia Pacific". Singapore, 4 June 2013.

———. Address by His Excellency the Prime Minister, Kay Rala Xanana Gusmão on the Occasion of the Lunch Hosted by International Enterprise Singapore. Singapore, 3 June 2013.

———. "g7+ Ministerial Meeting in Togo". Address by His Excellency the Prime Minister of the Democratic Republic of Timor-Leste Kay Rala Xanana Gusmão. Togo, 29 May 2013.

———. Address by His Excellency the Prime Minister and Minister of Defence and Security Kay Rala Xanana Gusmão at the Inauguration of the Building of the Ministry of Defence and F-FDTL Headquarters. Fatuhada, Dili, 3 April 2012.

———. "Military Operations Other than War: Regional and National Perspectives". Address by His Excellency the Prime Minister and Minister of Defence and Security, Kay Rala Xanana Gusmão, on the Occasion of the Second Jakarta International Defence Dialogue. Jakarta, 21 March 2012.

———. "Goodbye Conflict, Welcome Development: The Timor-Leste Experience". Address by His Excellency the Prime Minister of the Democratic Republic of Timor-Leste Kay Rala Xanana Gusmão at John Hopkins University. Washington D.C., 24 February 2011.

———. "Reviewing Resistance and Understanding the Present". Lecture by His Excellency the Prime Minister and Minister for Defence and Security Kay Rala Xanana Gusmão on the Strategic Framework Module for Timor-Leste Within the Pilot Course on Defence and Security. Dili, 9 November 2010.

———. Speech by His Excellency the Prime Minister and Minister for Defence and Security Kay Rala Xanana Gusmão at the Handover Ceremony of the Two Patrol Boats Class Jaco. Dili, 11 June 2010.

———. "New Year's Message". Dili, 31 December 2000.

Haacke, Jurgen. "South-East Asia's International Relations and Security Perspectives". In *East and Southeast Asia: International Relations and Security*

Perspectives, edited by Andrew T.H. Tan, pp. 154–66. Oxon: Routledge, 2013.

Habib, Benjamin. "Climate Change, Security and Regime Formation in East Asia". In *Non-Traditional Security in East Asia*, edited by Ramon Racheco Pardo and Jeffrey Reeves, pp. 49–72. London: Imperial College Press, 2016.

Hägerdal, Hans. "Servião and Belu: Colonial Conceptions and the Geographical Partition of Timor". *Studies on Asia* 3, no. 1 (Spring 2006): 49–64.

Hajek, John. "Language Planning and the Sociolinguistic Environment in East Timor: Colonial Practice and Changing Language Ecologies". *Current Issues in Language Planning* 1 (2000): 400–13.

Halper, Stefan. *The Beijing Consensus: How China's Authoritarian Model Will Dominate the Twenty-First Century*. New York: Basic Books, 2010.

Handel, Michael. "Weak States in the International System". In *Small States in International Relations*, edited by Christine Ingebritsen, pp. 149–92. Washington: University of Washington Press, 2006.

Hannum, Hurst. *Autonomy, Sovereignty, and Self-Determination: The Accommodation of Conflicting Rights*. Philadelphia: University of Philadelphia Press, 1990.

Harris, Vandra and Andrew Goldsmith. "The Struggle for Independence was Just the Beginning". In *Security, Development and Nation-Building in Timor-Leste*, edited by Vandra Harris and Andrew Goldsmith, pp. 3–16. Oxon: Routledge, 2011.

———, eds. *Security, Development and Nation-Building in Timor-Leste: A Cross-Sectoral Assessment*. Oxon: Routledge, 2011.

Hegarty, Matt. *China's Growing Influence in South-West Pacific: Australian Policies that Could Respond to China's Intentions and Objectives*. Canberra: Australian Defence College, March 2015.

Heiser, Anthony. "East Timor and the Joint Petroleum Development Area". *Australian and New Zealand Maritime Law Journal* 17 (2003): 54–79.

Heiser, Walter. "The Future of Hydropower Development in Timor Leste". *International Journal of Hydropower and Dams* 22, no. 2 (2015): 78–81.

Helman, Gerald and Steven Ratner. "Saving Failed States". *Foreign Affairs* 89 (Winter 1992–93): 3–20.

Henry, Iain. "Unintended Consequences: An Examination of Australia's 'Historic Policy Shift' on East Timor". *Australian Journal of International Affairs* 68, no. 1 (2014): 52–69.

Herz, John. "Rise and Demise of the Territorial State". *World Politics* 9, no. 4 (1957): 479–93.

———. "Idealist Internationalism and the Security Dilemma". *World Politics* 2, no. 2 (1950): 157–80.

Hey, Jeanne. "Introducing Small State Foreign Policy". In *Small States in World Politics: Explaining Foreign Policy Behaviour*, edited by Jeanne Hey, pp. 1–12. Boulder: Lynne Rienner Publishers, 2003.

Hicks, David. *Tetum Ghosts and Kin: Fertility and Gender in East Timor*. Long Grove, Illinois: Waveland Press, 2004.

Hill, Hal and Joao M. Saldanha, eds. *East Timor: Development Challenges for the World's Newest Nation*. Singapore: Institute of Southeast Asian Studies, 2001.

Hill, Helen. *The Timor Story*. Melbourne: Timor Information Service, 1976.

Hirst, Megan. *An Unfinished Truth: An Analysis of the Commission of Truth and Friendship's Final Report on the 1999 Atrocities in East Timor*. New York: International Center for Transitional Justice, January 2009.

———. *Too Much Friendship Too Little Truth*. New York: International Center for Transitional Justice, January 2008.

Hohe, Tanja. "The Clash of Paradigms: International Administration and Local Political Legitimacy in East Timor". *Contemporary Southeast Asia* 24, no. 3 (December 2002): 569–89.

Homer-Dixon, Thomas. "On the Threshold: Environmental Changes as Causes of Acute Conflict". *International Security* 16, no. 2 (1991): 76–116.

Horta, Loro. "Timor-Leste: The Dragon's Newest Friend". *Irasec Discussion Papers* no. 4 (May 2009).

Howard, Jessica. "Invoking State Responsibility for Aiding the Commission of International Crimes: Australia, the United States and the Question of East Timor". *Melbourne Journal of International Law* 2, no. 1 (2001).

Hughes, Caroline. *Dependent Communities: Aid and Politics in Cambodia and East Timor*. Ithaca: Cornell Southeast Asia Program, 2009.

Hull, Geoffrey. "East Timor and Indonesia: The Cultural Factors of Incompatibility". *Studies in Languages and Cultures of East Timor* 2 (1999).

Human Rights Watch. "Justice Denied in East Timor", 20 December 2002. Available at <http://www.hrw.org/legacy/backgrounder/asia/timor/etimor1202bg.htm> (accessed 24 March 2015).

Huntington, Samuel. *The Third Wave: Democratization in the Late Twentieth Century*. Oklahoma: University of Oklahoma Press, 1991.

Hutt, David. "Is China's Influence in Timor-Leste Rising?" *The Diplomat*, 19 November 2016.

Ikenberry, G. John. *After Victory: Institutions, Strategic Restraint, and the Rebuilding of Order after Major Wars*. New Jersey: Princeton University Press, 2001.

Ikenberry, G. John and Tsuchiyama, Jitsuo. "Between Balance of Power and Community: The Future of Multilateral Security Co-operation in the Asia-Pacific". *International Relations of the Asia-Pacific* 2 (2002): 69–94.

Inayatullah, Naeem. "Beyond the Sovereignty Dilemma: Quasi-States as Social Construct". In *State Sovereignty as Social Construct*, edited by Thomas Biersteker and Cynthia Weber, pp. 50–80. Cambridge: Cambridge University Press, 1996.

Ingebritsen, Christine. "Norm Entrepreneurs: Scandinavia's Role in World Politics". *Cooperation and Conflict: Journal of the Nordic International Studies Association* 37, no. 1 (2002): 11–23.

Ingram, Sue, Lia Kent and Andrew McWilliam, eds. *A New Era? Timor-Leste After the UN*. Canberra: Australian National University Press, 2015.

Institute for Economics and Peace. "Global Peace Index 2016". Available at <www.economicsandpeace.org> (accessed 11 February 2017).

International Center for Transitional Justice. *Unfulfilled Expectations: Victims Perception of Justice and Reparations in Timor-Leste*. Brussels: International Center for Transitional Justice, 2 December 2010.

———. *Security Sector Reform in Timor-Leste*. Brussels: Initiative for Peacebuilding Security Cluster, June 2009.

International Court of Justice. "Questions Relating to the Seizure and Detention of Certain Documents and Data (Timor-Leste v. Australia): Case Removed from the Court's List at the Request of Timor-Leste". Press Release, 12 June 2015. Available at <http://www.icj-cij.org/docket/files/156/18692.pdf> (accessed 27 February 2017).

———. "Case Concerning East Timor (Portugal v Australia): Judgement of 30 June 1995", 1995. Available at <http://www.icj-cij.org/files/case-related/84/6951.pdf> (accessed 2 February 2017).

International Criminal Court. "Rome Statute of the International Criminal Court". United Nations Document A/CONF. 183/9, 17 July 1998.

International Crisis Group. "Timor Leste: Oecusse and the Indonesian Border". *Asia Briefing* No. 104. Dili/Brussels: International Crisis Group, 20 May 2010.

———. "Timor-Leste: No Time for Complacency". *Asia Briefing* No. 87. Dili/Brussels: International Crisis Group, 9 February 2009.

International Energy Agency. *World Energy Outlook 2016: Executive Summary*. France: OECD, 2016.

International Monetary Fund (IMF). "Republic of Timor-Leste: Article IV Consultation – Press Release; Staff Report; and Statement by the Executive Director for Timor-Leste". International Monetary Fund Country Report No. 16/183. Washington D.C.: IMF, June 2016.

———. "Democratic Republic of Timor-Leste: Selected Issues and Statistical Appendix". Country Report No. 07/86. Washington D.C.: IMF, February 2007.

International Peace Academy. "The Security-Development Nexus: Conflict, Peace and Development in the 21st Century". New York: International Peace Academy, 2004.

Jackson, Robert. *Quasi-States: Sovereignty, International Relations and the Third World*. Cambridge: Cambridge University Press, 1990.

———. "Quasi-States, Dual Regimes, and Neo-Classical Theory: International Jurisprudence and the Third World". *International Organization* 41, no. 4 (Autumn 1987): 519–49.

Jackson, Robert and Carl Rosberg. "Why Africa's Weak States Persist: The Empirical and the Juridical in Statehood". *World Politics* 35, no. 1 (October 1982): 1–24.

Jakarta Post. "Truth at Last?", 2 April 2008.

Jannisa, Gudman. *The Crocodile's Tears: East Timor in the Making*. Lund: Lund University, 1997.

Jervis, Robert. "Cooperation under the Security Dilemma", *World Politics* 30, no. 2 (January 1978): 167–214.

Job, Brian. "Introduction". In *The Insecurity Dilemma: National Security of Third World States*, edited by Brian Job, pp. 1–21. Boulder: Lynne Rienner Publishers, 1992.

Jolliffe, Jill. "Ramos-Horta Shot Twice". *The Sydney Morning Herald*, 11 February 2008.

———. "East Timor says China is its Closest Ally". *The Sydney Morning Herald*, 11 July 2002.

———. *East Timor: Nationalism and Colonialism*. St. Lucia, Qld: University of Queensland Press, 1978.

Jomal de Notícias. "Timor-Leste aprova doação a Portugal de dois milhões de euros para ajuda aos fogos". *Jomal de Notícias*, 10 August 2016.

Jones, Lee. *ASEAN, Sovereignty and Intervention in Southeast Asia*. Houndmills, UK: Palgrave Macmillan, 2012.

Judicial System Monitoring Program (JSMP). "JSMP Appeals to Indonesian Government to Implement Keppres 71/2011 on Forced Disappearances". *East Timor Law and Justice Bulletin* (6 November 2012).

———. "Justice Not Served by Truth and Friendship Commission". *Justice Update*, July 2008.

———. "'Commission of Truth and Friendship' Seeks to End the Search for Justice Whilst 'Commission of Experts' Keeps It Alive". JSMP Press Release, 14 March 2005.

———. "'Truth and Friendship Commission': More Friendship, Less Truth, Impunity from the Law". JSMP Press Release, 14 January 2005.

Karl, Terry Lynn. "The Perils of the Petro-State: Reflections on the Paradox of Plenty". *Journal of International Affairs* 53, no. 1 (1999): 31–48.

Kartasasmuta, Sabana. *The Quest for a Solution*. Singapore: Crescent Design Associates, 1998.

Katzenstein, Peter. "Introduction: Alternative Perspectives on National Security". *The Culture of National Security: Norms and Identity in World Politics*. New York: Columbia University Press, 1996.

Katzenstein, Suzanne. "Hybrid Tribunals: Searching for Justice in East Timor". *Harvard Human Rights Journal* 16 (2003): 246–78.

Ken'ichi, Goto. "Multilayered Postcolonial Historical Space: Indonesia, the Netherlands, Japan and East Timor". Creation of a New Contemporary Asian Studies Working Paper 2. Tokyo: Waseda University, 2004.

Kennedy, Scott. "The Myth of the Beijing Consensus". *Journal of Contemporary China* 19, no. 65 (2010): 461–77.

Keohane, Robert. "'Lilliputians' Dilemma: Small States in International Politics". *International Organization* 23 (1969): 291–310.

Kessler, Oliver and Benjamin Herborth. "Recognition and the Constitution of Social Order". *International Theory* (2013): 155–60.

King, Peter. "Redefining South Pacific Security: Greening and Domestication". *The South Pacific: Problems, Issues and Prospects*, edited by Ramesh Thakur, pp. 45–64. Hampshire and London: Palgrave Macmillan, 1991.

Kingsbury, Damien. "China's Interest in East Timor". *Deakin Speaking*, 10 August 2012. Available at <https://blogs.deakin.edu.au/deakin-speaking/2012/08/10/chinas-interests-in-east-timor/> (accessed 19 February 2017).

―――. *East Timor: The Price of Liberty*. New York: Palgrave Macmillan, 2009.

―――. "Political Developments". In *East Timor: Beyond Independence*, edited by Damien Kingsbury and Michael Leach, pp. 19–28. Clayton: Monash University Press, 2007.

―――. "East Timor Border Security". In *Violence in Between: Conflict and Security in Archipelagic Southeast Asia*, edited by Damien Kingsbury, pp. 277–97. Clayton: Monash University Press, 2005.

―――. "The TNI and the Militias". In *Guns and Ballot Boxes: East Timor's Vote for Independence*, edited by Damien Kingsbury, pp. 69–80. Clayton, Victoria: Monash Asia Institute, 2000.

Kingsbury, Damien and Michael Leach. "Introduction". In *East Timor: Beyond Independence*, edited by Damien Kingsbury and Michael Leach, pp. 1–18. Clayton: Monash University Press, 2007.

Kingston, Jeffrey. "Balancing Justice and Reconciliation in East Timor". *Critical Asian Studies* 38, no. 3 (2006): 271–302.

Kinsella, Naomi and Soren Blau. "Searching for Conflict Related Missing Persons in Timor-Leste: Technical, Politics and Cultural Considerations". *Stability: International Journal of Security and Development* 2, no. 1 (2013): 1–14.

Klare, Michael. *Resource Wars: The New Landscape of Global Conflict*. New York: Holt, 2001.

KontraS, Timor-Leste National Alliance for an International Tribunal, and Amnesty International. "Timor-Leste/Indonesia: Calls on Truth and Reparation made by Bilateral Truth Commission 'Ignored'". ASA 57/002/2013, 7 July 2013.

Kraska, James. "China's Maritime Militia Upends Rules on Naval Warfare". *The Diplomat*, 10 August 2015.

Krasner, Stephen. "Recognition: Organised Hypocrisy Once Again". *International Theory* 5, no. 1 (2013): 170–76.

———. "Sharing Sovereignty: New Institutions for Collapsed and Failing States". *International Security* 29, no. 2 (2004): 85–120.

———. "Abiding Sovereignty". *International Political Science Review* 22, no. 3 (2001): 229–51.

Krieger, Heike. *East Timor and the International Community: Basic Documents*. Cambridge: Cambridge University Press, 1997.

Krishna, Sankaran. *Postcolonial Insecurities: India, Sri Lanka and the Question of Nationhood*. Minneapolis and London: University of Minneapolis, 1999.

Kyodo. "Japan, East Timor serve up Veiled Criticism of China over Maritime Rows". *Japan Times*, 15 March 2016.

Labs, Eric. "Do Weak States Bandwagon?". *Security Studies* 1, no. 3 (1992): 383–416.

La'o Hamutuk. "Timor-Leste's Private Investment Law and Policy", 30 March 2016. Available at <https://www.laohamutuk.org/econ/invest/16InvestPolicy.htm> (accessed 10 March 2017).

———. "La'o Hamutuk Submission on the Proposed Private Investment Policy", 29 March 2016. Available at <https://www.laohamutuk.org/econ/invest/LHSubMECAEInvestLaw29Mar2016en.pdf> (accessed 27 February 2017).

———. "2016 Budget Proposal Puts Fantasies Before People's Needs", 8 November 2015. Available at <http://laohamutuk.blogspot.com.au/2015/11/2016-budget-proposal-puts-fantasies.html> (accessed 26 February 2017).

———. "La'o Hamutuk: Oil Running Out is Reality, Not Propaganda". Dili, 15 June 2015. Available at <http://www.laohamutuk.org/econ/model/RespostaMina15Jun2015en.pdf> (accessed 26 February 2017).

———. "Timor-Leste's Oil and Gas are Going Fast". Dili, 15 April 2015. Available at <http://laohamutuk.blogspot.com.au/2015/04/timor-lestes-oil-and-gas-are-going-fast.html> (accessed 26 February 2017).

———. "Summary of New Tax Laws", 14 July 2008. Available at <https://www.laohamutuk.org/misc/AMPGovt/tax/NewTaxLaw08.htm> (accessed 10 March 2017).

———. *The La'o Hamutuk Bulletin* 6, no. 13 (August 2005).

Leach, Michael. *Nation Building and National Identity in Timor-Leste*. Oxon: Routledge, 2017.

———. "The Politics of History in Timor-Leste". In *A New Era? Timor-Leste After the UN*, edited by Sue Ingram, Lia Kent and Andrew McWilliam, pp. 41–58. Canberra: Australian National University Press, 2015.

———. "Talking Portuguese: China and East Timor". *Arena* 92 (2007–8): 6–8.

———. "Valorising the Resistance: National Identity and Collective Memory in East Timor's Constitution". *Social Alternatives* 21, no. 3 (Winter 2002): 43–47.
Leach, Michael and Damien Kingsbury, eds. *The Politics of Timor-Leste: Democratic Consolidation After Intervention*. Ithaca: Cornell, 2014.
Leach, Michael and Sally Percival-Wood. "Timor-Leste: From INTERFET to ASEAN". In *The Australia–ASEAN Dialogue: Tracing 40 Years of Partnership*, edited by Baogang He and Sally Percival-Wood, pp. 67–85. New York: Palgrave Macmillan, 2014.
Leadbeater, Marie. *Negligent Neighbour: New Zealand's Complicity in the Invasion and Occupation of Timor-Leste*. Nelson: Craig Potton Publishing, 2006.
Lebow, Ned. *Politics and Ethics of Identity: In Search of Ourselves*. New York: Cambridge University Press, 2012.
Leifer, Michael. *Singapore's Foreign Policy: Coping with Vulnerability*. London: Routledge, 2000.
———. "Southeast Asia". In *Foreign Policy Making in Developing States: A Comparative Approach*, edited by Christopher Clapham, pp. 17–41. New York: Praegar, 1977.
Lindemann, Thomas. *Causes of War: The Struggle for Recognition*. Colchester: ECPR Press, 2010.
Linklater, Andrew. *The Transformation of Political Community*. Cambridge: Polity Press, 1998.
Linton, Suzannah. "Cambodia, East Timor and Sierra Leone: Experiments in International Justice". *Criminal Law Forum* 12 (2001): 185–246.
Lipscomb, Leigh-Ashley. "Beyond the Truth: Can Reparations Move Peace and Justice Forward in Timor-Leste?" *Asia Pacific* 93 (Honolulu: East-West Centre, March 2010).
Lloyd, Grayson. "The Diplomacy on East Timor: Indonesia, the United Nations and the International Community". In *Out of the Ashes: Destruction and Reconstruction of East Timor*, edited by James J. Fox and Dionisio Babo-Soares, pp. 79–105. South Australia: Crawford House Publishing, 2000.
Locke, Sarina. "Australian Agricultural Researchers Help Lift Timorese Farmers Out of Dire Poverty". *Australian Broadcasting Corporation*, 2 May 2016.
Lowe, Vaughan, Christopher Carelton and Christopher Ward. "In the Matter of East Timor". *Legal Opinion on East Timor Maritime Boundaries provided to Petrotimor*, 11 April 2002.
Lowry, Bob. "After the 2006 Crisis: Australian Interests in Timor-Leste". *Strategic Insights* 38. Canberra: Australian Strategic Policy Institute, November 2007.
Lundahl, Mats and Fredrik Sjöholm. "The Oil Resources of Timor-Leste: Curse or Blessing?" *The Pacific Review* 21, no. 1 (2008): 67–86.
Lusa. "Cimeira CPLP: Declaração sobre Timor-Leste apoia independência", 18 July 2000.

Maass, Matthais. "Small Enough to Fail: The Structural Irrelevance of the Small State as Cause of its Elimination and Proliferation since Westphalia". *Cambridge Review of International Affairs* (2017): 1–12.

MacQueen, Norrie. "United Nations Integrated Mission in Timor-Leste (UNMIT)". In *The Oxford Handbook of UN Peacekeeping Operations*, edited by Joachim Koops, Noorie McQueen, Thierry Tardy and Paul Williams, pp. 755–66. Oxford: Oxford University Press, 2015.

———. "United Nations Transitional Administration in East Timor (UNMIT)". In *The Oxford Handbook of UN Peacekeeping Operations*, edited by Joachim Koops, Noorie McQueen, Thierry Tardy and Paul Williams, pp. 642–55. Oxford: Oxford University Press, 2015.

———. "A Community of Illusions? Portugal, the CPLP and Peacemaking in Guiné-Bissau". *International Peacekeeping* 10, no. 2 (June 2003): 2–26.

Madaus, Roman. "The Bear Returns to the South Pacific: Russia Sends Arms to Fiji". *The Diplomat*, 9 April 2016.

Magalhães, Fidelis. "Past, Present and Future". In *A New Era? Timor-Leste after the UN Intervention*, edited by Sue Ingram, Lia Kent and Andrew McWilliam, pp. 31–40. Canberra: ANU Press, 2015.

Makoni, Sinfree and Cristine Severo. "Lusitanization and Bakhtinian Perspectives on the Role of Portuguese in Angola and East Timor". *Journal of Multilingual and Multicultural Development* 36, no. 2 (2014): 151–62.

Marker, Jamsheed. *East Timor: A Memoir of the Negotiations for Independence*. Jefferson: MacFarland, 2003.

Marriott, Andrew. "The Justice Sector: Achievements, Challenges and Comparisons". In *Politics of Timor-Leste: Democratic Consolidation after Intervention*, edited by Michael Leach and Damien Kingsbury, pp. 99–120. Ithaca, NY: Cornell University Press, 2013.

Martin, Ian. *Self-Determination in East Timor: The United Nations, the Ballot, and International Intervention*. Boulder, Colorado: Lynne Rienner Publishers, 2001.

Marx, Susan. "Timor-Leste's Non-Oil Economy Must Look to Tourism". *Asia Foundation*, 22 July 2016.

Matsuda, Matt. "The Pacific". *The American Historical Review* 11, no. 3 (June 2006): 758–80.

Matsuno, Aksuno. "The UN Transitional Administration and Democracy Building in Timor-Leste". In *Democratic Governance in Timor-Leste: Reconciling the Local and the National*, edited by David Mearns and Steven Farram, pp. 52–70. Darwin: Charles Darwin University Press, 2008.

McCann, Linda. *The Future of Australia's Pacific Patrol Boat Program*. Canberra: Centre for Defence and Strategic Studies, Australian Defence College, August 2013.

McDonald, Hamish. "Boundary Row Escalates as Finances Deteriorate". *Nikkei Asian Review*, 20 November 2015.

McDonald, Hamish and Richard Tanter. "Introduction". In *Masters of Terror: Indonesia's Military and Violence in Timor-Leste*, edited by Richard Tanter, Desmond Ball and Geert Arend Van Klinken, pp. 1–12. Lanham, Maryland: Rowman and Littlefield Publishers, 2006.

McDougall, Derek. "The Security-Development Nexus: Comparing External Interventions and Development Strategies in Timor-Leste and Solomon Islands". *Asian Security* 6, no. 2 (2012): 170–90.

McGregor, Andrew. "Development, Foreign Aid and Post-development in Timor-Leste". *Third World Quarterly* 28, no. 1 (2007): 155–70.

McHugh, Babs. "Development of Greater Sunrise Gas Field in East Timor Could Be Decades Away". *Australian Broadcasting Commission*, 12 June 2017.

McWilliam, Andrew and Elizabeth Traube, eds. *Land and Life in Timor-Leste: Ethnographic Essay*. Canberra: ANU Press, 2011.

Mearns, David and Steven Farram, eds. *Democratic Governance in Timor-Leste: Reconciling the Local and the National*. Darwin: Charles Darwin University Press, 2008.

Mearsheimer, John. *The Tragedy of Great Power Politics*. New York: W.W. Norton: 2001.

Mendes, Nuno Canas. "Dilemas Indentitários e fatalidades geopoliticas: Timor-Leste entre o Sudeste Asiático e o Pacifico-Sul". In *Understanding Timor-Leste*, edited by Michael Leach, Nuno Canas Mendes, Antero B. da Silva, Alarico da Costa Ximenes and Bob Boughton, pp. 35–40. Hawthorn: Swinburne Press, 2010.

———. "Multidimensional Identity Construction: Challenges for State-building in East Timor". In *East Timor: How to Build a New Nation in Southeast Asia in the 21st Century?*, edited by Christine Cabasset-Semedo and Frédéric Durand, pp. 19–30. Thailand: Research Institute on Contemporary Southeast Asia, 2009.

———. *Multidimensionalidade da Construção identitária de Timor-Leste*. Lisbon: ISCSP, 2005.

Merican, Din. "Cambodia's Engagement with ASEAN: Lessons for Timor-Leste". *CICP Working Paper* 14. Cambodia: Cambodian Institute for Cooperation and Peace, 2007.

Migdal, Joel. "State Building and the Non-Nation-State". *Journal of International Affairs* 8, no. 1 (2004): 17–46.

———. *Weak Societies and Strong States*. Princeton: Princeton University Press, 1988.

Miller, David. *Citizenship and National Identity*. Malden, Massachusetts: Polity Press, 2000.

———. *On Nationality*. Oxford and New York: Oxford University Press, 1995.

Mitzen, Jennifer. "Ontological Security in World Politics: State Identity and the Security Dilemma". *European Journal of International Relations* 12, no. 3 (2006): 341–70.

Mohamed, Ali Nasser. *The Diplomacy of Micro-states*. Discussion Papers in Diplomacy, Netherlands Institute of International Relations, 2002.

Molnar, Andrea. *Timor-Leste: Politics, History, and Culture*. London and New York: Routledge, 2010.

Molyneux, Nicholas, Gil Rangel da Cruz, Robert Williams, Rebecca Andersen and Neil Turner. "Climate Change and Population Growth in Timor-Leste: Implications for Food Security". *AMBIO* 41, no. 8 (2012): 823–40.

Morrow, Jonathon and Rachel White. "The United Nations in Transitional East Timor: International Standards and the Reality of Governance". *Australian Year Book of International Law* 22, no. 1 (2002): 1–47.

Mottram, Linda. "Timor-Leste Navy Buys Chinese Boats". *ABC Radio National*, 7 June 2010.

Mouritzen, Hans. "Testing Weak-Power Theory: Three Nordic Reactions to the Soviet Coup". In *European Foreign Policy: The EC and Changing Perspectives in Europe*, edited by Walter Carlsnaes and Steve Smith, pp. 156–76. London: Sage, 1994.

———. "Tension between the Strong and the Strategies of the Weak". *Journal of Peace Research* 28, no. 2 (1991): 217–30.

Murdoch, Lindsay. "E. Timor counts cost of Chinese power plants". *Sydney Morning Herald*, 15 December 2010.

———. "Timor's Boats Buy Real Independence". *The Age*, 15 November 2010.

———. "Timorese Tweak Canberra with Patrol Boat Buys". *The Age*, 15 November 2010.

———. "Relations Strained as Timor-Leste Buys Chinese Navy Boats". *The Age*, 7 June 2010.

Nakamura, Toshi. *Reflections on the State-Institution-Building Support in Timor-Leste: Capacity Development, Integrating Missions, and Financial Challenges*. United Nations Development Programme, Oslo Governance Centre, November 2004.

Narine, Shaun. *Explaining ASEAN: Regionalism in Southeast Asia*. Boulder: Lynne Rienner, 2002.

Nashrillah, Faiz. "Jokowi Receives Highest Decoration from Timor-Leste President". *Tempo*, 26 January 2016.

National Council of Maubere Resistance. "East Timor Peace Plan". Available at <http://www.ci.uc.pt/timor/cnrm.htm> (accessed 11 February 2017).

Neves, Guteriano. "The Political Economy of Petroleum Dependency". *State, Society & Governance in Melanesia*, p. 2. Available at <http://dpa.bellschool.anu.edu.au/sites/default/files/publications/attachments/2016-04/ib-2016-6-neves.pdf> (accessed 20 February 2017).

Neves, Miguel Santos, Kusnanto Anggoro, José Amorim Dias, Alan Dupont, Francios Godement, Dato Hassan, Carolina Hernandez, Tim Huxley, Riefqi Muna, Roque Rodrigues, Leonard Sebastian and Kusuma Sntiwongse. *The Security of East Timor in the Regional Context Report*. Lisbon: Institute of Strategic and International Studies, 2002.

Nixon, Rod. *Justice and Governance in East Timor: Indigenous Approaches and the "New Subsistence State"*. Oxon: Routledge, 2013.

Non-Aligned Movement. "Members of the Non-Aligned Movement". Available at <http://www.nam.gov.za/media/040802b.htm> (accessed 14 February 2017).

Nordholt, H.G. Schulte. *The Political System of the Atoni*. The Hague: Martinus Nijhoff, 1971.

Norman, James. "Environmental Concerns for Timor-Leste Cement Project". *The Saturday Paper*, 11 February 2017.

Nye, Jr., Joseph S. "Soft Power". *Foreign Policy* 80, Twentieth Anniversary (Autumn 1990): 153–71.

Oatley, Thomas. *International Political Economy*. 5th ed. Oxon: Routledge, 2012.

Observatory of Economic Complexity. "Timor-Leste". Available at <http://atlas.media.mit.edu/en/profile/country/tls/> (accessed 27 February 2017).

Odgaard, Liselotte. "The South China Sea: ASEAN's Security Concerns about China". *Security Dialogue* 34, no. 11 (2003): 11–24.

Ohmae, Kenici. *The Borderless World: Power and Strategy in the Interlinked Economy*. New York: HarperCollins, 1994.

O'Keefe, Michael. "The Strategic Context of the New Public Diplomacy". In *The New Pacific Diplomacy*, edited by Greg Fry and Sandra Tarte, pp. 125–36. Canberra: ANU Press, 2015.

Organisation for Economic Cooperation and Development (OECD). *Fragile States 2014: Domestic Revenue Mobilisation in Fragile States*. Available at <https://www.oecd.org/dac/conflict-fragility-resilience/docs/FSR-2014.pdf> (accessed 11 February 2017).

──────. *The Paris Declaration on Aid Effectiveness and the Accra Agenda for Action*. 2005 and 2008. Available at <http://www.oecd.org/dac/effectiveness/34428351.pdf> (accessed 20 February 2017).

Organisation of African Unity. "Constitutive Act of the African Union". Lome, Togo, 11 July 2000.

Ortuoste, Maria. "Timor-Leste and ASEAN: Shaping Region and State in Southeast Asia". *Asian Journal of Political Science* 19, no. 1 (2011): 1–24.

Österud, Oyvind. "The Narrow-Gate: Entry to the Club of Sovereign States". *Review of International Studies* 23 (1997): 167–84.

Ó Súilleabháin, Andrea. *Small States at the United Nations: Diverse Perspectives, Shared Opportunities*. New York: International Peace Institute, May 2014.

Ottaway, Marina. "Rebuilding State Institutions in Collapsed States". *Development and Change* 33, no. 5 (2002): 1001–23.
Pacific-Australia Climate Change Science and Adaptation Planning Program. *Current and Future Climate of Timor-Leste*. Canberra: Australian Government, 2015.
Pacific Institute of Public Policy. "The Dili Consensus Calls For a New Deal on Global Development". Press Release, 28 February 2013. Available at <http://www.pacificpolicy.org/wp-content/uploads/2013/02/PRESS-RELEASE-Dili-Consensus1.pdf> (accessed 14 February 2017).
Pacific Island Development Forum. "Pacific Island Development Overview". Available at <http://pacificidf.org/overview/> (accessed 12 December 2016).
Pacific Islands Forum Secretariat. "The Pacific Islands Forum". Available at <http://www.forumsec.org/pages.cfm/about-us/> (accessed 14 February 2017).
Painter, Joe. *Politics, Geography and 'Political Geography'*. London: Arnold, 1995.
Palatino, Mong. "Is East Timor Now a Rich Country". *The Diplomat*, 22 August 2015.
———. "ASEAN Needs Timor-Leste". *The Diplomat*, 6 June 2011.
Pampalk, Madalena. "Accountability for Serious Crime and National Reconciliation in Timor-Leste: Progress or Wishful Thinking?" *Austrian Journal of Southeast Asian Studies* 3, no. 1 (2010): 8–30.
Panke, Diana. *Unequal Actors in Equalising Institutions: Negotiations in the United Nations General Assembly*. London: Palgrave Macmillan, 2013.
Parameswaran, Prashanth. "When Will Timor-Leste Join ASEAN?" *The Diplomat*, 6 October 2016.
Paris, Roland. "Saving Liberal Peacebuilding". *Review of International Studies* 36 (2010): 337–65.
Paris, Roland and Timothy Sisk, eds. *The Dilemmas of Statebuilding: Confronting the Contradictions of Postwar Peace Operations*. New York: Routledge, 2009.
Pasandideh, Shahryar. "Australia Launches New Pacific Patrol Boat Program". *The Diplomat*, 1 July 2014.
Passi, Sasha. "New Kid on the Bloc?" *ASEAN Focus*, 5 December 2013. Available at <http://focus-asean.com/east-timor-focus-asean/> (accessed 18 June 2014).
Pavkovic, Aleksandar and Peter Radan. *Creating New States: Theory and Practice of Secession*. Hampshire: Ashgate, 2008.
Pawelz, Janina. "Security, Violence, and Outlawed Martial Arts Groups in Timor-Leste". *Asian Journal of Peacebuilding* 3, no. 1 (2015): 121–36.
Peake, Gordon. "Timor-Leste Declares Open Season on the UN". *Lowy Institute*, 7 July 2011.

Pederson, Jon and Marie Arneberg, eds. *Social and Economic Conditions in East Timor*. New York and Oslo: Columbia University's International Conflict Resolution Program and The Institute for Applied Social Science, 1999.

Peel, Michael. "Philippines' Duterte Backs 'New Order' Led by China and Russia". *Financial Times*, 17 November 2016.

People's Republic of China Ministry of National Defence. "Defense Minister Meets with Guests from Sri Lanka, East Timor, Nepal and Thailand". Press Release, Beijing, People's Republic of China, 13 October 2016.

Percival-Wood, Sally. "Timor-Leste's ASEAN Aspirations Can Benefit From Pragmatic Indecision". *Australian Outlook*, 29 May 2015.

Pereira, Agio. "Government Reaffirms Commitment to UNCLOS as the 'Constitution of the Sea'". Government of Timor-Leste Media Release, Dili, 15 July 2016.

———. "Challenges and Opportunities: The View from Timor-Leste". *The Diplomat*, 19 January 2016.

———. "2015 Timor-Leste Update: Keynote Speech by His Excellency Agio Pereira, Minister of State and of the Presidency of the Council of Ministers, Government of Timor-Leste". Australian National University, Canberra, 19 November 2015.

———. "The Challenges of Nation-State Building". In *A New Era? Timor-Leste After the UN*, edited by Sue Ingram, Lia Kent and Andrew McWilliam, pp. 17–30. Canberra: ANU Press, 2015.

———. "Timor-Leste Transforming Belligerent Democracy into Consensus Democracy". *Tempo Semanal*, 26 January 2014.i

Permanent Court of Arbitration (PCA). "Conciliation between the Democratic Republic of Timor-Leste and the Commonwealth of Australia". PCA Press Release, The Hague, 26 December 2017.

———. "Conciliation between the Democratic Republic of Timor-Leste and the Commonwealth of Australia". PCA Press Release, The Hague, 2 September 2017.

———. "The South China Sea Arbitration". PCA Case Number 2013–19 In the matter of an arbitration before an arbitral tribunal constituted under annex VII to the 1982 United Nations Convention on the Law of the Sea between the Republic of the Philippines and the People's Republic of China: Award on Jurisdiction and Admissibility. The Hague, 12 July 2016.

———. "Arbitration under the Timor Sea Treaty (Timor-Leste v Australia)". PCA Case Repository, 2016. Available at <https://www.pcacases.com/web/view/37> (accessed 27 February 2017).

———. "Arbitral Award Rendered in Execution of the Compromis Signed at The Hague, April 3. 1913, between the Netherlands and Portugal Concerning the Subject of the Boundary of a Part of their Possession in the Island of Timor". Paris, 25 June 1914.

Perry, Robin. "Asia-Pacific: The Commission of Truth and Friendship and Justice for East Timor". *Alternative Law Journal* 34, no. 3 (2009): 199–200.
Pfaff, William. *The Wrath of Nations: Civilizations and the Furies of Nationalism*. New York: Simon & Schuster, 1994.
Phillips, Tom, Oliver Holmes and Owen Bowcott. "Beijing Rejects Tribunal's Ruling in South China Sea Case". *The Guardian*, 13 July 2016.
Philpott, Daniel. "Westphalia, Authority and International Society". *Political Studies* XLVII (1999): 566–89.
———. "In Defense of Self-Determination". *Ethics* 105, no. 2 (January 1995): 352–85.
Philpott, Simon. "Post-Colonial Troubles: The Politics of Transitional Justice". In *Timor-Leste: Challenges for Justice and Human Rights in the Shadow of the Past*, edited by William Binchy, pp. 237–60. Dublin: Clarus Press, 2009.
———. "East Timor's Double Life: Smells Like Westphalian Spirit". *Third World Quarterly* 27, no. 1 (2006): 135–59.
Pietsch, Sam. "Australian Imperialism and East Timor". *Marxist Interventions* 2 (2010): 7–38.
Pinto, Constâncio da Conceição. Statement by Constâncio da Conceição Pinto Minister of Commerce, Industry and Environment of the Democratic Republic of Timor-Leste to the High-level Signature Ceremony for the Paris Agreement. New York, 22 April 2016.
Pinto, Julio Tomas. "Government of Timor Leste and USA Discuss Defense Cooperation", 16 December 2010. Available at <http://juliotomaspinto.com/index.php?option=com_content&view=article&id=93:government-of-timor-leste-and-usa-discuss-defense-cooperation&catid=1:julio-pinto-news&Itemid=64> (accessed 4 April 2013).
———. "UNMIT Mission: Development or Destruction". *Tempo Semanal*, 7 June 2011.
———. "Reforming the Security Sector: Facing Challenges, Achieving Progress in Timor-Leste". *Tempo Semanal*, 18 August 2009.
Potter, Evan. "Canada and the New Diplomacy". *International Journal* 58, no. 1 (2002/3): 43–64.
Powles, Anna and José Sousa-Santos. "Xanana Gusmão – Mauk Moruk: Timor Struggles with Its Past and Future". *Lowy Interpreter*, 5 December 2013.
Prescott, Victor. "East Timor's Potential Maritime Boundaries". In *The Maritime Dimensions of Independent East Timor*, edited by Donald R. Rothwell and Martin Tsamenyi, pp. 70–105. Wollongong Papers on Maritime Policy No. 8. Wollongong: University of Wollongong, 2000.
Purdey, Jemma. "Legal Responses to Violence in Post-Soeharto Indonesia". In *Indonesia: Law and Society*, 2nd ed., edited by Timothy Lindsay, pp. 515–31. Annandale: The Federation Press, 2008.

Purnawanty, Jani. "Various Perspectives in Understanding the East Timor Crisis". *Temple International and Comparative Law* 14 (2000): 61–73.

Radio Australia. "East Timor and China Move Closer". Australian Broadcasting Corporation, 16 April 2014.

Ramalingam, Ben. *Aid on the Edge of Chaos: Re-thinking International Co-operation in a Complex World*. Oxford: Oxford University Press, 2013.

Ramcharan, Robin. "ASEAN and Non-Interference: A Principle Maintained". *Contemporary Southeast Asia* 22, no. 1 (2000): 60–88.

Ramo, Joshua Cooper. *The Beijing Consensus: Notes on the New Physics of Chinese Power*. London: The Foreign Policy Centre, 2004.

Ramos-Horta, José. "Why Timor-Leste Should Join ASEAN Now". *East Asia Forum*, 16 May 2011.

―――. "Address by the Hon. José Ramos Horta to The Lowy Institute for International Policy". Sydney, 29 November 2004.

―――. *Towards a Peaceful Solution in East Timor*, 2nd ed. Sydney: ETRA, 1997.

―――. "Ramos-Horta – Nobel Lecture", 10 December 1996. Available at <https://www.nobelprize.org/nobel_prizes/peace/laureates/1996/ramos-horta-lecture.html> (accessed 21 July 2014).

―――. *Funu: The Unfinished Saga of East Timor*. Lawrenceville, New Jersey: The Red Sea Press, 1987.

Ratuva, Steven. "A New Regional Cold War? American and Chinese Posturing in the Pacific". *Asia and the Pacific Policy Studies* 1, no. 2 (2014): 409–22.

República Democrática de Timor-Leste (RDTL). "Council of Ministers Meeting on November 22nd, 2016". Democratic Republic of Timor-Leste, Dili, 22 November 2016.

―――. "500th Anniversary of the Affirmation of the Timorese Identity". RDTL Press Release, Dili, 2016.

―――. *National Strategic Concept of Security and Defence*. Dili: Ministry of Defence, 2016.

―――. *Strategic Concept for Defence and National Security*. Dili: Ministry of Defence, 2016.

―――. "Launching of the Strategic Concept for Defence and National Security". Democratic Republic of Timor-Leste, Dili, 8 September 2015.

―――. "Program of the Sixth Constitutional Government 2015-2017". Dili: Government of the Democratic Republic of Timor-Leste, 3 March 2015.

―――. "Heineken Asia Pacific signs a Formal Investment Agreement with the Government of Timor-Leste". Minister of State and of the Presidency of the Council of Minister and Official Spokesperson for the Government of Timor-Leste, Dili, 10 January 2015.

―――. "Timor-Leste Participates in the Second Summit of the Pacific Islands Development Forum (PIDF) in Fiji". Press Release, 23 June 2014.

———. "Joint Statement between the People's Republic of China and the Democratic Republic of Timor-Leste on Establishing Comprehensive Partnership of Good-Neighbourly Friendship, Mutual Trust and Mutual Benefit". Minister of State and of the Presidency of the Council of Ministers and Official Spokesperson for the Government of Timor-Leste, Dili, 14 April 2014.

———. *Timor-Leste's Initial National Communication under United Nations Framework Convention on Climate Change*. Dili: Timor-Leste's State Secretariat for Environment, 2014.

———. "Timor-Leste and Indonesia Sign a Memorandum on Border Crossings". RDTL Press Release, Dili, 24 June 2013.

———. "Joint Conference on Peace and Reconciliation between ICAP-CAPDI". RDTL Press Release, Dili, 4 May 2012.

———. "The Dili Consensus". Dili, 28 February 2012.

———. *"Goodbye Conflict, Welcome Development": A Citizen's Guide to the 2012 State Budget of the Democratic Republic of Timor-Leste*. Dili: Democratic Republic of Timor Leste, 2012.

———. *Census of Population and Housing 2010: Suco Report*. Dili: National Statistics Directorate, 2011.

———. *Strategic Development Plan*. Dili: Government of Timor-Leste, 2011.

———. *National Adaptation Programme of Action (NAPA) to Climate Change*. Dili: Ministry for Economy and Development Secretary of State for Environment, December 2010.

———. *Law on National Security*. Dili: Government of Democratic Republic of Timor-Leste, 2009.

———. "Timor-Leste National Action Programme to Combat Land Degradation First Draft". Dili, November 2008, pp. 4, 7.

———. *First National Report Land Degradation in Timor-Leste*. Dili: Timor-Leste Ministry of Agriculture, Forestry and Fisheries, February 2007.

———. *IV Constitutional Government Program 2007–2012*. Dili: Democratic Republic of Timor-Leste Presidency of the Ministers Office, 2007.

———. *Force 2020*, 2007. Available at <https://www.locjkt.or.id/Timor_E/pdf/Forca202007.pdf> (accessed 11 February 2017).

———. *Census of Population and Housing 2004*. Dili: National Statistics Directorate, 2006.

———. "Commemorating the 10th Anniversary of Restoration of Independence of Timor-Leste". Available at <http://timor-leste.gov.tl/?p=6931&lang=en> (accessed 31 January 2017).

———. "Maritime Boundary Office". Available at <http://www.gfm.tl/> (accessed 24 February 2017).

———. "TradeInvest Timor-Leste". Available at <http://www.investtimor-leste.com/?q=node/1> (accessed on 27 February 2017).

RDTL Ministry of Finance. *State Budget 2016: Book One*. Dili: Democratic Republic of Timor-Leste, 2016.

———. "The Swearing-In of the New National Unity Government". February 2015. Available at <https://www.mof.gov.tl/the-swearing-in-of-the-new-national-unity-government/?lang=en> (accessed 30 January 2017).

RDTL Presidency of the Republic. "H.E. the President of the Republic, Taur Matan Ruak, Unveils Monument in Lifau". RDTL Press Release, Dili, 3 December 2016.

Rees, Edward. *Under Pressure: Falintil – Forças de Defesa de Timor-Leste. Three Decades of Defence Force Development in Timor-Leste 1975–2004*. Geneva: Centre for the Democratic Control of Armed Forces, 2005.

Refworld. "Timor-Leste (East Timor): Activists Say No to Proposed New Refugee Centre", 23 July 2010. Available at <http://reliefweb.int/report/timor-leste/timor-leste-activists-say-no-proposed-new-refugee-centre> (accessed 11 February 2017).

Reid-Smith, Kate. "Crocodile Oil: Dragon's Treasure – A Possible Future Southeast Asian Geopolitical Diaspora?" In *The Crisis in Timor-Leste: Understanding the Past, Imagining the Future*, edited by Dennis Shoesmith, pp. 65–72. Darwin: Charles Darwin University Press, 2007.

Reiger, Caitlin and Marieke Wierda. *The Serious Crimes Process in Timor-Leste: In Retrospect*. New York: International Center for Transitional Justice, March 2006.

Reis, Bruno and Pedro Oliveria. "The Power and Limits of Cultural Myths in Portugal's Search for a Post-Imperial Role". *The International History Review* (2017): 1–23.

Reisman, Michael. "Sovereignty and Human Rights in Contemporary International Law". *American Journal of International Law* 84, no. 4 (1990): 866–76.

Republic of Indonesia. "Indonesia–Timor Leste Relation Grows Because of Trust: President Yudhoyono". Republic of Indonesia Press Release, Jakarta, 20 March 2013.

———. *East Timor: Building for a Future: Issues and Perspectives*. Jakarta: Department of Foreign Affairs, 1996.

———. *Facts about East Timor*. Jakarta: Dewan Peerwakilan Rakyat, 1989.

———. *East Timor After Integration*. Jakarta: Department of Information, 1983.

———. *Government Statements on the East Timor Question*. Jakarta: Department of Information, 1976.

———. *Statement of the Government at the Republic of Indonesia on Portuguese Timor*. Indonesia: Departemen Luar Negeri, 10 December 1975.

Republic of Indonesia Defence Ministry. *Indonesia Defence White Paper 2015*. Jakarta: Ministry of Defence of the Republic of Indonesia, 2015.

Republic of Indonesia and Democratic Republic of Timor-Leste. "Fourth Senior Officials' Meeting between Indonesia and Timor-Leste". Joint Press

Statement of the Republic of Indonesia and the Democratic Republic of Timor-Leste, Bali, 21–22 January 2010.

———. "Terms of Reference for The Commission of Truth and Friendship". Jakarta, 10 March 2005. Available at <http://www.etan.org/et2005/march/06/10tor.htm> (accessed 24 March 2015).

Rice, Susan and Stewart Patrick. *Index of State Weakness*. Washington: Brookings Institution, 2008.

Ringmar, Erik. "Introduction: The International Politics of Recognition". In *The International Politics of Recognition*, edited by Thomas Lindemann and Erik Ringmar, pp. 3–24. Boulder: Paradigm Publishers, 2014.

Robie, David. *Blood on their Banner: Nationalist Struggles in the South Pacific*. London: Zed Books, 1989.

Robinson, Geoffrey. *East Timor 1999 Crimes against Humanity*. United Nations Office of the High Commissioner for Human Rights, July 2003.

Rogers, Felicity. "The International Force in East Timor: Legal Aspects of Maritime Operations". *University of New South Wales Journal of International Law* 37 (2005).

Roosa, John. "How Does a Truth Commission Find out What the Truth Is? The Case of East Timor's CAVR". *Pacific Affairs* 18, no. 4 (2007/8): 569–80.

Roque, Ricardo. "Mountains and Black Races: Anthropology's Heterotopias in Colonial East Timor". *The Journal of Pacific History* 47, no. 3 (2012): 263–82.

Rosser, Andrew. "Timor-Leste and the Resource Curse: An Assessment". In *Security, Development and Nation-Building in Timor-Leste*, edited by Vandra Harris and Andrew Goldsmith, pp. 185–94. Oxon: Routledge, 2011.

———. "The Transition Support Program in Timor-Leste". In *Making Aid Work in Fragile States*, edited by James Manor, pp. 59–84. Washington: World Bank, 2007.

Rotberg, Robert. "The Failure and Collapse of Nation-States: Breakdown, Prevention and Repair". In *When States Fail: Causes and Consequences*, edited by Robert Rotberg, pp. 1–50. New Jersey: Princeton University Press, 2004.

Rotberg, Roland, ed. *When States Fail: Causes and Consequences*. Princeton, New Jersey: Princeton University Press, 2003.

Roughneen, Simon. "Aid and Independence". *The Diplomat*, 29 September 2011.

Ryan, Stephen. "The Evolution of Peacebuilding". In *Routledge Handbook in Peacebuilding*, edited by Roger Mac Ginty, pp. 25–35. Oxon: Routledge, 2013.

Sahin, Selver, "Timor-Leste's Foreign Policy: Securing State Identity in the Post-Independent Period". *Journal of Current Southeast Asian* Affairs 33, no. 2 (2014): 3–25.

———. "Timor-Leste: A More Confident or Overconfident Foreign Policy Actor?" In *Southeast Asian Affairs 2012*, edited by Daljit Singh and Pushpa Thambipillai, pp. 341–58 Singapore: Institute of Southeast Asian Studies, 2012.

———. "Building the State in Timor-Leste". *Asian Survey* 47, no. 2 (2007): 250–67.
Sahin, Selver and Donald Feaver. "The Politics of Security Sector Reform in 'Fragile' or 'Post-Conflict' Settings: A Crucial Review of the Experience in Timor-Leste". *Democratization* 20, no. 6 (2012): 1056–80.
Salim, Tama. "Timor-Leste Looks to Benefit from ASEAN Membership". *The Jakarta Post*, 26 May 2016.
Sanches, Edalina Rodrigues. "The Community of Portuguese Language Speaking Countries: The Role of Language in a Globalizing World". *Atlantic Future Scientific Paper* 14 (June 2014).
Santos, Luís António. "Portugal and the CPLP: Heightened Expectations, Unfounded Disillusions". In *The Last Empire: Thirty Years of Portuguese Decolonisation*, edited by Stewart Lloyd-Jones and António Costa Pinto, pp. 67–81. Bristol: Intellect Books, 2003.
Santos, Sisto Dos. *Timor-Leste National Alliance for an International Tribunal Report*. Dili: Timor-Leste National Alliance for an International Tribunal, 1 March 2014.
Saragih, Bagus BT. "Marty Reiterates Support for Timor-Leste's ASEAN Bid", *The Jakarta Post*, 12 September 2012.
Scambary, James. "In Search of White Elephants: The Political Economy of Resource Income Expenditure in East Timor". *Critical Asian Studies* 47, no. 2 (2015): 283–308.
———. "Informal Security Groups and Social Movements". In *Politics of Timor-Leste: Democratic Consolidation after Intervention*, edited by Michael Leach and Damien Kingsbury, pp. 203–13. New York: Cornell University Press, 2013.
———. "Anatomy of a Conflict: The 2006–7 Communal Violence in East Timor". In *Security, Development and Nation-Building in Timor-Leste*, edited by Vandra Harris and Andrew Goldsmith, 59–79. Oxon: Routledge, 2011.
Scharfe, Sharon. *Complicity: Human Rights and Canadian Foreign Policy*. Montreal, New York and London: Black Rose Books, 1996.
Scheiner, Charles. "Can the Petroleum Fund Exorcise the Resource Curse from Timor-Leste?" In *A New Era? Timor-Leste after the UN Intervention*, edited by Sue Ingram, Lia Kent and Andrew McWilliam, pp. 73–102. Canberra: ANU Press, 2015.
Schofield, Clive. "Minding the Gap: The Australia–East Timor Treaty on Certain Maritime Arrangements in the Timor Sea (CMATS)". *The International Journal of Marine and Coastal Law* 22 (2007): 189–234.
Schofield, Clive and I. Made Andi Arsana. "The Delimitation of Maritime Boundaries: A Matter of Life or Death for East Timor?" In *East Timor: Beyond Independence*, edited by Damien Kingsbury and Michael Leach, pp. 67–85. Monash: Monash University Press, 2007.

Schulz, Carsten-Andreas. "Accidental Activists: Latin American Status-Seeking at The Hague". *International Studies Quarterly* 61, no. 3 (2017): 612–22.

Schweller, Randall. *Deadly Imbalances: Tripolarity and Hitler's Strategy of World Conquest.* New York: Columbia University Press, 1998.

Seabra, Pedro. "The Need for a Reshaped Foreign Policy". In *The Politics of Timor-Leste: Democratic Consolidation after Intervention,* edited by Michael Leach and Damien Kingsbury, pp. 145–61. Ithaca, NY: Cornell University, 2014.

Sebastian, Leonard C. "Timor-Leste's Road to ASEAN Membership". *In Asia.* San Francisco: The Asia Foundation, 9 March 2011.

Sebastian, Leonard C. and Isingdarsah. *Assessing 12-Year Military Reform in Indonesia.* RSIS Working Paper. Singapore: S. Rajaratnam School of International Studies, April 2011.

Secretariat of the Pacific Community in conjunction with CSIRO. *Food Security in the Pacific and East Timor and its Vulnerability to Climate Change.* Canberra: Australian Government, 2011.

Seeds for Life. "Seeds for Life Program Closing", June 2016. Available at <http://seedsoflifetimor.org/> (accessed 16 February 2017).

Severino, Rodolfo. The ASEAN Regional Forum. Singapore: Institute of Southeast Asian Studies, 2009.

———. *Southeast Asia in Search of an ASEAN Community.* Singapore: Institute of Southeast Asian Studies, 2006.

Sharman, JC. "Sovereignty at the Extremes: Micro-States in World Politics". *Political Studies* 65, no. 3 (2016): 559–75.

Shekhar, Vibhanshu. "ASEAN's Response to the Rise of China: Deploying a Hedging Strategy". *China Report* 48 (2012): 253–68.

Shoesmith, Dennis. *The Crisis in Timor-Leste: Understanding the Past, Imagining the Future.* Darwin: Charles Darwin University Press, 2007.

Siapno, Jacqueline. "Timor-Leste: On a Path of Authoritarianism?" *Southeast Asian Affairs* (2006): 325–40.

Sil, Rudra and Peter Katzenstein. "Analyical Eclectism in the Study of World Politics: Reconfiguring Problems and Mechanisms Across Research Traditions". *Perspectives on Politics* 8, no. 2 (2010): 411–31.

Sim, Edmund. "Wrap-up of the 2016 ASEAN Summit(s)". *ASEAN Economic Community Blog,* 7 September 2015. Available at <http://aseanec.blogspot.com.au/2016/09/wrap-up-of-2016-asean-summits.html> (accessed 12 February 2017).

———. "Can Laos Lead ASEAN in 2016?" *The Diplomat,* 10 June 2015.

Simões, Bruno. "Timor doa dois milhões de euros a Portugal para ajudar a combater incêndios". *Negocios,* 10 August 2016.

Simões, José Manuel Neto. "Novo modelo das Forças Armadas de Timor-Leste (FALINTIL-FDTL)". *Jornal de Defesa e Relações Internacionals* (2012).

Simonsen, Sven Gunnar. "The Role of East Timor's Security Institutions in National Integration – and Disintegration". *The Pacific Review* 22, no. 5 (2009): 575–96.

———. "The Authoritarian Temptation in East Timor: Nationbuilding and the Need for Inclusive Governance". *Asian Survey* 46, no. 4 (July/August 2006): 575–96.

Simpson, Brad. "Solidarity in the Age of Globalization: The Transnational Movement for East Timor and U.S. Foreign Policy". *Peace & Change* 29, nos. 3 and 4 (July 2004): 453–82.

Siqueira, Isabel Rocha de. "Measuring and Managing 'State Fragility': The Production of Statistics by the World Bank, Timor-Leste and the g7+". *Third World Quarterly* 35, no. 2 (2014): 268–83.

Smith, Anthony. "Constraints and Choices: East Timor as a Foreign Policy Actor". *New Zealand Journal of Asian Studies* 7, no. 1 (June 2005): 15–36.

———. "East Timor: Elections in the World's Newest Nation". *Journal of Democracy* 15, no. 4 (April 2004): 145–59.

Sørenson, Georg. "After the Security Dilemma: The Challenges of Insecurity in Weak States and the Dilemma of Liberal Values". *Security Dialogue* 38, no. 3 (2007): 357–78.

———. "An Analysis of Contemporary Statehood: Consequences for Conflict and Cooperation". *Review of International Studies* 23 (1997): 253–69.

Sousa, Helena and Manuel Pinto. *Lusophony: Communication in the Portuguese Speaking World*. Washington D.C.: International Communication Association, July 1999.

Sousa-Santos, José Kei Lekke. "Acting West, Looking East: Timor-Leste's Growing Engagement with the Pacific Islands Region". In *Regionalism, Security and Cooperation in Oceania*, edited by Rouben Azizian and Carleton Cramer, pp. 110–12. Honolulu: Asia-Pacific Centre for Security Studies, 2015.

Sovacool, Benjamin. "The Political Economy of Oil and Gas in Southeast Asia: Heading Towards the Natural Resource Curse?" *The Pacific Review* 23, no. 2 (2010): 225–59.

Steele, Brent. *Ontological Security in International Relations: Self-Identity and the IR State*. Oxon: Routledge, 2008.

Storey, Ian. *Southeast Asia and the Rise of China: The Search for Security*. New York: Routledge, 2011.

———. "China's Inroads into East Timor". *China Brief* 9, no. 6 (2009).

Strang, David. "Contested Sovereignty: The Social Construction of Colonial Imperialism". In *State Sovereignty as Social Construct*, edited by Thomas Biersteker and Cynthia Weber, pp. 22–49. Cambridge: Cambridge University Press, 1996.

Strating, Rebecca. "Timor-Leste in 2017: A State of Uncertainty". In *Southeast Asian Affairs 2018*, edited by Malcolm Cook and Daljit Singh. Singapore: ISEAS – Yusof Ishak Institute, 2018.

———. "A Sunset for Greater Sunrise?". *New Mandala*, 7 February 2017.

———. "Timor-Leste's Foreign Policy Approach to the Timor Sea Disputes". *Australian Journal of International Affairs* (2017).

———. "Timor-Sea Dispute: Timor-Leste is Running Out of Time". *Lowy Interpreter*, 11 October 2016.

———. *Social Democracy in East Timor*. Oxon: Routledge, 2015.

———. "Contested Self-determination: East Timor and Indonesia's Battle over Borders, International Law and Ethnic Identity". *Journal of Pacific History* 49, no. 4 (2014): 469–94.

———. "The Indonesia–Timor-Leste Commission of Truth and Friendship: Enhancing Bilateral Relations at the Expense of Justice". *Contemporary Southeast Asia* 36, no. 2 (2014): 232–61.

———. "East Timor's Emerging National Security Agenda: Establishing 'Real' Independence". *Asian Security* 9, no. 3 (2013): 185–210.

Strating, Rebecca and Beth Edmondson. "Beyond Democratic Tolerance: Witch Killings in Timor-Leste". *Journal of Current Southeast Asian Affairs* 34, no. 3 (2015): 37–64.

Strohmeyer, Hansjoerg. "Building a New Judiciary for East Timor: Challenges of a Fledgling Nation". *Criminal Law Forum* 11 (2000): 259–85.

Subotić, Jelena. "Narrative, Ontological Security, and Foreign Policy Change". *Foreign Policy Analysis* 12, no. 4 (2014): 610–27.

Sukma, Rizal. "Indonesia's Response to the Rise of China: Growing Comfort amid Uncertainties". In *The Rise of China: Responses for Southeast Asia and Japan*, edited by Jun Tsunekawa, pp. 139–55. Japan: National Institute of Defense Studies Joint Researches Services No. 4, 2009.

———. "Securing East Timor: Military and External Relations". In *Peace Building and State Building in Timor-Leste*, edited by Hadi Soesastro and Landry Haryo Subianto. Jakarta: Centre for Strategic and International Studies, 2002.

———. *Indonesia and China: The Politics of a Troubled Relationship*. New York: Routledge, 1999.

Sukma, Rizal and Edy Prasetyono. *Security Sector Reform in Indonesia: The Military and the Police*. The Hague: Conflict Research Unit, Netherlands Institute of International Relations Clingendael, February 2003.

Sutter, Patrick. "State-Building or the Dilemma of Intervention: An Introduction". In *Facets and Practices of Statebuilding*, edited by Julia Raue and Patrick Sutter, pp. 1–14. Leiden: Martinus Nijhoff Publishers, 2009.

Tanter, Richard, Mark Seldon and Stephen Shalom. "East Timor Faces the Future". In *Bitter Flowers, Sweet Flowers: East Timor, Indonesia and the World*

Community, edited by Richard Tanter, Mark Selden and Stephen Shalom, pp. 243–72. Sydney: Pluto Press Australia, 2001.

TAPOL. "Though Limited by its Mandate, the CTF Revealed a Great Deal". TAPOL Press Release, 21 July 2008.

———. "Submission to 2008 Universal Periodic Review of Indonesia by UN HRC", 27 November 2007.

———. "International Tribunal Proposal for East Timor Welcomed". TAPOL Press Release, 29 June 2005.

Tarling, Nicholas. *Regionalism in Southeast Asia: To Foster the Political Will*. Oxon: Routledge, 2006.

Tarte, Sandra. "A New Pacific Regional Voice? The Pacific Islands Development Forum". In *The New Pacific Diplomacy*, edited by Greg Fry and Sandra Tarte, pp. 79–88. Canberra: ANU Press, 2015.

Taur Matan Ruak. "State of the Nation". Speech by His Excellency Taur Matan Ruak to the National Parliament. Dili, 20 September 2016.

Tavares, Rodrigo and Luís Brás Bernardino. "Speaking the Language of Security: The Commonwealth, the Francophonie and the CPLP in Conflict Management in Africa". *Conflict, Security and Development* 11, no. 5 (2011): 607–36.

Taylor, John. *East Timor: The Price of Freedom*. Annandale, New South Wales: Zed Books, 1999.

———. "Emergence of a Nationalist Movement". In *East Timor at the Crossroads: The Forging of a Nation*, edited by Peter Carey and G. Carter-Bentley, pp. 21–32. London: Cassell/Social Science Research Council, 1995.

Taylor, Ruby. "Timor-Leste is PIDF Newest Member". *The Fiji Times Online*, 19 July 2016.

Taylor-Leech, Kerry. "Language and Identity in East Timor: The Discourses of Nation Building". *Language Problems and Language Planning* 32, no. 2 (2008): 153–80.

Thorhallsson, Baldur. "Small States in the UN Security Council: Means of Influence?" *The Hague Journal of Diplomacy* 7 (2012): 135–60.

Timor Gap E.P., *Annual Report & Accounts 2015*. Available at <https://timorgap.com/databases/website.nsf/vwAll/Resource-Full_TIMOR%20GAP%202015%20Annual%20Report_EN_Final/$File/TIMOR%20GAP%202015%20Annual%20Report_EN_Final.pdf?openelement> (accessed 26 February 2017).

———. *Timor Gap E.P. Annual Report 2014*. Available at <http://www.timorgap.com/databases/website.nsf/vwAllNew/Resource-AnnualReport_TIMORGAP_PubVer_English/$File/AnnualReport_TIMORGAP_PubVer_English.pdf?openelement> (accessed 26 February 2017).

Transparency International. "Timor-Leste". Available at <http://www.transparency.org/country/TLS> (accessed 26 February 2017).

———. "Timor-Leste: Overview of Corruption and Anti-Corruption". Available at <http://www.transparency.org/files/content/corruptionqas/Country_profile_Timor_Leste_2015.pdf> (accessed 26 February 2017).

Traube, Elizabeth. "Mambai Perspectives on Colonialism and Decolonization". In *East Timor at the Crossroads: The Forging of a Nation*, edited by Peter Carey and G. Carter-Bentley, pp. 42–55. London: Cassell/Social Science Research Council, 1995.

———. *Cosmology and Social Life: Ritual Exchange among the Mambai of East Timor*. Chicago: University of Chicago Press, 1986.

Ţuţuianu, Simona. *Towards Global Justice: Sovereignty in an Interdependent World*. The Hague: TMC Asser Press, 2013.

United Nations. "General Assembly Resolutions". Available at <http://www.un.org/en/sections/documents/general-assembly-resolutions/index.html> (accessed 14 February 2017).

———. "Issues Facing Small Island Developing States 'Global Challenges' Demanding Collective Responsibility, Secretary-General Tells Security Council". 7469th meeting, SC/11991, 30 July 2015.

———. "Paris Agreement". Paris: United Nations, 2015.

United Nations Commission of Experts. "Report to the Secretary-General of the Commission of Experts to Review the Prosecution of Serious Violations of Human Rights in Timor-Leste (then East Timor) in 1999". S/2005/458, 26 May 2005.

United Nations Development Programme (UNDP). *Human Development Report 2015*. New York: UNDP, 2015.

———. *New Solutions for a New Country: Timor-Leste's Future in Renewable Energy*. Case Study 16, September 2011.

———. *Timor-Leste Human Development Report 2011: Managing Natural Resources for Human Development: Developing the Non-Oil Economy to Achieve the MGDs*, 2011. Available at <https://www.laohamutuk.org/econ/HDI10/TLHDR2011En.pdf> (accessed 20 February 2017).

United Nations Economic and Social Commission for Asia and the Pacific (UNESCAP). "UNESCAP: 'Dili Consensus' Calls for Voices of Fragile and Conflict-affected States to be Heard in Reshaping Global Development Agenda". Press Release G/07/2013. Bangkok, March 2013.

United Nations General Assembly (UNGA). "Fourth Committee Approves 20 Texts for General Assembly Action, Passing 4 by Recorded Vote, 16 by Consensus". GA/SPD/612, 10 October 2016.

———. "Report of the Working Group on Enforced on Involuntary Disappearances: Mission to Timor-Leste". A/HRC/19/58/Add.1, 26 December 2011.

———. "Fourth Committee Approves Five Consensus Texts Reaffirming Inalienable Right to Self-determination and Independence". GA/SPD/482, 10 October 2011.

———. "Combating Defamation of Religions". A/RES/65/224, 11 April 2011.

———. "Combating Defamation of Religions". A/RES/64/156, 8 March 2010.

———. Fourth Committee. 37th session, 23rd meeting, 15 November 1982.

———. Fourth Committee. 37th session, 20th meeting, 11 November 1982.

———. Fourth Committee. 37th session, 18th meeting, 10 November 1982.

———. Fourth Committee. 37th session, 13th meeting, 5 November 1982.

———. Fourth Committee. 34th session, 17th meeting, 25 October 1979.

———. Fourth Committee. 34th session, 16th meeting, 24 October 1979.

———. Fourth Committee. 34th session, 15th meeting, 24 October 1979.

———. "International Covenant on Civil and Political Rights". United Nations General Assembly Resolution 2200A (XXI), 16 December 1966.

———. "International Covenant on Economic, Social and Cultural Rights". United Nations General Assembly Resolution 2200A (XXI), 16 December 1966.

———. "Territories under Portuguese Administration". United Nations General Assembly Resolution 1807, 17th Session, 14 December 1962.

———. "Declaration on the Granting of Independence to Colonial Countries and Peoples". United Nations General Assembly Resolution 1514 (XV), 15th Session, 14 December 1960.

———. "Voting Records". Available at <http://www.un.org/en/ga/documents/voting.asp> (accessed 14 February 2017).

United Nations Human Rights Office of the High Commissioner for Human Rights (OHCHR). "UN Human Rights Expert Urges Timor-Leste to Reconsider Dismissal of International Judges and Prosecutors", 25 November 2014.

———. *Moving Away from the Death Penalty: Lessons in Southeast Asia*. Bangkok: OHCHR, 2013.

———. "Report of the Commission for Inquiry on East Timor to Secretary-General". United Nations General Assembly, A/54/726, S/2000/59, January 2000.

———. "Good Governance and Human Rights". Available at <http://www.ohchr.org/EN/Issues/Development/GoodGovernance/Pages/GoodGovernanceIndex.aspx> (accessed 20 February 2017).

United Nations Mission in Timor-Leste. "Socio Economic Affairs", 20 August 2009. Available at <https://unmit.unmissions.org/socio-economic-affairs> (accessed 16 July 2012).

United Nations Peacebuilding Commission. "Review of the United Nations Peacebuilding Architecture". A/64/868, 2010.

United Nations Security Council (UNSC). "Resolution 1704. S/RES/1704", 25 August 2006.

———. "Report of the Secretary-General on the United Nations Transitional Administration in East Timor". S/2000/53, 26 January 2000.

———. "Resolution 1272". S/RES/1272, 25 October 1999.

———. "Report of the Secretary-General on the Situation in East Timor". RES/1999/1024, 4 October 1999.

———. "Resolution 1264". S/RES/1264, 15 September 1999.

———. "Debates Concerning UN Security Council Resolution 389 (1976)". Security Council Official Records, 31st year, 1909th meeting, 14 April 1976.

———. "Debates Concerning UN Security Council Resolution 384 (1975)". Security Council Official Records, 30th year, 1864th meeting, 15 December 1975.

United Nations Transitional Administration in East Timor (UNTAET). "On the Establishment of a Commission for Reception, Truth and Reconciliation in East Timor". UNTAET/REG/2001/10, 13 July 2001.

———. "On the Establishment of a National Council". UNTAET/REG/2000/24, 14 July 2000.

———. "On the Establishment of Panels with Exclusive Jurisdiction over Serious Criminal Offences". UNTAET/REG/2000/15, 6 June 2000.

———. "On the Establishment of a National Consultative Council". UNTAET/REG/1999/2, 2 December 1999.

———. "On the Organization of Courts in East Timor". UNTAET/REG/1999/1, 27 November 1999.

United Nations World Commission on Environment and Development. "Our Common Future". *Brundtland Commission Report*, 1987.

United States Agency for International Development (USAID). "Our Work (Timor-Leste)". Available at <https://www.usaid.gov/timor-leste/our-work> (accessed 20 February 2017).

———. "Timor-Leste Country Profile". Available at <https://www.usaid.gov/sites/default/files/documents/1861/TIMOR-LESTE_Country_Profile_2016.pdf> (accessed 20 February 2017).

U.S. Department of State. "U.S. Relations with Timor-Leste", 17 July 2018. Available at <https://www.state.gov/r/pa/ei/bgn/35878.htm> (accessed 5 January 2018).

———. "Timor-Leste Investment Climate Statement 2015", May 2015. Available at <https://www.state.gov/documents/organization/241976.pdf> (accessed 27 February 2017).

———. "East Timor and Human Rights in Indonesia: A Fresh Look". Telegram 02365 from U.S. Embassy Jakarta to State Department, 5 March 1993.

———. Telegram 1579 from the American Embassy in Jakarta, 6 December 1975.

U.S. National Security Council. "Indonesian Use of MAP Equipment in East Timor". Memorandum for Brent Scowcroft from Clinton E. Granger, 12 December 1975.

United States Senate. "Crisis in East Timor and U.S. Policy towards Indonesia". Hearing before the Committee on Foreign Relations. 102 Congress, 2nd session, 27 February and 6 March 1992.

Valters, Craig, Sarah Dewhurst and Juana de Catheu. *After the Buffaloes Clash: Moving from Political Violence to Personal Security in Timor-Leste*. Development Progress Case Study Report. London: Overseas Development Institute, 2015.

Vandenbosch, Amry. "The Small States in International Politics and Organization". *The Journal of Politics* 26 (1964): 293–312.

Verma, S.K. *An Introduction to Public International Law*. New Delhi: Prentice Hall of India, 2004.

Vitor, Antonio. "Progress and Challenges of Infrastructure Spending in Timor-Leste". In *A New Era? Timor-Leste after the UN Intervention*, edited by Sue Ingram, Lia Kent and Andrew McWilliam, pp. 103–15. Canberra: ANU Press, 2015.

Wainwright, Elsina with Alan Dupont, James J. Fox, Ross Thomas and Hugh White. *New Neighbour, New Challenge: Australia and the Security of East Timor*. Canberra: Australian Strategic Policy Institute, 20 May 2002.

Wallace, Luke, Baskaran Sundaram, Ross S. Brodie, Sarah Marshall, Samantha Dawson, John Jaycock, Gerard Stewart and Lindsay Furness. *Vulnerability Assessment of Climate Change Impacts on Groundwater Resources in Timor-Leste*. Record 2012/55. Canberra: Geoscience Australia, July 2012.

Wallis, Joanne. *Constitution Making During State Building*. New York: Cambridge University Press, 2014.

Walt, Stephen. "Alliances in a Unipolar World". *World Politics* 61, no. 1 (2009): 86–120.

———. *The Origins of Alliances*. Ithaca: Cornell University Press, 1987.

Waltz, Kenneth. *Theory of International Politics*. Reading: Addison-Wesley, 1979.

Watanabe, Sadachika. "Heineken Entry Could Open Taps on Foreign Investment". *Asia Nikkei*, 1 December 2015.

Weatherbee, Donald E. *International Relations in Southeast Asia: The Struggle for Autonomy*. 2nd ed. Lanham, Maryland: Rowman & Littlefield Publishers Inc., 2010.

Weber, Max. *From Max Weber: Essays in Sociology*. Edited, with an Introduction by H.H. Gerth and C.W. Mills. Oxon: Routledge, 1991.

Weir, Ben. "Interview: Ambassador Abel Guterres". *The Diplomat*, 20 April 2016. Available at <http://thediplomat.com/2016/04/interview-ambassador-abel-guterres/> (accessed 1 July 2016).

Weldes, Jutta, Mark Laffey, Hugh Gusterson and Raymond Duvall. "Introduction: Constructing Insecurity". In *Cultures of Insecurity: States, Communities, and the Production of Danger*, edited by Jutta Weldes, Mark

Laffey, Hugh Gusterson and Raymond Duvall, pp. 1–34. Minnesota: University of Minnesota Press, 1999.

Wendt, Alexander. *Social Theory of International Politics*. Cambridge: Cambridge University Press, 1999.

———. "Anarchy is What States Make of It: The Social Construction of Power Politics". *International Organization* 46, no. 2 (1992): 391–425.

Wesley, Michael. "The State of the Art on the Art of State Building". *Global Governance* 14 (2008): 369–85.

Whitlam, Gough. "The New Federalism: A Review of Labor's Programs and Policies". Speech by the Prime Minister, the Hon EG Whitlam QC PM, Opening Address to Conference of the Centre for Research on Federal Financial Relations. Australian National University, 27 August 1975.

Wilde, Ralph. "From Danzig to East Timor and Beyond: The Role of International Territorial Administration". *American Journal of International Law* 95, no. 3 (2001): 583–606.

Willis, David. "Timor-Leste's Complex Geopolitics: The Local, the Regional and the Global". In *Timor-Leste: The Local, the Regional and the Global*, edited by Sarah Smith, Nuno Canas Mendes, Antero B. da Silva, Alarico da Costa Ximenes, Clinton Fernandes and Michael Leach, pp. 237–43. Melbourne: Swinburne University Press, 2016.

Wilson, Bu V.E. "The Exception Becomes the Norm in Timor-Leste: The Draft National Security Laws and the Continuing Role of the Joint Command". *Centre for International Governance and Justice Issues Paper* 11. Canberra: Australian National University, September 2009.

Wimmer, Andreas. "Who Owns the State? Understanding Ethnic Conflict in Post-Colonial Societies". *Nations and Nationalism* 3, no. 4 (1997): 631–65.

WithOneSeed. Available at <http://withoneseed.org.au/> (accessed 8 March 2017).

Wivel, Anders, Alyson Bailes, and Clive Archer. "Setting the Scene: Small States and International Security". In *Small States and International Security: Europe and Beyond*, edited by Clive Archer, Alyson Bailes and Anders Wivel, pp. 3–25. Oxon: Routledge, 2014.

Wolf, Reinhard. "Respect and Disrespect in International Relations: The Significance of Status Recognition". *International Theory* 3, no. 1 (2011): 105–42.

Woodside. *Woodside Annual Report 2010*. Available at <http://www.woodside.com.au/Investors-Media/announcements/Documents/21.02.2011%20 Annual%20Report%202010.pdf> (accessed 26 February 2017).

Working Group on Reparations. "Concept Paper on a National Reparations Program for Timor-Leste". Prepared by the Working Group on Reparations for Parliamentary Committee A, July 2008.

World Bank. "2016 Country Policy and Institutional Assessments". Available at <http://pubdocs.worldbank.org/en/449561467141303352/Cpia15finalIDAxlsx.pdf> (accessed 26 February 2017).
———. *Doing Business 2016: Measuring Regulatory Quality and Efficiency. 2016 Economy Profile Timor-Leste*, 13th ed. Washington: World Bank, 2016.
———. *Timor-Leste: Key Issues in Rural Energy Policy*. Washington: World Bank, December 2010.
———. "Review of World Bank Conditionality: The Theory and Practice of Conditionality, a Literature Review". Development Economics World Bank, 6 July 2005.
———. "Ease of Doing Business Index". Available at <http://data.worldbank.org/indicator/IC.BUS.EASE.XQ> (accessed 10 March 2017).
———. "Population 2017". Available at <http://databank.worldbank.org/data/download/POP.pdf> (accessed 30 January 2017).
———. "Poverty Headcount Ratio at National Poverty Lines: Timor Leste". Available at <http://data.worldbank.org/indicator/SI.POV.NAHC?locations=TL> (accessed 14 February 2017).
———. "Timor-Leste". Available at <http://data.worldbank.org/country/timor-leste> (accessed 20 February 2017).
———. "Timor-Leste Overview". Available at <http://www.worldbank.org/en/country/timor-leste/overview> (accessed 24 April 2017).
Wright, Warren. "The Complexities of Timor-Leste–Indonesia Border Control". *Timor-Leste Law and Justice Bulletin*, 25 February 2013. Available at <http://easttimorlegal.blogspot.com/2013/02/the-complexities-of-timor-leste.html> (accessed 4 April 2013).
Wulan, Alexandra Retno. "Border Incident a Test Case for Jakarta–Dili Ties". *The Jakarta Post*, 14 January 2006.
Wurfel, David. "Democracy, Nationalism and Ethnic Identity". In *Democratization and Identity: Regime and Ethnicity in East and Southeast Asia*, edited by Susan Henders, pp. 201–24. Plymouth: Rowman and Littlefield Publishers, 2004.
Wyler, Liana Sun. *Weak and Failing States: Evolving Security Threats and U.S. Foreign Policy*. Congressional Research Service, 2008.
Xinhua. "Spotlight: Non-Aligned Movement Takes Stance on UN Reform, Terrorism, Multilateralism". *Xinhua*, 19 September 2016.
———. "China's Navy Warships Pay First Visit to Timor-Leste". *China Daily*, 16 January 2016.
———. "Chinese Defense Minister Holds Talks with Timor-Leste Counterpart". *Xinhua*, 19 October 2015.
Yoshimatsu, Hidetaka. "ASEAN and Evolving Power Relations in East Asia: Strategies and Constraints". *Contemporary Politics* 18, no. 4 (2012): 400–15.

Zaum, Dominik. "International Relations Theory and Peacebuilding". In *Routledge Handbook in Peacebuilding*, edited by Roger Mac Ginty, pp. 105–16. Oxon: Routledge, 2013.
───. *The Sovereign Paradox: The Norms and Politics of International State-building*. Oxford: Oxford University Press, 2007.
───. "The Authority of International Administrations in International Society". *Review of International Studies* 32 (2006): 455–73.
Zhang, Yongjin. "China and the Emerging Regional Order in the South Pacific". *Australian Journal of International Affairs* 61, no. 3 (2007): 367–81.

Index

A
Abe, Shinzo, 315
absolute external sovereignty, 10, 123, 127, 235, 237, 309, 318, 328–29
Acharya, Amitav, 163, 169, 172, 173
activist foreign policy strategy, 152, 244, 246–48
"Act of Free Choice", 48
African Community of Portuguese-Language Speaking Countries, 76
agricultural production, 319, 323
aid dependence problems, 237–41
Alagappa, Muthiah, 7
Alatas, Ali, 82
Alkatiri, Mari, 150, 209
Alliance for Parliamentary Majority (AMP), 16, 201, 210, 212, 213, 215, 225
Alliance of Small Island States (AOSIS), 142–43, 321
Amnesty International, 288, 290
Anderson, Benedict, 84
Annan, Kofi, 279
ANTI. *See* Timor-Leste National Alliance for an International Tribunal (ANTI)
anti-colonial nationalism, 247
anti-FRETILIN propaganda, 69

APEC, 102, 103
APODETI, 46, 47, 50
Araújo, Rui Maria de, 17, 131, 133, 137, 150, 181, 223, 247
Archer, Clive, 4
armed resistance movement, 203
ASEAN Charter, 165
ASEAN Coordinating Council Working Group (ACCWG), 166
ASEAN Economic Community (AEC), 166, 257
ASEAN People's Forum (APF), 167
ASEAN Political Security Community (APSC), 166
ASEAN Regional Forum (ARF), 164
ASEAN Socio-Cultural Community (ASCC), 166
Asia Infrastructure Investment Bank (AIIB), 310
Asian Development Bank (ADB), 251, 252, 256
Asian-Pacific region, challenges, 26, 304–5, 310, 316
aspirational foreign policy, 21, 23, 26, 124–25, 136–37, 149–50, 219, 244, 303, 308, 329. *See also* foreign policy
  external national identity and, 130

Associação Social Democratica Timorense (ASDT), 46
Association of Southeast Asian Nations (ASEAN), 10, 137
  anti-FRETILIN propaganda, 69
  membership, 163–74, 256, 276
  rights of states, 70
  security challenges, 67
  states, 72, 85, 102–4
  use of force, 68
  voting records, 70–71
Atoni, 41
Aubrey, Jim, 64
Aung San Suu Kyi, 173
AusAid, 324
Australia, 62–65, 84, 293
  alliance with United States, 101
  civil society, 247
  de jure recognition, 64
  diplomacy towards ASEAN, 62
  foreign policy, 63–64, 244
  leadership, 101
  logistic systems, 101
  maritime security interests, 216
  neocolonialism, 102
  policies, 244
  potential security risk, 311–12
  right to self-determination, 64–65
  security concerns, 64
  security interest, 312
  Timor-Leste and, 215, 236
  2009 Defence White Paper, 312
  UNGA resolution, 63
Australia–Indonesia Security Arrangement, 102
Australian Defence Force, 101
Australian Defence White Paper (2016), 135
Australian Pacific Maritime Security Program, 215
Australian stock exchange (ASX), 243
Australia–Timor-Leste bilateral agreement, 215, 218
Ayoob, Mohammad, 7, 9, 125

B
Babo-Soares, Dionisio, 132, 136, 140
Bailes, Alyson, 4
Bainimarama, Frank, 205
"Balibo Five", 63
Bali Democracy Forum (2013), 150, 164, 240
"Balkinization", 64
Bandung Conference, 72
Bangkok Declaration (1967), 67, 70, 165
Bartelson, Jens, 39, 110
Beauvais, Joel, 104, 111
Beeson, Mark, 171
Beijing, 310, 313
"Beijing Consensus", 309
Bellamy, Alex, 171
"Belt and Road" (BRI) initiative, 310–11
bilateral relations
  with Indonesia, 272, 274, 275, 285
  and multilateral relationships, 138
Blunt, Peter, 252
Boothe, Douglas, 320
border disputes, 42, 135, 287
border security, 273, 287
Boxing Day Tsunami, 149
Brant, Philippa, 238
Bretton Woods institutions, 310
BRICS New Development Bank, 310
Brundtland commission report (1987), 320
Bull, Hedley, 18
Burke, Roland, 10
Buzan, Barry, 7
"bypass normal systems", 259

C
Cambodia, 167
Cape Verde, 74, 76
"Carnation Revolution", 46
Carrascalão, Mario, 48
Carter, Jimmy, 66
Certain Maritime Arrangements in the Timor Sea (CMATS), 243–45, 317

China
  hedging relation with, 306–15
  soft loans, 309–10
  Soviet Union and, 78–79
Chinese "maritime militia", 314
Chinese Ministry of National
    Defence, 314
Chinese Nuclear Industry 22nd
    Construction Company, 326
Chong, Ja Ian, 307–8
Chopra, Jarat, 9
civil society organizations, 282, 283,
    285, 289, 290
Clapham, Christopher, 138
climate change, 26, 305–6, 318–19,
    321–23, 327, 328
Clinton, Bill, 80, 98, 101
Clunan, Anne, 129
Coelho, Hernâni, 143, 164
cognitive dissonances, 239
Cold War, 143
colonial boundaries, 45
Colonial Boundary Treaty (1859), 42
colonialism, 172. *See also* Portuguese
    colonialism
Commission for Disappeared
    Persons, 289
Commission of Reception, Truth and
    Reconciliation (CAVR), 273, 281
Commission of Truth and Friendship
    (CTF), 274–75, 281–85
  beneficial relations with
      Indonesia, 282, 283
  conclusive truth, 283, 285
  democratization, 286
  human rights culture, 286
  human rights violations, 286,
      290–92
  independent judiciary, 284
  institutional reform, 286
  international reconciliation,
      281–85, 287, 293
  Per Memoriam ad Spem, 285–92
  political legitimacy, 284
  security and border policies, 287
  Security Sector Reform, 286–87

terms of reference, 282–83
Commission of Truth, Reception and
    Reconciliation (CAVR) Report,
    61
Committee for the Popular Defence
    of the Democratic Republic of
    Timor-Leste (CPD-RDTL), 221
Community of Portuguese-
    Language Speaking Countries
    (CPLP), 24, 74–76, 133, 137, 145,
    163, 177–79, 181–84, 188
"comprehensive and collective
    engagement", 136
conclusive truth, 274, 283, 285
*Congresso Nacional de Reconstrução de
    Timor* (CNRT), 16, 111, 179–80,
    206, 240
ConocoPhillips, 259
Consensus Democracy, 151
Constitutive Act of the Union, 129
constitutive localization, 171
constitutive norms, 170, 173
constructivism, 180, 182
contemporary international law, 242
"Copenhagen Agreement", 245
core national interest, 124
Costa Rican model, 140
Cotton, James, 62, 102, 103
Country Policy and Institutional
    Assessment (CPIA), 239, 253
Cristovão, Cirilo José, 134, 313, 317
Crouch, Harold, 282

D
da Costa, Helder, 185, 240
da Costa, Zacarias, 164, 205
Da Silva, Estanislau, 313
Declaration on Decolonization, 44,
    45
declaratory recognition, 38
declaratory theory, 39
decolonization, 8, 104–6
defence cooperation, 218
Defence Cooperation Program
    (2001), 218
defence force, 207, 218

central mission of, 216
    Southeast Asia, 203
    Timor-Leste, 204–6
defence planning, 275
defence strategy, 205–6, 209, 219
de los Santos, Jaime, 103
democracy, 167, 173, 182–83
    institutions, 220
    legitimacy, 109
    promotion, 149–51
Democratic Republic of Timor-Leste (RDTL), 1, 2, 22, 46
democratization, 286
developmental nationalism, 170
Dili Consensus, 186–87
diplomacy, 217
diversified approach, 124, 215
Documentation and Conflict Resolution Centre, 288
domestic politics, 14–17
dominant foreign policy, 130
donor–recipient relationship, 237
Downer, Alexander, 101
draft investment law, 259
Draft Law on National Security, 211–12
Dunn, James, 48, 63
Dupont, Alan, 102, 166
Durand, Frédéric, 43
Dutch–Portuguese relationships, 42–43
Duterte, Rodrigo, 318

E
Eanes, Ramalho, 73
East Asia Summit (EAS), 164
East Timor and Indonesia Action Network, 283
economic ambitions, 241–49
economic dependence, 276
economic diversification, 236
economic growth, 320, 322
economic independence, 236
economic plans, 306, 320
economic sovereignty
    absolute external, 235
    aid dependence problems, 237–41
    ambitious economic plans, 236, 241–49
    challenges, 236
    development plans, 243
    foreign direct investment, 237, 258–59
    fragile state measure, 239
    key issues in, 259
    multilateral economic forums, 237
    oil exports, 248, 255–58
    Petroleum Wealth Fund, 243
    recognition, 247
    resource curse, 249–55, 260
    Strategic Development Plan, 236
    United Nations Transitional Administration in East Timor, 238
Electricidade de Timor-Leste (EDTL), 325–26
El Niño weather events, 322
Emmerson, Donald, 165, 166
empirical sovereignty, 96, 104–8
energy diplomacy, 182, 260, 329
energy policies, 325–27
English-speaking diplomatic staff, 166
Equatorial Guinea, 182
Erman, Eva, 38, 39
Estimated Sustainable Income (ESI), 252
"eternal vigilance", 127
ethnic heterogeneity, 41
European colonialism, 181
European Economic Commission (EEC), 73
Evans, Gareth, 140
Exclusive Economic Zone (EEZ), 200, 216, 313
export markets, 257
"extending solidarity", 147
external security, 275, 277, 284
    threats, 24, 200, 204, 210–16
Extractive Industries Transparency Initiative, 252

F
Fabry, Mikulas, 38–39
"failing state", 105
fait accompli, 61, 63, 69
FALINTIL, 47, 203, 208
FALINTIL-Defence Forces of Timor-Leste (F-FDTL), 200, 203, 205, 206, 208, 209, 218
Farram, Stevens, 43
Federer, Juan, 108, 112
Feijó, Rui Graça, 151, 203
fiscal consolidation, 255
Flitton, Dan, 314
food insecurity, 323
Forcas 2020, 272
Force 2020, 205–10, 217, 219, 292
Ford, Gerald, 66
foreign direct investment (FDI), 237, 258–59
foreign policy, 3, 163–64, 166, 172, 174, 176, 216, 217, 235, 327, 412
  activist strategy, 246, 248
  actors, 16
  approach, 123, 124, 132–39, 226, 236
  Australia, 244
  "comprehensive and collective engagement", 136
  declarations, 146
  domestic politics, 14–17
  dominant, 130
  exceptionalism, 125
  expansive, 137
  fragile state exceptionalism, 129–32
  "friendship and cooperation", 134
  Gusmão, Xanana, 124, 130, 132, 135
  history, culture and identity, 19–22
  Indonesia–Australia relations, 134–36
  international citizenship, 140–48
  international speeches, 130, 131
  key relational circles, 138
  multilateralism and rules-based order, 17–19

National Development Plan, 133
  objective, 128, 133
  relational circles, 138
  rules-based order for, 142
  in Singapore, 126–27
  small state, 11–12, 17, 248
  Strategic Development Plan, 128
  strategies, 129
  systemic factors, 12–14
  systems *vs.* domestic approaches, 12
  United States, 239
fragile states, 5–6, 184–87
  democratic institutions, 209
  exceptionalism, 129–32, 163, 250
  identity, 241
  national security interests, 10
  political institutions, 201
  security dilemma for, 7–8
fragility to resilience, 132
Franck, Thomas M., 109
Fraser, Malcolm, 64
free and fair elections (2012), 220
FRELIMO (*Frente de Libertação de Moçambique*), 76
FRETILIN, 15, 16, 72, 76, 83, 114, 210, 215, 223
  communist leanings, 78–79
  declaration, 49
  pro-independence political party, 46, 48
  resistance against, 209
  unilateral declaration of independence, 46, 73
"friendship and cooperation", 134
functional independence, 7
Fundasaun Mahein, 216
Fund for Peace Failed State Index, 221

G
g7+, 184–87
Gama, Jaime, 73
geostrategic position, 65, 207, 311
Ghani, Ashraf, 105
Gillard, Julia, 205

"global rules-based order", 18, 140
good governance, 238, 239, 249
"good international citizenship", 140
Greater Sunrise gas field, 25, 312, 329
Green Climate Fund, 327
gross domestic product (GDP), 166
Gross National Income, 254
Group of 77 (G77), 321
Guedes, Armando Marques, 67
Gusmão, Xanana, 16–17, 80, 111–15, 124, 130, 132, 135, 150, 172, 175, 187, 200–202, 204–6, 210, 212–14, 217, 220–23, 236, 240, 243, 246, 249, 256, 258, 261, 277, 281, 283, 286, 291, 308, 320–21
    economic development plan, 183
    emerging economies, 169
    geopolitical positioning, 162
    goal of 'g7+', 186
    membership in ASEAN, 166
    Portuguese language, 180
    regionalism and solidarity, 170
    state-building processes, 185
Guterres, Abel, 83, 247

H
Haacke, Jurgen, 104
Habib, Benjamin, 323
Habibie, B.J., 60, 81, 82, 98, 103, 104
Hägerdal, Hans, 43
Handel, Michael, 14–15
hedging strategy, 14, 26, 161, 305, 316, 328
    Asian-Pacific states, 307
    relations with China, 306–15
hegemonic transition theory, 306
Helman, Gerald, 105, 106
Herz, John, 6
Hirst, Megan, 285
Hong Long Fisheries, 314
Howard, John, 81
Hughes, Caroline, 239
Hull, Geoffrey, 77
humanitarianism, 149–51
human rights, 173
    culture, 286
    violations, 273–74, 279–82, 284, 286, 292
human security, 104
Hussein, Abdul Razak, 68
"hybrid" tribunal, 279

I
identity debates, 60
"identity hedging", 161, 163, 188
Ikenberry, G. John, 330
"imagined community", 173
Import Substitution Industrialisation (ISI), 257
inclusive growth, 306, 320
incremental socialization, 173
independence movement, 3, 22, 50–51, 78, 97, 175, 180, 246
    China's support for, 79
    in 1974–75, 201
    success, 79–84
independence referendum, 273
independent judiciary, 284
Indonesia, 47, 82–83
    Australia–Indonesia Security Arrangement, 102
    Australia's cooperation with, 204
    bilateral relationship with, 272
    China's relations with, 79
    colonialization and oppression, 277
    defence and security, 276
    democratic transition, 282
    East Nusa Tenggara province, 256
    East Timor invasion by, 37, 46, 49, 202
    in foreign policy, 275–78
    foundational states, 168
    "genocidal policy", 74
    human rights tribunal, 279
    human rights violations, 274, 280, 286
    incorporation with, 170
    internal and external security, 275, 277
    international tribunal, 279

Konfrontasi against Malaysia, 70
memorandums of understanding, 280
military modernization, 316
multinational force, 98
national security, 168
Philippines support for, 68
political instability, 206
political reconciliation, 291
Portuguese literacy, 179
recognition of sovereignty, 60, 61
reconciliation, 277
security forces, 288
solidarity, 277
sovereignty, 45, 102
Strategic Development Plan, 275
substantive justice, 273, 287
Timor Gap Treaty with, 73
Timor-Leste's membership, 167
Indonesian military (TNI), 97, 98, 280, 282, 292
Indonesian National Human Rights Commission, 280
Indonesian rule, 48, 254, 272, 277
Indonesia–Timor-Leste Commission of Truth and Friendship, 25
industrialization, 249
Initial National Communication, 322
institutional reform, 286
intergovernmental organizations, engagement with, 163
    Association of Southeast Asian Nations membership, 163–74
    g7+, 184–87
    Lusophone connection, 177–84
    Pacific Island region, 174–77
internal reconciliation, 273
internal security, 210, 218, 275, 277, 284
    Australia and Indonesia for, 213
    challenges, 209, 212
    developing, 225
    foreign policy and, 216
    intervention in, 210
    management, 221
    problems, 205, 220–24
    threats, 201
international actors, 239
international assistance, 104
international blasphemy law, 144
International Center for Transitional Justice, 287
international citizenship, 140–48
international community, 1, 2, 4, 15, 44, 61, 80
    ASEAN states, 67–72
    Australia, 62–65
    China and Soviet Union, 78–79
    independence movement, 79–84
    Portuguese-speaking countries, 72–77
    South Pacific states, 77–78
    United States, 65–67
International Court of Justice (ICJ), 73, 244
International Covenant of Economic, Social and Cultural Rights (ICESC) 1966, 44
International Covenant of Political and Civil Rights (ICPRC) (1966), 44
International Crisis Group (2009), 211
international diplomacy, 141
International Force for East Timor (INTERFET), 96, 99, 101–3
international human rights instruments, 274
International Institute of Portuguese Language, 177
international institutions, 24
international intervention, 97, 104, 115
international justice, 25, 274
international law, 36, 44–45
international legal rights, 50
international legal sovereignty, 8
international legitimacy, 104–8
international maritime law, 204
international missions, 99–100
International Monetary Fund (IMF), 24, 98, 237, 310

international non-governmental
  organizations (INGOs), 238
international political community,
  104, 202, 209
international political system, 6, 18,
  125
international reconciliation, 276, 287,
  293
  Commission of Truth and
    Friendship, 281–85
  Timor-Leste's foreign policy,
    275–78
international relations, 5, 12, 16, 18,
  23, 101, 124, 236, 304
  debates in, 38
  as "grand strategy", 206
  identities in, 20
  issues, 137
  public relations in, 129
  "two-pronged" approach to, 204
International Stabilisation Force
  (ISF), 2, 100, 114, 218
international state-building
  ASEAN states, 102–4
  Australia support, 101
  civil society, 110, 114
  democratic legitimacy, 109
  empirical sovereignty, 96, 104–8
  "functional independence", 107
  humanitarian crisis, 97, 98, 102,
    104, 107
  international community
    intervention, 97–104
  international legitimacy, 104–8
  international relations, 101
  legitimate statehood, 96, 105
  liberal-democracy, 96, 108–14
  national security, 107
  neo-trusteeship, 108–9
  participatory intervention, 109,
    110
  political institutions, 107
  post-World War Two, 104, 106
  self-determination, 97, 108–14
  shared sovereignty, 110
  state institutions, 108

timorization, 112
International Tribunal for the Law of
  the Sea (ITLOS), 243

J
Jackson, Robert, 8, 105
Jakarta, 47, 167–68
  annexation, 67–69
  ASEAN support for, 103
  invasion, 68
  public criticism, 172
  Woolcott, Richard, 63
Jakarta International Defence
  Dialogue, 164, 217
Jakarta Post, 284
Job, Brian, 7
John Paul II, 80
Joint Petroleum Development Area
  (JPDA), 241, 242, 248
"Joint Plan of Action", 289
Jones, Lee, 103
José Manuel Neto Simões, 206

K
Kartasasmuta, Sabana, 48, 49
Katzenstein, Peter, 4
Kissinger, Henry, 66
Konfrontasi, 68, 70, 171
KOTA, 46, 47
Krasner, Stephen, 8, 106, 112, 114
Krieger, Heike, 43
Krishna, Sankaran, 40
KRM. *See* Maubere Revolutionary
  Council (KRM)
Kyoto Protocol (2008), 321

L
Labs, Eric, 13
La'o Hamutuk, 238, 248, 251, 252, 257
Law of the Sea agreements, 65
Leach, Michael, 101, 182
Least Developed Countries (LDC),
  321, 327
Lee Hsien Loong, 127
legal self-determination rights, 51,
  83

legal system, 95
legitimate statehood, 96, 105
Leifer, Michael, 15, 126, 127, 170
Lere Anan Timur, 222
Lesser Sundas (Nusatenggara), 36
liberal rights discourses, 80, 81
linguistic diversity, 41
Lipscomb, Leigh-Ashley, 283
Lisbon Convention, 42
Liurias, 41
Lobato, Lucia, 254
Lockhart, Clare, 105
Lowry, Bob, 312
Lusitanization, 177
Lusophone connection, 77, 177–84

M
Macau Forum Ministerial Conference, 310
Malacca, 41–42
Malaysia
 Indonesia's *Konfrontasi* against, 70
 invasion of Dili, 68
maritime boundary law, 243, 247
maritime security, 200, 313
Maritime Silk Road (MSR), 311
Martial Law, 98
Maubere Revolutionary Council (KRM), 201, 221, 222
McDougall, Derek, 224, 230
"Melanesian independence struggles", 77
Melanesian Spearhead Group (MSG), 176, 219
Memorandum of Understanding, 276, 279, 280, 287
Mendes, Nuno Canas, 39–40
"mental colonialism", 223
Migdal, Joel, 110
military force, 202–5
military modernization, 218, 316
Millennium Development Goals (MDGs), 186, 320
Ministry of Foreign Affairs and Cooperation, 126, 139, 288, 289, 308

"modern diversified economy", 241
Montevideo Convention (1933), 35, 38
Moruk, Mauk, 221
Mouritzen, Hans, 13, 14
Mozambique, 74, 76
multilateral economic forums, 237
multilateralism, 17–19, 24, 140, 142
Murdoch, Lindsay, 213–15
Myanmar
 ASEAN membership, 167
 military regime, 174

N
Narine, Shaun, 102, 173
Natalegawa, Marty, 276
National Adaptation Programmes of Action (NAPA), 321, 327
National Congress for Timorese Reconstruction (CNRT), 16, 111, 179–80, 206, 240
National Constitution, 112, 128, 130, 147
National Consultative Council (NCC), 111
National Defence Policy, 212
National Democratic Institute, 112
National Development Plan (NDP), 133, 205
national electricity grid, 325
national gendarmerie, 203
national identity, 5, 20, 84, 130, 131, 180, 247, 273
National Museum in Dili, 130
National Police Force, 201
national political elites, 239
National Reparations Programme, 288, 290
national security, 6, 24, 211
 challenges, 200
 conventional approach to, 199
 Defence Cooperation Program (2001), 218
 defence policy, 221
 defence self-reliance, 199
 Exclusive Economic Zone, 200

external security threats, 200, 210–16
FALINTIL-Defence Forces of Timor-Leste, 200, 203, 205, 206, 208, 209
Force 2020, 205–10
Gusmão, Xanana, 200–202, 204–6, 210, 212–14, 217
internal security. *See* internal security
Jakarta International Defence Dialogue, 217
military, 202–5
naval power, defence and, 217
problems, 220–24
Transitional Cabinet of East Timor, 203
National Security Act (2/2010), 211
National Security Law legislation, 212
National Security Policy Workshop, 210, 214
"national unity", 151, 222, 223
National Unity government, 151
nation-branding strategies, 150
natural gas, 325
natural prolongation, 242
neo-colonialism, 62, 192, 238
neoliberal tax reforms, 257, 258
Netherlands, 42
Neves, Guteriano, 252
New Deal, 184–85
Newly Industrializing Economies (NIE), 249
Nixon, Rod, 251
non-aligned movement (NAM), 70, 143
non-interference, 10, 67, 70, 128–29, 162, 170–73
non-oil private sector, 255
non-petroleum economy, 253
non-renewable resources, 251, 252
non-self-governing territory, 2, 45, 51, 85, 148
non-state threats, 213

O

OECD Peacekeeping Database, 219
Oecussi, 36, 42, 135
oil and gas revenues, 223, 224, 241, 248, 261
oil exports
economic multilateral institutions, 255
import dependence, 252, 256
industrialization plans, 241, 243, 244
over-dependence on, 254
reliance on, 252
trade policy, 255–58
O'Keefe, Michael, 176
Ombai-Wetar Strait, 65, 134, 311
"one nation, one vote" principle, 19
Operasi Komodo, 72
"Operation Clean Sweep" campaign, 97–98, 104, 203, 278
Organisation Internationale de la Francophonie (OIF), 178
Organisation of Economic Cooperation and Development (OECD), 184
Ortuoste, Maria, 165
Ottaway, Marina, 105

P

Pacific Economic Monitor, 253
Pacific Island Forum (PIF), 163, 175
Pacific Island region, 174–77
Pacific Islands Developing States (PSIDS), 175
Pacific Islands Development Forum (PIDF), 175–77, 321
Pacific Patrol Boats Program, 207, 215, 216
Palestine's self-determination rights, 146
Pampalk, Madalena, 289
Papua New Guinea, 41, 62, 78, 315
Paris Agreement on Climate Change (2016), 325
Paris Declaration (2005), 239
partido Trabalhista, 46, 47

patronage system, 222, 254
peacekeeping forces, 98, 102–4, 219
Percival-Wood, Sally, 101, 257
Pereira, Agio, 51, 84, 141, 179, 181, 223
Permanent Court of Arbitration (PCA), 311, 317
Per Memoriam ad Spem, 285–92
"Petitioners Group", 209
petrochemical refining industries, 250
PetroChina, 310
petroleum refining ambitions, 242
Petroleum Wealth Fund, 241, 248, 252, 253, 255, 326
Philippines
 domestic leadership in, 318
 East Timorese solidarity movement, 69
 proceedings against China, 311
 support for Indonesia, 68
Philpott, Simon, 37, 44, 83
Pintang Marine Enterprises, 314
Pinto, Julio Tomas, 115, 212, 215, 223
Pinto, Manuel, 178
Pires, Emilia, 185, 241, 254
Pitsuwan, Surin, 103
political economy, 247, 254, 255
political independence, 38, 95, 106, 113–14, 127
political institutions, 96, 107
political legitimacy, 60, 247, 261, 284
political reconciliation, 126, 273, 274, 291
Popular Representative Assembly, 47–48
Portugal, 45–46, 72, 85, 162, 166, 177
 artificial pseudoethnic divisions, 43
 Community of Portuguese Speaking Countries, 183
 influence in Timor-Leste, 41–42, 180
 National Congress for Timorese Reconstruction, 180

 negotiated borders between Dutch and, 42
 neo-colonial behaviour, 183
Portuguese Armed Movement (AMF), 46
Portuguese colonialism, 1, 20, 40–43, 51, 177, 180, 181
Portuguese language, 76, 178–80, 182
Portuguese-speaking countries, 72
 ascension to European Economic Commission, 73
 assimilation policies, 76
 Community of Portuguese Language Countries, 74–76
 FRETILIN's declaration of independence, 73
 Lusophone-Catholic cultural influence, 77
 Operasi Komodo, 72
 Timor Gap Treaty, 73
Portuguese Timor, 1–2, 46, 62, 65, 72–73
positive sovereignty, 110
post-ballot violence, 98
"post-carbon" international economy, 325
post-colonial states, 8, 9–10, 108, 162
poverty eradication, 322
power dynamics, 4, 12, 226, 304–5
Powles, Anna, 222
"pragmatic realist" approach, 204
pro-Indonesia militia, 98, 204
"public diplomacy" campaign, 81, 129, 244, 246
Public Memory Institute, 288, 289

Q

quid pro quo, 245

R

Ramo, Joshua Cooper, 331
Ramos-Horta, José, 15, 72, 74, 76, 77–78, 83, 85, 135, 139–41, 147, 149, 151, 162, 168, 202, 205, 210, 220, 221, 223, 235, 240, 243, 246, 283, 285, 290, 750

Ratner, Steven, 105, 106
RDTL. *See* Democratic Republic of Timor-Leste (RDTL)
"real" independence, 9, 10, 115, 123, 201, 208, 224, 240
recognition acts, 39
Regional Comprehensive Economic Partnership (RCEP), 310
regional security, 168, 169, 315–18
Reinado, Alfredo, 210, 221
resource curse, 249–55, 260
"revolutionary legitimacy", 203
right to self-determination, 24, 44, 45, 48, 59, 63, 67, 84–85, 214
Ringmar, Erik, 10
Robinson, Mary, 280
Rocha de Siqueira, Isabel, 185, 187
Rome Statute, 274, 279
Rosser, Andrew, 252
Rotberg, Robert, 5
"rules-based order", 244

S
Sahin, Selver, 20, 181, 240
Sampaio, Luis de Oliveira, 289
Santa Cruz massacre (1991), 80
Scambary, James, 247, 254
Schweller, Randall, 306
Secretariat of the Pacific Community (SPC), 176
security and defence policy, 214
"security-development nexus", 235
security environment, 14, 176, 305, 318, 328
security interests, 2, 63, 72, 104, 134, 303
security issues, 3, 200, 275, 276, 284, 313
Security Sector Reform (SSR), 202, 286–87, 289
"Seeds for Life" programme, 324
self-determination, 21, 22, 38–40, 97, 106, 126, 132, 148, 225, 235, 239, 240, 246, 309
  challenges, 108–14
  emphasis on, 187

  human rights and, 63
  for independence, 44
  under international law, 44–45
  international relations and, 72
  rights, 36–37, 49–50, 59, 60, 72–74, 84, 85, 214, 329
  struggle for, 130, 147
  use and abuse of, 45–51
"sense of self", 127
"Sentenca Arbitral", 42
17th Non-Aligned Summit, 143
Severino, Rodolfo, 168
Shangri-La Dialogue, 164
Sharman, JC, 13
Silk Road Economic Belt (SREB), 310
Sil, Rudra, 4
Simonsen, Sven Gunnar, 202
Singapore
  colonialism by British, 250
  economic growth, 257
  foreign policy, 126, 127, 169
  independence, 126
  Indonesia's invasion, 69
  Lee Hsien Loong, 127
  major factor in, 126
  population, 126
  reliance on ASEAN, 169
  territorial sovereignty, 126
  Timor-Leste's membership, 166
  vulnerabilities, 126
Singapore Model, 258
Small Island Developing States (SIDS), 143, 321
small state foreign policy, 11–14, 17, 126, 248
small states, 3, 5, 13, 18–19
Smith, Anthony, 276
Soares, Mario, 73
Soares, Roberto, 169, 188
socialization process, 238–39
Soesastro, Hadi, 204
soft idealism, 143
soft-institutionalism, 173
solar panels, 326
solidarity, 175, 181, 182, 184
Solomon Islands, 175

Songkitti Jaggabatara, 103
Sousa, Helena, 178
Sousa-Santos, José Kei Lekke, 222, 238
South China Sea dispute, 317
Southeast Asian states, 15, 85
    defence force, 203
    Timor-Leste's connections with, 20
    "unsettled relations", 307
    voting records of, 71
South Korea, 102, 214
South Pacific Forum. *See* Pacific Island Forum (PIF)
South Pacific island states, 77–78
Southwest Pacific Dialogue, 176
sovereignty, 1, 9, 23, 38, 59, 96, 162, 171–73, 188, 208, 216, 273
    absolute external state, 123, 127
    economic. *See* economic sovereignty
    empirical concept, 249
    external, 162, 171
    of "fragile" states, 237
    independence, 249
    international relations, 128
    language, 128
    legitimacy, 110
    principles of territorial integrity, 127
    recognition, 247
    secure state, 123
    sovereign status, 36, 38, 39
    symbolic concepts of, 248
    territorial and symbolic concept, 248, 249
    "Westphalian" conceptions, 10
sovereignty-security conception, 199
Soviet Union, East Timor's independence and, 78–79
Special Regime for Greater Sunrise, 245
state-based identity, 37, 43, 130, 131, 137, 142, 152
statehood, 8–9, 26, 35–36
    territorialization and, 37–40
state identity, 20, 23, 186

state sovereignty, 8, 123, 129, 132
status quo powers, 306
Storey, Ian, 311
strategic culture, 20
Strategic Development Plan (SDP), 128, 136–37, 139, 141, 164, 174, 176, 187, 214, 221, 236, 241–42, 275, 320, 321, 326
Strohmeyer, Hansjoerg, 278
Structural Adjustment Programs, 257
"struggle for recognition", 246
Subianto, Prabowo, 292
substantive justice, 273, 281, 283, 287
Suharto, 49, 60, 62, 81
Sukarno, 65
Sukma, Rizal, 313
Sunrise International Unitization Agreement (Sunrise IUA), 242, 243
sustainable development, 305, 306, 320
Sustainable Development Goals (SDG), 143, 320
symbolic sovereign narratives, 236

T
Taiwan
    de facto authority, 61
    sovereignty, 311
Tasi Mane, 242, 243, 247, 253, 260
Taur Matan Ruak, 141, 151, 181, 202, 206, 220, 256, 261, 315
Teme, Jorge da Conceição, 276
territorial constitutions, 39
territorialization, 35, 36
    statehood and, 37–40
territorial sovereignty, 9, 10, 126, 127
Thorhallsson, Baldur, 142
"Thucydides Trap", 304
Timor Gap Treaty, 73
Timor-Leste Defence Force, 308
Timor-Leste National Alliance for an International Tribunal (ANTI), 289
Timor Sea, 236

activist strategy, 247
boundaries, 243
dispute, 244
oil and gas revenues, 241, 261
Timor Sea Treaty (TST), 241
Topasses, 42
"To Resist is to Win!", 130
Trade Invest website, 258
trade policy, 255–58
traditional security dilemma, 101, 218, 316, 323
transitional justice, 273, 274, 282, 289, 292
international dimensions, 278–81
Transition Support Program, 237
transnational crimes, 142, 200
transparency reputation, 254
Traube, Elizabeth, 41
"Treaty of Neutrality", 203
Treaty on Amity and Co-operation (TAC), 165
Trump, Donald, 328
Truth and Reconciliation Commission, 25
Tsuchiyama, Jitsuo, 330
28/2011 Government Resolution, 211
22nd Session of the COP (COP22), 321
"two-pronged" approach, 204, 215

U
UN Commission of Human Rights, 73
UN diplomacy, 142
UN Forum of Small States, 11
UNGA Fourth Committee, 69
UN General Assembly Resolution (1807), 45, 50
UN General Assembly's Declaration on the Granting of Independence to Colonial Countries and Peoples, 44
União Democrática Timorense (UDT), 46, 47
United Nations (UN), 1, 19, 37, 61, 79, 80, 96, 97, 100, 107, 185

United Nations Administration in East Timor (UNTAET), 96, 99, 103, 109–14
United Nations Compulsory Conciliation (UNCC), 245, 246
United Nations Convention on the Law of the Sea (UNCLOS), 242, 243, 245, 311, 317, 318
United Nations Development Programme (UNDP), 253, 324
United Nations Framework Convention on Climate Change (UNFCCC), 321, 322
United Nations General Assembly (UNGA), 60, 61, 66, 68–70, 142–45
resolution, 63
West Papua in, 148
United Nations Integrated Mission in Timor-Leste (UNMIT), 2, 100, 114, 201, 210, 220, 223
United Nations Mission (2012), 218
United Nations Mission in East Timor (UNAMET), 97, 107
United Nations Mission of Support in East Timor (UNMISET), 99, 113, 114
United Nations Office in East Timor (UNOTIL), 100, 113
United Nations Security Council (UNSC), 98, 100, 109
United Nations Security Council Resolution 384 (1975), 67, 68, 73
United Nations Security Council Resolution 1704 (2006), 210, 278
United Nations Transitional Administration in East Timor (UNTAET), 2, 238, 278, 279, 281
United States, 65, 80
alliance with Australia, 101
Indonesia's *de facto* incorporation, 66–67
invasion of Dili, 65–66
Portuguese Timor, 65
"Thucydides Trap", 304

United States Agency for International Development (USAID), 239
UN Security Council, 50

V
value-added benefits, 249
Vanuatu Conference, 78
Vieira de Mello, Sergio, 110
Vienna Convention of the Law of Treaties, 244
vulnerabilities, 125–29

W
Wahid, Abdurrahman, 290
Walt, Stephen, 307
Waltz, Kenneth, 13, 17
"Washington Consensus", 186, 309
water scarcity, 324
"Weberian" state, 105
Weiss, Thomas, 9
Wesley, Michael, 105
West Papua
  Pacific Island Coalition on, 148
  in UNGA debates, 148
Whitlam, Gough, 62
Widodo, Joko, 292, 313
"Wilsonian idealism", 63
Wiranto, 104, 280, 281, 290, 292
'WithOneSeed', 324–25
Wivel, Anders, 4
Woolcott, Richard, 63
World Bank, 24, 237, 252, 310
World Trade Organization, 310

Y
Yudhoyono, Susilo Bambang, 133, 276, 285, 287, 289–92

Z
Zaum, Dominik, 101
"Zone of Peace", 140, 203

ABOUT THE AUTHOR

Rebecca Strating is a Lecturer of Politics in the Department of Politics and Philosophy at La Trobe University, Melbourne, Australia.

www.ingramcontent.com/pod-product-compliance
Lightning Source LLC
Chambersburg PA
CBHW070008010526
44117CB00011B/1461